The Effective Local Government Manager

THIRD EDITION

Contributors

The third edition of *The Effective Local Government Manager* contains material adapted from the 1983 edition, edited by Wayne F. Anderson, Chester A. Newland, and Richard J. Stillman II, and the 1993 edition, edited by Charldean Newell.

First Edition	Second Edition	Third Edition
Wayne F. Anderson	David N. Ammons	N. Joseph Cayer
F. Gerald Brown	David R. Berman	Raymond W. Cox III
E. H. Denton	N. Joseph Cayer	David Coursey
Chester A. Newland	E. H. Denton	Mary Ellen Guy
Joe P. Pisciotte	James J. Glass	William H. Hansell
Richard J. Stillman II	Patrick Manion	William Earle Klay
	Charldean Newell	Michael McGuire
	Joe P. Pisciotte	Charldean Newell
	James H. Svara	Ronald W. Perry
		James H. Svara
		Martin Vanacour
		Craig M. Wheeland

The Effective Local Government Manager

INTERNATIONAL
CITY/COUNTY
MANAGEMENT
ASSOCIATION

THIRD EDITION

Edited by
Charldean Newell

International
City/County
ICMA
Management
Association
icma.org

**Textbooks in the Municipal Management Series
of the International City/County Management Association**

Library of Congress Cataloging-In-Publication Data

The effective local government manager / edited by Charldean Newell.
   —3rd ed.
        p.   cm.
     Includes bibliographical references and index.
     ISBN 0-87326-143-7
     1. Municipal government by city manager—United States.
   I. Newell, Charldean. II. International City/County Management
   Association.
   JS344.C5E44 2004
   352.3'214'0973—dc22
                                                              2004010976

Printed in the United States of America

08 07 06 05 04

5 4 3 2 1

#04-150

The International City/County Management Association (ICMA) is the professional and educational organization for appointed managers and administrators serving cities, towns, counties, regional entities, and other local governments throughout the world. The mission of ICMA is to create excellence in local government by developing and fostering professional local government management and leadership worldwide. To further this mission, ICMA develops and disseminates new approaches to management and leadership through training programs, information services, and publications.

Local government managers and administrators—carrying a wide range of titles—serve at the direction of elected councils and governing boards. ICMA serves these managers and local governments through many programs that aim at improving the manager's professional competence and strengthening the quality of local governments. While ICMA recognizes professional management in all forms of local government, ICMA's origins lie in the council-manager form of local government, which combines the strong professional experience of an appointed local government manager or administrator with the strong political leadership of elected officials in the form of a council, board of selectmen, or other governing body.

ICMA was founded in 1914, adopted its Code of Ethics in 1924, and established its Institute for Training in Municipal Administration in 1934. The Institute provided the basis for the Municipal Management Series, popularly known as the "ICMA Green Books." By 1994, the institute had evolved into the ICMA University, which provides professional development resources for members and other local government employees.

ICMA's programs and activities include providing professional development; establishing guidelines for voluntary credentialing and standards of ethics for members; managing a comprehensive information clearinghouse; conducting local government research and data collection and dissemination; providing technical assistance; and producing a wide array of publications focused on local government management issues, including *Public Management magazine*, newsletters, management reports, and texts. ICMA's efforts toward the improvement of local government—as represented by this book—are offered for all local governments and educational institutions.

International City/County ICMA Management Association icma.org

Contents

Figures and Tables

Foreword

The professional local government manager is distinguished by commitment to high performance and ethical conduct. The work itself is both leadership and management, and the balance between the two is constantly shifting. In the opening years of the new millennium, the velocity of change is more complex and challenges force the professional local government manager to lead.

This third edition of *The Effective Local Government Manager* reflects the changes taking place in democracy at the local level, the fierce competition among communities for a dwindling share of the global economy, the increasing number of relationships to be juggled in the course of managing local projects, and the personal pressures that managers can expect to face in their careers.

In addition to describing the political context in which local government managers work and the expectations of elected council and the wider community, this book describes exactly what managers do: how they help elected officials provide effective leadership, how they make themselves a bridge between the community and the local government, how they help the community design its future, how they leverage resources, and how they promote quality in the delivery of local government services.

Like its predecessor volumes, this third edition of *The Effective Local Government Manager* looks at both

pieces of the manager's work: leadership and management, with the emphasis on the manager's role as standard bearer for high performance and ethical conduct. It is intended for all local government managers and all professionals whose aim is one day to serve as a city, village, town, or township manager; as a county manager; as a director of a council of governments; or in one of many other executive positions in local government. It is intended equally for assistant managers and department directors, whose responsibilities complement and support those of the manager.

The third edition of *The Effective Local Government Manager* owes its currency and comprehensiveness to Charldean Newell, Regents Professor Emerita of Public Administration, University of North Texas, and Honorary Member, ICMA, who served as editor for both the second and third editions. Her wise and good-humored guidance shaped the themes of the new book and brought out the best in each author's chapter.

This book builds on the work of many people. The editors of the first edition, Wayne F. Anderson, Chester A. Newland, and Richard J. Stillman II, laid the foundation. A glance at the long list of practitioners and professors who contributed valuable suggestions for the second edition reveals the breadth of use and review that in turn formed the platform for this third edition. The following people reviewed the second edition and offered important ideas for its updating: Kurt Bressner, city manager of Boynton Beach, Florida; Alex Briseño, former city manager of San Antonio, Texas; Raymond W. Cox III, professor and chair of the Department of Public Administration and Urban Studies, University of Akron; Delmer Dunn, Regents Professor of Political Science, Vice President for Instruction, and Associate Provost, University of Georgia; Michael Letcher, deputy city manager of Tucson, Arizona; Henry Moore, Building Communities, Inc., Savannah, Georgia, and former assistant city manager of Savannah; Chester A. Newland, Duggan Distinguished Professor of Public Administration, University of Southern California; Karl Nollenberger, Vice President, PAR Group, Ltd., and longtime local administrator, most recently as county administrator of Lake County, Illinois; James B. Oliver Jr., Corporate Executive Vice President of CI Travel in Norfolk, Virginia, and former city manager of Norfolk; Raymond R. Patchett, city manager of Carlsbad, California; Jorge Rifa, assistant city manager of Salinas, California; and Martin Vanacour, Dynamic Relations, LLC, Glendale, Arizona, and former city manager of Phoenix and Glendale, Arizona.

Their suggestions provided invaluable help in making sure that *The Effective Local Government Manager* is tracking the actual experience of managers and those who prepare future managers for their work.

We are grateful to the chapter authors, not only for their contributions but also for their responsiveness, patience, and cooperation during the stages leading to publication.

A number of ICMA staff members contributed to the project: Barbara H. Moore, former director of publications; David M. Childs, director, Western United States; Christine Ulrich and Mary Marik, who served as development editor and copy editor, respectively; Dawn M. Leland, who coordinated production; and Will Kemp, who designed the cover for the third edition.

Robert J. O'Neill Jr.
Executive Director
ICMA

Preface

The Effective Local Government Manager, originally published in 1983, was revised in 1993 and now, again, in 2004. All three editions have many commonalities—the vitality of local government, the great variety of communities, the multiple roles managers must master, the need to adapt to current socioeconomic and political trends, and the evolving nature of the structure of local governments themselves. All three editions examine the skills and abilities that local government managers need to be successful. Beginning in the first edition and continuing through the next two, the legacy of Richard Childs,[1] the reformer considered to be the conceptual father of council-manager government, is evident, but the evolution of the profession beyond Childs is also apparent. Reflected too are the prescriptions found in the Model City Charter, first published in 1915 and most recently in 2003 in its eighth edition.[2]

Like earlier editions of The Effective Local Government Manager, this edition is designed to meet the needs of both practicing managers and graduate students who aspire to local government management careers. Some but not all of the authors from the first edition participated in the second. Similarly, some but not all of the authors from the second edition contributed to the third, thus providing continuity to the book. Throughout, the authorship of the book has reflected a mix of academic and practitioner perspectives.

But each edition is also different. The first edition took pains to define public management and to establish criteria for measuring effectiveness. ICMA in 1983 was still the International City Management Association, without the county component, so that emphasis was on successful municipal management. The individual chapters reflected fairly orthodox thinking about The Plan, that is, the council-manager form of government; emphasized traditional intergovernmental relations; and concluded with a look at the manager as a person. At the same time, it broached the thinking of ICMA about the likely future conditions under which managers would have to provide leadership.

The second edition built on the excellent foundation of the first, but acknowledged the introspective study by ICMA leading to "New Worlds of Service" and the incorporation of the county as the other unit of general government that used the model of a professional administrator. The growing consequences of heterogeneous communities were introduced, along with intrusions on the classic council-manager structure, and the entry of single-issue politics and politicians. Ways in which elected officials and the professional executive share power, the growing concern for growth management, and the manager's need to execute the term of service effectively were other concepts that were added to the book. In addition, each chapter ended with a self-test or exercise to verify the understanding of concepts and ensure that the ideas were grounded in practice.

By the time the third edition was prepared, the work of the ICMA Task Force on Continuing Education and Professional Development was obvious. ICMA had amended the Code of Ethics to include a mandatory annual 40 hours of professional development. It had initiated not only the ICMA University as a means of structuring professional development but also the Voluntary Credentialing Program to provide a mentored and recognized variant to professional development. Part of this emphasis on professional development was identification of a list of 18 competencies and skills that collectively constituted essential management practices that the modern local executive needed to master and the parallel development of means of assessing mastery of them. ICMA's emphasis on professional development appears in various ways in this edition of the book. The work of ICMA in the area of continuing education gave further impetus to viewing local government management as a true profession.

The third edition puts more emphasis on ethics, new-century concepts of leadership, strategic planning, and economic development. It modernizes traditional intergovernmental relations by presenting a discussion of organizational networking. E-government, assessment and evaluation, and the difficulties of modern agenda setting are included. Particularly noticeable are discussions of variations in the council-manager plan as it is practiced in specific communities and as these variants reflect the growing power of mayors even in council-manager governments as well as the broader

definitions of recognized governments by the International City/County Management Association. At the same time, the third edition returns to its roots by adding a chapter on essential management skills that include human resources, finance, and technology management; also, the final chapter restores the more personal look at the human side of professional local government management and managers. The book also is more inclusive, emphasizing that executive leadership occurs not only in the top executive's job but in the next tier as well and in individual departments of a given jurisdiction.

Whether the reader is a graduate student looking forward to the excitement of a local government management career, a relative newcomer to general management who may have risen through the technical ranks and now seeks a broader base of knowledge, or an experienced manager who wants to review concepts and test knowledge and skills against managers of similar backgrounds, *The Effective Local Government Manager,* third edition, should offer something of value. More than anything, each subsequent edition of the book reflects the realities of local public management at the time of its writing.

Charldean Newell
Regents Professor Emerita
   of Public Administration
University of North Texas
Honorary Member, ICMA

Notes

[1] Richard S. Childs, Civic Victories: The Story of an Unfinished Revolution (New York: Harper, 1952), and The First Fifty Years of the Council-Manager Plan of Municipal Government (New York: National Municipal League, 1965).
[2] Model City Charter, 8th ed. (Denver: National Civic League, 2003).

The profession of local government manager: evolution and leadership styles

Local government is the most dynamic, innovative, and organizationally diverse level of all governments. It employs more people, provides more direct services, and is the most likely point of contact between government and citizens. Whether citizens are concerned about the quality of drinking water, the speed with which snow is removed from streets, opportunities for recreation, or the response time of emergency medical services, the service in question is most likely to have been funded or provided (or both) by municipal and county government. Everyday life is bound to the services and programs of local government more inextricably than to other levels of government. Citizens depend on the effectiveness and quality of local government to make their lives safer, healthier, and more livable.

Because of the close bond between citizens and local government, the nature of local government has changed (and keeps changing) to mirror the changes in society. In particular, the twentieth century was a time when the demands placed on government rose dramatically, as did the expectations of citizens. Thus, the public's need for professional and effective government was never more apparent. And the ever more varied and complex role of public service created a parallel need for managers who could see the issues, create a vision of what a community could be, take charge, and manage effectively.

In 1918, at the annual convention of what was then called the International City Managers' Association (now ICMA), Richard Childs predicted:

> Some day we shall have managers who have achieved national reputation, not by saving taxes or running their cities for a freakishly low expense per capita, but managers who have successfully led their commissions into great new enterprises of service. . . . The great city managers of tomorrow will be those who pushed beyond the old horizons and discovered new worlds of service.[1]

Rarely has a speaker been more prescient. The role of the local government manager is decidedly more complex at the beginning of the twenty-first century than it was in 1918. The contemporary local government manager is still concerned with potholes and sewer systems, but those responsibilities are now supplemented with others: supervising and managing co-workers, involving and accommodating citizens, and interacting with elected officials. These new responsibilities have required the entire profession to (in Childs's words) "push beyond old horizons" and "discover new worlds of service."[2]

At this point in the evolution of local government, as modern relationships and ways of doing business are replacing the methods and practices of earlier times, new skills are required. In fact, the changes come so fast that the question of how to be an effective manager elicits a different response decade by decade. This chapter focuses on the evolution of the profession of local government management and on the distinctive aspects of the professional manager as leader.

The profession of local government management

City and county management is called a profession. But what exactly does being a profession mean? Professions are marked by

- Practices
- Norms or values
- Perspectives.

Professions evolve as a specific set of practices, and shared norms or values are first taught (often in what are characterized as professional schools) and then emerge as proper or accepted behavior. Shared credentials and ultimately a shared language separate those whose training enables them to understand from those who lack such training. According to Frederick C. Mosher, professions have their

> own particularized view of the world and of [their institution's] role and mission in it. The perspective and motivation of each professional are shaped at least to some extent by the lens provided him by his professional education, his prior professional experience, and by his professional colleagues.[3]

A profession, then, is a defined career that usually requires a college degree and often a graduate degree. Mosher goes on to note that professions are characterized as having an "evolving and agreed-upon body of knowledge," as promoting socialization among members, and as sometimes reflecting norms different from those of the organizations that employ their practitioners.[4] Additional features of a profession are client recognition, professional identity, professional culture, a code of ethics (one of the critical distinguishing features of a profession), formal measures of professional competence, and sufficient discretion to perform at a professional level.[5] The local government management profession is characterized by all these features and by the fact that the practices, norms or values, and perspectives that distinguish a profession are carefully laid out.

The birth of a profession   "Grassroots professionals in America often developed from particular events. The need for passable streets and sidewalks, after the old ones had turned into quagmire with the appearance of the new automobile, led Staunton, Virginia, to hire the first city manager, Charles Ashburner. Thus, a new profession began quite literally out of potholes in roads created by cars."

Source: Richard J. Stillman II, Preface to *Public Administration: A Search for Themes and Directions,* 2nd ed. (Burke, Va.: Chatelaine Press, 1999), 92–93.

The local government management profession was born in the twentieth century, but it was born with ancient precepts and notions of governance and management that heavily influence it to this day. Furthermore, local government management is arguably the first self-conscious profession in that it represents the first effort to shape a job to notions of professionalism. There is no predecessor occupation for the local government manager. The profession's creators had to define the norms or values and perspectives of the profession and then determine the practices.

In a very real sense, therefore, local government management was a profession before it was an occupation. To this day the fundamental characteristics that distinguish the professional local government manager are not occupational but center on credentials, recognition, and experience. Local government management is not and never has been an occupation with a narrow range of duties and responsibilities. Rather, the work environment varies with the economic, social, and cultural differences among local governments. The day-to-day practices of managers vary as well. Certain technical skills (finance or public works management) may be more critical or less, depending on the community; and certain skills may be paramount for a period (for example, public works in the early years of the profession, public finance during the Great Depression, growth management in the 1980s) until events demand new skills.

In other words, like most professions, local government management redefines itself in relation to changing perceptions and values. (An example of such redefinition is the medical profession's reaction to the patients' rights movement.) But although the local government manager changes practices, he or she does so in order to remain true to the values or norms of the profession, some of which go back to its founding.[6] This historic continuity of purpose and values is both the greatest strength and the greatest weakness of local government management. Therefore, it is to this history that we turn first.

Local government management in historical perspective

The profession of local government manager emerged in the late nineteenth and early twentieth centuries from two separate but related intellectual movements, one political and one organizational: the urban reform movement and what was called scientific management. This odd coupling remains relevant to the profession to this day. The new profession combined a zealous commitment to transforming the very structures of government with support for new, "scientific" theories of management (the modern notion of the manager comes from this period). The new profession required the transformation of governmental structures so that it could put into practice its vision of the new urban society. The vision began with the attempted separation of political activities from administrative functions so that local governments would largely operate as though they were apolitical.

In short, the new profession arose from efforts to reform governmental structures and make them less blatantly political than their unreformed cousins. The ultimate embodiment of that vision of new government was the council-manager form of government. For many decades that form and its placement in cities and towns helped define the profession. The managers' professional society was originally called the International City Managers' Association.

A central feature of the ideal of the council-manager form of government is the unitary style of government—cooperation between council and manager.[7] This style was effective because policy issues were the responsibility of the council, and the execution of policy and the administrative details of government were the responsibility of the manager. The manager and the council worked as one, seamlessly shifting from policy to practice. This type of government was effective as long as the organizational structure reflected the intended relationship between council and manager. It was also effective as long as administration was left to the chief executive officer (CEO)—that is, the manager.[8] The rationale for this type of government was that the professional city manager was the ultimate administrator, separated from politics (policy making) but possessing the skill and acumen to ensure that the city worked well. Although such a pure separation between administration and politics rarely exists, the council-manager plan did at least make clear which type of official had primary responsibilities for policy making and which for administration. However, even in the earliest days of council-manager government, the engineer-managers knew that recommending Avenue A instead of First Street as a candidate for rebuilding had political implications. Indeed, L. P. Cookingham, the dean of city managers until his death in 1992, was fond of observing that one of the initial tasks of a manager was to determine just how political the council wanted the manager to be.

Because the local government manager was a professional generalist, the creation of an ethics code in 1924 was a necessary step: the code became the primary basis for judging performance and practice. The primacy of integrity in the local government management profession is connected partly to the fact that local government management is a matter of public trust and partly to the fact that quantitative performance measures are often hard to identify. The integrity of the manager was and is more important to how the occupation is understood than is true for most professions, especially for professions that emphasize specialization. Basically, the reason few professions take their codes of ethics as seriously as local government managers do is that for the latter there is less latitude and the need to enforce the code is more critical. Without the code there is no profession.

The ICMA Code of Ethics sets the local government managers' professional organization apart from many others. The code provides communities and elected officials with confidence that managers—at all levels and serving local governments in a wide range of capacities—who belong to ICMA nationally and internationally are required to maintain high ethical and professional standards. The managers' code helps them to do the right thing right. The council-manager form of government was created to remove politics from the day-to-day management of local government. The code was established and exists as the sole mechanism to achieve this goal, and through its aggressive enforcement by local government peers, it stays current, relevant, and effective. Our members have embraced the Code of Ethics and work very hard at keeping it alive and robust.

Gordon Anderson and
Anton "Tony" Dahlerbruch

What were the implications of melding this form of government with a professional practice based on a code of ethics? Ultimately, there were (and are) at least five:

- The profession is linked to a particular form of government (council-manager).
- The profession cannot be defined as a single occupation.
- The profession's practices are more varied and idiosyncratic than the practices in other professions.
- Diversity increases as governments evolve.
- Norms of behavior are critical.

Although the mind-set of the profession was focused on the council-manager form of government, reality was never so clear-cut. Beginning in the 1950s, membership in the profession (through its professional society[9]) slowly changed, eventually including city administrators, county administrators and managers, clerks of board, and international variants. Even without such changes in membership standards, this was a profession on the rise.

In sum, the nature and character of local government have changed radically since the beginning of the twentieth century. The level of professional and technical skill needed to be a competent manager is quite different in 2004 from what it was in 1920 or even 1960. During the first three decades of the twentieth century, for example, the responsibilities of local governments

> were generally confined to housekeeping or systems maintenance issues; sewage and waste disposal, water supply, public safety, and building and road construction; and other public works projects. The training required of local government managers was largely technical. In 1934, more than three-quarters of managers with college degrees had received them in engineering.[10]

In the first decade of the twenty-first century, it is generally recognized that the core values of the profession are no longer expressed through form of government or specific technical skills but through ethical practices and professional development. Nevertheless, a considerable residue of older views remains because the most reformed plan of government, the council-manager form, was originally inseparable from a suspicion of politics. Many managers still feel most comfortable at some distance from local politics; they sometimes achieve this distance by claiming special expertise in a functional area such as financial management or infrastructure management that seems remote from politics. In fact, the ICMA Code of Ethics (discussed in more detail on page 12) demands a separation from true political involvement. Yet the behavior of successful managers—behavior that includes giving policy direction and exercising community leadership (see Chapter 2)— sometimes belies separation. Clearly, walking the fine line between ethical behavior (which includes providing policy and community leadership) and unethical behavior (which is defined by the code as "political activities") raises the importance of professional education to a new level.

New political context: The revolution of the 1980s and 1990s

In the 1980s and 1990s charter reform began to move away from, instead of toward, pure council-manager government. In a few cities, mostly very large ones, the shift was to some form of mayor-council government. In most other cities, however, elements of nonreform government—chiefly the direct election of the mayor and the district election of council members—were introduced. But the most significant shift in form of government was the addition of a chief administrative officer (CAO) in what had been pure mayor-council cities. CAOs generally lack the authority to hire and fire but in all other respects fill the role of a professional local government manager. Thus, since the early 1980s a blurring of the lines between forms of government has been occurring.

There are several explanations for this evolution. First, many cities that adopted the council-manager form early in the twentieth century had changed economically, socially, and politically since deciding to adopt the innovative plan. Rather than being the new approach, the council-manager form was now the status quo. Accordingly, some of the reformers who in earlier times might have been advocates of the council-manager plan and therefore of the profession were now looking for alternatives, especially for more identifiable and accountable political leadership. However, even the more zealous reformers urged elected officials in traditional nonreformed (mayor-council) cities to add a professional CAO.

Second, a small change that was to have a lasting effect on the council-manager form was the shift to a separately elected mayor rather than a mayor who was appointed from within the council. Although many separately elected mayors had no more formal power than mayors appointed from councils, this change was to prove significant because it would pit the political ambitions of the legislators (the council) against those of the new executive (the mayor). Moreover, many directly elected mayors began to seek additional powers, mainly with regard to budgeting and key appointments. A parallel development was the shift from at-large to district election of council members. Indeed, district elections were second only to the addition of a CAO as the most common form of structural change in local government.[11]

I don't like to get involved in politics. The job is difficult enough with what lands on my desk.

Dave Osberg

The third change that came to fruition in the last two decades of the twentieth century had its roots in the 1960s and 1970s, a time of rising insistence that government do more, especially for those with the least political clout. The street-level bureaucrat, seen as the advocate for and voice of the disadvantaged, was frequently praised in the 1960s and 1970s. Academics and political activists, at least, held in high esteem those who were closest to the people.[12] Those at the top were suspect; they were part of the problem.

By the 1980s this discontent had broadened. The very concept of public service was held in considerable disdain. Politicians at every level of government and across a broad ideological spectrum found that the best way to get elected was to run against the government and, especially, against the careerists in government.[13] The label "bureaucrat" was virtually an expletive. Being a professional bureaucrat was even worse than being a professional politician. The local government manager was soon painted with the same broad brush of disrespect and anger as other careerists. Under such circumstances, the council-manager form with its emphasis on professionalism and apolitical administration struck many as a formula for old-fashioned and unresponsive government. The intensity of the arguments is conveyed by the points (and counterpoints) made in comments featured in newspapers in two cities—Fort Lauderdale and Cincinnati—that still have professional local government but where fierce campaigns for change have been waged:

> The proposed strong mayor system undermines the desired objectivity and professionalism of a county administrator. . . . My point is that consistently, and historically, the council-manager plan has maintained a more stable, ethical and efficient administration of the taxpayers' business than any other form of local government. The checks that are established in such a form of government do not allow absolute power in the hands of the chief administrative officer without responsive action to the legislative body.
> —George Hanbury in the *Sun-Sentinel* (Fort Lauderdale), February 28, 2000

> Under Issue 4, the mayor will be able to initiate the hiring and firing of the city manager; veto legislation, subject to override by six council members; and be able to appoint all council committee chairs. . . . Coming Together for Cincinnati, the pro-Issue 4 campaign committee, maintained that the new system would give the mayor's office credibility and political accountability.
> —Howard Wilkinson, in the *Cincinnati Enquirer,* May 5, 1999

> Strong mayors know votes put them in office because of their agenda. . . . By electing the mayor, the voters gave him a mandate to get the job done. "Beyond the issues, the mandates and the art of consensus building," David Axelrod told me, "electing a strong mayor boils down to electing a strong personality."
> —Cliff Radel, in the *Cincinnati Enquirer,* May 7, 1999

In the early twenty-first century, drawing a picture of what constitutes a particular form of local government has become complicated. Victor DeSantis and Tari Renner, explicating work by Bill Hansell, have identified three variants of council-manager government and four variants of mayor-council government; the distinctions depend on the relative authority of the mayor and of the administrator.[14] Figure 1–1 shows an approximation of the power of the professional administrator across the myriad forms of government.

ICMA has reported that the proportion of governments classified as council-manager rose from 34.7 percent of all city governments in 1984 to 53 percent in 2001 (the equivalent form in county government, the council-administrator form, remained constant at 12.2 percent from 1988 through 2002). These findings reflect the continuing robustness of professional local government management, particularly in communities with populations between 5,000 and 250,000. At the same time, however, the percentage of mayor-council cities and of counties with an appointed CAO also grew.[15] In 2003 Susan McManus and Charles Bullock concluded that "the council-manager form has continued to gain in popularity while the commission form [in which elected commissioners serve as directors of one or more functional departments] has faded somewhat; use of the mayor-council form has regained some ground, especially in larger jurisdictions [but the] position of chief appointed official increasingly has broad appeal across various forms of government."[16]

The greatly expanded powers of mayors in larger council-manager cities has eroded managerial authority. When the mayor controls or shares in the appointment to certain politically sensitive positions such as police chief and city attorney and

Figure 1-1   Professional administrator's authority in local government

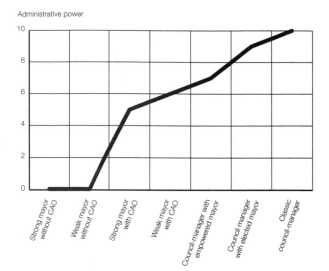

Source: Based on Victor S. DeSantis and Tari Renner, "City Government Structures: An Attempt at Clarification," *State and Local Government Review* 34, no. 2 (Spring 2002): 95–104.

has growing control over the budget, managerial authority is eroded. Nevertheless, many mayors and managers forge successful partnerships, sometimes at the expense of the council members.

In the smaller and midsize communities, where the council-manager plan continues to flourish, one may still see the breadth of authority envisioned by Richard Childs and the other early advocates of the profession. Yet there is no doubt that during the latter part of the twentieth century and the early years of the twenty-first, managerial authority was challenged not only in large cities (such as Cincinnati, San Diego, San Antonio, and Dallas) but also in smaller communities where newly established council-manager or council-administrator charters required long-powerful mayors to cede some authority to a chief administrative officer.

New politicians

While the political context has changed, research by James Svara and others notes that the makeup and character of those who serve on councils has also changed.[17] Most commonly cited in this respect are the single-issue candidates who have emerged at all levels of government. The presumed problem is that such candidates, when elected, have little regard or concern for, and provide little input on, most of the policy issues and practical service-delivery problems of local government. Their regard and input are directed only to the issues and problems that relate to their single concern.

A more critical problem is that many newly elected officials focus on issues of implementation. After all, often the core of campaigns for election or reelection is some issue of constituent service. Two interrelated attitudes shape the outlook of many council members: existing management practices must be challenged and privatization is a progressive solution to public sector problems.

Council members' new interest in implementation has put the manager much more in the spotlight, and at some point the desires and goals of managers and councils inevitably collide (this is the one profession where being fired is almost a badge of honor; see Chapter 8 for a discussion of being "IT"—that is, of being in transition). In some cases management practices even become a subject of political debate. The first action of some new councils is to fire the manager and bring in their own, someone with a different perspective on running the local government. Many council members, particularly those who have been elected on single issues, assume that careful scrutiny of the managerial and administrative decisions of the manager is their primary task. Judgments are based on specific decisions, not on performance in a broader sense.

Antagonism between council and manager can be exacerbated by a mayor seeking to consolidate power. When denied political leadership by a strong mayor, council members focus more heavily on administrative issues. However, antagonism between council and manager and between mayor and council is presumed by the public to be healthy and appropriate rather than an aberration.[18]

City government is becoming more about process and less about outcomes. Government cannot solve the problems facing some of our largest cities; they are too complex, too expensive, too highly charged. . . . Citizens want a visible leader who will lead them to the right solution and that leader is not seen as the low profile, technically competent, professional manager.
Mark M. Levin

Where has all this left the manager? Although the role has broadened just as Richard Childs predicted in 1918, the outlook is quite different from the one Childs anticipated. The need for professional knowledge and understanding to execute the policy directives of the council is replaced by the need for survival skills that will enable the manager to juggle the competing demands of mayor and council. Changes in municipal and county government have transformed the local government manager from the technical administrator of the early twentieth century into a manager of diverse interests and perspectives.

As mentioned above, managers in the twenty-first century are much more deeply engaged in policy making.[19] Success as a manager now depends on skills and relationships that have more to do with leadership than with administration. The skills and competencies implied by the distinction between administration and leadership are certainly not mutually exclusive (just the opposite), but the emphasis and application have changed. The profession in the early years of the twenty-first century is distinguished by

- A new emphasis on policy making
- Recognition that leadership skills are broader and more critical than administrative or managerial skills
- Realization that management positions are more precarious than they once were, and more subject to influences beyond the control of the manager
- The need to emphasize core values, standards of practice, and ethical behavior.

The real question is how can a city council and manager come to terms with leadership roles, separating the political leadership from the organizational leadership roles, and the manager keeping him/herself from being sucked into the former.
Charley Bowman

New leadership styles

At the start of the twenty-first century, the primary skills of the effective local government manager are the skills that characterize modern organizational leadership. The literature on management and leadership, even if studies directed to the private sector are filtered out, is quite extensive; and a cursory look at the body of work would consume far more space than is available here. Chapters 2 and 5 return to this topic in considerably more detail. This survey of two decades of change highlights new perspectives on the manager's role.

Managerial roles   The 1991 ICMA FutureVisions Consortium identified the following 13 important managerial roles:

- Consensus builder
- Educator on community issues
- Translator/interpreter of community values
- Problem solver
- Process leader
- Convener of interested parties and diverse community groups

- Team builder/mentor
- Source of empowerment
- Change agent
- Champion of new technologies
- Facilitator of conflict resolution
- Bearer of ethical standards
- Champion of leadership development within the community.

In 1991 ICMA's FutureVisions Consortium described managerial leadership as the

> ability to help people see more clearly their own desires and goals. Leadership is continuing quietly to instill in people the belief that they can successfully contend with the future. . . . Managers [in the future] will rely much less on fixed legal parameters— much more on political realities and strategic thinking and persuasiveness. . . . The manager as broker and negotiator, or unobtrusive leader, will dominate the time and resources of the top professional. . . . The more traditional internal management functions—that often require entirely different skills, knowledge, and experience— will fall to a new group of specialists.[20]

The key elements of management as leadership include, at a minimum, both an appreciation of how to frame problems and an understanding of the need for flexibility and experimentation in implementation of policy directives. Six elements of management practice that represent minimum competencies are

- Basing decisions on facts, including being fully aware of the context as both a public event and a specific circumstance
- Understanding the consequences of any action
- Recognizing obligations to others, whether teammates, subordinates, or citizens
- Visioning and creativity
- Preventing problems
- Demonstrating leadership.[21]

These competencies fall into two categories: the first three relate to how a manager defines problems, and the second three relate to how a manager decides what to do.

The way we define a problem shapes the solution to that problem, and the first step toward freedom to be creative in defining problems is to understand the facts broadly. Recognizing that facts may hide more than they reveal is the starting point for those who have the ability to define problems clearly when others can only list symptoms.[22]

The public nature of any problem confronting a public manager requires the manager to focus on citizens (not merely on clients or constituents) and on democratic process. The manager has a mandate to begin problem solving by creating a vision of an idealized future. To do this, the manager must be creative and sensitive to community sentiment.

Defining and solving problems is a collective job in a democracy. A team has the capability to address problems more creatively than an individual. Knowledge and participation are prerequisites for everyone involved in decision making, whether the decision-making team is limited to others within the organization or includes all citizens. Just as important, the perception by the public that decisions and actions are fair is critical for the public to support those decisions and actions.[23]

Carla Day recommends that organizational leaders (managers) use what she calls "value statements" to define an ethic that can serve as the basis for organizational action.

> Translating values into practice begins with developing an understanding of the normative practices that go with each value orientation. . . . Values that engage and empower employees and give clear direction are likeliest to succeed in bringing about behavioral change. But to guarantee compliance with new policies, values should also be supported by coherent and congruent regulatory practices within the framework of the existing culture.[24]

ICMA's Code of Ethics and Guidelines are an excellent starting point for developing an organizational ethic.

Together [concepts of ethics and democracy] form for me the backdrop of every decision I make at work every day. In government, you can't always make the decision that is the quickest or least expensive or most popular. Truly understanding that comes from ingrained concepts of ethics and democracy.
Wally Bobkiewicz

Borrowing from physics what is popularly referred to as chaos theory, Douglas Kiel developed a management perspective to help managers succeed in a chaotic world.[25] Chaos theory for management addresses organizational dynamics and change. It says that variability of performance is the norm and that trying to make employees fit into narrow confines of behavior (the "one best way" of scientific management) may only create problems. The goal is to take advantage of chaos (Kiel prefers the term "instability") to impel change. Just as luck, for some people, can mean the ability to recognize opportunity,[26] instability in the local government environment gives the good manager an opportunity to promote positive change. Managers must understand their role in fostering stability or instability and must use disorder to promote change and innovation.

Good and bad luck was the lot of Austin, the second-fastest-growing city in the country but one whose rapid growth was heavily dependent on high technology. Facing a 20th month of negative sales tax figures and a negative property evaluation for the first time in 12 years for FY 04, the city manager noted that "the higher you fly, the farther you can fall." The budget and its consequences are a "helluva" challenge, but the city had made its own luck by careful development of publicly owned utilities.
Toby Futrell

Two ways to apply chaos theory to management are to encourage participation and to create a diverse workforce. Encouraging participation is a way of stirring the pot; and the conflict of ideas and cultures gained through diversity helps achieve instability. The nonstable organization is a creative organization. Rather than use the energies of management to control and direct the organization toward a defined future (one that is unlikely to be achieved), managers should focus on looking for opportunities to destabilize the organization through change and innovation. These are not easy notions for managers who have been taught that control is key. Yet one senses intuitively the connection between instability and change even as one resists, or fears, trying to foster instability in practice.

Strategic management applies some of the same principles about the uncertainty and elusiveness of the future. Strategic management emphasizes working toward a broadly defined future, not taking a narrow path to a single point.

Helping an organization follow an unknown path through change and innovation is not an easy task. It requires a manager who has insight and courage. When goals are so far into the future that those who set them will not be around to be judged by the outcome, a controlling style seems a wise course. However, James MacGregor Burns, in a book titled simply *Leadership,*[27] suggests an alternative approach. He introduces the idea of transformational leadership; the key tenets are that

- Active leadership is important
- The way to change an organization's performance is to change its culture
- The leader must look ahead.

Burns argues that the key responsibility of the leader is to foster an organizational culture that seeks and supports the values of the people in it. Change itself is neither good nor bad. What can be evaluated is how the organization anticipates and responds to change. With one eye on an obscure future and the other on a commitment to a way of acting, leaders help organizations face change not as a problem but as a necessity and an opportunity.

Generally, I want to continue to build a team atmosphere where everyone's input is valued and considered. Ultimately, I expect the team approach to result in better organization and coordination within the county and better customer service.
Jan Christofferson

Burns emphasizes that a leader accomplishes transformation by

- Articulating a vision that defines the direction, values, and outlook for the organization
- Developing, in cooperation with others, a mission that defines the outcomes to be achieved
- Empowering all employees by granting them authority to make decisions and encouraging decision making at the lowest possible level
- Encouraging broad participation in all planning and decision making.

The ability to help an organization achieve its goals may be the best definition of leadership. John Gardner suggests that "leaders must look beyond the systems they are heading and grasp the relationship to larger realities." They must be able to craft agreements, network, exercise power beyond their official jurisdiction, and build institutions.[28]

The successful leader promotes an organizational culture that permits the organization to navigate a complex of issues, perspectives, perceptions, and ideologies. Luck, instability, and organizational change make a heady mix. The environment within which public managers work requires considerable skill and interpersonal acumen. Under these circumstances, the manager must be firmly grounded in the values and core understandings of the profession.

The traits needed by the leader in today's environment include

- A sense of commitment to the job, the goals, and the purpose of whatever the manager undertakes
- Attention to the broad picture, that is, to the overall results for which the organization is striving
- Personal self-assurance
- Faith in the people in the organization and a willingness to let them excel

- Attention to resources, including people, money, information, and opportunities
- Awareness of important relationships and institutions outside the organization.[29]

On being an ethical leader

Most professions emphasize academic degrees and credentials, but the local government profession has always concerned itself first and foremost with ethical action. The ICMA Code of Ethics found in Appendix A embodies the mission and core values of the local government management profession. These core values are

- Representative democracy
- The highest standards of honesty and integrity in local governance
- Professional management as an integral component of effective local government
- The council-manager form of government as the preferred form
- The value of international association
- Diversity in local government and in the association.[30]

Members of ICMA place a great deal of importance on personal integrity and adherence to the ICMA Code of Ethics, which was first approved in 1924 and supplemented with guidelines in 1972. All members of the association (including about 5,300 appointed managers at various levels) agree to abide by the code and are "subject to sanctions for any violations thereof which occur during their membership."[31] The professional local government manager takes responsibility not only for personal adherence to the Code of Ethics but also for the adherence—in values, actions, and behaviors—of all persons the manager appoints or supervises.

Fundamental to our service to our communities and our professional values is the need to consider thoughtfully when we as managers are morally, ethically, and/or legally required to confront misconduct.
Kevin Duggan

The ICMA Committee on Professional Conduct regularly investigates questionable conduct by members to determine whether it violates the code, and it recommends sanctions to the ICMA's executive board. Sanctions can include private censure, public censure, expulsion from ICMA, and a bar against reinstatement. (In 2002, ICMA expelled and barred from membership one member, publicly censured three members, and privately censured two members.) Infractions of the code that are sanctioned by the organization typically involve inappropriate personal relationships, violations of the public trust, encroachments on the role of elected officials, campaign contributions to local and federal candidates, and failure to fulfill commitments. The actual number of sanctions is always small, but the fact of the sanctions dramatically demonstrates the importance of the code.

An ethical problem   Scenario: The city has a sports arena and plans to work with a consultant to come up with a state-of-the-art lighting plan for the facility. The consultant has completed a similar project in another state and has offered to fly the public works director out to see it. The public works director thinks this is a good idea and argues that it won't cost the city any money and will ensure that the city gets what it expects. The city manager, however, has some doubts about the offer and has asked for guidance.

This ethics inquiry, along with the unofficial response to it, was posted in the May 2003 issue of *Public Management.* The inquiry and response are a useful subject for discussion.

The effective professional

As emphasized above, the profession of local government management is anything but static. The nature and structure of the governments within which managers work have expanded and changed, and public expectations have changed. In this context it is vital that managers continually review and assess their capabilities to manage, to lead, and to promote ethical behaviors. ICMA has acknowledged the importance of continual self-assessment in Tenet 8 of the Code of Ethics, which says that every member of ICMA has the "duty continually to improve the member's professional ability and to develop the competence of associates in the use of management techniques." The guidelines for this tenet specify

Self-assessment   Each member should assess his or her professional skills and abilities on a periodic basis.

Professional development   Each member should commit at least 40 hours per year to professional development activities that are based on the practices identified by the members of ICMA.

To support Tenet 8, during the 1990s the ICMA membership developed three interrelated programs:

- A set of practices or core content areas essential to effective local government management
- The ICMA University, "a comprehensive delivery system for professional development offerings"
- Voluntary Credentialing Program, which is a means of identifying and recognizing ICMA members who demonstrate a combination of education and experience, adherence to high standards of integrity, and a commitment to lifelong learning and professional development.

These three programs provide a solid foundation for local government managers who want to explore the concepts of leadership, ethics, and management. The 18 core content areas, or practices, were developed and approved by the entire membership of ICMA and represent the state of the local government management profession. The practices essentially correspond to the precepts and skills of leadership and ethics described above and examined in more detail in subsequent chapters. These areas lay out the key approaches and activities that make local government more effective. The detailed list appears in Appendix B; the list below presents only the labels given to the core content areas.

Practices for effective local government management

- Staff effectiveness
- Policy facilitation
- Functional and operational expertise and planning
- Citizen service
- Quality assurance
- Initiative, risk taking, vision, creativity, and innovation
- Technological literacy
- Democratic advocacy and citizen participation
- Diversity
- Budgeting
- Financial analysis
- Human resources management
- Strategic planning
- Advocacy and interpersonal communication
- Presentation skills
- Media relations
- Integrity
- Personal development.

The ICMA University offers programs and resources centered on these 18 practices that have been identified as essential to effective local government management. ICMA members are, of course, responsible for assessing their own skills and abilities and determining what continuing education activities to pursue.

The Voluntary Credentialing Program was a significant step toward providing the same kind of guidance and perspective on management and leadership that the guidelines adopted for the ICMA Code of Ethics do on ethics. The program helps interested members quantify the unique expertise they bring to their communities. It also guides ICMA members in focusing their lifelong professional development. Members who complete the program are recognized by the ICMA executive board and are awarded the designation of ICMA Credentialed Manager (or, for those who lack the full experience required, Credentialed Manager Candidate). The program's key attribute is its emphasis on both expertise (born of experience and education) and the need for lifelong learning and professional development.

In summary, a code of ethics implies continual self-assessment, which the local government management profession carries out by means of a list of core competencies, a comprehensive training agenda, and a credentialing program. On behalf of its membership, ICMA has developed a support system to ensure the competence and skill of members of the profession. The expectation is that managers who adhere to ICMA's Code of Ethics and pursue lifelong professional development will display the managerial and leadership traits necessary to create effective local government.

Looking ahead

The primary purpose of this chapter has been to establish the meaning of professional local government management and thereby foreshadow key, recurrent themes of the book. The focus has been on the near term, that is, how the changes of the last decades of the twentieth century have influenced the profession and what skills and abilities its practitioners need in order to be effective. Particular importance has been paid to ethics and leadership. The chapters that follow discuss the details of how to be an effective local government manager.

Chapter 2 examines the characteristics of community (broadly defined to include not only government but also citizens and organizations other than government) and the processes involved in exercising community leadership. The chapter also examines the manager's responsibilities for helping both to shape the policy agenda and to create programs to implement those policies.

Chapter 3 focuses on the manager's relations with the governing body. Not only have the charter-defined relationships between the manager and elected officials changed, but so also have citizens' and elected officials' expectations for managerial behavior. The chapter emphasizes the importance of a strong partnership between the appointed professional manager and elected officials in the effort to create and maintain an effective local government; at the same time, the chapter also acknowledges that one of the manager's important roles is helping governing board members improve their own effectiveness.

Chapter 4 focuses on the role of the manager in shaping the future of the community. Although the chapter notes the importance of traditional planning processes (for example, strategic planning), it emphasizes economic development, the sustainable community, and community visioning. The element common to all these topics is community building.

Chapter 5 addresses the essential skills that mark a good manager and considers the three sets of resources for which managers are continually responsible:

people, finances, and information. How the manager allocates each set of resources determines the manager's capacity to accomplish goals, to respond quickly to changing circumstances, and to ensure that each resource is mined to the fullest.

Chapter 6 introduces the idea of service-oriented management. Whereas the preceding chapter looks at the inner resources of the local government, this chapter looks at the program planning that results in services provided to the community. Of equal importance is how the manager enhances productivity and orchestrates the evaluation of performance and the success of programs.

Chapter 7 takes an expansive view of relationships between and among governmental and nongovernmental organizations, with an emphasis on the importance of networking. The effective manager must develop appropriate interactions with the people in key organizations in the community. Overall, managers must learn how to capitalize on the many different resources available from organizations outside the government.

Chapter 8 looks at the personal side of management, including various career paths and levels of local government management. It deals with the realities of how to manage self, health, family relations, career disruptions, and professional networking. In short, the chapter allows the reader a glimpse of what it is like on a personal level to be a local government manager.

Recap

- Professions are characterized by practices, norms or values, and perspectives as well as by educational level, client recognition, professional identity, professional culture, a code of ethics, formal measures of competence, and discretion. Commitment to professionalism is the hallmark of local government managers.

- The local government management profession has evolved from focusing on engineering solutions for public works problems to orchestrating complex relations with diverse councils, other governmental and nongovernmental organizations, and citizens who have divergent interests.

- The local government management profession is distinguished by its generalist nature and the importance it places on ethical behavior. For members of the International City/County Management Association, the Code of Ethics is a guide to daily decision making and behavior. The special emphasis on and institutional commitment to ethical conduct are distinguishing features of this profession.

- The theory and practice of local government management revolve around leadership.

- The changing political climate and the resulting alterations in forms of government profoundly affect the profession. Managers increasingly find themselves sharing power in various ways with mayors, a sharing that creates strains between the administrator and the political executive, but the number and proportion of jurisdictions with professional administrators is growing.

- The skill set for a manager keeps evolving, but the modern local manager is aided by a set of essential practices and skills identified by peers and reinforced by requirements for annual professional development activities.

Sample performance evaluation

Confidential
City Manager Performance Evaluation
City Of Garden City, Kansas

Responsibility or Characteristic	Rate from 1–10, 10 being excellent Circle Rating

General Administration

Manpower Development   Does he/she appoint and train effective subordinates? Is he/she able to recruit and retain quality employees?

1 2 3 4 5 6 7 8 9 10

Leadership   Does he/she motivate others to maximum performance? Is he/she respected as demanding but fair? Does he/she get enthusiastic response to his/her new ideas and needed reorganizations?

1 2 3 4 5 6 7 8 9 10

Supervision   Does he/she adequately supervise and direct the activities of the Department Heads and staff? Is he/she able to control the operational activities of the City through others? Is he/she available to his/her employees for guidance and counseling? Does he effectively develop Department Heads and staff people?

1 2 3 4 5 6 7 8 9 10

Job Organization   Does he/she delegate responsibility effectively? Does he/she use his/her time productively? Does he/she program activities in an orderly and systematic way?

1 2 3 4 5 6 7 8 9 10

Execution of Policy   Does he/she understand and comply with the overall policies, laws and philosophy of the City? Do his/her efforts lead towards successful accomplishment of goals? Does he/she measure results against goals and take corrective action?

1 2 3 4 5 6 7 8 9 10

Planning   Does the Manager translate polices and objectives into specific and effective programs? Does the Manager independently recognize problems, develop relative facts, formulate alternate solutions and decide on appropriate recommendations.

1 2 3 4 5 6 7 8 9 10

Budget   Is the budget developed in a systematic and effective manner? Is the budget proposal for the Manager normally reasonable and appropriate? Does he/she carry out the budget satisfactorily and control expenses within the levels set in the budget?

1 2 3 4 5 6 7 8 9 10

Communication   Does he/she keep appropriate people informed? Does he/she present his/her thoughts in an orderly and understanding manner? Is he/she able to be persuasive?

1 2 3 4 5 6 7 8 9 10

Reporting   Does he/she submit accurate and complete staff reports on schedule? Do the reports adequately convey information on the City?

1 2 3 4 5 6 7 8 9 10

Commission Communication   Does the Manager provide the Commission with adequate information to make decisions?

1 2 3 4 5 6 7 8 9 10

Written Communication   How effective are the Manager's letters, memoranda and other forms of written information?

1 2 3 4 5 6 7 8 9 10

Response to Commission   Does the Manager respond in a positive way to suggestions and guidance from the Commission? Is the Manager attuned to the Commissions attitudes, feelings and needs?   1 2 3 4 5 6 7 8 9 10

Productivity   Can the Manager be depended on for sustained productive work? Does the Manager readily assume responsibility? Does the Manager meet time estimates within his/her control?   1 2 3 4 5 6 7 8 9 10

Stress Management   Is the Manager able to resolve problems under strain and unpleasant conditions? How well does the Manager tolerate conditions of uncertainty? Does the Manager respond well to stressful situations and adequately deal with the stress inherent to the position?   1 2 3 4 5 6 7 8 9 10

External Relationships

Community Relations   Is the Manager skillful in his/her dealing with the News media? Does he/she properly avoid politics and partisanship? Does he/she show an honest interest in the community? Does he/she properly convey the policies and programs of the City?   1 2 3 4 5 6 7 8 9 10

Community Reputation   What is the general attitude of the community to the Manager? Is he/she regarded as person of high integrity and ability? Is his/her public credibility an asset or liability to the City?   1 2 3 4 5 6 7 8 9 10

Professional Reputation.   How does the Manager stand among his/her colleagues? Does he/she deal effectively with other public managers? Is he/she respected by professional and staff representatives of other cities and counties? Does he/she attend and participate in seminars and conferences for professional development?   1 2 3 4 5 6 7 8 9 10

Intergovernmental Relations   Does the Manager work effectively with federal, state, and other local government representatives? Is the relationship with other local government officials beneficial to the City? Is he/she able to facilitate cooperative efforts among various local agencies and the City?   1 2 3 4 5 6 7 8 9 10

Personal Characteristics

Imagination   Does he/she show originality in approaching problems? Does he/she create effective solutions? Is he/she able to visualize the implications of various alternatives?   1 2 3 4 5 6 7 8 9 10

Objectivity   Is he/she unemotional and unbiased? Does he/she take a rational and impersonal viewpoint based on facts and qualified opinions? Is he/she able to divide his/her personal feelings from those which would most effectively convey the City's interest?   1 2 3 4 5 6 7 8 9 10

Drive   Is the Manager energetic and willing to spend the time necessary to do a good job? Does he/she have good initiative and is he/she a self-starter? Does he/she have good mental and physical stamina?   1 2 3 4 5 6 7 8 9 10

Judgment and Decisiveness   Is he/she able to reach quality decisions in a timely fashion? Are his/her decisions generally good? Does he/she exercise good judgment in making decisions and in his/her general conduct?   1 2 3 4 5 6 7 8 9 10

Attitudes   Is he/she enthusiastic? Cooperative? Willing to adapt? Does he/she have an enthusiastic attitude toward the City, both professional and personally?   1 2 3 4 5 6 7 8 9 10

Integrity   Does the Manager fulfill his/her responsibilities and duties in accordance with the ICMA Code of Ethics? Is he/she honest and forthright in his/her professional capacities? Does he/she have a reputation in the community for honesty and integrity?   1 2 3 4 5 6 7 8 9 10

Self-Assurance   Is the Manager self-assured of his/her abilities? Is he/she able to be honest with himself/herself and take constructive criticism? Does he/she take responsibility for mistakes which are his/her? Is he/she confident enough to make decisions and take actions as may be required without undue supervision from the Commission?   1 2 3 4 5 6 7 8 9 10

Composite Performance Rating

General Administration   _____

External Relationships   _____

Personal Characteristics   _____

STRONG POINTS

WEAK POINTS

SUGGESTIONS AND SPECIFIC DIRECTION

GENERAL COMMENTS/DIRECTION FOR IMPROVEMENT

Notes

1 Leonard White, *The City Manager* (Chicago: University of Chicago Press, 1927), 149.

2 See Chester A. Newland, "The Future of Council-Manager Government," in *Ideal and Practice in Council-Manager Government,* ed. George W. Frederickson (Washington, D.C.: International City Management Association, 1989), 257–271.

3 Frederick C. Mosher, *Democracy and the Public Service* (Englewood Cliffs, N.J.: Prentice-Hall, 1968), 106.

4 Ibid., 122.

5 Daniel W. Fitzpatrick, "City Management: Profession or Guild," *Public Management* (January/February 1990): 32.

6 The distinction between the city manager and the city administrator that was codified in the definition of full membership in ICMA through the 1960s is an example of preserving values and norms that were critical in 1920 but are increasingly less relevant.

7 The idea of a unitary system is borrowed from discussions with David Y. Miller, formerly a city manager and now an academician. Miller noted that in the council-manager form the success of the government rests on cooperation between the manager and the council. When the two work as one, the form is most successful. However, when a form that includes a separately elected—and particularly strong—mayor is substituted, the government effectively has three parts, with the manager in the middle. Each of the two sides has its own goals and aspirations. Being in the middle requires quite different behaviors and skills from being part of a cooperative unitary effort. See

also Greg J. Protasel, "Abandonment of the Council-Manager Plan: A New Institutional Perspective, in *Ideal and Practice in Council-Manager Government*," 22–32.

8 James Svara, "Dichotomy and Duality: Reconceptualizing the Relationship between Policy and Administration in Council-Manager Governments," *Public Administration Review* 45, no. 1 (January–February 1985): 221–232; Svara, "Complementarity of Politics and Administration as a Legitimate Alternative to the Dichotomy Model," *Administration and Society* 30, no. 6 (January 1999): 676–705.

9 The name of the society until 1969 was the International City Managers' Association, when it was changed to International City Management Association. Only since 1991 has it been the International City/County Management Association.

10 Tari Renner, "The Local Government Management Profession at Century's End," *The Municipal Year Book 2001* (Washington, D.C.: International City/County Management Association, 2001), 35.

11 Susan McManus and Charles S. Bullock III, "The Form, Structure, and Composition of America's Municipalities in the New Millennium," in *The Municipal Year Book 2003* (Washington, D.C.: International City/County Management Association, 2003), 1–18.

12 Frank Marini, ed., *Toward the New Public Administration* (Scranton, Pa.: Chandler Publishing, 1971).

13 Charles Goodsell, *The Case for Bureaucracy*, 4th ed. (Chatham, N.J.: Chatham House Publishers, Inc., 2004) is among the many who explore this phenomenon.

14 Victor S. DeSantis and Tari Renner, "City Government Structures: An Attempt at Clarification," *State and Local Government Review* 34, no. 2 (Spring 2002): 95–104; Bill Hansell, "Is It Time to 'Reform' the Reform?" *Public Management* 80, no. 12 (December 1998): 15–16; see also H. George Frederickson and Gary Alan Johnson, "The Adapted American City: A Study of Institutional Dynamics," *Urban Affairs Review* 36 (July 2001): 872–884; James H. Svara, *Official Leadership in the City: Patterns of Conflict and Cooperation* (New York: Oxford University Press, 1990); Craig M. Wheeland, "An Institutionalist Perspective on Mayoral Leadership: Linking Leadership Style to Formal Structure," *National Civic Review* 91 (Spring 2002): 25–39.

15 See, for example, Tari Renner, "The Local Government Management Profession at Century's End," *The Municipal Year Book 2001* (Washington, D.C.: International City/County Management Association, 2001); Kimberly Nelson, *Structure of American Municipal Government*, Special Data Issue, no. 4 (Washington, D.C.: International City/County Management Association, 2002); and "Council-Manager Government . . . The Most Popular Form of U.S. Local Government Structure," drawn from ICMA's *The Municipal Yearbook 2002* and available at www.icma.org by clicking on "Council-Manager Form of Government," then "Form of Government Statistics" among the available e-Library documents.

16 McManus and Bullock, 17.

17 Svara, "Dichotomy and Duality," and "Complementarity of Politics and Administration"; Protasel, "Abandonment of the Council-Manager Plan"; Kimberly Nelson, *Elected Municipal Councils*, Special Data Issue, no. 3 (Washington, D.C.: International City/County Management Association, 2002); McManus and Bullock, 16.

18 David Y. Miller, interview, March 30, 2003.

19 See, for example, Greg J. Protasel, "Leadership in Council-Manager Cities: The Institutional Perspective," in *Ideal and Practice in Council-Manager Government*, ed. H. George Frederickson (Washington, D.C.: International City Management Association, 1989), 114–122; and Charldean Newell and David N. Ammons, "City Managers Don't Make Policy: A Lie, Let's Face It," *National Civic Review* (March/April 1988): 124–132.

20 Amy Cohen Paul, *Future Challenges, Future Opportunities: The Final Report of the ICMA FutureVisions Consortium* (Washington, D.C.: International City Management Association, 1991), 4.

21 Raymond W. Cox III, "Creating a Decision Architecture," *Global Virtue Ethics Review* 2, no. 1 (Summer 2000).

22 Gareth Morgan, *Imagines of Organization* (Newbury Park, Calif.: Sage Publications, 1986).

23 Stuart Gilman, "Public Sector Ethics and Government Reinvention: Realigning Systems to Meet Organizational Change," *Public Integrity* 1, no. 2 (Spring 1999): 175–192.

24 Carla Day, "Balancing Organizational Priorities: A Two-Factor Values Model of Integrity and Conformity," *Public Integrity* 1, no. 2 (Spring 1999): 162–164.

25 L. Douglas Kiel, *Managing Chaos and Complexity in Government: A New Paradigm for Managing Change, Innovation, and Organizational Renewal* (San Francisco: Jossey-Bass, 1994).

26 Robert Behn, *Leadership Counts: Lessons for Public Managers* (Cambridge: Harvard University Press, 1991).

27 James MacGregor Burns, *Leadership* (New York: Harper and Row, 1979).

28 John Gardner, "The Changing Nature of Leadership," *Independent Sector* (July 1988): 14.

29 Summary of Patrick Manion, "Promoting Excellence in Management," *The Effective Local Government Manager*, 2nd ed. (Washington, D.C.: International City/County Management Association, 1993), 81–105.

30 ICMA Strategic Plan, approved July 2000.

31 ICMA Code of Ethics: Rules of Procedure for Enforcement, II.A.

Achieving effective community leadership

Community leadership is not a new role for managers, but trends in local politics make it more important than ever that the local government manager bring to this role the distinctive qualities of responsible professionalism. Furthermore, in their interactions with citizens, managers need to develop a new awareness of the changing dynamics of community life; they also need to use new organizational methods and personal skills. The question, therefore, is not whether managers are involved in the community but rather how much they are involved and, above all, how effectively.

Local government managers are significant figures not only in their governments but also in their cities or counties as a whole. They may be more visible or less, but by virtue of their positions they are at the center of efforts to identify and address the needs of their communities. Although the title "manager" implies an emphasis on carrying out the policies adopted by elected officials and an internal and organizational focus, in reality the people who fill the position of top manager or administrator in cities and counties are community leaders in three respects. First, they help shape the agenda of the city or county and propose policies for adoption by elected officials. Second, as both individuals and representatives of their governments, they interact with people outside of government and thereby contribute to the life of the community. Third, they shape the orientation of their governmental organization to citizens: how the organization treats citizens and how it facilitates citizens' participation in governmental affairs.

Another way to describe the three ways in which local government managers are community leaders is to point out that, alone among public administrators, they interact directly with three key sets of actors (see Figure 2–1). First, the local government manager works for and interacts directly with the governing board or the mayor or both. Second, the manager also handles a wide range of interactions with the people and organizations within the city or county and outside it. Finally, the manager is the head of the administrative organization—not the assistant to the head—and therefore shapes the way local government staff members deal with the citizens they serve.

There can be tension among the three aspects of the manager's leadership role—leadership vis-à-vis elected officials, in the wider community, and within the organization—and some managers choose to give greater emphasis to one aspect than to others. The distinctive challenge of local government management is to blend these three dimensions of the position to fashion comprehensive community leadership.

After first considering whether community leadership is appropriate, this chapter explores the three respects in which local government managers provide community leadership; assesses the changing political context in which managers operate in the new millennium; and offers guidelines for assessing one's own personal style, the dynamics of the community, and the characteristics of the major actors in community politics. The chapter concludes with a consideration of key behavioral components of effective community leadership.

Figure 2–1   Key relationships of local government
managers

Source: Based on Victor S. DeSantis and Tari Renner, "City Government Structures: An Attempt at Clarification," *State and Local Government Review* 34, no. 2 (Spring 2002): 95–104.

Appropriateness of community leadership by local government managers

It is possible to minimize the community-leadership role of the local government manager. Some people would argue that the manager's job is to work for elected officials, give them the information they need to make decisions, and direct the organization. In this view, the manager lets elected officials handle the community-leadership dimension of local government. The manager focuses on the internal organization and seeks to keep outside forces from interfering with the work of local government. This approach is characterized by a passion for anonymity. It is commonly believed that most managers before World War II took this low-profile approach and confined themselves to the administrative sphere. In fact, however, community leadership has a long tradition in local government management.

From the beginning of the council-manager form to the present, community leadership has been recognized as a central responsibility of local government managers. The origins of this view can be traced to Richard Childs and his call (in 1918) for managers to create "new enterprises of service" (see Chapter 1) and to the drafters of the second Model City Charter (in 1915), which endorsed the council-manager plan of government. The drafters of that charter expected the manager to exert great influence on "civic policy" and urged the manager to "show himself to be a leader, formulating policies and urging their adoption by the council."[1] C. A. Harrell of Norfolk, Virginia, in his presidential address to ICMA in 1948, endorsed this approach.

When offering leadership in the community, managers will naturally be concerned to do so in a professional way.[2] Professionalism should characterize the manager's objective, methods, and standards of conduct. The objective should be to advance the public interest. The methods should facilitate discussion, obtain feedback from citizens, and contribute to strategic planning. The standards of conduct should produce behavior that promotes inclusiveness and equal opportunities for citizens to participate, ensures fairness and impartiality when demands are assessed and conflicts resolved, and advances equity in the distribution of resources within the community. When managers have a professional objective and adhere to professional methods and standards of conduct, they will be operating within a professional framework in their community-leadership activities.

The values and standards that guide community leadership are clearly articulated in the organizational norms of ICMA; and, building on its traditions, the local government management profession has committed itself to offering multifaceted community leadership. The ICMA Code of Ethics (Appendix A) and Declaration of Ideals (Appendix C) oblige the manager to promote the welfare of the community, serve all the people, promote equity and social justice, support citizen participation, and create diversity in that participation. Also, a set of standards for community leadership has been articulated as part of ICMA's Practices for Effective Local Government Management (see Chapter 1): 10 of the 18 core content areas deal directly with citizens and the community, and this count does not include areas relevant to community leadership but applicable to all aspects of the manager's work (e.g., integrity, presentation skills, and personal development).[3] The full text of the practices appears in Appendix B.

Finally, although the manager's job is obviously grounded in the relationship with the council, two current trends that affect the work of local government professionals are "building and maintaining a sense of community" and "modernizing the organization."[4]

The ideal manager is a positive, vital force in the community. He spends a great deal of his time thinking of broad objectives which would greatly improve community life. Why should he hesitate to initiate policy proposals and submit them to the council? Neither the mayor nor individual councilmen can give much time to this task and if the manager also shies away from such leadership the community stands still and important matters are allowed to pass by default. . . . [The manager] visualizes broad objectives, distant goals, far-sighted projects.
C. A. Harrell

Community-leadership aspects of local government management

Community leadership entails monitoring all aspects of the interaction between the local government and the community served. Local government managers are community leaders when they shape the council's agenda and propose policy, when they relate directly to individuals and groups in the community, and when they make administrative and managerial decisions within their organizations. Community leadership is a long-standing role of local government managers, and its scope has expanded over time in response to new conditions in communities.

Shaping the agenda and proposing policy

Local government managers are not neutral bystanders when it comes to setting the agenda for their governments and making policy proposals. (See Chapter 6 for other perspectives on agenda making.) Surveys of city and county managers over the years have indicated a widespread acceptance of their obligation to provide policy leadership. City and county managers generally agree (80 percent or more) that a manager should advocate major changes in policies, assume leadership in shaping policies, and advocate new services in order to promote equity and fairness for low-income groups and minorities.[5] Consistent with these views, a majority do not agree that the manager should remain neutral on any issues on which the community is divided. The manager complements the political leadership of the governing board with a professional perspective on the community's needs and on ways to address them,[6] and on the basis of his or her knowledge, experience, and independent monitoring of community sentiments and conditions, the manager may be led to raise issues or propose alternatives that the board would not have considered.

Agenda setting involves both broad decisions about mission and specific policy decisions. Mission decisions determine the basic purposes and role of government within the community and the goals that are pursued.[7] In making such decisions, managers favor extensive involvement by elected officials. Managers must recognize, however, that it is often hard to get serious consideration for major changes despite (or because of) the high stakes involved. The manager must decide whether and how to raise an issue that is being ignored or is unpopular and how to help groups that are having difficulty getting a matter on the political agenda.

Policy decisions involve deciding how to spend money, design a program, or develop the details of a plan. Concrete policy proposals are likely to draw the attention of many participants with specific interests. Staff members play a large role in developing these proposals because they typically have in-depth knowledge about the matter, but local government managers must ensure that consultation occurs with, and input is invited from, all the groups that will be affected by a policy decision.

Local government managers are highly involved in shaping the mission of their communities and in making policy recommendations, and they have an effect that both they and elected officials recognize. In the 1997 survey referred to in note 5, city managers in council-manager cities rated their own influence as greater than the mayor's or council members' in both the budgetary and economic development processes; city administrators in mayor-council cities rated the mayor's influence as higher than their own in economic development but lower in budgeting.[8] When council members are interviewed, they see things somewhat differently, although they recognize the manager's contributions. They do not view the city manager's influence as greater than theirs, but, in a 2001 survey of cities over 25,000 in population, more than half of the council members in council-manager cities considered the city manager to be a very important initiator in the policy process, and another 38 percent saw the manager as an important source of initiation. City administrators in mayor-council cities were considered to be very important by 30 percent of council members, and an additional 49 percent rated their contribution as important.[9]

With changing trends in the social and political characteristics of communities (discussed in greater detail below), local government managers are expected to contribute even more broadly to their communities in terms of setting the agenda and proposing policy. Community groups are becoming more contentious in pushing for specific favored programs, and governing boards more fragmented—and both developments make it harder for elected officials to set goals and establish policies that are consistent with the goals.[10] Thus, it is even more important for the manager to monitor the community independently and pay close attention to the policy-making process. The manager must put long-term questions on the table for consideration, secure continuing support for previous commitments, and critically examine the contribution of new initiatives to overall goals and purposes. Local government managers do not dictate what matters are on the agendas of their communities, but they are the keepers of the agenda who help ensure that important matters receive attention.

Relating directly to the community

The second aspect of community leadership is relating to the community, or community relations, and it entails participating in organizations and civic affairs generally. It includes explaining what local government is doing and exploring the possibility of new needs and approaches. In addition, the manager may be instrumental in helping forge partnerships between government and the community. The manager negotiates with private citizens and organizations to get support for local government projects and seeks help from the community in dealing with problems that government cannot fully address. Roughly half of local government managers think they should work through powerful members of the community to achieve policy goals.[11] Managers also are involved in mediating differences and helping resolve controversies among groups. In addition, they can help promote a sense of community.

There is a trend toward the use of comprehensive community-based strategies to address social and economic challenges. For example, more and more professional managers—whether at the city, county, or state level—are being called on to provide leadership in redesigning programs to better meet the needs of families and children. This trend requires managers and agency directors to be creative and flexible, at times even donning the hats of community organizers to mobilize neighborhood groups and other citizens to be more involved in policy and planning.[12]

More generally, local government managers have extensive interactions with a variety of individuals and groups in the community, although from country to country the amount of interaction varies. Compared with chief administrators in 13 other countries (in Europe plus Australia), U.S. managers have a very high overall involvement with citizens, business leaders, leaders from voluntary and nonprofit associations, and journalists (see Table 2–1). In all, 14 countries were studied: Australia, Belgium, Denmark, Finland, France, Great Britain, Ireland, Italy, Netherlands, Norway, Portugal, Spain, Sweden, and the United States.

These interactions serve two purposes. First, managers are soliciting input by informing a wide range of actors in the community about the work of local government and by receiving information in return about the ideas and concerns of these actors. Second, managers are building a constituency—people in the community who are interested in what managers are trying to accomplish and are willing to provide help. This is not a political following that permits the manager to stand against the council, but a network of individuals and groups through which the manager can communicate to the larger community and from which the manager can receive information and suggestions. Although local governments have extensive formal channels of communication, these do not eliminate the need for extensive informal channels as well.

U.S. local government managers can be divided into two broad groups according to the extent and nature of their networking with the community and with other governments. In the 14-country study mentioned above, managers fell into four groups of approximately equal size, each based on the managers' own assessments of what kinds of actors were important to their success. One group of managers was largely isolated from all actors, including elected officials in their own governments (this group is called "isolates"). A second group focused only on the mayor, council, and staff; no other external relationships were very important ("internal networkers"). A third group focused primarily on relationships with other governments but had relatively little contact with other actors within the government or in the community ("intergovernmental networkers"). The fourth group was made up of managers who were inclusive in their networking behavior; they considered elected officials, other governments, and a wide range of individuals and groups in their own communities all to be important to their success ("inclusive networkers").

Table 2–1   Extent of chief administrators' communications with actors in the community

Communication with:	U.S. score*	U.S. rank among countries	Mean for 13 other countries
Citizens	83.3	1.5	62.1
Private business interests	45.9	1	28.8
Leaders from voluntary and nonprofit organizations	39.3	3	23.1
Journalists	53.6	1	31.2
Composite index	55.5	1	36.3

Source: Adapted from James H. Svara, "U.S. City Managers and Administrators in a Global Perspective," *The Municipal Year Book 1999* (Washington, D.C.: ICMA, 1999), Table 3/6.

*Involvement is measured on a 100-point scale, with the highest score indicating daily contact; 75, several times a week; 50, weekly contact; 25, once or twice a month; and 0, no contact.

Note: Weighted number of U.S. respondents is 285–287, depending on the item; weighted number of respondents from other countries is 3,440–3,721. The other countries are Australia, Belgium, Denmark, Finland, France, Great Britain, Ireland, Italy, Netherlands, Norway, Portugal, Spain, and Sweden.

Almost all U.S. managers in the survey fell into the second and fourth groups. Over half—55 percent—had primarily internal networks. These managers focused on the elected officials and their own organizations and gave little attention to others. In contrast, 42 percent were inclusive networkers—the highest percentage for all countries except Finland—who assigned higher than average importance to community leaders and other governments as well as to elected officials. This proportion is high compared with the total of 27 percent for all the countries.[13] Although it can be argued that community relations is a key ingredient of effectiveness as a local government manager, more than half of U.S. managers are largely inside players, offering community leadership primarily through their interactions with the council and their own staff but with only modest direct links to other actors in the community. The average of 27 percent for all countries indicates that, despite the fact that community relations is the second of the three aspects of community leadership, most managers do not have broad, inclusive networks in the community.

Orienting the organization to the community

The third aspect of local government management that points to community leadership as a role for managers is the orientation managers give to their organization in its treatment of citizens. Many elements of local government managers' leadership of the organization—both their administrative and their managerial decisions—are relevant in this regard.

Administrative decisions involve delivering services, implementing policies, and undertaking projects. These decisions impinge directly on the citizens who will receive the service or are affected by the policy or project. These decisions are usually made by administrative staff according to the technical, legal, and organizational criteria appropriate to the type of decision being made. Nevertheless, under the guidance of the manager, staff in the implementing department have to consider what kind of citizen involvement is needed to ensure that the implementation is effective and that citizens will meet it with responsiveness and acceptance. For example, the police can be more effective and can work more cooperatively with citizens when the type of policing adopted is community based. Another example involves permitting and inspections in subdivision development: these can be more effective and efficient if administrators seek input from builders. A third example: consulting with residents and operating in accordance with fair criteria for siting facilities can reduce conflict over who gets something desirable (such as a community center) or something undesirable (such as a landfill). In other words, when an organization ignores citizens' reactions, the likelihood of controversy and extensive involvement by the governing board increases.

The traditional way in the U.K. is to appoint an in-house public relations manager to herald the dawn of a new empire of assistants, support staff, and escalating publications budgets. . . . My approach . . . proceeds from the simple proposition that all staff should be involved in publicising their services, and it should be a part of the job of all local government managers (not just top managers) to develop proactive PR skills as part of their core jobs.
Michael Ball

Furthermore, managers need to set high standards for service delivery and for staff relations with citizens. They should instill the attitude that all staff members are responsible for positive interaction with the community.

Management decisions, too, can be linked to community leadership. These decisions involve the coordination and control of the resources of the organization.

Management decisions largely affect internal matters and are guided by systems and procedures. They concern personnel, hiring, promotion, and appraisal; contracting and purchasing; and the technical aspects of governmental functions, such as engineering standards for street construction. Normally these management decisions are made by staff and are handled internally. But if the decisions affect outside groups or if elected officials or citizens become involved in them, they can generate community issues. A minority contracting program affects outside groups and can engender support and opposition from firms that are affected positively and negatively. An investigation of alleged police brutality and the dismissal of an employee with political connections can embroil staff in a community controversy. When either kind of situation arises, the boundaries between the internal and the external become blurred. While maintaining the integrity of the organization's procedures, the manager must be attentive to outside groups.

Changes in the political context of community leadership

The manager's role of community leader has expanded in response to new political realities. Populist politicians—politicians critical of government action—have become more common, and interest groups have become more influential. More special interest groups have spokespersons on the governing board, and the groups' activity has become more intense. In addition, the number of communities (even small ones) that have more ethnic groups and more immigrants has grown since 1900.

At the same time, fiscal stress has heightened debate about the role of local government and has increased conflict about scarce resources. Since September 11, 2001, new security challenges have added to the load of services that local governments must provide, and in many communities these challenges have put further strain on intergroup relations. All these forces—the growing prominence of interest groups, the growth in number of immigrants and ethnic groups, fiscal stress, and security responsibilities—put pressure on the local government manager to provide greater and more sensitive leadership.

This pressure needs to be understood in the context of two sorts of changes affecting the local government manager. One is a change in the relationship between local government and outside actors. The other is a change in the behavior of local government leadership itself.

Changes in the relationship between local government and outside actors

Present-day managers should neither underestimate the community challenges their predecessors encountered nor overestimate the difficulties they face in the early twenty-first century in exercising leadership to bring expertise to bear on the problems of their communities. Still, managers must recognize that the number of community activities they should be involved in is increasing, and the range of groups with which they need to communicate effectively is broader. Fragmentation within the community is one trend drawing managers in that direction. Two others are the emergence of new approaches to governance, and the rapid growth in information technology. With new approaches to governance, some of the local government manager's responsibilities have become more diffuse—less a matter of law and more a matter of influence exerted informally. Information technology has affected governance by greatly increasing citizens' ability to access information from government and to respond to it.

Divisions and the dwindling sense of community An important dimension of the shifting politics at the turn of the millennium is changes in communities themselves. The divisions within communities are sharper, and the political activism is more intense. The NIMBY (not in my backyard) attitude appears to be more deeply entrenched as neighborhood groups assert their interests and block government action more effectively.

At the same time, general support for a broad public agenda has declined, and the sense of community that could be a counterweight to divisive forces is dwindling. Residents' time, energy, and inclination for involvement in the community are diminished by more frenetic lifestyles, longer workdays, more households with both spouses working or with single parents, fewer children, increased relocation at retirement, and a larger number of people over 75. Regionalization of some activities, new technologies that permit more things to be done from a residence, and the disappearance of places for informal gathering reduce the engagement of residents with each other. "In several surveys in 1999 two-thirds of Americans said that America's civic life had weakened in recent years, that social and moral values were higher when they were growing up, and that our society was focused more on the individual than the community. More than 80 percent said there should be more emphasis on community, even if that put more demands on individuals."[14]

There are some modest countertrends. Developers' and planners' increased interest in "new urbanism" suggests a recognition that the design and location of facilities are important in promoting a sense of community. More public spaces are being created. Interest in service is rising, and the numbers of community volunteers are increasing. The same technologies that permit people to work at home also connect people in new ways.

New approaches to governance   Since 1990, new approaches to governance have unmistakably emerged, changing key features of the world of local government administrators. The new governance, as it is called, is based on the increasing devolution and decentralization of the way societal needs are met.[15] In the past, governance largely occurred within the governmental process, and there was some clarity about which governmental levels or units were responsible for action. In contrast, under the new governance, responsibilities are diffused across levels of government, across units of government at the local level, and across public-private partnerships. In the delivery of services, contributions by nonprofit organizations, community groups, and businesses have increased; and functions have been transferred from government to the private sector.

The authority of public administrators in general, and of local government managers in particular, is diminished under the new governance. Ironically, both the administrators and the managers still have great responsibility, but they exercise it less and less in direct relationships with their own elected officials and subordinate staff. Local government managers increasingly need to act on their own initiative to be the facilitators of people and organizations they do not control, the brokers of resource acquisition from sources other than their own governments, and the builders and sustainers of informal networks.

Three examples highlight the manager's altered position in the new governance. First, welfare reform put county managers in the midst of an array of public, non-profit, and for-profit providers of services with no one clearly in charge. Second, brownfields redevelopment requires pulling together a wide array of actors in federal and state government, local groups, and potential investors, none of whom can be compelled to act; instead, they must be brought together and kept together in an extended, complex process of renewal.[16] Third, in relationships with other governments focusing on such regional matters as air-quality control, local government managers are working with people who are outside their control and their jurisdiction; among neighboring governments and governments in urban regions, it is at the professional level that much informal communication and cooperation take place.[17] (For an extended discussion of interorganizational networking, see Chapter 7.)

Changes in information technology The continued acceleration of change in the uses of information technology (IT) has been mentioned above. Although IT may not be creating the revolution in the political process or the equalization of power and resources that some had predicted,[18] it has vastly increased the amount of information readily available to citizens and has widened the channels of communication and quickened its speed. As the use of IT as a whole has expanded, access to it has become broader.[19] The digital divide, however, remains a reality and affects the extent to which local government managers can rely on electronic media. Still, a manager who fails to recognize the importance of the information explosion is ignoring a fundamental reality: in 2001, 93 percent of those between the ages of 9 and 17 used the computer, and 69 percent used the Internet. Electronic communication has altered the way people relate to each other and to government.

When these three factors (fragmentation, new governance, and IT) are combined, the inescapable conclusion is that greater collaboration is required within and across organizations. When information, ideas, resources, and power are shared, the result can be increased leverage over problems that no one organization can solve on its own.[20]

Changes in the behavior of local government leadership

Just as the relationship between local government and outside actors has changed, so too have the relationships among the players in local government itself: the members of the council, the local government manager in relation to the council, and the local government manager in relation to the mayor.

Governing boards' greater focus on the particular and the specific The characteristics and attitudes of members of governing boards have changed. Typically council members, particularly in council-manager cities, have been viewed as trustees who were concerned about the well-being of the entire community and who served from a sense of civic duty. But in the early years of the twenty-first century, more council members are activists who seek to tackle particular problems. It is still true that almost all council members have a desire to serve the city as a whole, but increasingly they also serve particular neighborhoods and promote specific projects and interests.[21] Council members spend more time on their elected positions than previously, but much of that time is spent acting in the role of an ombudsman: providing services to citizens, responding to complaints, and helping obtain information, as indicated in Table 2–2. Consequently, the manager and staff will have extensive interactions with council members about specific matters dealing with constituencies and constituent relations.

Reflecting the increased diversity of and divisiveness within the communities they serve, governing boards are more fragmented, and achieving leadership within

Table 2–2   City council–member workload by city size, 2001

	Average for cities of all sizes	Small 25,000– 70,000	Medium 70,000– 200,000	Large larger than 200,000
Total hours work on council-related matters per week (average number)	22.2	19.1	25.0	42.0
Hours per week spent doing services for people (average number)	7.7	6.2	8.9	17.5
Service hours as percentage of total	35%	32%	36%	42%

Source: Computed from survey conducted in 2001 by James H. Svara for the National League of Cities.
Note: Number of council members interviewed: 670.

them is more difficult, although it does not follow that all governing boards are lead-
erless or fragmented. In a 2001 survey of city council members in cities over 25,000
in population, seven council members in ten expressed the view that they provided
their city governments with sufficient overall leadership. Still, half of the council
members agreed that they focus too much on short-term problems and give too little attention to long-term concerns. Over two-fifths cited conflict among council
members as a serious problem. Finally, one-third indicated that a lack of clear political goals negatively affected their ability to perform their jobs as elected officials.
These changes in the orientation of governing board members mean that the manager bears more of the responsibility to respond to the needs of the entire community, balance competing demands, and take a long-term perspective.

Managers' greater focus on the council   There is evidence that managers are
giving more to their relationship with the council despite the increasing need to
interact with other groups and attend to community problems. In a 1965 survey,
managers in cities over 100,000 in population were asked to indicate the relative
importance of a policy role (including relating to the council), a political role
(including relating to the community), and a management role. One-third of the
managers indicated that community leadership was most important to their success, compared with 22 percent who chose council relations. By 1985 a dramatic
shift had occurred. Over half—56 percent—now indicated that council relations
were the most important, and the proportion choosing community leadership had
dropped to 6 percent.[22] In both surveys, just under two-fifths chose the management role as most important to success. In 1997, 79 percent of the city managers
in large cities chose the policy role (including council relations); only 21 percent
saw the management role as most important. No city managers in these large cities
identified community leadership as the factor most important to their job success.[23]
Certainly, many managers spend a considerable amount of time working with citizens and leaders in the community, as the evidence on networking indicates. It is
not community leadership, however, that determines the manager's job success.
Whereas many local government managers were previously able to concentrate on
community leadership with a clear understanding of the policy priorities of a cohesive council, increasingly they devote their attention to working with council members to develop agreement on policy and to respond to the members' constituency
concerns.

The emphasis on council relations to the exclusion of community relations as
indicated by these responses may be somewhat misleading. To some extent, managers must bring community relations into their work with elected officials on
projects that the mayor and council members want to advance and on constituent
problems. In this respect, the two roles overlap. Furthermore, in smaller cities,
managers assign somewhat less importance to council relations. Still, managers
face a major dilemma. They must be active in community relations, but their job
success increasingly depends on how they handle council relations.

For city administrators in mayor-council cities, the situation is somewhat simpler.
Administrators are more likely to leave council relations to the mayor, but they are
also much more likely to see management rather than active community involvement as their key role. These administrators, like their city manager counterparts,
face the hard choice of deciding how much time to spend on a crucial role that, by
itself, will usually not lead to success.

Managers' and administrators' relationships with mayors   An important aspect
of the manager's community leadership is the relationship with the mayor. It seems
likely that most citizens would identify the mayor as the official who is (or should

be) the most important person in city government. When the local government manager is active in setting the agenda, relating to the community, and orienting the organization to the community, is there a risk that the manager will come into conflict with the mayor, especially if the mayor is also active? The question must be answered separately for the two major forms of government in which appointed administrators work.

In the council-manager form, the mayor potentially handles three sets of roles: the traditional or "automatic" roles of the office, such as presiding over and being spokesperson for the council; the role of coordinator who promotes effective working relationships and team building within the council; and the role of policy guide who helps the city council shape an agenda that incorporates citizen preferences and the goals of the mayor and members of the council. If mayors fill all these roles well, they can be effective facilitative leaders.

On the basis of survey responses by city managers about the mayor's performance, one can identify three groups of mayors, depending on the level of facilitative leadership displayed. Group one combines caretaker mayors (who do not handle any role very well) and symbolic heads (who play only the traditional roles and are ineffective at helping the council adopt policies and at promoting communication within the city council). This group represents about two-fifths of the mayors in council-manager cities over 5,000 in population. Group two consists of mayors who are coordinators (i.e., they are effective at improving the governmental process but offer little policy leadership). The coordinators represent almost two-fifths of the mayors. Group three consists of the director type of mayor (mayors who are process leaders and, in addition, help chart the course for the community). Such leaders, like former Wichita, Kansas, mayor and National League of Cities president Bob Knight,[24] are effective as both coordinators and policy innovators. These visionary facilitative mayors are found in only one city out of five. The mayors in groups two and three (the coordinator and the director types) also have strong relationships with citizens, as shown in Table 2–3. The more effective the mayor is in filling all three aspects of the office, the better the council functions, the clearer the division of labor between the council and the manager, and the better the relationship between the council and manager. Thus, more effective mayors do not diminish the manager's position. In fact, they enhance it.[25]

Local government managers must adjust their leadership to match the leadership coming from the mayor. As indicated above, in cities where mayors have limited effectiveness, a leadership vacuum is created that others, including the city man-

Table 2–3   Types of council-manager mayors, and ratings of mayors' citizen relations

Type of mayor	Cities with this type mayor (%)	Roles filled effectively	Rating: Mayor is effective at relating to citizens (% with excellent or good ratings)
Caretaker	22	None	31
Symbolic head	21	Traditional/automatic (presiding, spokesperson)	55
Coordinator	37	Above roles plus coordination and communication	75
Director	20	Above roles plus policy guidance	85

Source: Prepared from data in James H. Svara, "Mayors in the Unity of Powers Context," In *The Future of Local Government Administration: The Hansell Symposium*, ed. H. George Frederickson and John Nalbandian, eds. (Washington, D.C.: ICMA, 2002).
Note: Survey in 1997 covered 447 cities with populations greater than 5,000.

ager, must try to fill. In other cities, the mayor makes a substantial contribution by helping other officials work well together but is not an effective policy leader. In a minority of cities, one finds a comprehensively effective mayor, and the council members, manager, and citizens benefit from having a political leader who is able to identify a course of action for the community. In these cities, managers contribute to both shaping and accomplishing the goals set by the mayor and council, and they build on the mayor's strong public leadership. These managers are just as active in all three aspects of community leadership as those who work with less-effective mayors, but managers who work with these effective mayors are moving with the current, so to speak, rather than paddling upstream in their community-leadership tasks.

Even though a positive or at least not a negative relationship between the mayor and the manager is common in council-manager cities, it is important to recognize that, in a few cities, expanding the power of the mayor has been linked to reducing the manager's authority and changing the form of government. When the constitutional question is how the executive position will be defined, the strong-mayor model and the city-manager model conflict. As a commentator put it in Dallas in 2003 when a charter commission was at work in that city, "In the beginning was the question: Should the mayor of Dallas have more power and the city manager less?"[26] Although city administrators in mayor-council governments are professional leaders who contribute to their governments (as discussed below), a change in form confers upon the mayor executive power that, in the council-manager form, is exercised by the city manager.[27]

In some cities, such as Cincinnati, Ohio; Kansas City, Missouri; and San Jose, California, the powers of the mayor have been expanded without necessarily reducing the authority of the city manager. These cities have "empowered" their mayors, as Hansell puts it,[28] by adding to the mayor's office the power to do one or more of the following: appoint citizens to serve on boards and commissions without council concurrence, exercise a veto, receive the annual budget prepared by the city manager and present it to the council with the mayor's own comments and suggestions (or prepare a mayoral budget in addition to the managerial budget), nominate the city manager for approval by the council, and initiate the dismissal of the manager. There is debate about whether these changes constitute a shift in the form of government, especially in the case of Cincinnati, where charter change gave all these powers to the mayor. In large council-manager cities and counties, the respective responsibilities of the chief elected official and the city manager or county administrator, and the political dynamic accompanying their formal duties, are likely to be sensitive constitutional issues for the foreseeable future.

In mayor-council cities with a city administrator or chief administrative officer—an office found in 38 percent of mayor-council cities[29]—the method of appointing the administrator makes a big difference. When the administrator is nominated by the mayor and approved by the council, the administrator serves to bridge—but does not eliminate—the separation of powers. Results from a 1997 survey of administrators indicate that when the council approves the appointment, most city administrators feel they should be equally accountable to the mayor and the council, and most feel they can have sufficient power to bring the values of professional management to the administration of city government.[30] When the mayor appoints the city administrator without council approval, on the other hand, the administrator feels accountable to the mayor. Still, most city administrators, whether approved by the council or not, feel that they are increasingly the agent of the mayor and that the scope of their office is shaped by the mayor. Regardless of how they are appointed, administrators are active in policy making and community relations at levels very similar to those of city managers.

Setting priorities   [In the midst of preparations for city-county consolidation, on October 1, 1997, the International Speedway Corporation asked Kansas City, Kansas, for a proposal for a new racetrack, to be developed in three weeks.] Dennis Hays, chief administrative officer, recalls: "It wasn't until that point that I realized how serious this was and how much time and energy would have to be devoted to it. I got to the mayor [Mayor Carol Marinovich], and I remember saying, 'Mayor, do we want this? Do we throw everything we have at it?' She was facing a September election, and she couldn't know how this would affect her chances to become mayor of the consolidated government. But she looked at me, and she said resolutely, 'Yes, we are going for it.' " The city administrator got the political direction he needed. The mayor would work with the council, and Hays now knew where his priorities lay: NASCAR first, transition [to consolidated government] second.

Source: John Nalbandian, "The Manager as Political Leader: A Contemporary Challenge to Professionalism?" *Public Management* 82 (March 2000): 9.

Council approval of the appointment of the administrator appears to increase the likelihood that the city administrator will play an integrative role, helping both the mayor and city council. Council approval was endorsed in the eighth edition of the Model City Charter, but having a city administrator, no matter the method of appointment, is preferred over not having an administrator. The city administrator helps the mayor or the mayor and council set the policy agenda, takes care of the community-relations activities the mayor wants the administrator to handle, and sets the tone for the administrative organization, incorporating themes the mayor emphasizes. Like the city manager, the city administrator is a community leader, although in filling this leadership role the city administrator operates to a greater extent as the agent of the mayor.

Sizing up one's own community-leadership style

To be effective in dealing with others, a local government manager or administrator needs to size up personal values, ideals, and qualities and needs to be honest in recognizing personal preferences, strengths, and weaknesses. Only by personal understanding—in terms of individual traits and also in relation to a typology of community-leadership styles—can the manager hope to match performance to the characteristics of the community served.

Four salient dimensions of personality

Four dimensions of personality are particularly salient to an understanding of community-leadership style: internal versus external orientation, degree of innovation (extent to which innovation is initiated or fostered), technical orientation (degree of reliance on expertise), and degree of flexibility. On each dimension, a manager can be low, medium, or high.

Internal versus external orientation   The issue here is whether the manager relates primarily to members of the organization and the city council or is highly active in community affairs. The question is not whether the manager is involved outside the organization, since such involvement is unavoidable. Rather, it is whether the manager enjoys, is good at, and is extensively engaged in community affairs. As noted in the above discussion of networking, managers can locate themselves on this dimension by listing the actors inside and outside government whom they consider to be important to their performance of their duties as well as the actors they do not consider to be important.

A personal characteristic that can affect the orientation to community relations is the extent to which the manager is engaged in, and energized by, relating to other people face-to-face. Managers who seek out contact with other people and enjoy the give-and-take of verbal exchange probably find it more natural and enjoyable to have extensive dealings with citizens and groups. Those who prefer to have enough distance to be able to reflect on information they have received, who prefer written reports to discovery through dialogue, and who need time to themselves to recharge their batteries are going to be less drawn to involvement in the community. They will also be drained rather than energized by extensive interaction. These contrasting types might be labeled "extroverts" (people who are drawn to relating to others) and "introverts" (people who prefer to reflect on the information they have received).[31]

Degree of innovation   The second salient dimension of personality is the degree to which the manager initiates and fosters innovation. How creative, change oriented, and visionary is the manager? Some managers focus on the concrete, the here and now, and the facts of the situation. Others look at the same information and see patterns and possibilities. They focus on how things can be different, and they develop plans for the future. These two types are "sensors" (the realists) and "intuitives" (the visionaries).

Technical orientation   The third dimension is technical orientation: how much emphasis does the manager place on using administrative and managerial expertise? The manager who has a strong technical orientation incorporates management systems in the organization and, in decision making, emphasizes the collection and analysis of information. Managers who are low on this dimension place more emphasis on the art of management and their feel for the situation. A technically oriented manager is more comfortable with data about community conditions and citizen attitudes and looks for logical analyses and reasoned conclusions about what is the "best" approach or solution to a problem. The less technically oriented manager puts more trust in knowing how people are affected by a decision and how they feel about it. This manager would be comfortable bargaining to find mutually acceptable solutions and compromising to find the basis for agreement. These two types are "thinkers" (or analysts) and "feelers" (or empathizers).

Degree of flexibility   The final dimension—degree of flexibility—can interact with any of the others. Some people like order, predictability, and closure. Others are happier with spontaneity and surprises; they like to keep their options open, and they postpone making decisions. Most managers might be called "closers," who like to get decisions made and problems resolved.[32] The "processors," on the other hand, want to delay decisions and keep their options open. It should be noted that the political process tends to produce delays that the processor may be better able to tolerate. Decisions are frequently postponed and are sometimes reopened after being made. Frequently, citizen groups will want to raise new factors and reconsider decisions.

Typology of community leaders

From variations on the four dimensions (particularly the first three), one can develop a typology of community leaders. The following descriptions of hypothetical managers are designed to highlight the distinctions among the types. Many additional types can be imagined, and, in reality, the combinations of qualities do not form clearly differentiated types. An individual manager is likely to be a blend of the characteristics of several of the types. The examples here may suggest how managers can think about their own characteristics and tendencies.

The complete *community leader* has an external focus, is highly innovative, and has a high technical orientation. This is the ideal type for those who think the manager should be actively involved in community affairs, a creative leader, and highly proficient in the technical aspects of the position. Even though the community-leader type of manager, like most others, may think council relations are the key to success, managers of this type still devote a considerable degree of attention to community relations as well as to the management aspect of the leadership role and are able to make all three aspects work to support each other.

Also with a strong external focus are the *coalition builder* and the *arbiter*. The coalition builder is happiest working with people and groups in the community to build agreement to meet community problems. This manager is very attuned to the feelings of others and picks up on negative vibrations that others often miss. But because of a low technical orientation, this manager finds the details of the job to be dull and uninspiring. The arbiter is similar to the coalition builder but ranks lower on innovation. This manager negotiates with groups and helps them compromise but is not innovative in approaching problems.

The *chief executive* is similar in many ways to the community leader but has a stronger internal orientation. Thus, this manager relies more on staff to develop proposals and is somewhat detached from the community.

The *administrative innovator* is highly innovative when it comes to making the organization work better and has a strong technical orientation. Even more than the chief executive, however, this manager avoids community involvement.

The *administrative stabilizer or improver* also likes to work on the inside but places more emphasis on making the existing systems work better than on introducing new systems. These managers are pragmatists interested in how to get the job done. They are most inclined to examine new ideas that have been tested in other cities and then adapt them to fit the circumstances in their own cities. Both the administrative innovator and the administrative stabilizer/improver rely on the council as their channel to the community. They are inclined to view elected officials as the ones who will speak for the community and secure the public support needed for the implementation of decisions.

Finally, a manager who ranks low on all three dimensions is a *caretaker*. With an internal focus, low innovation, and low technical orientation, this manager concentrates on housekeeping or maintenance functions. The caretaker certainly does not want to make waves in the community.

Assessment of one's own style

As stated above, developing a good sense of one's own characteristics and tendencies is important to one's effectiveness as a local government manager. People who fit almost any of the types described here can be effective managers if they recognize their weaknesses and blind spots, on the one hand, and appreciate their strengths, on the other. Furthermore, a person can certainly develop attributes that do not come naturally and are not acted on with as much facility as other attributes.

One approach to assessing style is to develop a self-portrait of community leadership. Practicing managers can describe what they actually do. Future managers can project how they think they would handle the position.

Another approach to self-assessment is to use an inventory that identifies key traits. One instrument that is commonly used to gain personal insights is the Myers-Briggs Type Indicator.[33] The traits typically manifested by managers who have completed this inventory suggest that if managers' behavior were determined entirely by their own preferences, most managers would fall into the administrative stabilizer/improver type. There are many exceptions, but managers tend to be introverts—reflectors rather than relaters—and therefore are more likely to be somewhat

---

Assessing your community-relations style

- What parts of your job do you like most? Least?

- What actors inside and outside of government do you consider to be important in the performance of your duties? You can also list the actors whom you consider not important. What do the two lists tell you about the extent and inclusiveness of your networking?

- How comfortable are you dealing with the council? Do you like it when they look to you for explicit leadership (whether or not it is wise for you to lead)?

- Are you comfortable interacting with groups in the community? Which groups do you like to deal with and which do you not?

- Do you look at situations and think about how things can be changed in fundamental ways or do you concentrate on specific actions that can

improve how the organization operates?

- Are you interested in dealing with the big problems and needs facing the community and in developing a vision for this community?

- Are you interested in using the best available methods and adhering to the highest standards of practice in your organization? Do you pay as much attention to practices that pertain to citizen and community relations as you do to internal operations?

- How flexible are you? How do you feel about adapting the decision-making process to involve diverse groups and opinions?

- Which type of community leader described in the text is most like you? Which other types have some characteristics that you demonstrate? Which type do you most want to be like?

---

removed from people and groups in the community rather than highly involved with them.[34] They are typically concerned about concrete problems in the present (the sensors, or the realist characteristic) rather than highly innovative and visionary (the intuitives). They prefer rational, logical approaches to decision making (the "thinking" characteristic) rather than being highly empathic (the feelers). Finally, they have a strong preference for being orderly, maintaining control, anticipating and preparing for problems, and bringing decisions to closure (the "closer" characteristic) rather than being spontaneous, flexible, and willing to postpone decisions (the processors). All these traits have advantages in community leadership. Still, it is the atypical traits (i.e., being outgoing, innovative, empathic, and flexible) that are associated with facility and comfort in community relations.

Anyone can develop the "shadow" trait that is the opposite of his or her own natural tendency. Doing so involves identifying the characteristics associated with the shadow trait and assessing which of them could be used to soften the natural tendency or make interaction in atypical ways easier. For example, a naturally outgoing and expressive person could make the effort to pause after making a point and ask the other person for feedback. After local government managers have assessed their own tendencies, they may need to make special efforts to strengthen the characteristics that bear on their community-leadership role.

Local government managers adopt the community-relations style that is based on their personal traits, the skills they have developed, the circumstances they face in particular situations, and the (changing) characteristics and needs of the community. They have probably felt the need to adopt the styles of many or all of the types at different times in their careers. The mode of behavior that is closest to one's personal preferences will be the one most commonly used and the one to which the manager tends to revert. Nevertheless, effective managers need to be able to understand all the types and styles and adopt them when necessary. Furthermore, local government managers can supplement their community-relations style with a comprehensive community-leadership approach, one that includes setting the agenda and orienting the organization to the community. This approach will address the needs of the community and meet professional standards.

Understanding community dynamics

A comprehensive community-leadership approach requires the manager to understand the community's dynamics: what the community as a whole expects of government, and what the configuration of the community's political landscape is.

Expectations of government

Some communities, usually small ones, have a dominant orientation toward, or expectation of, government. Others, particularly larger communities, have a number of differing expectations about what local government is and what it does. Managers must be able to understand the characteristics of their own community and adapt their style to the expectation and needs of the community. Disparities between the manager's expectations and the community's will diminish effectiveness and produce tension in the relationship.

Three pure types of expectation Citizens and communities as a whole differ in what they demand from government and public officials (i.e., the services provided, the degree of governmental activism, and the level of expenditures). At one time it might have been possible to identify three types of communities, depending on whether the government was expected to focus primarily on being an instrument of growth, a provider of amenities, or a provider of caretaker functions.[35] A challenge to local government management in the twenty-first century is that most jurisdictions are characterized by conflicting orientations.

Citizens and groups that stress economic growth and development ask their local jurisdiction and its officials to serve primarily as catalysts for community and regional growth. Here public managers are busy promoting population expansion, fostering industrial development, encouraging commercial activities, and building the essential infrastructure (roads, sewers, and so on) to further business development and economic progress. A local public manager's community involvement therefore entails a good deal of promotion; participation in the planning of industrial and residential site development; and effort to keep costs low, provide tax advantages or other incentives for local business development, and ensure adequate utility, transit, labor, and other necessary services for rapid economic expansion.

The commitment to development can weaken, however, if residents come to feel that there has been enough growth. For example, the town of Cary, North Carolina, next to Raleigh and Research Triangle Park, ballooned from 8,860 residents in 1972 to 103,260 in 2002. In 2000 a new majority on the city council adopted a growth management plan. The same city manager who had helped the city grow since 1994 shifted to leading the staff in implementing the plan to contain growth.[36]

Other citizens and groups emphasize quality of life and urge local government to focus on providing life's amenities. Here public managers must be involved in offering residents an attractive, desirable, comfortable community in which to live. Consumption as opposed to production or growth is therefore the principal and most cherished value of these communities. In a consumption-oriented community, the present way of life is preferred over the possibility of attaining a new or better one tomorrow. Thus, a local public manager in these communities emphasizes such activities as the provision of adequate parks, recreation, and leisure activities; prompt and courteous responses to citizens requiring public services; strict enforcement of zoning; the quiet and safe flow of traffic; and abatement of noise and pollution.

In communities with this orientation, an important part of the local government manager's job is being able to supply public goods and services in innovative ways at a reasonable cost to citizens. The manager and staff must be prepared to devote a fair amount of attention to involved citizens who are interested in particular services (e.g., a library board and support group) and want special attention given to "their" service in order to make it as good as possible, with little regard to the impact on the total budget.

A third orientation comes into play when citizens and groups prefer that government provide minimal services, or when the community's fiscal resources may force the government to restrict what it offers. In responding to this orientation, managers must demonstrate that they are keeping the costs of government down and keeping the size of government as a whole to a minimum.[37] The preferred approach here would be to rely largely on the private sector or on other levels of government to supply such necessary public goods and services as refuse collection and recreation—if these services are supplied at all. If new projects are to be undertaken, private rather than public funding would be preferred.

The minimalist orientation could be linked to an opposition to professional local government management itself. Even so, the manager needs to maintain extensive ties with the community as a positive representative of government. To persuade elected officials and the community that the local government is being operated frugally and effectively, the manager will need to be both a good communicator and an accomplished organizational leader who looks for ways to cut costs and improve productivity.

Overlapping expectations in communities in crisis and transition   Citizen orientations commonly overlap when the community is in crisis and in transition because of a sudden change in economic fortunes. In these communities, forces that favor limited growth and enhancement of quality of life counter pro-growth forces. Economically disadvantaged groups press for a wider range of services directed toward their needs. Groups that want lower taxes and less government activity tend to oppose everything. In this situation, the local government manager needs the skills and sensitivities appropriate to interacting with each group separately and must also be effective at linking dissimilar groups, promoting the identification of common interests, and, of course, resolving conflicts without getting caught in the cross fire. In a transitional or crisis setting, the manager's role is particularly important because the governing board is likely to reflect the divisions among groups and be unable to serve as the unifying force.

Examples of situations in which communities are in crisis and transition can be taken from recent history. Despite the economic boom of the 1990s, one-third of central cities in the United States continued to struggle with high levels of poverty, and one in six experienced unusually high unemployment at the end of that decade.[38] Then during the economic downturn that started in the second half of 2000, conditions worsened. Although the 2000 census showed that population trends in older central cities were not as negative in the 1990s as they had been in the 1980s, the change represents a slowing of decline rather than a reversal of fortune.[39] In distressed urban areas, local government managers seek to arbitrate differences among the competing groups in a diverse population and to discover ways of expanding opportunities. The public manager's job is especially difficult because of pressure on local government to provide extensive services to a population increasingly marked by poverty and dependence and to expand opportunities in the face of negative forces. The job involves managing conflict—sometimes quite intense conflict—among groups and interests over the allocation of scarce public goods and services. In distressed communities, the public manager's community-relations skills are often tested to their utmost because much of the manager's time is spent negotiating, compromising, and bargaining in order to build common ground on which to act. Symbolic actions on the part of the manager—the "right" gestures, proclamations, or appointments—can be as important as solid managerial results.

Although these conditions are commonly linked with central cities, an increasing number of inner-ring older suburbs are experiencing the same conditions. In any community where a major employer shuts down or economic opportunities are limited, the need and demand for services are very high and resources are few. Local government managers in these communities must not only be adept at resolving conflict but also must develop close personal ties within the community to try to offset feelings of alienation from and distrust of local government.

These managers must also develop measures to reverse decline and promote economic development. In both the central city and older suburbs, success depends on a dual strategy of encouraging the reuse of underused land and buildings within the community while forging regional partnerships. Redevelopment and revitalization can transform blighted areas into magnets for shoppers and tourists from outside the city and for new residents in rehabilitated housing. Managers must take care, however, that revitalization not produce a dislocation of low-income residents or of local merchants and companies. In addition, single communities must work with others in the region to reap the benefits of industry clusters.[40]

Redevelopment and revitalization

"Successful redevelopment of first-tier suburbs . . . will exert strong positive impact both inward, toward the center city, and outward, to aging outer ring suburbs, helping them learn how to avoid decay. The great hope: healthy metro regions. . . ."

William Hudnut developed a list of "urban acupuncture" tips in which some suburbs already excel—and many more could.

Examples from his book:

- Rebuild Main Street—a strategy that's already worked for such towns as

Bethesda, Maryland; Merchantville, New Jersey; Webster Groves, Missouri; and Pasadena, California.

- "DeMall" failing shopping centers for second-generation uses such as offices (Whitehall, Ohio) or even demolish them for radically redesigned, pedestrian-friendly, full-service town centers (Park Forest, Illinois).

Source: Neal Peirce, "Overdue Limelight for Inner-Ring Suburbs," review of William Hudnut, *Halfway to Everywhere* (Washington, D.C.: Urban Land Institute, April 2004), www.postwritersgroup.com/archives/peir0707.htm.

Small towns in rural areas also face challenges, although generally different ones. The lifeblood of a small community can slowly drain away as main-street businesses close and young people leave to seek opportunities elsewhere. Or life can be suddenly disrupted when a major employer shuts down. Small towns have a narrow resource base, limited services, and limited transportation linkages. Small-town revitalization requires a multifaceted approach that includes fostering new investment, growing new businesses in empty storefronts, and training dislocated workers. These approaches, like those in metropolitan areas, require extensive community leadership from the local government manager.

Configurations of the community's political landscape

In addition to being attentive to a community's expectations of local government, the manager should be attentive to basic configurations of the community's political landscape. This is important because the degree of fragmentation in the community can affect the scope of local managerial action.

In communities that are small and homogeneous, that is, where differences in ethnicity, race, and income are minimal, conflict is relatively rare. Here the public manager usually has considerable latitude for active leadership in community affairs and finds citizens generally willing to cooperate on a broad range of initiatives and activities. In fact, because of the manager's full-time involvement and specialization in public affairs, citizens frequently look to the manager for leadership and direction, and local leaders often have great confidence in the manager and give that person considerable latitude. A study published in 2003 shows that local government managers with tenures of 20 years or more tend to be found in this kind of community.[41]

With greater size, diversity, and a changing population, the situation facing the local government manager is more challenging and less predictable. Midsize communities with more diverse populations are sometimes divided into two roughly equal interest groups or factions. Examples of such divisions are pro-growth people and environmentalists, blacks and whites, members of the old ethnic group and the new minority, established people and newcomers, Democrats and Republicans, and progressives and conservatives. Obviously in this type of community the manager's maneuverability is severely limited because the manager cannot become too closely identified with either side.

For a manager, the most dramatic example of a fluid shift in power between the factions is when a council controlled by one group hires a manager and the opposition group wins the next election. The manager may suddenly be without a job or at the very least confront the challenge of winning the trust of a council whose majority comes from a different faction than did the hiring.

Managers should develop ties with both factions and should treat them equally and fairly. In the case of factions aligned with political parties, the manager should avoid any partisan connection with either party and, as required by the Code of Ethics, should be scrupulously neutral in elections. The code also requires that the manager provide information equally to all members of the council and implement with equal faithfulness the policies adopted by either group when it is in the majority. At the same time, the manager should not take actions that the group in the minority will view as detrimental.

In council-manager governments, the level of political stability varies and has some effect on managerial turnover.[42] Even in stable situations, however, conditions can change, and managers are often unable to anticipate a coming shift in political control.

Managers need to continually monitor community groups and the dynamics of relations among them. Managers should also assess how community conditions match their personal style. In general, the greater the divisions in the community, the more externally oriented the manager needs to be. The more diverse the population, the more carefully the manager needs to balance a strong technical orientation with empathy for others and sensitivity to how groups with different backgrounds and values will respond to actions taken. Innovative managers need to ensure that their vision is widely understood and shared. Managers should also take stock of their ability to work with specific groups and of their community-relations skills.

Identifying the actors in community politics

In addition to understanding one's own community-leadership style and the general dynamics of the community, a local government manager needs to understand the individual and group actors in community politics. Communities are made up of a variety of actors: groups, institutions, and networks. Developing an inventory of actors involves identifying general patterns of influence, general patterns of participation, and specific groups.

Sources of power and influence in the community

People with the capacity to tackle a big problem alone are rare. Some actors attempt to exert "power over" others and impose their wills, but they are often checked by those other actors. Progress is more likely to be made when two or more actors combine their "power to" contribute to an accomplishment in order to achieve a shared purpose.[43] In assessing sources of influence, managers should look beyond the governing board because in the new millennium council members are less likely than in the past to come from or have ties to influential organizations in the community. They are now more likely to be political activists with neighborhood or issue-based followings. In working with the governing board, therefore, the manager does not necessarily have much access to community elites.

In the process by which a community action is accomplished, different groups are likely to have influence at different stages. The first question is: How do ideas originate; that is, what are the sources of change in the community? The answer is that both public officials and interest group leaders as well as economic elites figure prominently at this stage. In mayor-council governments, mayors are particularly important "entrepreneurs," but in other forms of government, with less fanfare, mayors and board chairpersons, governing board members, and local government managers also help identify problems, issues, and goals. For example, at the time of the opening of a new center for the performing arts, the *News & Observer* in Raleigh, North Carolina, recognized the many people who had helped shape the project. Included in the list identified by the newspaper was the city manager, whose contribution was described in this way: "He conceived the idea for an affordable performing arts center and sold it to other city leaders."[44]

The second stage in the process of accomplishing community action is legitimation and decision. If significant opinion makers and value shapers oppose a proposal, it may not secure a place on the issue agenda or, if it does, it is unlikely to receive support. Other groups will have to work harder and seek public support for their cause by taking direct action. A wide range of groups can be involved in seeking to win acceptance of or to reject the proposal.

The next stage is the provision of resources. When an idea or project needs resources beyond those that government can generate, the sources of support obviously exert great influence over whether that project comes to fruition.

Finally, new ideas or projects need to be implemented. The activists who will play the key roles in implementation are likely to come from government, a range of civic and nonprofit organizations, and interest groups. Although these actors are not typically thought of as being holders of power, they are usually crucial to the actual success of a new project or program, that is, they have the "power to" make the initiative a reality. When planning the early stages of community action, the local government manager needs to consider the perspectives of the actors who are crucial to the final stage.

Thus, the participants—those who have some influence over affairs in the community—are varied in their backgrounds and prominence. Local government managers should carefully assess all those whose support and contributions are necessary for specific projects. It is a mistake simply to assume that the major economic interests in the community control all decisions; however, it is also a mistake to ignore those interests.

Approaches to expanding citizen participation

In addition to identifying sources of influence and resources in the community, the local government manager should also be concerned with reaching out to and fostering involvement by a broad range of citizens.

Most citizens do not participate directly in community affairs. A small segment of the population will be attentive and active, some of the population will be attentive to a specific interest and active in their efforts to advance that interest, and most of the population will be inattentive and inactive unless an issue arises that directly affects them. Organized interest groups, for example, generate intense participation but represent only a small minority of the population. Those who vote in local elections also represent only a small minority of the population, typically only 12 to 20 percent of adults (or 20 to 30 percent of registered voters).[45] Citizens with higher levels of education and income and with professional occupations are more likely to feel they have a duty as citizens to take part and more likely to think their participation will make a difference. Citizens who have fewer resources and weaker motivation to take part are not likely to participate in community affairs in the absence of either special efforts to involve them or events that have a direct effect on their lives. Local government managers should always be aware of the differences among the activists, the attentive electorate who will choose the governing board members, and the general citizenry. Managers also need to solicit input about the quality and impact of local government services directly from consumers and not rely on the opinions of activists or voters to determine whether programs are being run well.

In addition, interest in new conceptions of citizenship and attention to the social conditions that support them are increasing, and here, too, the manager has a role to play. Citizens are commonly seen as individualistic claimants who press for government action; expanding citizen participation means seeking to ensure that all voices are heard and all groups can express their demands. However, there are other ways of looking at citizen participation: A social-contract approach balances shared responsibilities against individual rights. The republican roots of the American revolution stressed civic virtue and the common good, not simply a commitment to individualism.[46] In the new (or newly rediscovered) definitions of citizenship, a central element is the emphasis on building community as a collection of formal and informal institutions and organizations that connect people and provide the setting for collective actions to address needs.[47] Service and volunteerism are important because "people helping people" is an essential quality of community. Citizenship involves people coming together on their own initiative to work on common projects and goals.[48] Managers can help foster these efforts to build community.

Managers also have an important role as citizen educator. In informal gatherings, presentations to civic groups, classroom appearances as a visiting speaker or instructor, and, of course, the interactions with elected officials and staff, the manager has the opportunity to broaden knowledge as well as understanding of local government affairs. The teaching should move beyond explaining current problems and projects to examining the reasons for problems in the community, the rationale for alternative actions, and the possibilities for the future. In addition, the manager should provide lessons in democracy to help citizens of all ages understand how government operates and how people can work together to improve the community. (See also Chapter 4.)

Types of groups and constituents

A wide range of groups is active in local affairs. The larger the community, the more groups there will be and the more likely they are to be well organized. Table 2–4 provides a general picture of the relative influence of certain major types of groups as seen by city council members who responded to a National League of Cities survey conducted in 2001. Most council members view neighborhoods and business organizations as being influential, and roughly half of the council members in cities of all sizes consider women and environmentalists to be influential. Elderly

Table 2–4 Percentage of council members who believe interest groups influence council decisions

Interest groups	Average for cities of all sizes	Small (25,000– 70,000)	Medium (70,000– 200,000)	Large (over 200,000)
Neighborhoods	90	88	92	92
Business interests	79	76	85	85
Elderly	71	74	71	53
Realtors/developers	58	53	70	71
Women	55	57	55	48
Racial minorities	54	51	58	69
Environmentalists	49	47	52	56
Ethnic groups	49	46	51	62
Labor unions	39	32	47	71
Municipal employees	39	32	47	71
Political parties	29	25	33	47

Source: James H. Svara, *Two Decades of Continuity and Change in American City Councils* (Washington, D.C.: National League of Cities, 2003), 18, Table III.4.
Note: 670 council members were interviewed in 2001.

people are given greater influence ratings in small and midsize cities than in large cities. For a number of other groups, the proportions are reversed: as city size increases, racial minorities, ethnic groups, labor unions, municipal employees, and political parties are more influential. Groups that are part of national movements (e.g., pro-choice or right-to-life organizations) can exert substantial pressure if they are able to mobilize allies regarding a concrete issue in a particular community. Similarly, groups and organizations that are peripheral to local government can be galvanized into action over a specific issue (e.g., churches over zoning for "adult" establishments, or garden clubs over removal of trees). The challenge to local officials is to be accessible to all groups, yet to reach sound decisions despite the pressures and cross pressures. The rest of this section discusses eight groups in more detail.

Neighborhood groups Neighborhood groups are among the most numerous and, in the view of council members, the most influential in local government affairs. Many of the most intense issues that arise deal with the characteristics of neighborhoods (e.g., what kind of housing will be permitted) and with providing services that will make neighborhoods more attractive (e.g., a community center), protecting them from threats (e.g., drug trafficking), and resisting changes that will have adverse effects (e.g., widening a street and thereby increasing the traffic). Not only do residents seek to protect the lifestyle of their chosen neighborhood, but they also, in the case of homeowners, seek to maintain the value of a major investment in property. The increased use of district elections has increased the influence of neighborhoods. In addition, many local governments have created formal mechanisms for input, such as neighborhood-based citizen advisory committees. For example, the city of Richmond, Virginia, created a Neighborhood Team Process (NTP) in 1988 to bring residents from more than 100 neighborhoods into nine working teams organized into nine districts.[49] These teams continue to address service complaints by citizens, provide ideas for the operating and capital improvement budgets, and find ways to help the police prevent drug sales. NTP has fostered a partnership approach with community development corporations, leveraging private- and public-sector resources and targeting them to a limited number of strategically selected neighborhoods to maximize impact.

Neighborhood organizations can provide the base for resisting changes that are viewed as actually or symbolically detrimental. The NIMBY phenomenon is a powerful force to be reckoned with when siting decisions are made. It is imperative, therefore, to consult the neighborhood before making a decision, to recognize the concerns of residents, and to address those concerns. Taking these and other measures to resolve conflicts (a topic discussed below) will not ensure acceptance by the neighborhood, but failure to take these actions will certainly lead to strong resistance from the area affected.

Business community   The business community is divided roughly into two groups: (1) businesspeople with firms whose ownership is located elsewhere and whose markets are national and international, and (2) businesspeople with firms whose markets are local, who therefore have a vital stake in local development since their livelihoods depend on it directly. The challenge with the former group can be to get them involved in the local community and keep them from relocating or disinvesting. Members of the latter group, especially when the business is locally owned, are normally active in the local Chamber of Commerce and other such organizations for promoting local growth. They include department store owners; utility company executives; real estate developers and salespeople; and small-business owners whose economic survival requires them to press local government for downtown redevelopment, better roads, improved trash collection, mass transit, and better services overall to lure customers to their businesses. Thus, business leaders are often great supporters of physical-improvement projects and initiatives to improve municipal management. Chambers of commerce and city governments commonly form close partnerships.[50]

Because the business community has influence and a critical role in any community's economic prosperity and job opportunities, the local public manager interacts with it extensively. With the clout that businesses have, local government managers must take care that actions reflect need. The demands of business must be justified and balanced against the broader needs of the entire community.

Racial and ethnic groups   Communities are experiencing a transformation of their racial and ethnic composition as a result of population shifts and expanding immigration. Although cohesive European ethnic groups continue to be important participants in the local politics of cities, they are found primarily in the Northeast and Midwest. African Americans, formerly living mainly in the rural areas of the South, are a major segment of the population in communities throughout the country. The large number of immigrants from Latin America and Asia are adding new ethnic groups to communities, and these groups are moving into all parts of the country, even though more than 50 percent of the Hispanic population is still found in Texas, California, and New York,[51] and the largest Asian concentrations are in large cities.

It has been common to think of small cities as being relatively homogeneous and large cities as diverse. This generalization is getting weaker over time, and the 2000 census shows that minority groups are found in cities of all sizes. As indicated in Table 2–5, in one-third of the urban places between 2,500 and 10,000, minorities make up less than 5 percent of the population; none of the largest cities is this homogeneous. At the other end of the scale, however, one-quarter of the urban places between 2,500 and 10,000 have minority populations greater than 35 percent. It may be common to think that it is only the city administrators of very large cities who have to be adept at dealing with diversity, but 566 towns that are under 10,000 in population and 372 cities with populations from 10,000 to 499,000 have sizable (35 percent or greater) minority populations. Thus, a significant number of small and moderate-size jurisdictions face the challenges that come from having a high proportion of minorities. In comparison, 31 of the 72 largest cities (more than 500,000 inhabitants) have these population characteristics. Local government man-

Table 2–5   Minority population percentage by size of urban place, 2000

Percentage minority	Size of urban place						Average for cities of all sizes	Number
	2,500–10,000 (N = 2,238)	10,000–19,000 (N = 683)	20,000–49,000 (N = 245)	50,000–99,000 (N = 198)	100,000–499,000 (N = 193)	More than 500,000 (N = 72)		
Under 5%	32.2	18.3	4.5	3.5	1.0		23.9	866
5–9%	16.0	18.0	21.6	19.7	7.8		16.2	589
10–19%	13.8	22.3	26.9	27.3	31.1	15.3	17.9	651
20–34%	12.7	14.3	17.1	22.2	29.0	41.7	15.3	554
35–49%	8.8	9.4	14.3	17.7	17.1	20.8	10.4	379
50% and over	16.5	17.7	15.5	9.6	14.0	22.2	16.3	590

Source: Calculated from Census 2000 Summary File 1 (SF1).
Note: An urban place has a population equal to or greater than 2,500 and is defined by the census as an urban cluster or urban area. Some urban places combine two or more municipalities.

agers in cities of all sizes must be prepared to work with people from many different ethnic groups and with large, well-established groups as well as with growing minorities.

The presence of diverse groups in communities has always created dynamic forces for change and renewal. Diversity has also produced tensions over competing values and conflict over how resources are distributed, as new groups seek to get a share. Members of minority groups have often suffered from discrimination, although members of European ethnic groups have found it easier to avoid discrimination than have members of identifiable racial groups.

The dynamics of racial and ethnic relations must be assessed carefully with attention to the specific combinations of groups and local traditions in each city and county. Managers need to be attuned to the potential for clashes between large ethnic minorities over electoral office, government jobs, and services. As the size of the Hispanic population grows to equal and surpass the number of African Americans in the general population,[52] clashes in the electoral arena and in the competition for jobs are increasingly likely.[53] In the early years of the millennium, however, the overlap of substantial African American and Hispanic population groups is still relatively uncommon. In 2000, in only 6 percent of the urban places (a total of 199) did both groups have a population share that was 10 percent or greater. On the other hand, one in six urban areas over 500,000 in population had this combination, and the number of communities with sizable numbers of both groups will be growing in the future.

When any non-English-speaking immigrant group grows, language becomes a salient issue for the local government; and where there are large numbers of immigrants, it is necessary to be able to communicate with at least some citizens in their native tongue. In many communities, therefore, managers will need to be bilingual.

The issue of unequal provision of or access to services, or both, is magnified when differences in provision or access correspond to racial and ethnic divisions. The nation's underlying economic conditions continue to reflect racial and ethnic inequality. Whereas African Americans and Hispanics together represented 26 percent of the population in 2001, they accounted for 49 percent of the population below the poverty line.[54] Access to housing and the provision of credit reflect disparities in income as well as discrimination.

In relating to all groups, local government managers need to promote recognition and inclusion. They should also determine whether there are problems in the community that relate to race or ethnicity. Such problems may include the following: a systematic bias in living conditions and opportunities, discrimination against and exclusion of any groups, tension and conflict among groups, and acts of intolerance and violence directed toward members of minority groups. Local government managers are committed by professional values to promoting equality, fair provision of services, service delivery that is sensitive to the characteristics of citizens served, affirmative action to expand opportunities, full participation by all groups, and protection of the rights of minorities.

Issue and interest groups   The number of groups that promote specific issue agendas is very large. These groups may be nationally oriented, taking up local issues only when the issues are relevant to the group's concerns (e.g., the Sierra Club) or may be organized specifically around local issues (e.g., a save-the-park organization). A general phenomenon that affects local government (as well as the national government) is the increasing ability of organizations to mobilize members by phone, direct mail, and the Internet to apply intense pressure regarding a specific issue. The pressure may take the form of lobbying as well as supporting candidates for the governing board. The activity of these groups has expanded the local government agenda and injected many new voices into public discussions, but it has also increased the possibility that a response to one issue will create imbalances in other areas and that some of the people elected to the governing board will have a very narrow agenda. Managers need to communicate more extensively with governing board members to help them be aware of the general needs and policies that should be kept in mind when the board is handling specific decisions.

Gay and lesbian people   Gay and lesbian organizations are increasingly important in large cities, but measures to expand gay rights are extending beyond large cities. Initially the goals of these groups focused on city services and protection from violence and from police entrapment. Over time, the groups' political concerns have expanded to include issues of personal safety, civil rights, and recognition of same-sex domestic arrangements.[55] In 2003, more than 160 local jurisdictions, including cities, counties, and school districts of all sizes, recognized domestic partnerships.

Elderly people   The elderly (over-65) population grew by 3.7 million people in the 1990s, an increase of 12 percent (and the over-75 population increased by 26 percent). As a share of the total U.S. population, however, the over-65 group actually shrank a bit, dropping from 12.6 percent in 1990 to 12.4 percent in 2000.[56] This surprising decrease is important only because it means that far more change will be experienced in the future: between 2000 and 2010, the over-65 population will grow both numerically and proportionally from 35 million (or one in eight Americans) to 40 million (or one in 7.5). By 2030, 70 million (or one in every five) Americans will be over the age of 65.[57] The elderly are a growing segment of the population in communities of all sizes and in all areas, although in the 1990s the greatest growth occurred in the West (19.9 percent) and the South (16.0 percent), with much slower rates of growth in the Midwest (6.6 percent) and the Northeast (5.4 percent).[58] Local government managers should recognize that people over 65 have distinct characteristics and needs and that they vote at higher rates than younger people.

As an interest group, elderly people may push for services that benefit themselves, and they may withhold support for programs—such as public education—that raise their taxes but do not benefit them directly. Local officials will need to rethink how they approach and involve elderly people as their numbers grow and their attitudes shift. Large numbers of elderly people are not familiar or comfortable with computer use; although this proportion will decline as more people carry their computer literacy into older age, age is still one source of the digital divide that affects the implementation of e-government.

Volunteers   Local governments already make extensive use of citizen volunteers in their programs, but there are contradictory indicators regarding this use (as well as the use of volunteers in nonprofits). On the one hand, the potential sources to be tapped for service work are growing. A new generation of high school and college students seeks opportunities for community service. And members of the so-called Generation X can be drawn to service work if it has a hands-on aspect and produces clear-cut results.[59] Furthermore, already some of the 76 million baby boomers are looking for ways to give something back to society. They and others among the growing number of retired persons may be looking for activities to occupy their time. However, busy work lives, economic pressures, and values centered on self decrease the availability of volunteers to many organizations, which have to hire staff for work that volunteers once performed. Today's over-65 population has the lowest volunteerism rate of all age groups.[60] To attract more volunteers, particularly among the Generation Xers and baby boomers, organizations must engage volunteers and give them ways to make meaningful contributions to the organization as whole, not just perform specific tasks.[61] Nonprofit organizations generally have greater flexibility to make these adjustments, so local government managers will need to be more effective in the competition to identify, reach, motivate, and manage volunteers.

Poor people   Poor people are different from the members of other groups in having a low level of participation in community affairs. Feelings of alienation, apathy, and exclusion make them less likely to vote and less attentive to government. As individuals, many lack the knowledge, skills, time, and resources for effective participation. Few job skills and a lack of mobility limit their employment options, and illegal immigrants without papers can take only the most menial jobs. As a group, poor people are fragmented (e.g., some are elderly, some are mothers with children, men without jobs, people without homes, and ill and disabled people) and are divided by race and ethnicity. They have limited organization and leadership.

Local governments are severely constrained in their capacity to respond to the underlying problems of poverty. Restricted budgets and increasing needs in all areas limit the ability of local governments to allocate more funds to programs for poor people, particularly in cities with the greatest problems. Any substantial redistribution of income must be undertaken by higher-level governments because localities that provide extensive services and benefits may find themselves with much higher costs per resident and a more dependent population than those that do not.

City of Phoenix strategic approach to neighborhood revitalization   Phoenix has committed to concentrating community development resources primarily in five noncontiguous Neighborhood Initiative Areas. . . . The five Neighborhood Initiative Areas are primarily residential and contain at least 51 percent lower income residents.

The strategy is to comprehensively address the social, economic, and physical needs of the neighborhoods, complete revitalization activities, and move on to other neighborhoods.

Revitalization is accomplished through:

- Neighborhood residents defining success and developing completion plans

- Community-based nonprofit partnerships providing additional resources to support neighborhood revitalization efforts

- Multiyear funding commitments

- Interdepartmental city service delivery teams

- Multiple economic development activities that assist small businesses to add physical improvements to and/or expand their operations, provide training and job opportunities for lower-income neighborhood residents, and that leverage private resources to the greatest extent possible.

Source: City of Phoenix Consolidated Plan for 2000–2005, chapter 7, Strategic Plan, www.ci.phoenix.az.us/GRANTNSD/cp00vii.html.

There are, however, seven effective general strategies that local government managers can use to promote social equity: (1) fair and prompt responsiveness to problems of and complaints by individual citizens regarding local services, (2) effective and impartial delivery of basic services (fire, police, recreation, refuse collection, social services) to all parts of the community, (3) equal opportunity for jobs and promotion in the government workforce, (4) special efforts to identify, support, and seek input from leaders of groups that speak for poor people, (5) sustainable development strategies that locate jobs near workers and invest in public transportation, (6) renewal of low-income neighborhoods, and (7) prohibition of discriminatory practices by public employees and constant monitoring for unintended exclusionary impacts. Effective strategies require coordination and the concentration of limited resources.

One of my mottos is *"Gerencia con corazon."* Management with a heart. Having the skills needed to run city government, but also having the best interest of the community at heart. I think it's a formidable combination that has worked well for me.

Alex Briseño

Behavioral components of effective community leadership

Exercising community leadership effectively in the new millennium requires the local government manager to understand

- Changes in the political context
- Styles of community leadership
- Dynamics of the particular community
- Actors in community politics.

Exercising effective community leadership also means understanding and manifesting certain principles of behavior.

Four key behavioral aspects of community relations are facilitation, conflict resolution, communication with the public, and leadership in a diverse community.

Facilitation

Facilitators help a group come together and improve its interactions.[62] Facilitation is guided by four core values about the way people relate to each other in solving problems. First, interchange is based on valid information, with participants sharing all information relevant to the issue under consideration. Second, participants make a free (unconstrained) and informed choice. People are able to define their own objectives and the methods of achieving them, and choices are based on valid information. Third, participants feel personally responsible for the decisions they make, and their commitment to the decisions is based on the intrinsic value of action rather than on possible inducements or sanctions. Fourth, participants feel compassion for each other. They are concerned about what is good for one another and for themselves. Facilitators help groups act in a way that is consistent with these four core values, and they also use the core values to guide their own behavior.

The role of the facilitator is to

- Establish ground rules for effective group process
- Identify behavior that is inconsistent with the ground rules, as well as behavior that is consistent with them
- Help group members learn more effective behavior.

Facilitation takes training and practice, and it starts with a commitment to promote the core values that support facilitation. Managers who undertake facilitation with the intention of leading citizens to an outcome preferred by the manager are undermining the integrity of the process. In addition, effective facilitation includes skills such as remaining objective, listening actively, soliciting balanced participation, achieving group agreement, and responding to feedback.[63]

Conflict resolution

Conflict resolution is necessarily divided into two separate tasks. First, the parties must agree or be persuaded to come to the table and engage in dialogue. Second, the parties need to be helped to find some basis for agreement. The first task entails building a forum for the cooperative resolution of disputes.[64] The key participants must be persuaded that the process will be open and fair and that no outcome will be imposed on them. They must agree to a set of ground rules about how to proceed. (Ground rules cover the openness of the meetings, the members' relationship to the media, and the way decisions are made; and participants must agree to the use of a facilitator or mediator.) Establishing the ground rules provides an opportunity for the groups to reach agreement before turning to the substantive issues that divide them.

The second task involves facilitating discussion according to certain principles that have been designed to change the tone of interaction (from negative to neutral to positive) and to identify common ground.[65] It is important to separate the people from the problem and avoid personalizing attacks. Disagreement should be invited, and the inferences drawn from statements as well as the assumptions made about other participants should be explicitly tested. It is also useful to seek an understanding of underlying concerns and interests rather than defend preferred positions. At this early stage there may be more agreement than the participants realize. The process leads participants to think of new options that satisfy the concerns and interests of both sides. Seeking consensus for solutions prevents a win-lose mentality and ensures that each side and each participant has an equal role in shaping the agreements that emerge.

Local government officials can also develop structures that will promote communication and understanding among citizens and between citizens and officials. Traffic and parking issues, for example, often turn out to be loaded subjects that touch on serious underlying differences about how the city should function and develop. The parties in dispute can engage in hostile exchanges, and the city council can devote considerable time to those issues, with only minimal success in coming up with satisfactory resolutions. To promote the desired communication and understanding, the Sonora, California, city council created the Sonora Parking and Traffic Commission, where these differences could be explored in a constructive fashion and deliberative decisions made. The commission's membership includes council members, representatives of key departments, and at-large members from the community. The place chosen for the commission meetings allows no physical separation between the commission members and the people who come to its meetings: there is no dais, and no raised seating for commissioners. All sit at a round table, and conversations are constructive rather than confrontational and argumentative. The whole approach has prompted "a renewed sense of community."[66]

Communication with the public

Communication with the public encompasses most of what local government does, but two functions are singled out here: media relations because it is so central to the manager's connection with the community, and e-government because it is steadily growing in importance.

Media relations   Managers can easily fall into the trap of viewing the media as the enemy and thinking that it is impossible to influence coverage. Managers can take steps, however, to improve media relations and the news coverage of local government.[67]

A media relations strategy   Good media relations start with a strategic plan for the organization that can be easily explained to the media, and a communications strategy that is part of that plan. The following pointers are for the local government manager as well as for the information officer and the assistant manager.

- **Start with the reporters.**   Get to know them and ask them to attend periodic briefings. Be as available as possible—for either good times or bad—and always be frank and honest.

- **Give reporters opportunities.** Provide them with good news items and, especially, with well-planned informational events that enable them to do good context work.

- **Get to know the circumstances of the local media.**   Develop an understand-ing of the pressures and constraints under which reporters and editors are working.

- **Get to know the editors.**   Start with a social event or with a request for an initial editorial board briefing and continue periodic briefings.

- **Provide spaces for meeting with reporters where you can display context information (maps, graphs, photographs).**   Do this especially with your office and at least one conference room.

- **Use retreats or other special opportunities to work with the press.**   Try to assure good coverage that doesn't distort the process.

Source: Adapted from James E. Kunde and David W. Tees, "Media Relations: The Manager's Role," *IQ Report* (Washington, D.C.: ICMA, December 1999).

First, the manager should recognize and accept the fact that the public has a right to know what goes on in local government. It is professionally responsible, as well as effective, to respect the letter and spirit of freedom of information acts rather than engage in contests with the media over how much will be hidden and how much will be revealed.

Second, the local government should establish a clear policy for press relations. Press relations should be coordinated by one person, with a clear assignment of responsibilities for releasing various types of information. Reporters should be encouraged to talk to any officials, but officials and employees should know what information is public and when comments on policy questions are appropriate and inappropriate.

Third, the local government manager should take time to orient reporters to local government operations and explain who does what, what the various acronyms mean, and how and why certain decisions are made. If a news story is inaccurate, the manager should not hesitate to tell the reporter but should respect the reporter's news judgment and ignore minor inaccuracies.

Finally, the manager must accept the fact that criticism of local government, the manager, and other officials will appear in the media and that skepticism is built into reporters' professional training. The media are not in the business of quietly informing local government when a problem is discovered. Instead, their job is to inform the public. Nonetheless, with careful attention to media relations, managers can help make the media's coverage more focused, accurate, and positive.

E-government   Relating to the community and providing expected services increasingly calls for information to be distributed electronically.[68] The challenge is to fully integrate the new technologies of communication with reorganized internal processes. Chapter 5 discusses e-government in detail.

Transforming city hall " 'There are four phases Internet migration goes through,' [Meisburg] says. 'The first is a very simple demographic thing, where with pictures and names you make more people aware of the things the city does, the key players, the names of the commissioners. Then there is the query phase. That's when you give them simple information about what these entities do: Who do you call if . . .? Then there's the transactional phase, which is where we are now. In this stage, your customers can begin to do their work, pay their bills, get their services, change their services, track their billing over the internet.' The final phase, [he] says, is the hardest: 'the transformational phase, in which city hall is reconfigured.' "

Source: Rob Gurwitt, "Behind the Portal," *Governing* 14 (August 2001): 56, quoting Steve Meisburg, Tallahassee (Florida) city commissioner.

A specific application of information technology (IT) is the paperless council meeting.[69] Preparing council packets with electronic files makes the information used by the council accessible in the same form to staff and citizens, while it also saves time and money.

The next challenge is applying IT to the process of citizen participation. E-democracy, as it is called, offers the promise of opening new channels of input and strengthening the interaction between citizens and officials in the decision-making process. For example, the Web site "Have Your Say" announces that the city council in Wellington, New Zealand, "relies on the people of Wellington to help us make the right decisions on policy and projects." It not only asks for opinions on identified issues but also offers background information on these issues and, in the particular case of a possible change in the method of electing council members, offered an online survey form that examined a range of issues related to representation as well as to preferences for the method of election.[70]

The manager should be wary of overblown promises for a new "virtual town meeting," however. The electronic medium may be misused.[71] Overcoming barriers to computer access and allowing alternative methods of input for people unfamiliar or uncomfortable with computers will be essential to incorporating electronic citizen participation into the governing process. Furthermore, e-democracy cannot be permitted to crowd out other elements of sound governance. Representative democracy places council members, in their decision making, under the obligation to reflect and deliberate about how to advance the public interest of the community as a whole, not just electronically count hands. Professionalism requires that administrators present recommendations based on knowledge, best practices in other communities, impact on stakeholders, and analysis of long-term needs and trends, not just respond to easily transmitted popular pressures. In the future, therefore, local government managers will have to guide their communities toward finding new ways to blend citizen participation—both computer-assisted and traditional—with representation and with professionalism.

Leadership in a diverse community

The fourth key behavioral aspect of community relations is leadership in a diverse community. Ethnic and cultural diversity have been linked to a community's ability to attract the "creative class" who contribute to economic dynamism.[72]

As mentioned above, effective leadership in a diverse community requires that the manager perceive and relate to citizens in distinctive ways. The manager's orientation to groups should stress inclusion, appreciation of diversity, and representation in the processes of local government.

Inclusion   Leadership involves creating a sense of community out of diversity rather than dividing or polarizing groups. Efforts to identify common ground and overarching principles that all accept must start with a willingness to encompass all groups. The challenge is to make inclusion a reality, not just an assembly of representatives of different groups. The test is getting results; that is, managers must not just be open to participation but must actually get participation and achieve a broader perspective on the nature of problems and their solutions.

Appreciation of diversity   Appreciating differences among people leads one to understand not only the reasons for behavior but also the effect of cultural traditions or experience on a group's values and on its participation in community affairs. The challenge for local government officials is to achieve a depth of understanding that will overcome stereotypical assumptions and prejudices. It is one thing to be aware of an ethnic group's traditions in its original homeland. It is more difficult to understand how those traditions and values affect behavior in the group's present circumstances.

Representation of diversity in local government   With the increased use of district elections, a wider range of groups are securing membership on city and county governing boards. Still, the representation of minority groups typically lags such groups' proportions in the population. New and less-organized groups have difficulty getting members elected, as do groups that are too small or too geographically dispersed. Councils can use appointments to government boards and commissions to broaden participation. Leaders can create forums for the expression of diverse views. Many cities have used study circles to involve ordinary citizens in discussions about improving human relations. Local government managers, as part of their commitment to citizen participation, must act to ensure that all groups have a voice.

Building bridges: A community process to heal racism   Wichita, Kansas, used a dialogue process to increase respect among people from different races, cultures, and religions and to encourage citizens to contribute to community problem solving.

Nearly 300 citizens participated in dialogue groups representing over 75 organizations from business and industry, social services, educational institutions, government, law enforcement, and faith and community groups. Dialogues were held in churches, schools, police substations, bookstores, companies, and museums. Over 23 businesses and civic groups hosted the dialogue groups.

In each group, 8 to 15 community members from different racial and socioeconomic backgrounds discussed challenging topics as introduced in a written curriculum developed by the Study Circles Resource Center (SCRC). Two trained facilitators of different racial or ethnic backgrounds moderated. Each group met for six consecutive weeks for two hours. The conversations moved through important trust-building exercises to discussions of the root causes of problems identified and the actions needed to address the problems effectively. Participants made commitments towards direct action individually and as part of a larger group.

Source: www.wichitagov.org/News/Announcements/2001/12-06-2001b.htm.

Recap

- Local government managers lead their communities by helping shape the policy agenda, actively networking with citizens and groups, and orienting the staff and organization toward being open and responsive to all citizens.

- Local government managers not only lead, but they also seek to promote leadership by others, for example, by supporting elected officials in carrying out their roles and by empowering citizens to address their own problems.

- Professional managers are obligated to ensure that all groups have access to the decision-making process and are treated fairly, whether or not they are directly represented on the city council or participate actively in local politics.

- As governing boards become more diverse and members are more focused on specific areas and groups, the local government manager must assert a perspective that encompasses all segments of the community.

- Local government managers should be outgoing and inclusive in their community relations, although more than half of the local government managers in the United States focus on internal actors in their networking.

- Local government managers, regardless of their typical personality characteristics, should extend themselves beyond being pragmatic problem solvers to become visionary innovators.

- It is important to size up the community's orientation to local government and assess which groups exist in the community and their level of involvement in community affairs.

- Local government managers should develop the capacity to be effective in handling facilitation, conflict resolution, communication with the public, and diversity within the community.

Community assessment for project initiation

When local government managers work to get a major project under way, they fill several roles:

- The initiator, who helps get an issue on the public agenda and seeks to secure effective action

- The catalyst, who brings others into the process and who works through others

- The responsible professional, who seeks to ensure that the decisions are (1) clearly related to and advance the mission of the organization; (2) based on appropriate information about needs, alternatives, and impacts; and (3) reached in a legitimate way by the governing board with broad-based participation of all those affected.

The following are questions the manager can use to assess and monitor the involvement in the project of various individuals and groups in the local government and community.

Local government

Where did the project originate?

Is there complete and objective analysis of the need and the alternative approaches?

What other departments will be affected? What input do they have or should they have in developing a proposal?

Is there an appropriate level of understanding and support for the project in the organization?

Governing body

What is the stance of elected officials with regard to the project? Are they in agreement, divided by constituency, opposed, or waiting for a decision to be presented to them?

If they are supportive, how firm is their support?

How much do they know about the project? (Have you been the only source of information?) Who might sway them in different directions?

What would happen if something goes wrong or a new issue appears?

Are you too far out in front of the governing body? As you venture into the community, is the governing body behind you?

The active community

Who constitutes your network of supporters through whom information about the project can be disseminated and general support can be obtained?

Whose support is needed? What kind of support?

1. Non-opposition

2. Approval

3. Endorsement/publicity

4. Participation

5. Resources

How will support be obtained? Who is the best contact?

Who will oppose the project? When? At the beginning, middle, or end of the project? If opposition will occur late in the process, should participation be invited earlier to secure the input of opponents? On what grounds is the opposition based? Is common ground possible? How can it be secured? Are opponents willing to engage in conflict resolution efforts?

The inactive community

Who will be affected by the project but not necessarily participate in the decision-making process?

How will they be affected?

Will they support or oppose the project?

Should they be left alone or involved? Are they being left alone to make it simpler to get the project approved? (If so, they should be brought into the process.)

Who should contact them?

To capture the steps and interrelationships in the process, develop a Gantt chart (bar graph plotting of action by start and completion date) or flow chart for the process. Be particularly attentive to the sequencing of actions. Asking the question "Who should be contacted before I take this action?" helps the manager identify people who might otherwise be left out and steps that might be overlooked.

Notes

1 Clinton Rogers Woodruff, ed., *A New Municipal Program* (New York: D. Appleton and Company, 1919), 31 and 130.

2 Some fear that, by engaging in community leadership and being active in the policy role, managers are operating outside the bounds of their professionalism. See Bill Kirchhoff, "Babbitt Could Have Been a Manager," *Public Management* 72 (September 1990): 2–6; and James R. Griesemer, "Restoring Relevance to Local Government Management," *Public Management* 72 (September 1990): 7–12.

3 The nine areas are 2. policy facilitation; 4. citizen service; 6. initiative, risk taking, vision, creativity, and innovation; 7. technological literacy; 8. democratic advocacy and citizen participation; 9. diversity; 11. financial analysis; 13. strategic planning; 14. advocacy and interpersonal communication; 16. media relations.

4 John Nalbandian and Carol Nalbandian, "Contemporary Challenges in Local Government," *Public Management* 84 (December 2002): 6–11.

5 James H. Svara, *Official Leadership in the City* (New York: Oxford University Press, 1990), 188–192. In a 1997 survey of city managers and city administrators in cities over 5,000 population, 86 percent agreed that the administrator should assume leadership in shaping municipal policies. Calculations from survey conducted by author; for information on the survey, see James H. Svara, "U.S. City Managers and Administrators in a Global Perspective," *The Municipal Year Book 1999* (Washington, D.C.: ICMA, 1999), 25–33.

6 James H. Svara, "The Myth of the Dichotomy: Complementarity of Politics and Administration in the Past and Future of Public Administration," *Public Administration Review* 61 (March/April 2001): 176–183.

7 The levels of decision are defined in Svara, "Dichotomy and Duality: Reconceptualizing the Relationship between Policy and Administration in Council-Manager Cities," *Public Administration Review* 45 (January/February 1985): 221–232.

8 James H. Svara, "U.S. City Managers and Administrators in a Global Perspective."

9 James H. Svara, *Two Decades of Continuity and Change in America's City Councils* (Washington, D.C.: National League of Cities, 2003).

10 James H. Svara, "The Shifting Boundary between Elected Officials and City Managers in Large Council-Manager Cities," *Public Administration Review* 59 (January/February 1999): 44–53.

11 Svara, *Official Leadership in the City.*

12 National Civic League, "Building Communities That Strengthen Families," *Governing* (October 1998): 2.

13 Poul Erik Mouritzen and James H. Svara, *Leadership at the Apex: Politicians and Administrators in Western Local Governments* (Pittsburgh: University of Pittsburgh Press, 2002), 99–102. The other percentages for U.S. managers were 2 percent isolates and 1 percent intergovernmental networkers. The breakdown for all countries was isolates, 24 percent; internal networkers, 27 percent; intergovernmental networkers, 21 percent; and inclusive networkers, 27 percent.

14 Robert Putnam, *Bowling Alone: The Collapse and Revival of American Community* (New York: Simon & Schuster, 2000), 25.

15 Donald F. Kettl, *The Transformation of Governance: Public Administration for Twenty-First Century America* (Baltimore: Johns Hopkins University Press, 2002).

16 "Preserving Cultural and Historic Resources through Brownfields Redevelopment," E-Library document, ICMA, 2002.

17 H. George Frederickson, "The Repositioning of American Public Administration," *Political Science & Politics* 32 (1999): 701–711.

18 Alexei Pavlichev and G. David Garson, *Digital Government: Principles and Best Practices* (Hershey, Pa.: Idea Group Publishing, 2004), chap. 1.

19 Between 1997 and 2001, the increase in computer use among African Americans and Hispanics was 28 percent, compared with 22 percent among whites. Racial differences in use were still substantial, however: among whites and Asian Americans/Pacific Islanders, 71 percent used computers; among African Americans, 56 percent; and among Hispanics, 49 percent. Similar racial patterns can be observed for income and educational levels. *A Nation Online: How Americans Are Expanding Their Use of the Internet* (Washington, D.C.: National Telecommunications and Information Administration and the Economics and Statistics Administration, U.S. Census Bureau, 2002).

20 Russ Linden, "The Promise and Challenge of Collaboration," *Public Management* 85 (August 2003): 8–11.

21 Svara, *Two Decades of Continuity and Change.*

22 Charldean Newell and David N. Ammons, "Role Emphasis of City Managers and Other Municipal Executives," *Public Administration Review* 47 (May/June 1987): 246–252.

23 James H. Svara, "Metamorphosis of Government and the Importance of New Governance" (presentation, ICMA Annual Conference, 2002).

24 Roy Wenzl, "Bob Knight Profile: All about Bob, How a Lonely Kid from Wichita Became Our Mayor Seven Times," *Wichita Eagle,* October 17, 1999.

25 James H. Svara, "Mayors in the Unity of Powers Context," in *The Future of Local Government Administration: The Hansell Symposium,* ed. H. George Frederickson and John Nalbandian, 50–52 (Washington, D.C.: ICMA, 2002). The managers' self-rating of influence was slightly higher in the director-type cities than in other cities.

26 Victoria Loe Hicks, "Stronger City Council Proposed: Charter Review Panel's Preliminary Draft Seeks More Accountability," *Dallas Morning News,* February 24, 2003.

27 James H. Svara, "Do We Still Need Model Charters? The Meaning and Relevance of Reform in the Twenty-First Century," *National Civic Review* 90 (Spring 2001): 19–33. The change in form also has important implications for the council and tends to make it a more reactive body responding to proposals from the mayor rather than a body that shapes the policy agenda through give-and-take with a city manager who serves at the pleasure of the council as a whole.

28 Bill Hansell, "Revisiting the Reform of the Reform," *Public Management* 81 (January 1999): 27–28.

29 Kimberly L. Nelson, *Structure of American Municipal Government,* Special Data Issue, no. 4 (Washington, D.C.: ICMA, 2002).

30 Svara, "Do We Still Need Model Charters?"

31 Terms used in this discussion are drawn from the Myers-Briggs Type Indicator (MBTI). See Sandra Krebs Hirsh and Jean M. Kummerow, *Introduction to Type in Organizational Settings* (Palo Alto, Calif.: Consulting Psychologists Press, 1987).

32 The corresponding Myers-Briggs types for this dimension are termed "judgers" and "perceivers."

33 For those who have completed the inventory and know their types, the approximate connection between the categories of managers we have just described and the MBTI types is as follows: community leader-ENTJ; chief executive-INTJ; administrative innovator-INTJ; administrative stabilizer/improver-ISTJ; coalition builder-ENFP; arbiter-ESFP; caretaker-ISTJ. Information about the MBTI is available in David Keirsey, *Please Understand Me II: Temperament, Character, Intelligence* (Del Mar, Calif.: Prometheus Nemesis Book Co., 1998).

34 Charles K. Coe, "The MBTI: A Tool for Understanding and Improving Public Management," *State and Local Government Review* 23 (Winter 1991): 37–46. The breakdown of types for city managers in North Carolina is as follows: extroversion 39 percent, introversion 61 percent; sensing 76 percent, intuition 24 percent; thinking 87 percent, feeling 13 percent; judging 82 percent, perceiving 18 percent.

35 Oliver P. Williams, "A Typology for Comparative Local Government," *Midwest Journal of Political Science* 5 (May 1961): 150–164. A fourth type was the arbiter of conflicting interests.

36 William B. Coleman started work in Cary as assistant town manager in 1988 and became city manager in 1994.

37 William D. Eggers and John O'Leary, *Revolution at the Roots: Making Our Government Smaller, Better, and Closer to Home* (New York: Free Press, 1995).

38 U.S. Department of Housing and Urban Development (HUD), *Now Is the Time: Places Left Behind in the New Economy* (Washington, D.C.: HUD, 1999).

39 G. Thomas Kingsley and Kathryn L. S. Pettit, "Population Growth and Decline in City Neighbor-

hoods," in *Neighborhood Change in Urban America* (Washington, D.C.: Urban Institute, 2002).

40 An industry cluster can be defined as a geographically concentrated group of interdependent firms and supporting institutions. See Michael E. Porter, "Clusters and Competition: New Agendas for Companies, Governments, and Institutions," in *On Competition,* ed. Michael Porter, chap. 7 (Boston: Harvard Business School Publishing, 1998).

41 Wendy L. Hassett and Douglas J. Watson, "Long-Serving City Managers: Why Do They Stay?" *Public Administration Review* 63 (January/February, 2003): 71–78.

42 Gordon Whitaker and Ruth Hoogland DeHoog, "City Managers under Fire: How Conflict Leads to Turnover," *Public Administration Review* 51 (March/April 1991): 156–165. Managers completed a survey in 1986 that included questions about the political stability of the community. The managers who then left their positions were reinterviewed by telephone three years later.

43 Clarence Stone, "Power and Governance in American Cities," in *Cities, Politics, and Policy: A Comparative Analysis,* ed. John P. Pellissero, 130–131 (Washington, D.C.: CQ Press, 2003).

44 *News & Observer* (Raleigh, North Carolina), February 18, 2001, 3I. The city manager was Dempsey Benton, who served in the position from 1983 to 2000.

45 Nationally, approximately 64 percent of the population 18 years of age and over was registered to vote in 2000 (U.S. Census Bureau, Voting and Registration in the Election of November 2000, issued February 2002, P20-542). In Virginia, local elections had a 25 percent turnout of registered voters in May 2000 (Commonwealth of Virginia, Local Elections—Voter Turnout, May 2, 2000, www.sbe.state.va.us/web_docs/election/results/2000/may_local/l_loc_turnout.html). In California for off-cycle and odd-year November local elections in 2000 and 2001, 28 to 30 percent of registered voters turned out (Research Brief, Public Policy Institute of California, March 2002).

46 David Greenberg, "Debunking America's Enduring Myths," *New York Times,* June 29, 2003, section 4, p. 3.

47 The term "civil society" is sometimes used to refer to all institutions that are not part of either the market or the government (e.g., family and religious organizations, nonprofits, and other voluntary associations).

48 See, for example, the Alliance for National Renewal fostered by the National Civic League; the Center for Democracy and Citizenship at the University of Minnesota and Public Achievement, which it sponsors; and other partner organizations of the Civic Practices Network.

49 For information, see the Web site of Richmond, at www.ci.richmond.va.us/citizen/neighborhoods/cmxxs_process.asp.

50 Alan Ehrenhalt, "For Chambers of Commerce and Cities, the Days of Conflict May Be Over," *Governing* (November 1989): 40–48.

51 Lynette Clemetson, "Hispanics Now Largest Minority, Census Shows," *New York Times,* January 21, 2003. The political impact of Hispanic growth is diminished somewhat by the fact that roughly one-quarter of Hispanics living in the United States are not U.S. citizens.

52 Ibid.

53 Ron Nissimov, "Some Blacks Irritated by Immigrant Influx," *Houston Chronicle,* September 19, 2002.

54 U.S. Census Bureau, Current Population Survey, 2001 and 2002 Annual Demographic Supplements.

55 Steven H. Haeberle, "A Curricular Guide to Gay/Lesbian/Queer Studies; U.S.: State and Local Government" (American Political Science Association Online, 1998), www.apsanet.org/_lgbt/state.cfm. A list of the local governments that provide domestic partner benefits can be found at "Domestic Partner Benefits," Human Rights Campaign Foundation, www.hrc.org/worknet/dp/index.asp.

56 Liza Hetzel and Annetta Smith, *The 65 Years and Over Population: 2000, Census 2000 Brief* (Washington, D.C.: U.S. Census Bureau, 2001). Census 2000 was the first time in the history of the census that the 65-and-over population did not grow faster than the total population.

57 "Projections of the Total Resident Population by 5-Year Age Groups, and Sex with Special Age Categories: Middle Series, 2025 to 2045" (NP-T3-F)(Washington, D.C.: Population Projections Program, Population Division, U.S. Census Bureau, 2000).

58 Hetzel and Smith, *The 65 Years and Over Population: 2000.*

59 One example is the organization, Content of Our Character, www.contentofourcharacter.org/.

60 Ken Dychtwald, "The Age Wave Is Coming," *Public Management* 85 (July 2003): 6–10.

61 Laura B. Wilson and Jack Steele, *Marketing Volunteer Opportunities to Baby Boomers: A Blue Print from the Field.* 2001. Accessed through National Service Resource Center, www.nationalserviceresources.org/filemanager/download/727/boomers.pdf.

62 Roger Schwarz, *The Skilled Facilitator,* 2nd ed. (San Francisco: Jossey-Bass, 2002), 46–50.

63 Gordon McIntosh, *The Local Government Leadership (LGL) Facilitator Program Tool Kit.* Victoria: LGL Institute at Royal Roads University, 2003.

64 William Potapchuk, "Building Forums for the Cooperative Resolution of Disputes in Communities," *National Civic Review* 77 (July–August 1988): 342–349.

65 In addition to Potapchuk, see Roger M. Schwarz, "Groundrules for Effective Groups," *Popular Government* (Spring 1989): 25–30; and Roger Fisher and William Ury, *Getting to Yes* (New York: Penguin Books, 1982).

66 Liz Bass and Greg Applegate, "Come, Let Us Reason Together," *Public Management* (November 2001): 20–22.

67 Many of these points were drawn from Stribling P. Boynton, "A Dozen Tips for Working with the Media," *Public Management* (March 1989): 27–28.

68 Evelina Moulder, *E-Government: What Citizens Want; What Governments Provide* (Washington, D.C.: ICMA, 2002).

69 "The Paperless Council," *ICMA IQ Report* 34, no. 10 (October 2002).

70 www.wcc.govt.nz/yoursay/.

71 Pavlichev and Garson, *Digital Government,* 6, note this negative assessment: "Santa Monica's seminal and much-vaunted example of e-democracy, PEN, which could be said to have started it all, after an initial tsunami of publicity and flurry of actual use soon fell into relative disuse as elected officials came to see it as a vehicle for hecklers and political junkies not representative of the community and not helpful as a forum for their exposure for purposes of re-election."

72 Richard Florida, "The Rise of the Creative Class," *Washington Monthly* 34 (May 2002): 15–25.

3 Enhancing the governing body's effectiveness

A bond exists between the elected governing body and its appointed manager in the form of their common obligation to make local government work for the good of the citizens in the community. Citizens usually judge how well their local government officials meet this obligation on the basis of the community's economic vitality and quality of life and the local government's responsiveness to their needs. The success of the local government in meeting citizens' expectations and community goals often depends on the manager's ability to enhance the governing body's effectiveness.

This chapter explores ways in which appointed professional managers and elected officials can achieve a successful partnership in their mutual effort to create and maintain an effective government. It examines the changing roles of both the governing body and the local government manager and explores ways in which the manager can help members of the governing body become more effective policy makers with a broad view of community affairs. In addition, the chapter discusses the importance of the governing body's confidence in the manager and describes possible sources of conflict between the manager and governing body, as well as among elected officials. The chapter also offers ways of measuring the manager's and the governing body's effectiveness.

The governing body's role

National governments worldwide delegate specific authority and responsibilities to lower levels of government. In the United States, enhancing local government authority has been the stated goal since the 1980s. As a consequence, local governing bodies are required to demonstrate a greater degree of political leadership. As local governments receive less state and national financial assistance, local elected officials must innovate to generate revenue. As they prepare to compete in an increasingly global economy, local officials must develop an international outlook. To avoid service duplication, improve the quality and efficiency of services and the equity of service delivery, and develop a much-needed sense of community, policy makers in rural areas, townships, and smaller municipalities will need to cooperate with neighboring jurisdictions toward innovative approaches.

As local elected officials confront the challenges that arise from social, political, and economic change, they must ask the basic question of whether they should lead by influencing citizen attitudes and opinions (act as trustee) or by faithfully representing public opinion as expressed in polls and public forums (act as a delegate). Edmund Burke, the English political leader, in the eighteenth century argued that the elected leader must exercise independent judgment when voting on legislation and would be held accountable by voters at each election.[1] While serving as a United States senator in the 1950s, John F. Kennedy wrote *Profiles in Courage,* in which he also observed:

> The voters selected us, in short, because they had confidence in our judgment and our ability to exercise that judgment. . . . This may mean that we must on occasion lead,

inform, correct and sometimes even ignore constituent opinion, if we are to exercise fully that judgment for which we were elected.[2]

Effective leadership as a trustee is not an automatic consequence of elected officials' positions and authority; it is instead an applied art. Warren Bennis has stated that leaders should exercise a "transformative power" that does not spring from the formal structures of governments but derives instead from the ability of the leader to empower others through vision, purpose, belief, and organizational culture.[3] Like appointed professional managers, elected officials need to reinterpret traditional models of leadership and develop the proactive and anticipatory leadership qualities discussed in Chapter 1 in order to meet the demands they will face.

Courageous leaders set the tone by making hard decisions and moving the organization forward; they set a good example by showing the courage of their own convictions.

Les White

These newer models of leadership may increase conflict rather than decrease it. In the constant struggle over which services local governments are to provide for whom and over how they are to be funded, the conflict resolution emerges as a central focus of leadership and management. Despite leaders' efforts to diminish it, conflict will remain a constant as the demand for services increases, resources shrink, and the need for change challenges the status quo. In communities around the world, municipal officials operate in a new political culture infused with single-issue leaders, extensive media coverage, and active citizens.[4]

This new political culture has caused local elected officials to stress their representational function—their delegation—rather than the governing body's governance function. Governance "involves the determining of goals and policy for the city, whereas the representational function stresses the articulation of citizen views and the assisting of citizens in their dealings with government."[5] This trend toward the role of delegate rather than trustee among many members of today's governing bodies presents a special challenge to professional managers who must encourage their governing bodies to think about mission, long-term policy choices, and community-wide interests.

Pervasive social, political, and economic changes require successful partnerships between the governing body and the local government manager to sustain achievements and maintain the momentum of progress. Professional managers are positioned to help their elected officials become effective decision makers. Professional local government managers "must continually relate specific institutions and practices to the broader constitutional order. This activity defines and redefines appropriate relations among themselves and the people as policies and circumstances change."[6]

The professional manager's responsibilities toward the governing body

Contemporary local government managers are responsible for serving their governing bodies, providing for the citizens residing in their communities, and upholding the high standards of conduct found in the ICMA's Code of Ethics and Declaration of Ideals.[7] The chief appointed professional is primarily responsible to the governing body but is also a community leader and is therefore encouraged to assist elected officials in working with the citizens.[8] John Nalbandian argues: "In the future the legitimacy of professional administrators in local government will be grounded in the tasks of community building and enabling democracy—in getting things done collectively, while building a sense of inclusion."[9]

In the process of determining the policy the manager can and should play a most important role. . . . If the manager shies away from such leadership, the community stands still and important matters are allowed to pass by default.
C. A. Harrell

Among the 18 core content areas in "Practices for Effective Local Government Management" developed by ICMA (see Appendix B for list of all practices), two focus on working with the governing body and citizens.[10] Number two, policy facilitation, asks local government managers to help "elected officials and other community actors identify, work toward, and achieve common goals and objectives. . . ." Number eight, democratic advocacy and citizen participation, asks local government managers to demonstrate "a commitment to democratic principles by respecting elected officials, community interest groups, and the decision making process; educating citizens about local government; and acquiring knowledge of the social, economic, and political history of the community. . . ." These two core content areas, and the general practices listed with them, form the foundation of many more specific practices that enable local government managers to improve the policy making of their governing bodies.

Strengthen policy-making capabilities

The manager and the manager's staff can help strengthen the policy-making capabilities of the governing body by thinking strategically to guide decision making, structuring the budget process, creating an annual policy calendar, using citizen input and expertise, and focusing the governing body on mission and policy.[11]

Use strategic thinking to guide decision making

To lay the groundwork for policy making by the governing body, the manager can marshal the resources of the staff and the community to help develop a strategic agenda. In localities large and small, properly assembled information can provide the basis for projecting the future of the community. Informed citizens can then choose positive change to improve their communities. Strategic planning works both within government and outside in the community.

In Sarasota County, strategic planning is not a product; it is a process. By encouraging a culture in which everyone thinks strategically, works strategically, and reports progress toward goals within a strategic framework, the county is able to strike a balance between organizational rhetoric and the reality of its strengths, weaknesses, and resources applied to community needs.
Jim Ley

The following four questions can stimulate strategic thinking:

- What is the community like now?
- What are the community's strengths and weaknesses, its opportunities, and threats to its well-being?
- What will the community be like in 10 years if no action is taken?
- What will the community be like in 10 years if a strategic plan is developed and implemented?

Strategic planning in Blagoevgrad, Bulgaria   City Manager Douglas Watson of Auburn, Alabama, and his staff assisted the officials of Blagoevgrad in creating a strategic plan to help improve citizen participation and solid-waste management. They used a traditional approach that featured citizen participation and consensus building.

Four committees comprising volunteers, members of nongovernmental organizations, elected officials, and city staff stud-

ied "economic development, ecology and solid waste, and urbanization and infrastructure." They issued reports stating long-term, middle-term, and short-term goals and the strategies to implement the plan. One immediate success involved developing a technical solution to the solid-waste crisis facing Blagoevgrad by extending the life of the existing landfill.

Source: "2001 ICMA Annual & Service Awards: Celebrating Excellence in Local Government," *Public Management* 83 (September 2001): 5.

Structure the budget process

After goals are established, the manager can structure the budget preparation, review, and adoption process so that the governing body understands the budget and feels that it addresses the goals and agreed-upon service levels. The manager needs to integrate the annual operating and capital improvements budgets, debt service, and state and federal grants so they relate to the achievement of community goals. For example, City Manager Thomas Brymer and his management team in College Station, Texas, integrated the city's strategic plan into the budget process to ensure that specified policies and programs would be implemented.[12] ICMA's Financial Trend Monitoring System[13] is another tool many communities have used to restructure and improve the budget process.

Create an annual policy calendar

Incorporating an annual policy calendar into the governing body's operating procedures will help coordinate long-range policy issues, and budgeting should be the cornerstone of the policy calendar. The governing body should be involved in the budgeting process at an early stage and set goals before staff prepares working documents. The policy calendar should provide time for the governing body to study issues and responsibilities in greater depth. Special meetings and retreats can be used to:

- Evaluate performance of the chief executive administrative officer and other appointees
- Review internal operations and procedures, especially after the election of new members to the board
- Reconsider and refine community goals and major policy statements
- Consider intergovernmental and legislative matters such as joint budgeting, intergovernment cooperation, and key legislation pending in the state legislature or in Congress.

Retreats should be held for one or two days in a relaxed setting that permits participants to get away from business as usual. All elected officials as well as the manager should be present, but staff should be limited to those members whose presence is absolutely necessary. An outside facilitator—someone experienced in leading public organizations through goal-setting discussions and familiar with the background of the government, the governing body, and the issues—can lead the discussion, giving everyone an opportunity to participate. Media representative should be invited to attend, and organizers should keep in mind their logistical needs and deadlines. Participation by the media will improve their awareness and understanding of local government and may increase their support, not only for the retreat as a policy-making device but also for the issues involved. The retreat should be located nearby and in a not-too-elegant facility; if not, media representatives may criticize it as not in accord with community values or economic conditions.

Use citizen input and expertise

The new political culture expects that citizens will participate. Citizens want to be involved in the policy-making process and are less trusting of elected officials and professionals to make decisions for them.[14] Managers can involve citizens in structured ways beyond the traditional public hearing, which has only limited value as a forum for obtaining citizen input. The traditional public hearing is best used to hear citizens comment on a specific issue such as a zoning variance instead of on the adoption of major new program or policy.[15] Neighborhood councils, town meetings, a community policy calendar, citizen surveys, focus groups, task forces and advisory committees can all structure citizen participation and obtain useful information that can affect the governing body's major mission and policy choices.

Neighborhood councils The manager can encourage citizens to form neighborhood associations to advise the governing body on policy matters and refer citizen service requests. In many communities, neighborhood organizations also participate in the delivery of services to residents.

Town meetings In cooperation with local colleges and other institutions, some communities organize town meetings on issues of local importance. These meetings empower citizen groups, and the governing body receives important information on policy-related issues.

Community policy calendar Community groups should be encouraged to schedule their activities according to the annual policy calendar and provide their views to elected officials and the appointed manager.

Citizen surveys The citizen survey is frequently used to gather data about program demand, program quality, level of service, and new services that are needed. One affordable option is The National Citizen Survey™ sponsored by ICMA in partnership with National Research Center, Inc.[16] This service uses a standard instrument that allows comparisons across communities.

Using citizen survey results

- Refer to results whenever citizens tell you they know what the community thinks

- Bring results into discussions with elected officials about strategic planning

- Monitor results to track the quality of service delivery; allocate resources where they seem most needed

- Compare results with results for similar communities; help identify opportunities to benchmark service performance

- Consider holding department directors to agreed targets for consumer satisfaction

- Decide whether to press for a community policy that has been tested in a citizen survey

- Jawbone the results in your citizen newsletter and at press conferences.

Source: Thomas I. Miller and Michelle Kobayashi, "The Voice of the Public: Why Citizen Surveys Work," *Public Management* 83 (May 2001): 9

Focus groups A focus group usually comprises approximately 10 to 12 citizens specially chosen so that their comments can be interpreted to reflect part of the larger population in the community.[17] Examples of criteria often used are race, gender, age, residential area, education, and user of a particular service. Several focus group discussions usually provide more accurate information than only one. The group discusses several questions presented by a facilitator. A summary of the discussion provides useful insight into how the public views policy choices and the performance of the government.

Task forces/advisory committees   Leaders of local business, community, and service agencies are usually willing to donate time to advise the governing body and the manager on budgeting, financial forecasting, and methods of assessing effectiveness and efficiency. Asking citizens with a particular expertise to serve on a task force or advisory committee has several benefits: they frequently recommend changes and improvements on the basis of their professional perspectives and their experiences in the private and volunteer sectors. Establishing links with leaders in the community also tends to promote communication between community leaders and elected officials, which can be useful when critical decisions are before the governing body.

In reporting the outcomes of citizen participation to the governing body, the manager must report both positive and negative results. Elected officials most often appreciate good executive summaries with more detailed backup material for those inclined to study it.

Focus the governing body on mission and policy

Governing bodies usually spend the greater share of their time on routine administrative matters and less time on the purpose for which they were elected—focusing on mission and policy (see Chapter 2). Indeed, today's political culture encourages elected officials to stress their responsiveness to citizen complaints rather than to broader concerns. Maintaining relations with boards and commissions and responding to citizen complaints are necessary but time-consuming, and over-allocation of time to routine activities detracts from policy making. To facilitate the flow of information and shift the workload from administration to policy making, local government managers can:

- Shift the emphasis of meetings from administrative routine to policy considerations by setting time limits on public agenda items and speakers

- Develop a consent agenda of administrative or routine matters that can be acted upon by a single motion unless individual members call for exceptions for special consideration

- Schedule informal public meetings with government staff in neighborhoods to answer residents' questions and resolve problems prior to any formal hearings and government action

- Hold hearings with citizen boards on zoning, property-related matters, traffic engineering and control, and public utilities; recommendations can be reviewed and action taken

- Use short executive summaries of staff position papers on an annotated agenda; documentation—preferably electronic—can be made available for later review by elected officials

- Establish regular sessions to deal solely with planning issues and/or reserve three- or four-hour blocks of time or one meeting each month to focus on one broad policy area of local concern

- Delegate non-policy-related duties and responsibilities to administrative staff and appointed citizen bodies

- Include in policy statements formal criteria for exceptions; this discourages capricious disregard of adopted policies.

Staff communication on policy matters should be streamlined: materials on policy issues submitted by staff should be well organized, concise, relevant to the agenda, and formatted to include at least:

- A clear identification of an item as a policy issue
- A clear statement of the issue
- A discussion of feasible alternatives
- A presentation of the strengths and weaknesses of each alternative
- The identification of relevant social, economic, political, and environmental implications for the various alternatives.

Staff must anticipate and be prepared to answer questions on the policy issues.

Maintain a good work environment

Effective managers keep open the lines of communication by meeting with individual members of the governing body, provide a central base of operations, schedule orientation for new members, and institutionalize annual evaluations.

Meet individually with members of the governing body

The manager can help individual members develop their policy-making capabilities. The manager should inventory council members regularly to determine whether their individual goals as elected officials are being addressed or, if appropriate, what new objectives or programs are of concern. Discussion of individual goals within the group tends to reinforce confidence in the manager and the decision-making process. In some communities, the manager can meet periodically with individual members to discuss their concerns and goals. Managers serving governing bodies whose members have their own staffs may use individual meetings less frequently because the members' staffs are available to help members pursue their concerns and goals.

It is important to provide structured meetings and opportunities to keep council staff in the loop and feeling well-informed and a part of the team. Orientation and training should be a priority. These staff do a great deal of constituent service work and the more they understand the organization and its systems, the better they can serve their bosses . . . which makes for happier council members.

Del Borgsdorf

Provide a base of operations

As resources permit, even in small local governments, the governing body should be provided a central base of operations:

- Provide a central file and an office or a space for elected officials to meet with citizens in private
- Adopt some or all of the features of a paperless council—e-mail accounts, laptop computers, printers, software licenses, and a support staff
- Furnish an aide and secretary (under direction of the manager) to maintain the central office, handle certain correspondence and telephone calls, maintain appointment calendars, and receive citizen requests on behalf of governing body members
- Establish weekly office hours for members of the governing body and publish these for constituents.

The paperless council in Galesburg, Illinois   As part of its e-packet initiative, Galesburg provides each council member, legal adviser, and staff member a laptop at a total cost of $53,176; each council member an inkjet printer at a cost of $2,984; and software licenses for each council member and legal adviser at a cost of $1,367. The city also purchased at a cost of $4,999 a projector to display e-packets on screen during council meetings. The total initial direct cost of the e-packet initiative was $62,526.

Other costs included information technology improvements, such as wiring and cabling council chambers; remote access service; and new copiers/scanners, all of which are only partly attributed to the e-packet initiative. Additional indirect costs include $3,240 for staff time devoted to setup and implementation.

Galesburg estimates that this paperless approach "saves 100 reams of paper, photocopy charges, and 150 labor hours annually, for a dollar value of $5,830." Galesburg believes citizens and council members benefit from better access to information and easier ways to communicate.

Source: Sheldon Cohen, "The Paperless Council," *IQ Report* (Washington, D.C.: ICMA, October 2002).

In some larger communities, especially those with full-time elected officials, members of the governing body have their own offices and hire their own staffs. This practice will present challenges for the local government manager if the governing body staff emerges as a rival to the appointed executive and the executive's staff. Nurturing working relationships among all staff members on the basis of mutual respect and a partnership is one approach that can avoid potential problems.

Schedule orientation for new members

Newly elected members should receive an orientation soon after election; refresher courses should be provided for continuing members. Some newly elected members will have had prior experience, while others will be new to public office. An orientation process should be in place for both newcomers and continuing governing body members; some communities conduct orientation sessions for candidates as well. The basic orientation can be customized according to current needs, policies, and issues.

Board member orientation   Appointed professionals use a variety of approaches to orientating new members of the governing body.

- Peggy Merriss, city manager of Decatur, Georgia, provides an informal review of finances, personnel, and operating policies and procedures that lasts about four hours. After this review, officials tour all city facilities and meet department heads.
- Ed Daley, city manager of Winchester, Virginia, provides a half-day review of public safety, utilities, planning and development, finance and administration, recreation, social services, schools, and public works. Visits to various facilities are spread over a two-week period. Incumbent members of the council and the press can also attend the tours.

- David Limardi, city manager of Highland Park, Illinois, provides new members with an orientation binder before their first meeting, when they are sworn in. The binder contains information about Highland Park's mission statement, employee code of organization values, organization structure and contact lists of employees, the city council's code of ethics and rules of procedure, the paperless agenda process, the city's master plan, and a budget overview, among other topics. Limardi schedules a breakfast with new members and devotes that day to individual meetings with department heads, who provide tours of facilities.

Source: Each manager provided descriptions to author.

If time and resources are available, the orientation session should be held as a retreat, allowing for reviews of the formal structure of the local government and existing policies and programs and opportunities for governing body members to get acquainted with each other as well as with the manager and key staff.

Local colleges and universities can be valuable for conducting the orientations and for developing manuals and training sessions. Government, political science, communications, and management departments might be able to assist. Many state institutes of government also provide training for elected officials, but state-level training cannot take the place of local orientation.

The orientation has been helpful because I at least know that there is a baseline of information that each commissioner has, and it gives me some time to meet with them and determine their particular interests.
Peggy Merriss

Following orientation, one or more members of the manager's staff can be designated as a temporary liaison with individual elected members to facilitate the flow of information, obtain answers to questions, assist with constituent requests, and conduct research.

Institutionalize annual evaluations

Annual evaluation of the city manager provides a means for continuing dialogue on the management of local affairs. The manager can suggest a structure for evaluating effectiveness and performance of the manager and of others appointed by or under the direct supervision of the local governing body. The evaluation should include:

- Review of the past year's performance to see whether the expectations of the governing body and the manager coincided and were realized
- Specific feedback to the manager about areas in which the manager could have served more effectively
- Establishment of definite objectives and a plan and/or contract for the upcoming year.

No single evaluation method predominates in the United States.[18] Cities continue to experiment with different combinations of features. Research suggests that four specific features in the annual evaluation are especially useful:

- Requiring an evaluation in an employment agreement to ensure that one occurs at least annually
- Using a form to document the evaluation
- Training members of the governing body to do an evaluation
- Using a two-way evaluation, which involves reviewing the governing body's performance as well as the appointed manager's performance.[19]

The governing body evaluation form provided at the end of this chapter works effectively in a two-way evaluation. Having every member of the governing body evaluate their personal contributions to the effectiveness of the governing body can also be useful (see page 66). Although standard human resources practice recommends separating the tasks of evaluation and adjusting salary, linking the manager's evaluation to the discussion of the manager's salary can be useful because members of the governing body often need an incentive to carry out the evaluation.

Evaluation of individual board members In Book 2 of the *Elected Officials Handbooks,* the following checklist of questions is presented as a way for individual governing body members to assess how they contribute to meetings. It is suggested that members answer the questions after a meeting using a five point scale: 1 means "rarely," and 5 means "most of the time."

___Did I help create an informal, relaxed atmosphere?

___Did I participate in the discussion?

___Did I help keep the discussion on track?

___Did I understand and accept the task(s) entailed in the discussion?

___Did I listen to others?

___Did I feel comfortable disagreeing with others?

___Did I feel comfortable when others disagreed with me?

___Did I seek consensus when working toward agreement?

___Did I use my skills and knowledge at the session?

A score of 25 or less indicates room for improvement. If a majority of members score 25 or less, team-building activities could be helpful.

Source: "Team-Building Skill Checklist," in *Elected Officials Handbooks,* book 2 (Washington, D.C.: ICMA, 1994), 24.

To be sure, no particular method will be a panacea and solve all the problems that may prevent a governing body from evaluating the manager thoroughly and communicating results clearly. Ultimately it is the people using the method who make it work.

As a supplement to a formal evaluation by the governing body, or as a substitute for such an evaluation, appointed professionals can use the 360-degree tool often used for professional development. ICMA's Management Practices Assessment Program uses a performance-based assessment tool developed by ICMA and the Andrew Young School of Policy Studies at Georgia State University. It is a multi-rater—a 360-degree instrument—that gathers feedback on managerial performance from the subject's supervisor(s), staff, elected officials, and others the manager selects. The manager conducts a self-rating and asks up to 14 other individuals to do the same on the basis of questions in an easy-to-use booklet. All ratings are analyzed confidentially and act as feedback to the administrator. This approach is not identical to a formal evaluation by the governing body, but it does generate a learning opportunity for the manager and may stimulate the governing body to take annual evaluations seriously.

Build confidence

The foundation of a successful manager-council relationship is confidence. In some countries, this principle is institutionalized at the national level; the prime minister, for example, serves only while enjoying the confidence of the parliament, the governing body. Few other comparisons between parliamentary prime ministers and local government managers are valid, but the principle of confidence in the manager is worth noting.

The governing body's confidence in the manager usually depends on the skill with which the manager handles key issues and makes critical decisions. Managers find that decisions that make a large impact on governing body confidence are often complex and have long-term implications—for example, labor negotiations, selection of key staff members, annual budgets, capital improvement programs, comprehensive planning, independent audits, and credit ratings. Managers also may be judged on how well they handle the media and interest groups on high-visibility and conflict-inducing issues.

Most professional managers are skilled technicians, effective communicators, and often gifted and trusted advisers. But governing body–manager relations that are regarded as successful (judged by tenure of the manager) may depend on how well only 5 percent of the business is conducted: managers should help their governing body maximize time spent on important mission and policy matters and minimize time spent on administration.

You can make a great team with the council, you can offer policy recommendations on a variety of local affairs, and you can have frank discussions with the council. Bottom line, however, is that you play a subordinate role to the council. This situation is not bad or evil; in fact, in a democracy we anticipate that elected officials will wield control and authority over appointed officials. Just remember that is so!
James Thurmond

No quantitative measures exist to gauge governing body effectiveness, save perhaps effective budget policy, but the level of confidence in the manager can be increased by the skillful manager's ability to maintain a team spirit to resolve conflict and carry out responsibilities. Experienced managers with stable tenure and effective elected policy makers often recommend the following team-building techniques.

Avoid peaks and valleys

The length and intensity of regular governing body meetings vary by jurisdiction and by the issues, but members should always know what to expect at meetings. Short, routine meetings alternating with marathon sessions convey the impression that no one is in charge. Policy makers will be unable to give adequate time to some critical issues, while they devote too much time to others. Short agendas invite excursions into administrative detail; on the other hand, managers who stack the agenda with complicated issues are often accused of manipulating the agenda to force the governing body—out of sheer fatigue or frustration—to adopt staff recommendations. Even if a hidden staff agenda is absent, heavy agendas do not build a team spirit or confidence.

Prepare good agendas

Agenda items should be accompanied by clear, concise, timely, written evaluations that exhibit careful preparation and competent analysis. A manager who fails to meet this requirement may cripple the ability of the governing body to function in even routine matters.[20] Because of the continuing and often routine nature of agenda preparation, managers may lose interest or the motivation to maintain quality control. Perceptions by appointed and elected officials of the importance of individual agenda items also may differ. Managers must monitor the quality of the agenda through frequent and open communication with members of the governing body. Weekly agenda communications can be improved if the manager and staff try to:

- Give all elected officials prior knowledge of agenda items
- Deliver all agenda packets at the same time
- Give the same information to all elected members (if one asks for something special, share it with everyone)
- Discuss key issues informally before formal meetings (within the limitations of open meeting laws)
- Make recommendations, and include with each recommendation the advantages and disadvantages.

The effective manager should be able to suggest tactfully to elected officials how they too can improve the weekly agenda preparation process; suggestions to elected officials can be based on the following guidelines:

- Be prepared—study the issues before the meeting, not during it
- Recognize that staff often have little time to prepare the agenda, which can explain the last-minute inclusion of perhaps unpredictable items
- Do not embarrass the staff in public; instead discuss any problems with an agenda item before or after the meeting
- Inform the manager if members of the governing body want to meet with other staff members about agenda items
- Tell the manager whether the agenda and supporting information meet expectations; if they do not, tell the manager what changes are needed.

Identify alternatives

The manager should communicate to the governing body several tenable policy alternatives and note objective arguments for and against each one. Even though the manager is expected to recommend an optimal solution, the manager's failure to list alternatives and discuss their advantages and disadvantages brings the motives of the manager into question, possibly risks converting the manager's role from a professional to a partisan one, and often undermines the governing body's confidence in the policy-making process as well as in the manager.

Withdraw from the final decision

Withdrawal of the manager from debate in the last stages of the decision making is fair, fitting, and necessary. The manager is in the privileged position of being able to recommend decisions without being held directly responsible, through the electoral process, to the people of the community. The governing body does not enjoy this luxury. Staff also have an unusual advantage through their advance communications and access to information about any given issue or policy. It is finally the right and responsibility of the governing body to make its own decisions on the basis of all input.

I always gave council at least three alternatives. I emphasized the one I felt was best. I listed that one first, but you must let council decide. If they asked for my recommendation I always gave them one, but I also let them know that they may have good reasons not to accept my advice.
Roland Windham

Respect council decisions

Respecting the decisions of those with whom we agree is easy; it is not as easy to respect the decisions of those with whom we disagree. The professional manager who seeks the confidence of the governing body must keep personal opinions private in order to maintain a public and continuous display of fidelity to the democratic process of decision making. Acknowledgement of the right of elected officials to differ vigorously with staff recommendations, regardless of whose position prevails, is best stated openly and with conviction.

Lose gracefully

Floating coalitions form in every governing body; last week's winner may be next week's loser. The confident manager is both a graceful loser and a modest winner.

It is an axiom that losing erodes confidence to a greater degree than winning builds it, but battles gracefully lost can increase the stature of the manager. Managers gain by trying twice as hard to implement what they did not recommend, thereby demonstrating the professional mettle that builds trust, respect, and admiration. The manager needs governing body support; equally, policy makers must be secure in the knowledge that they will have staff support.

Be generous with credit

The manager who credits the governing body when things go right builds confidence on both sides. Only rarely is the manager native to the jurisdiction, and the manager usually owns no property other than a car and house and has no historical connection to or family position in the community. Success for the manager, then, lies in the reflected glory of the governing body.

More than one manager has lost the council's confidence not because of failure, but because of too much recognition of the manager or of other appointed staff members, whose stars outshone those of the elected policy makers. Every manager should be aware that recognition may become increasingly difficult to avoid, especially if the manager achieves success as described in the report of ICMA's Council-Manager Plan Task Force, which calls on the manager to play an expanded and more visible role in the policy-making process.[21]

Members of the governing board often enter electoral politics to pursue personal as well as altruistic goals—if not also to qualify for election to a higher office—and these goals are not served by anonymity. Managers who crave public credit or who ensure high visibility for their own recommendations run the risk of labeling their governing bodies rubber stamps and themselves as dictators, which can be risky for managerial tenure.

Take the heat

Not only should the manager be free with credit, the manager must also be ready to take the heat when things go wrong. Failure to do so sometimes sends a message of cover-up, if not complicity. Quick acknowledgement, however, of any misconduct, policy failure, or nonperformance shifts public concern from fixing the blame to correcting the problem. Mistakes are inevitable, but few are intentional. When a policy adopted by the governing body fails, the wise manager remembers that policies usually are proposed by the staff, the manager, or both; the governing body most often reacts rather than acts. Thus, blaming such policy adoption solely on the policy makers usually distorts the truth and undermines confidence in the manager. The manager's candor and obvious dedication to prompt corrective measures shift public attention from the action the governing body is going to take against the manager to what the manager proposes to do to solve the problem. Governing body members will be more likely to shield the appointed executive when they are confident that the executive will shoulder the blame, not shift it, when the going gets tough.

Pay attention to timing

Effective public management depends on three critical factors: timing, timing, and timing. An acute sense of timing derives from both intuition and experience. Experience tells the manager when it is time to press hard, time to pull back, or time to move on; it is not possible to create a checklist. Timing is significant in the success or failure of managers, governing bodies, and communities. History is replete with people and institutions that misjudged critical timing and were left behind. A gifted leader can say with conviction, "This is the time, and this is the place."

Understand the governing body's incentives

The formal features found in local government structure create incentives for certain kinds of candidates to run for office and for certain governing styles to be adopted. Timothy Bledsoe suggests "different environments are conducive to different types of individuals securing political office. A person who is successful in a city of the Northeast may be totally out of place in a Western city; a person who thrives in the demanding government of a big city may be thoroughly bored on the council of small city; an at-large-elected council member may find the constituent demands of a district seat intolerable. Thus, it is not just who is pursuing the political career, but where or under what conditions the career is pursued."[22] James March and Johann Olsen's theory explaining how institutions affect our behavior is also a useful guide to understanding how the formal structure of government can influence members of the governing body.[23]

The logic of appropriateness

March and Olsen suggest that "political institutions define the framework within which politics takes place." They argue that rules are the means by which institutions affect behavior. Rules are the "routines, procedures, conventions, roles, strategies, organizational forms, and technologies around which activity is constructed." Rules also include the "beliefs, paradigms, codes, cultures, and knowledge that surround, support, elaborate, and contradict those roles and routines." They explain that rules "define relationships among roles in terms of what an incumbent of one role owes to incumbents of other roles."

They argue that the "logic of appropriateness associated with obligatory action" shapes how individuals follow the rules supported by the political institutions in which they work. In other words, an official shapes activities and positions by defining the situation, determining a personal role, assessing the appropriateness of different actions in the situation, and carrying out the most appropriate action. Discretion of course applies to the use of rules because rules are not monolithic and may be contradictory and ambiguous; therefore, conformity to as well as deviation from rules can occur in political institutions. March and Olsen conclude that trust, defined as "a confidence that appropriate behavior can be expected most of the time," supports the network of rules and rule-bound relations. Deviation from the rules (i.e., violating the "logic of appropriateness") will undermine trust among officials and will potentially erode support for the political institutions as well.

Forms of government

In the United States, the two main forms of local government are the mayor-council form and the council-manager form (see page 71 for county government structures). Raymond Cox introduced the evolving nature of these two forms in Chapter 1. Some scholars today find the simple typology of council-manager and mayor-council inadequate to capture alterations of these original forms of government in the United States. Victor DeSantis and Tari Renner use survey data from 1996 on form of government to identify seven main variations: classic council-manager, council-manager with at-large mayor, council-manager with empowered mayor, strong mayor with chief administrative officer (CAO), strong mayor without CAO, weak mayor with CAO, and weak mayor without CAO.[24] H. George Frederickson, Gary Johnson, and Curtis Wood use survey data to identify a cluster of cities that mixes electoral features and the powers of the mayor to become "adapted cities" that do not conform to either of the two traditional forms.[25]

County government structures The three traditional forms of county government in the United States are the commission, the commission-administrator, and the council–elected executive.

The majority of counties continues to use the commission form, which provides both legislative and executive powers to the commissioners. Each commissioner assumes administrative authority for one or more departments. This form lacks an appointed professional responsible for the general administration of government.

The commission-administrator form—used by approximately 40 percent of the 3,000 counties in the United States—is similar to the council-manager form. Appointed professional managers working in this form will find the ideas discussed in this chapter most useful.

The council–elected executive form is used in about 480 counties. The elected executive has powers similar to a strong mayor. Appointed professional managers working in this form have much in common with professionals appointed by mayors in strong-mayor council communities.

Electoral systems in county government feature district elections on a party basis more than systems for city government. About 72 percent of counties use district elections and 82 percent use partisan elections. And in counties using the commission form or the commission-administrator form, commissioners choose their presiding officer instead of voters electing one. The appointed professional serving in county government is likely to find the environment more highly charged politically than in cities. Members of the governing body in counties focus on serving district needs rather than think about mission and long-term planning.

Source: Beverly A. Cigler, "Administration in the Modern American County," in *The Future of Local Government Administration: The Hansell Symposium*, ed. H. George Frederickson and John Nalbandian (Washington, D.C.: International City/County Management Association, 2002), 157–174.

If March and Olsen are correct about the "logic of appropriateness" influencing the behavior of elected and appointed officials, mixing of institutional features offers challenges and opportunities. The main challenge is for officials to understand their roles in governing when institutional incentives are ambiguous. Conflict may increase among members of the governing body, between the governing body and the elected executive, and with the appointed professional as each official acts on the basis of individual understanding of the rules. The best situation is activist members of the governing body working effectively together with an empowered mayor and an appointed professional manager who form an executive team. The three subsections that follow capture the institutional variation relevant to understanding the incentives affecting the governing body: the governing body's powers, the electoral system, and the governing body's stature.

The governing body's powers The trend in the United States is to enhance the role of the mayor, especially in council-manager communities. The move to empower the chief elected official (CEO) in council-manager communities can affect how members of the governing body do their jobs. Some of the changes in recent years include giving the CEO the power to veto ordinances, the power to review and comment on the budget prepared by the professional manager, the power to nominate and/or approve the dismissal of the professional manager, the power to offer a legislative program through a state-of-the-city speech and other means, and the authorization to be directly elected by the voters. These changes are intended to enhance the ability of the CEO to guide the policy-making process, and they are popular in communities with large populations such as Cincinnati, Kansas City, and Charlotte.[26] These changes are intended to encourage members of the governing body to look to the CEO for leadership in performing the governance function, much as members of the governing body in mayor-council communities, especially strong-mayor communities, look to the CEO.

This effort to enhance the status of the mayor in council-manager communities has met with some success, but most council-manager communities in the United States have not moved in this direction:

- Only 12 percent of CEOs have the power to veto ordinances.
- The professional manager develops the budget and presents it to the governing body in 81 percent of communities.
- The CEO receives the budget developed by the professional manager in 30 percent of the communities.
- The governing body appoints and dismisses the professional manager in 77 percent of the communities.
- The CEO has the authority to initiate the appointment and dismissal of the professional manager in 41 percent of the communities.
- The CEO reports annually to the governing body in 41 percent of the communities.
- The CEO is directly elected by the voters in 65 percent of the communities.[27]

The governing body in council-manager communities in the United States continues to have significant powers that make performing the governance function a key obligation. And the council-manager form continues to be the preferred form featured in the eighth edition of the National Civic League's *Model City Charter.*

The governing bodies in mayor-council communities usually have less formal executive-type powers, although differences exist between the weak-mayor forms and the strong-mayor forms. The governing bodies in weak-mayor forms, such as borough governments in Pennsylvania, have powers more like governing bodies in council-manager communities with empowered mayors. For example, the borough council can appoint a professional manager who will have extensive administrative authority, while the mayor has the veto power and administrative authority over only the police department. The strong-mayor, with powers that establish this official as the center of governance activity, has several legislative and executive powers, including the veto, preparing the budget, proposing a legislative program, reporting on the city's performance, appointing department heads and the CAO, and executing the law. Philadelphia, New York, Boston, and Cleveland are examples of communities with the strong mayor–council form.

Given these differences in governing bodies' formal powers, one would expect to see differences in the performance of the governance function. Recent survey research indicates this is indeed the case. Members of governing bodies in council-manager communities give themselves higher ratings when performing governance activities such as "handling visioning, goal setting, setting objectives, reviewing the budget, and overseeing administrative effectiveness" than do their counterparts serving in mayor-council communities.[28] Members of governing bodies serving in both forms of government give themselves high ratings when it comes to the representational function. Regardless of form of government, elected officials now stress their responsiveness to citizens by devoting a lot of time to constituent service. Appointed professionals working in council-manager communities may find it easier than their counterparts working in mayor-council communities to get their governing bodies to focus on mission, but they will also find members increasingly interested in citizen complaints and demands. If the focus is constituent service above mission, members of governing bodies often try to micromanage the professional.

The electoral system   Campaigns for seats on the governing body are affected by the rules featured in election law. These electoral rules attract certain kinds of people to be candidates and influence how they act if they are elected.[29] Three important variables of electoral systems are party affiliation on the ballot, at-large or district (ward) elections, and term limits. Data .from 2002 on electoral systems affirm the continued popularity of nonpartisan elections.[30] Only 33 percent of mayor-council communities and 15 percent of council-manager communities list the partisan affiliation of candidates on the ballot. However, partisan elections are popular in certain states—Pennsylvania, New Jersey, and New York—so appointed professionals serving in those states need to understand the incentives that partisan elections create. Partisan elections do not necessarily attract candidates who are more motivated to further party interests, but they do attract people who enjoy politics, who pursue personal advancement through public office, and who are more likely to seek a political career.[31] In nonpartisan elections, too, candidates often use appeals to party loyalty to gain votes. Appointed professionals working in communities with strong political party activity can insulate themselves from such activity by including the ICMA's Code of Ethics in their employment agreements and in orientation programs for newly elected and already serving members, and by not expressing opinions about candidates during elections.

Neighbors and friends would constantly ask my opinion on how to vote. It takes some discipline to not give an opinion when you believe strongly that there is a good-government ticket that you want to support. The downfall of many good managers has been their unwillingness to accept the results of an election. At times it is difficult to respect the persons in office, but we must always respect the office, and the fact that they are duly elected by the people.
Larry Comunale

Data from 2002 also indicate that 51 percent of mayor-council communities and 72 percent of council-manager communities use at-large elections exclusively.[32] In 24 percent of mayor-council communities and 9 percent of council-manager communities a district system is used exclusively. A combination of at-large and district elections is used in 25 percent of the mayor-council communities and 19 percent of the council-manager communities. District elections attract candidates who pursue personal advancement through public office and who seek office in order to help people—family, friends, and neighbors—with whom they share a personal connection.[33] In contrast, candidates in at-large elections are more likely to be motivated not by a love of politics or personal success but out of a sense of community service and a commitment to abstract values such as honesty, efficiency, and good government. It is usually easiest for appointed professionals to work on mission and long-term planning with a board elected at-large because the structural incentives are more supportive of this approach.

Term limits on local governing bodies are still rare in the United States. Only 5 percent and 13 percent of mayor-council and council-manager communities, respectively, use term limits. Term limits increase turnover among members of the governing body, which may lead to governing bodies with inexperienced members who pursue a limited vision of the job. The longer a council member serves in office, the broader the range of interests that member represents; representing a political party becomes less important and promoting business interests becomes more important. Effective governing bodies are therefore more likely to be free of term limits. Appointed professionals can turn to veteran members of the governing body to help steer first-term members toward a greater appreciation of mission and policy making and away from single-issue politics and micromanagement.

The governing body's stature   The importance of the governing body in community politics compared with other government institutions can be estimated in variety of ways. Three useful indicators of the governing body's stature are support facilities, salary, and term limits.[34] Governing bodies with offices, staff, expense allowances (support facilities), higher salaries, and no limits on the number of terms they may serve are high-stature governing bodies because they have institutional resources to support independence from the CEO or CAO. High-stature governing bodies are more likely to attract talented and motivated officeholders and also are more likely to be found in mayor-council communities, communities with partisan elections, and larger cities.

Individual members

The effectiveness of the governing body often depends on reconciling the differences among members arising from career orientations and personal characteristics.

Career orientations   The majority of citizens seeking election to local governing bodies in the United States are newcomers to community and government leadership who have not previously held leadership positions in any governmental or community organization.[35] Once they are elected and begin to work as members of the governing body, they continue to respect the institution and enjoy the work, but they think the public does not appreciate the effort they make. People most likely quit office or do not seek reelection because they want more time for business and family; this is especially true for low-stature councils. For appointed professionals, the challenge often is to motivate members of the governing body to do the work, especially in low-stature governing bodies.

Personal characteristics   Governing bodies are more diverse today than in the past although women, minorities, blue-collar and nonprofessional occupations continue to be underrepresented.[36] Smaller communities with part-time positions also elect a large number of retired citizens. Susan MacManus suggests that women and minorities are more successful in larger communities, and women usually win office in larger communities "with racially and ethnically diverse, more affluent and better-educated, populations."[37] Diverse governing bodies produce a wider range of personalities, approaches to the job, and issues resulting in higher rates of conflict. Appointed professionals must help their governing bodies learn to manage this conflict.

Understand and resolve conflict

Managers responding to surveys indicate that most governing bodies in the United States, especially those serving smaller communities, experience low levels of conflict and only occasionally experience high conflict over some agenda matter.[38] Common cleavages include economic philosophy (slow growth versus pro-growth), expanding programs versus hold-the-line on taxes, and racial and ethnic inclusion versus protecting residential enclaves.

Conflict is often perceived to have only negative consequences for the community, members of the governing body, and the relationship of the manager with the governing body. However, conflict can often lead to positive consequences, such as stimulating a search for creative solutions.[39] The challenge for elected and appointed officials is to manage conflict constructively and steer differences toward an agreement. Conflict management is a skill that can be learned by elected officials and professionals. An effective governing body is one whose members understand the sources of conflict and practice approaches and skills that will enable them to resolve the conflict.

More and more councils are fragmented. Diversity is the word, so you try to get them to work together.

O. Wendell White

Sources of conflict

It is well established that social and political changes have brought about a blurring of the relationship between elected officials serving on the governing body and the appointed professional manager. As James Svara suggests in Chapter 2, elected and appointed officials share work in all dimensions of the governing process, from determining mission to management practices. Consequently, the manager–governing body relationship, although ideally cooperative, has a potential for conflict that can affect the performance of all officials. Conflict often arises from miscommunication and misunderstanding. Conflict more difficult to remedy stems from population diversity, electoral incentives, role perceptions, and governmental form.

Population diversity   The more socially and economically diverse the population, the more likely the members of the governing body are to see the community interest as pluralistic. Each member defends and promotes a particular interest so that it is not underrepresented in the political process and ultimately underserved by the government. A diversity of interests gives rise to ideological, partisan, and single-issue politics. The challenge for the governing body is to balance concern for particular group interests with the universal interests shared by all citizens. The professional manager must also be sensitive to working in a multicultural context, especially in communities with a large population of Spanish-speaking (or other non-English-speaking) residents and in racially diverse communities.

Electoral incentives   In at-large elections (the most common method of electing local governing bodies), candidates try to create a coalition of supporters by appealing to universal interests or by crafting a platform that includes particular interests.[40] The inclusive-coalition approach to winning at-large elections increases the chances that diversity will find its way into governing-body deliberations, thus making conflict more likely. In heterogeneous communities, even if the inclusive-coalition approach is used, the at-large election system may not provide representation for the range of social and economic interests present in the community.

In recent decades, many communities changed at-large electoral systems to either single-member-district systems or to mixed systems, which designate some seats on the governing body for single-member-district representatives and some seats for at-large representatives. The use of single-member districts to elect members of the governing body creates incentives for officials to see the community interest as pluralistic. In many heterogeneous communities, neighborhoods often have concentrations of residents of similar economic, racial, and ethnic characteristics; single-member districts increase the chances of these diverse interests achieving representation on the governing body.

Defending and promoting the interests of the district become the representative's approach. Conflict over parochialism is common among governing body members.

Role perceptions   Perhaps the most subtle source of conflict between elected officials and the appointed executive lies in their perceptions of how the other carries out the job.[41] It is not surprising that their perceptions will sometimes concur and sometimes differ. All work in the same political environment, share values, and often share in victory and defeat. However, each individual comes to the position via a different route and with different motivations; and each may have a different perspective toward governing. Each has different relations with and loyalties to the community and the electorate, and each has different needs for interaction with the others of the governmental group.

To be successful in this reality, we must make clear to the governing body what they can expect from us as managers and administrators—particularly as it relates to our roles in their domain; and we should agree on ground rules for their participation in our domain.

Julia D. Novak

Managers and elected officials often do not fully appreciate each other's roles. Some elected officials complain that the manager cannot think like an elected official. Elected officials may think the managers are withholding information in order to dominate the policy-making process. They may suggest that managers are not sensitive to citizen demands. In contrast, managers may see elected officials as too political, yielding to popular pressure in order to retain office rather than staying the course on policy matters, and too often concerned about single issues. Managers also complain that some elected officials inject favoritism and partisanship into management processes by trying to micromanage personnel and other administrative matters.

Governmental form   Some local governments may experience persistent conflict because of the form of government in place.[42] Conflict will be more common in mayor-council and county-executive forms of government because they are based on the separation of powers and use checks and balances to hold government officials accountable. Struggle over policies and credit for government successes are built-in. Because council-manager government rests on a unification-of-powers approach, "elected and administrative officials have compatible goals, and therefore, do not actively seek to block the goals of others."[43] As the position of mayor in council-manager government gains additional formal powers (such as the veto) over the legislative process and over the appointment or removal of the manager, conflict may increase as elected officials and the appointed manager struggle to sort out their roles.

Approaches to resolving conflict

Sue Faerman identifies five approaches individuals can use to manage conflict: avoiding, accommodating, competing, compromising, and collaborating (see page 77).[44] Compromising helps officials who disagree over goals to find a solution that gives each party some benefit in exchange for some loss. Collaborating can produce win-win solutions by nurturing the exploration of interests and the creative search for solutions. Two well-known forms of collaboration are principled negotiation and problem solving.

Approaches to managing conflict

Sue R. Faerman defines five approaches along two dimensions:

- Assertiveness is "taking action to satisfy one's own needs and concerns."
- Cooperativeness is "taking action to satisfy the other party's needs and concerns."

Avoiding is "low on assertiveness and low on cooperativeness. It is used when one does not wish to confront or explore the issues behind the conflict."

Accommodating is "low on assertiveness but high on cooperativeness. Like avoiding, it is sometimes seen when one or more parties do not wish to confront or explore the issues behind the conflict. Unlike avoiding, however, it is also seen when one party decides that the issue at hand is not as important to him or her as it is to the other party."

Competing is "high on assertiveness and low on cooperativeness. Individuals who consistently use this approach are basically interested in their own position and see the world in terms of a zero-sum game."

Compromising "lies in the middle of both dimensions; it is characterized by a moderate amount of assertiveness and a moderate amount of cooperativeness."

Collaborating is "high on assertiveness and high on cooperativeness. This approach assumes most organizational conflicts emerge as a result of interdependence, not incompatible goals."

Source: Sue R. Faerman, "Managing Conflicts Creatively," in *Handbook of Public Administration*, ed. James L. Perry (San Francisco: Jossey-Bass, 1996), 635–638.

Principled negotiation Roger Fisher and William Ury developed principled negotiation through the Harvard Negotiation Project and featured this approach in *Getting to Yes*.[45] The method consists of four principles: separate the people from problem; focus on interests, not positions; invent options for mutual gain; and insist on using objective criteria to resolve differences. Using principled negotiation allows the individual to learn about the problem and the different interests during the negotiation, to be creative in finding solutions, and still be able to avoid making one-sided agreements.

For example, when the city of Wichita, Kansas, needed to find a solution to the polluted underground lake located beneath its central business district, City Manager Chris Cherches invented options that led to a creative solution.[46] Instead of asking the U.S. Environmental Protection Agency (EPA) to add the site to the superfund list or pursuing litigation against property owners who might be responsible, City Manager Cherches suggested that the city of Wichita take responsibility for the cleanup. He proposed paying for the cleanup with a variation of tax increment financing and sharing the cost of the cleanup with Coleman Company, Inc. This solution required the agreement of the state legislature, the governor, the Sedgewick County council, the Wichita school board, the city council, banks and other lending institutions, Coleman Company, Inc., the Kansas Department of Health and Environment, and the EPA. Eventually all parties agreed to participate and the crisis was resolved. The city manager's search for a creative solution and his focus on the interests of the parties, not their positions, helped to resolve the problem.

Problem solving Christine Altenburger has developed a problem-solving manual that offers practical advice on how to find a resolution when "honest and honorable public officials, elected and appointed, . . . disagree on how problems and issues should be resolved." Her four-step problem-solving method is summarized on page 78. Above all, it is important for the manager to search for alternative solutions and clearly define the benefits and drawbacks of the solutions for others to consider.

Altenburger also provides seven rules that she has drawn from the large body of literature on the art of problem solving:

- Be both smart and wise
- Don't be a power wielder; lead
- Guard against arrogance
- Seek first to understand, then to be understood
- Seek alternative approaches to resolve a problem
- If you find yourself in a hole, stop digging
- Don't get mad; don't get even; get the problem resolved.[47]

A four-step method for problem solving

1. Diagnose the problem
   - Describe the problem
   - Assemble the facts
   - Identify gaps in information
   - Identify the stakeholders
   - Define the position of each party involved
   - Describe the history of the problem
   - Identify factors that might limit the local government's control of the problem
   - Define the issues that are central to solving the problem.

2. Diagnose the environment for problem resolution—examine the levels of hostility and misinformation that exist.

3. Diagnose the unknown—consider consequences of various alternatives and the risks involved.

4. Diagnose yourself—how objective can you be on the issue and how does it relate to your core values?

Source: Christine Altenburger, *Attaining a Wise Outcome: Problem-Solving for Public Officials* (Washington, D.C.: ICMA, 2001), 66–69.

Recap

- Expectations embedded in the new political culture have blurred the lines defining the roles performed by the appointed professional manager, the mayor, and the governing body and have increased the responsibilities each has for governance.

- Professional managers can help their governing bodies effectively perform their duties by:

  Using practices that strengthen the policy-making capabilities of the governing body;

  Using practices that establish confidence in the manager and that nurture the spirit of teamwork needed to assist the governing body in carrying out its responsibilities;

  Educating the governing body about the institutional and personal incentives motivating local government officials; and

  Educating members of the governing body about the main sources of conflict arising in local government and encouraging them to use constructive approaches to resolving disputes.

Governing body evaluation

The following questionnaire (adapted if necessary to suit individual needs) may be used by governing bodies for self-evaluation or by local government managers as they attempt to assess and enhance their governing body's effectiveness.

Goal setting
1. Are established governing body goals realistic and doable within the time frame stated?

   Almost always _____Sometimes_____Never_____

2. Do governing body members participate sufficiently in implementing goals once established?

   Almost always _____Sometimes_____Never_____

3. Is the public adequately informed about the governing body's goals?

   Almost always _____Sometimes_____Never_____

Policy making
1. Are governing body positions and policies communicated effectively?

   Almost always _____Sometimes_____Never_____

2. Does the governing body have the capacity to make hard choices and politically unpopular decisions when required or necessary?

   Almost always _____Sometimes_____Never_____

Budgeting
1. Does the governing body clearly understand the city's financial resources in order to make sound decisions on prioritizing public spending?

   Almost always _____Sometimes_____Never_____

2. Is there adequate opportunity for a cross section of public participation in the budgeting process?

   Almost always _____Sometimes_____Never_____

3. Does the governing body avoid unbudgeted appropriations?

   Almost always _____Sometimes_____Never_____

4. Does the governing body consider the budget their budget as opposed to the staff's budget?

   Almost always _____Sometimes_____Never_____

Council meetings
1. Does the governing body provide for adequate public input at public meetings?

   Almost always _____Sometimes_____Never_____

2. Does each governing body member effectively participate in the governing body's meetings?

   Almost always _____Sometimes_____Never_____

3. Does the staff have adequate opportunity for input before making its decision?

   Almost always _____Sometimes_____Never_____

4. Is the governing body's meeting time well utilized?

   Almost always _____Sometimes_____Never_____

5. Are relevant facts and opinions expressed before decisions are made or governing body positions stated?

Almost always _____Sometimes_____Never_____

6. Is direction given to staff clear and concise?

Almost always _____Sometimes_____Never_____

Advisory commissions and committees
1. Is there adequate public participation in commission and/or committee member selection?

Almost always _____Sometimes_____Never_____

2. Are commission members and committee members selected on the basis of ability to serve the community rather than personal friendships?

Almost always _____Sometimes_____Never_____

3. Does the governing body place sufficient emphasis on balancing memberships on commissions and committees in order to assure the total community is represented?

Almost always _____Sometimes_____Never_____

4. Does the governing body give sufficient weight to commission and committee recommendations?

Almost always _____Sometimes_____Never_____

Relationship with staff
1. Does the governing body establish reasonable time frames for staff to accomplish assignments?

Almost always _____Sometimes_____Never_____

2. If it changes its priorities, does the governing body consider the impact on staff time?

Almost always _____Sometimes_____Never_____

3. Does the governing body give adequate consideration to staff recommendations?

Almost always _____Sometimes_____Never_____

4. Do governing body members limit contacts with staff members to inquiries and suggestions as opposed to giving direction?

Almost always _____Sometimes_____Never_____

Council relationships
1. Allowing for differences of philosophy and opinions on given issues, do governing body members respect each another's opinions?

Almost always _____Sometimes_____Never_____

2. Does the governing body function as a team?

Almost always _____Sometimes_____Never_____

3. Do individual governing body members avoid unduly consuming the governing body's meeting time?

Almost always _____Sometimes_____Never_____

4. Do governing body members deal with issues openly?

Almost always _____Sometimes_____Never_____

5. Do individual governing body members avoid over-politicizing the public process?

Almost always _____Sometimes_____Never_____

6. Do governing body members in their attitudes reflect a sense of public service over personal interest?

Almost always _____Sometimes_____Never_____

Relationship with the professional manager

1. Is the relationship among governing body members and the professional manager open and honest?

Almost always _____Sometimes_____Never_____

2. Does the governing body function as a unit in giving direction to the professional manager?

Almost always _____Sometimes_____Never_____

3. Is there mutual respect between the governing body and the professional manager?

Almost always _____Sometimes_____Never_____

4. Is there opportunity for the professional manager to offer input into the decision-making process?

Almost always _____Sometimes_____Never_____

Notes

1 Edmund Burke, "Speech to the Electors of Bristol," in *American Government: Readings and Cases,* ed. Peter Woll (New York: Longman, 1999), 373–375.

2 John F. Kennedy, *Profiles in Courage* (New York: Harper, 1955), 16–17.

3 Warren Bennis, "Transformational Power and Leadership," in *Leadership and Organizational Culture,* ed. Thomas H. Sergiovanni and John E. Corbally, 70 (Urbana: University of Illinois Press, 1986).

4 Terry Nichols Clark, "Overview of the Book," in *The New Political Culture,* ed. Terry Nichols Clark and Vincent Hoffmann-Martinot, 3 (Boulder, Colo.: Westview, 1998).

5 James H. Svara, "City Council Roles, Performance, and the Form of Government," in *The Future of Local Government Administration: The Hansell Symposium,* ed. H. George Frederickson and John Nalbandian, 214 (Washington, D.C.: ICMA, 2002).

6 Richard Green, Larry Keller, and Gary Wamsley, "Reconstituting a Profession for American Public Administration," *Public Administration Review* 53 (November/December 1993): 516–524.

7 Craig M. Wheeland, "City Management in the 1990s: Responsibilities, Roles, and Practices," *Administration & Society* 32 (July 2000): 255–281.

8 "Council-Manager Plan Task Force, A Look at Our Evolving Profession: The Report of the Council-Manager Plan Task Force" (Washington, D.C.: ICMA, 1995), A4.

9 John Nalbandian, "Facilitating Community, Enabling Democracy: New Roles for Local Government Managers," *Public Administration Review* 59 (May/June 1999): 189.

10 Visit www.icma.org to read more about the ICMA University Practices for Effective Local Government Management.

11 Parts of this discussion are adapted from "Setting Goals," in *Elected Officials Handbooks,* Book 1 (Washington, D.C.: ICMA, 1994); and from Booz Allen Hamilton Inc.,

"Strengthening Policy-Making Capabilities of the City Commission" (Wichita, Kans.: City of Wichita, 1975).

12 Dana Ingman, Jeff Kersten, and Thomas Brymer, "Strategic Planning that Uses an Integrated Approach," *Public Management* 84 (May 2002): 16–18.

13 See Sanford M. Groves and Maureen Godsey Valente, *Evaluating Financial Condition: A Handbook for Local Government,* 4th ed., revised by Karl Nollenberger (Washington, D.C.: ICMA, 2004).

14 John Clayton Thomas, *Public Participation in Public Decisions: New Skills and Strategies for Public Managers* (San Francisco: Jossey-Bass, 1995), 1.

15 Tom Lando, "The Public Hearing Process: A Tool for Citizen Participation, or a Path Toward Citizen Alienation," *National Civic Review* 92 (Spring 2003): 73–82.

16 www.icma.org provides additional information about the National Citizen Survey™.

17 Susan Welch and John Comer, *Quantitative Methods for Public Administration: Techniques and Applications,* 3rd ed. (New York: Harcourt College Publishers, 2001), 64–65.

18 Craig M. Wheeland, "Council Evaluation of the Manager's Performance: An Inventory of Methods," in *The Municipal Year Book 2002* (Washington, D.C.: ICMA, 2002), 3–9.

19 Ibid.

20 The discussion of agenda preparation is adapted from Elizabeth K. Kellar, "Communicating with Elected Officials," in *Effective Communication: Getting the Message Across,* ed. David S. Arnold, Christine S. Becker, and Elizabeth K. Kellar (Washington, D.C.: ICMA, 1983).

21 "A Look at our Evolving Profession: The Report of ICMA's Council-Manager Plan Task Force" (Washington, D.C.: ICMA, 1995), A4.

22 Timothy Bledsoe, *Careers in City Politics: The Case for Urban Democracy* (Pittsburgh, Pa.: University of Pittsburgh Press, 1993), 37.

23 The March and Olsen theory of institutional effect on behavior is found in James G. March and Johann P. Olsen, *Rediscovering Institutions* (New York: The Free Press, 1989). Quotations are from pages 18, 22, 23, and 30.

24 Victor S. DeSantis and Tari Renner, "City Government Structures: An Attempt at Clarification," *State and Local Government Review* 34 (Spring 2002): 95–104.

25 H. George Frederickson, Gary A. Johnson, and Curtis Wood, "Type III Cities," in *The Future of Local Government Administration: The Hansell Symposium,* ed. H. George Frederickson and John Nalbandian, 85–97 (Washington, D.C.: ICMA, 2002). Adapted cities are also called Type III cities (Type I cities are mayor-council cities, and Type II cities are council-manager cities.

26 Craig M. Wheeland, "An Institutionalist Perspective on Mayoral Leadership: Linking Leadership Style to Formal Structure," *National Civic Review* 91 (Spring 2002): 25–39.

27 Kimberly Nelson, "Structure of American Municipal Government," Special Data Issue no. 4 (2002) (Washington, D.C.: ICMA, 2002).

28 Svara, "City Council Roles," 221.

29 Bledsoe, *Careers in City Politics,* 41.

30 Kimberly Nelson, "Elected Municipal Councils," Special Data Issue no. 3 (2002) (Washington, D.C.: ICMA, 2002).

31 Bledsoe, *Careers in City Politics,* 75, 78–79.

32 Nelson, "Elected Municipal Councils," provides the basis for this discussion.

33 Bledsoe, *Careers in City Politics,* 74–75, 78, 110.

34 Ibid., 42, 51.

35 Ibid., 58, 111–112, 127, 129.

36 Nelson, "Elected Municipal Councils."

37 Susan MacManus, "The Resurgent City Council," in *American State and Local Government: Directions for the 21st Century,* ed. Ronald E. Weber and Paul Brace (New York: Chatham House Publishers, 1999), 186–187.

38 Wheeland, "Council Evaluation."

39 Sue R. Faerman, "Managing Conflicts Creatively," in *Handbook of Public Administration,* ed. James L. Perry (San Francisco: Jossey-Bass, 1996), 632–646.

40 For a classic discussion of electoral incentives political coalitions, see Edward C. Banfield and James Q. Wilson, *City Politics* (New York: Vintage Books, 1963).

41 Margaret S. Carlson and Anne S. Davidson, "After the Election: How Do Governing Boards Become Effective Work Groups?" *State and Local Government Review* 31 (Fall 1999): 190–201.

42 James H. Svara, *Official Leadership in the City: Patterns of Conflict and Cooperation* (New York: Oxford University Press, 1990).

43 Ibid., 29.

44 Faerman, *Managing Conflict.*

45 Roger Fisher and William Ury, *Getting to Yes: Negotiating Agreement without Giving In* (New York: Penguin Books, 1991), xix.

46 Susan Rosegrant, "Wichita Confronts Contamination," in *Public Administration: Concepts and Cases,* 7th ed., ed. Richard J. Stillman, 147–154 (Boston: Houghton Mifflin Company, 2000).

47 Christine Altenburger, *Attaining a Wise Outcome: Problem-Solving for Public Officials* (Washington, D.C.: ICMA, 2001), 61–63.

Promoting the community's future

Promoting the community's future, creating a positive community legacy, and striving for economic viability and sustainability are ongoing and vital functions for local government managers. These tasks require new ways of thinking because of today's rapid social, demographic, economic, and technological changes.

Since the previous edition of this book, the world has changed dramatically. Ushered in by the watershed events of September 11, 2001, and a prolonged weak economy, "the first decade of the twenty-first century is not a happy time for state and local governments. Most of the states and many localities face stringent financial times."[1] Global economic competition, serious social concerns, decaying and inadequate infrastructure, and persistent environmental problems present enormous challenges to local government.

Other, more positive changes need just as much attention: a growing and more diverse population, new technological advances in communication, e-government, and increasing citizen participation in all aspects of local government. The community-building process has broadened to encompass many new participants.

Unlike their historical counterparts who often viewed the future as a linear extension of the past, today's local government professionals, elected officials, and community residents are beginning to accept the necessity of developing plans and strategies that guide the community through present-day change toward an acceptable future. The goal should be to create a positive community legacy.

Planning the community's future is a broad-based activity that compels managers to engage citizens, retool their organizations regularly, and reevaluate their roles and relationships with elected officials. Local government managers need to know how to react fast to changing circumstances and plan skillfully for a variety of contingencies. Willingness to share information with the community and knowledge of public relations and marketing are necessary skills for managers.

John and Carol Nalbandian note:

> Of the many forces affecting local governments, two emerging trends will shape the future of local government professionals. The first is the movement to modernize the organization. The second is the movement to build and maintain a sense of community, capturing the essence of governing at the local level.[2]

This chapter explores what local government managers can do to create community, build sustainable economic development projects, develop viable community visioning and planning mechanisms, and promote their communities in a positive, ethical manner consistent with ICMA's professional development management practices.

The expanding role of the manager

Local government managers are ideally positioned to affect the future. Working with the governing body, they help shape public events by helping policy makers decide what to do and how to do it. Good management, like good planning, anticipates the future as well as affects the future. Making the right decisions today leads to the right things tomorrow.

New challenges and expectations for leaders in local government are greater than they were in the early days of the profession, but the rewards and contributions are also much greater. Local government managers need to have a better understanding of the world of elected leaders and of the disappearing boundaries between managing an organization and participating in policy leadership.

Promoting and leading

The manager must identify opportunities to promote the community, and thereby promote the local government's strategic goals and enhance its image as an effective organization. The role the manager assumes should reflect the community's culture, structure, and politics as well as the manager's skills and personality.

Managers must overcome the profession's traditional passion for anonymity. Public relations, community relations, and economic development have become critical components of the local government strategic planning process.
Mark M. Levin

Building a viable, sustainable community requires technical skills and political savvy, especially when high-profile economic opportunities present themselves to the community. Special projects demand a great degree of political skill in dealing with elected officials, developers, media, citizens, and neighborhood groups. In smaller communities without designated economic development staff, the local government manager needs to be involved from the very beginning of economic development activities. Managers who are well-grounded in the history and culture of their communities and who can express the policy preferences of their elected bodies will be able to speak with authority to potential developers. Number 3 of ICMA's "Practices for Effective Local Government Management," Functional and Operational Expertise and Planning, addresses the necessary skills (see Appendix B).

The manager's job is to market the community, build community, and interact with the community.
Jan Dolan

When controversial projects come forward, the local government manager takes on mediating and negotiating difficult issues. Most elected officials try to avoid controversy and look to the manager to articulate the guiding policy of the elected body. The local government manager must accept these responsibilities and serve as an enthusiastic spokesperson without supporting anything that puts the community at economic or financial risk.

Watching the big picture

Governance requires public managers to look two directions at once—both inward towards their jurisdictions and its day to day operation, and also toward the broader environment in order to produce a wide range of social goals and services that could not have been produced through jurisdictional prerogatives alone.[3]

In the past, managers were mainly concerned with the internal organization and left the translation of the community's desires to elected officials. Managers—and their staffs—need to build political capacity so they can assist the elected body in framing community issues. They need to seek and explore community-wide collaborative relationships as the scope of government continues to change.

Managers have an obligation to take the road less traveled on occasion, and I believe city councils expect this type of attitude in working through the issues in the community and leading the organization.
Gary Sears

In a rapidly changing environment, the local government manager can anticipate, react, and adapt quickly only by keeping the big picture in view. The manager cannot afford to think only about local issues because regional, state, federal, and global issues affect every community. For example, the competition for new jobs is no longer confined to one community. A successful manager must spend mental and even physical time outside the community (see Chapter 7 on the importance of networking) in order to meld local concerns with outside trends to achieve a viable, sustainable community.

Supporting planning activities

How does the manager reconcile active promotion of the community's future, taking into account physical, economic, social, and environmental factors as well as regional and global issues, with the everyday reality of traditional organizations, which are sometimes slow to respond and willing to accept short-term gains at the expense of long-term benefits?

If a city generally does the right thing consistently, citizens will realize the government is competent and, therefore, when you have a problem, they will usually give you some slack when it occurs.
Terry Ellis

Without question, significantly more planning is now done in the United States than at any other time in the country's history. Although the success stories about regional transportation, air quality, firefighting, crime-fighting activities, and even economic development projects are becoming better known, planning efforts between levels of government, even within a single jurisdiction, are too often disjointed and fragmented.

Coordinating jurisdictions' master plans so that artificial boundaries do not hinder regional planning is a major task. Coordinated local planning that receives adequate funding, that expands and combines comprehensive planning with strategic and contingency planning to include social and environmental issues, and that unites economic development and managed growth with other planning activities is a tremendous asset for the local government manager.

Another major task is making sure that community plans are based in economic reality. Plans should express the community's ideals—for example, smart growth and limited sprawl—but they must also take into account the market environment. A plan that ignores market realities is not likely to succeed.

Bridging the gap between theory and politics

The local government manager's job is apolitical although it exists in the midst of a highly charged political system. Local government administrators who help develop and implement policy must understand the political context in which they work. Because the best solution, idea, or project, no matter how well developed, will go nowhere without political support from the majority of elected officials, it is no longer possible to imagine separating administration from politics.

A manager may at times be required to take the lead on behalf of the mayor and the council on issues that have major political implications. For example, the chief administrative officer (CAO) of the unified government of Wyandotte County/ Kansas City, Kansas, became the point person during International Speedway Corporation's search for a site to construct a NASCAR track in the Kansas City area. The mayor asked the CAO to take the lead in researching the project, making the presentations, and speaking for the elected officials. The administrator was cast in a role he never thought a manager would perform: simultaneously lead staff in an objective analysis of a complex project and build political support for it.[4]

Political savvy is the ability to see all sides of an argument, to know who will be for and against the issue at hand, to maneuver the issue through the policy maze, to understand where members of the elected body stand on the issue and why, and to navigate the process issues—who to tell, when to tell, and how much to tell.

Professional managers seek a planning process that is a technical, rational, orderly procedure, based on guiding principles developed over the years as well as local and national standards applied to master planning, community facilities, and standard zoning issues. What makes the job of local government administrators so interesting, however, is that the decision-making process is sometimes irrational. A politically savvy manager understands that other issues, some obvious and some not, come into play and, in many cases, the technical recommendations of staff should not and do not override the political views of the elected officials. "One of the best ways to have top staff develop political savvy is to provide opportunities for interactions and communication among elected officials and top staff, and to maintain continuous discussion with your staff about the relationships between you and the elected officials."[5]

Managers must be on firm ground, constantly reaffirming with your elected officials how you are doing.

Bill Pupo

The local government manager needs to be able to translate important technical information for the elected body, and also translate the political desires of the elected officials back to staff. The manager translates council goals into actions and helps the council formulate new goals. It is also the job of the manager to help resolve political conflicts in the community.[6]

ICMA's Professional Development Management Practices address some of these issues in number two, Policy Facilitation: facilitative leadership, facilitating council effectiveness, and mediation/negotiation.[7]

The changing scene in local government

A number of critical issues within cities, towns, and counties need equal attention: the pace of change, tolerance for diversity, rejuvenation of downtowns, generating revenue sufficient to meet needs, maintaining the viability of neighborhoods, preventing urban decay, dealing with smart growth issues, and involving all residents in the community in decision making.

Demographic change and cultural diversity

To accommodate the needs of an increasingly diverse population, local governments must show flexibility in the mix of services they deliver. They must also develop new communication and information systems so that all residents can participate in the building of community.

As their populations become a "majority of minorities," many U.S. cities are following the paths of Miami, Los Angeles, San Francisco, Houston, Newark and Trenton, New Jersey, and Montgomery, Alabama, where elected and appointed officials are developing new and stronger outreach programs to encourage minorities to actively participate in community building and policy development. All managers also face the aging of America. In 2000, 12.4 percent of the population was 65 years of age or older. That percentage is projected to grow to 13.2 percent by 2010, 16.5 percent by 2020, and 20 percent by 2030.[8] (See Chapters 2 and 5 for more extended discussion of diversity issues.)

Economic globalization and competition

A community's efforts to attract or retain businesses will succeed depending on how well it competes—not only with neighboring jurisdictions but also with cities in China, India, Korea, Mexico, Europe, and elsewhere.

> For the first time in centuries, metropolitan regions throughout the world, rather than nations, have emerged as cohesive economic units that operate as important players in the world economy. . . . Economic activity does not come to a halt when it reaches a jurisdictional line. Political boundaries, though important to local leaders, are artificial and don't reflect the way global economies operate.[9]

Jurisdictions need to cooperate and gain economic power by sharing their tax bases.

Economic development is one of the most challenging activities of local government because competition for a stable, sustainable tax base is controversial and politically charged. For the local government manager, economic development offers the opportunity to exercise entrepreneurial leadership, and as in the private sector, entrepreneurship brings both rewards and risk.

The sharing of resources and consolidation of services with nearby cities will become a necessity, and the traditional territorial lines will have to be crossed in cooperation, not competition.

Leonard Martin

Infrastructure concerns

The ability of a community to promote its future is linked directly to the existing and future quality and capacity of its infrastructure: streets, highways, parks and recreational facilities, civic centers, sports stadiums, water and sewer systems, and fiber-optic networks. High-speed data transmission networks are important not only to potential high-tech companies, but also to local fire, police, public utility departments, and even to other local entities such as school districts and the community college. Communities must combine capital facilities planning, programming, and budgeting with other strategic and contingency planning.

A city or county is probably doing the best it can for its long-term economic growth and viability if it concentrates first on basic needs—making sure that basic services and infrastructure are competitive in terms of both quality and price. Extending infrastructure ahead of development within planned-growth boundaries can place a jurisdiction at a competitive advantage for attracting new businesses. But this option must be weighed against the risks of tying up capital funds and pushing up tax rates and fees charged to current payers to cover the cost of new development and future benefits.

Infrastructure improvements can be defined differently when they are meant to attract e-business companies. E-business companies do not need to be near central transportation corridors or close to other businesses; they do however need high-speed data transmission capabilities:

> Indeed, the story of second and third tier markets and rural communities all over America is the ability of forward-thinking governmental officials to level the economic playing field by providing the kind of high-speed connectivity that fast-moving companies need.[10]

Both Cedar Falls, Iowa, and Hawarden, Iowa, have developed cooperative municipal telecommunications utility ventures in rural areas where market and technology services can be limited. Through creative financing and with their voters' hearty approval, they have invested in fiber-optic technology to provide cable television and high-speed Internet service. Competing head-to-head with incumbent utilities, they helped lower average rates charged to their citizens and met an underserved need for responsive, local customer service in a nonmetropolitan setting.[11]

Managers need to insure there is a real consensus on what type of community the locality wants to be, and to have a good master plan, adequate infrastructure, and the personnel capable of efficiently executing its policies.
John L. Maltbie

Environmental concerns

The environment has been a perennial issue on the agendas of local governments, but air and water pollution, erosion of natural resources, depletion of open space, and rapidly filling landfills are still common challenges facing city and county officials. Cities and counties designated as "nonattainment areas" by the U.S. Environmental Protection Agency will be restricted in their economic development because of the various compliance mandates they face. To recruit businesses as well as retain firms already in residence, communities need to retain a good quality of life and high environmental standards—a delicate balance. On the one hand, quality of life and a healthy environment can attract and retain businesses; on the other hand, both can be adversely affected by the results of successful economic development.[12]

The capacity of the environment to take punishment is limited. To preserve and protect both the environment and the quality of community life, local governments must factor in the environmental impact of economic decisions and programs.

Regionalism

The problems faced by local governments are not confined to the boundaries of existing jurisdictions (see Chapter 7). Transportation, water supply and quality, solid-waste disposal, land use, and economic development are among the issues with regional ramifications.

A manager cannot promote a community's future in isolation from the future of surrounding communities, especially if the jurisdiction is near a core city. Because the formal consolidation of local governments remains politically unacceptable, it is the regional councils of government that serve as the vehicle for regional cooperation and coordination. Local government managers therefore need to participate in their region's council of governments. For example, transit and transportation—with their high costs, need for connectivity, and need for economies of scale—usually cross jurisdictional boundaries, especially in metropolitan areas, and should be treated regionally.

Citizen involvement

In addition to cooperating with leaders of other jurisdictions in the region, local government managers must also work closely with citizens and neighborhood groups to create as broad a base as possible for local government decision making.

Syracuse, New York, for example, put together a successful citizen involvement program called Tomorrow's Neighborhoods Today (TNT), which involves neighborhood residents, businesses, and organizations in comprehensive planning for their neighborhoods. TNT identifies and builds upon community assets, and develops workable plans and priorities for Syracuse's neighborhoods. The plans direct the city's resources in the most important areas in the most cost-effective way. Their process strengthens the democracy that is critical for a healthy city, improves the quality of life, and builds Syracuse's capacity to solve problems and create a desirable future.[13]

The professional expertise of the government staff must be blended with the values, perceptions, and desires of local residents to arrive at a successful plan for development patterns, land use configuration, public services, recreational amenities, and other facilities. Officials have to find out what residents want the community to look like and then they have to figure out how they can contribute to that vision. (A more comprehensive discussion of community power and citizen involvement is provided in Chapter 2).

The planning function and community strategic planning

The manager's central place in the community makes the manager a key player in the community's efforts to chart the future. Local government managers have to understand the broad goals and strategies involved in comprehensive planning, strategic planning, and contingency planning, processes differentiated from other managerial activities primarily by their focus on the future.

Types of planning

Comprehensive planning takes a long-range look at a community and provides general concepts and a vision of how the community should develop and how proper land use designations can affect the health, safety, and welfare of the community. The comprehensive plan should be an expression of citizen preferences and a guide to public and private decision making. The comprehensive plan must include requirements mandated by state law and other elements that the elected body and the citizens feel are necessary to build the community: a transportation plan, open space development, redevelopment goals and objectives, urban design elements, a housing plan, quality-of-life issues, economic development elements, and a fiscal element. Zoning ordinances and land use designations must be consistent with the goals and vision developed in the comprehensive plan.

The role of the local government manager is to assist and guide elected officials and citizens in the development of a comprehensive municipal planning document and vision statement. The manager ensures that all stakeholders in the community have ample opportunity to participate in this important process. Also, the manager, with the guidance of elected officials, coordinates the comprehensive plan with adjacent jurisdictions, agencies of the county (or, if a county, agencies of municipalities), the state, and, when possible, with the regional association of governments. Although comprehensive plans largely involve technical planners, the local government manager must oversee the plan because it sets the tone for the physical development of the community and receives the most attention from the public.[14]

Strategic planning involves a shorter time span, and the critical issues and available resources that a community faces determine the orientation. A strategic plan may embrace all aspects of the local government or may address critical issues of one department. One example of an item to be decided strategically would be the number of police personnel and fire stations needed over the next five to ten years. The strategic plan is a management tool that helps assess direction on important issues.

A contingency plan is a more flexible, dynamic plan. It is a resource investment plan, based on immediate and future what-if scenarios, that usually involves a human resources plan, a capital plan, and an action plan that evolves as unanticipated conditions occur. Most contingency planning focuses on disaster preparedness and recovery, and contingency plans are used to understand and anticipate the potential impact of a disaster by testing, training, and observing the effects of holding back or shifting resources when necessary. This chapter deals with contingency planning only to the extent that it is a component of a comprehensive strategic plan.

Community strategic planning

Effective strategic planning identifies the critical current issues that an organization—in this case a community—must confront. Community-wide strategic planning often serves as a supplement to—but not a replacement for—comprehensive planning. Strategic planning can provide managers with the cornerstone they need to develop effective processes to promote their community's future.

Strategic planning cannot predict the future; it is a guide that uses somewhat different techniques than traditional planning to help create a vision for the community. "The external environment changes so rapidly and so unpredictably that the capacity to get a fix on it is severely limited. Planning under these conditions must be fluid. . . . Thus plans are best reviewed as 'strategic guides' rather than fixed paths to the future."[15] Memphis 2006 (Tennessee), and Scottsdale Vision 2000 (Arizona) are two successful examples of major community visioning efforts.

Strategic planning has weaknesses and limitations as well as strengths. If managers recognize the weaknesses and limitations inherent in the process and do not expect miracles, strategic planning can be an effective management tool in conjunction with contingency planning and community-visioning processes.

Table 4–1 compares the characteristics of comprehensive planning and strategic planning. Except for the concept of widespread participation that is critical to both processes, the two are significantly different.

Comprehensive planning tends to be long range (20 years or more), oriented toward the community's physical development, and idealistic. Strategic planning has a much shorter time horizon (usually about three to five years), focuses on critical issues, and advocates realistic change. It is designed as a management as well as a planning tool.

> Strategic management emphasizes an ongoing process that integrates systematic planning with other management systems. It employs a strategic-planning process that is

Table 4–1   Comprehensive and strategic planning

Comprehensive planning	Strategic planning
1. Long-range	1. Short-range
2. Land use/physical orientation	2. Orientation determined by critical issue
3. Not tied to available resources	3. Tied to available resources
4. Rational model base	4. Rational and institutional elements
5. Strategies omitted from plan	5. Strategies as part of the plan
6. Widespread participation	6. Widespread participation
7. Planner driven	7. Executive driven

Source: Charldean Newell, ed., *The Effective Local Government Manager*, 2nd ed. (Washington, D.C.: ICMA, 1993), 139.

externally oriented, issue focused, and opportunity seeking. It entails active leadership that can direct organization-wide systems of strategic management and be capable of mastering the events and consequences of rapid change.[16]

A common thread runs through comprehensive, strategic, and contingency planning. Necessary overlaps occur in each process, and elements of one plan are often referenced during the development of other planning documents. For example, while a municipal utility department develops a long-range water supply plan for 2050, it must have a concurrent strategic plan to guide it in determining whether to buy natural gas for the power plant on the spot market or develop a contract with a supplier at a locked-in price that could, depending on future spot-market prices, result in higher costs. The same department must have contingency plans for water rationing in case of drought and for enhanced security in case of terrorist attacks.

The strategic-planning process Unlike traditional planning in which the base elements of the plan—land use, housing, transportation, and open space—are essentially predetermined, the focus of a community's strategic plan depends on issues that emerge from an initial environment scan. Strategic plans vary significantly from city to city and from county to county. A community whose tax base has eroded because of a decline in population or the loss of a key business may identify economic development as critical to community survival. In contrast, a community that is close to a growing metropolitan area, has land available for development, and has maintained a balance between resources and demand for services may see the need to control growth as more critical.

Local planners often make assumptions about community goals and frame them in terms of improved housing, transportation, land use, and general quality of life. In strategic planning, however, the development of a mission and goal statement is crucial. When the mission statement is being developed, it is imperative that all affected parties become involved. The resulting statement, although general, charts the direction of the community.

The following statement from Carlsbad, California, is typical: "Our mission is to provide top-quality services to our citizens and customers in a manner that enhances the quality of life for all who live, work, and play in Carlsbad."[17] The Carlsbad city council took this process one step farther and developed more elaborate guidelines to enhance the mission and vision statement (Figure 4–1).

The SWOT process The essential features of local government strategic planning are captured in the acronym, SWOT: strengths, weaknesses, opportunities, and threats. The community assesses its strengths, weaknesses, opportunities, and threats and then devises strategies to address critical issues.

Table 4–2 presents a simple SWOT analysis after economic development had been selected as a key issue facing a community with a declining population and a declining tax and business base. The city intends to use its existing economic development department to obtain new, high-technology businesses. If a jurisdiction is too small to have its own department, it may need to work with the local chamber of commerce or form a partnership with an existing agency that specializes in economic development. Even when the city has its own economic development operation, it will need to cooperate with external agencies. Table 4–2 implies that community-wide efforts should focus on upgrading the school system, developing economic incentives, and developing a modern infrastructure system to accommodate new e-business. Individuals involved in strategic planning must consider intercity competition and, possibly, a divided council. If its economic development program is successful, the city should be able to expand its economic and tax bases.

Figure 4–1
Statement of
Carlsbad, California

CARLSBAD CITY COUNCIL | FIVE-YEAR VISION STATEMENTS
City Council continues to clarify and pursue the vision of Carlsbad that reflects
the pride and quality of life for all who live, work, and play here.

Carlsbad…
1. Diverse and healthy economic base provides opportunities for employment to
   the residents of Carlsbad, economic vitality to the community, and the
   necessary revenues to support City services.
2. Policies and decisions implement the General Plan, enforce the Growth
   Management Plan, maintain the safety and security of its citizens, and are
   based on what is best for Carlsbad.
3. Leadership role in local and regional planning issues actively involves
   addressing governmental issues at the local, state, and national levels.
4. Open government provides for the betterment of the community in a nonpartisan manner while encouraging active citizen participation and
   involvement with the City Council, and the City's Boards and Commissions.

Carlsbad Efficiently and Effectively…
5. Delivers top-quality public services.
6. Manages environmental concerns proactively, including:
   - open space
   - water quality/conservation
   - beach erosion
   - air quality
   - resource conservation and waste reduction
   - wildlife habitat
7. Has a safe and efficient integrated transportation system.
8. Maintains citywide "small town" community spirit.
9. Has a community where continuous and life-long learning are supported and
   embraced for people of all ages.

Source: Raymond Pachett, city manager, Carlsbad, California, February 2003.

Once the SWOT analysis is complete, planners must move on to develop an
action plan that includes goals, objectives, and strategies for each critical issue.
Implementation may be assigned to existing governmental units, such as the economic development office, or new organizational mechanisms may be created.
For example, an economic development committee consisting of representatives
from different city departments, the council, the business community, and un-
affiliated residents could be established to oversee the city's economic development activities. Continual monitoring and updating complete the strategic
planning cycle.

The desired outcome is that substantial progress be made toward addressing the
critical issues within a two- to five-year period. Strategies and programs designed to
address most critical issues are not likely to be terminated after two or three years.

Table 4–2   SWOT analysis

Critical issue: Economic development		
SWOT	External analysis	Internal analysis
Strengths	High-tech concentration	Economic development office
Weaknesses	Education system	No city-chamber cooperation
Opportunities	Economic expansion	Expanded tax base
Threats	Intercity competition	Split city council

If significant progress has been made, however, those programs can continue as regular local government activities while other issues assume critical status.

The specificity and direct-action orientation of the strategic planning process make it distinct from comprehensive planning. Managers have at their disposal action strategies tailored to address the critical issues as they attempt to guide the community toward identified goals. Moreover, strategic plans are flexible and can and should be amended when a new opportunity or a new threat arises.

The participants   Public-sector strategic planning begins with the recognition that a high level of participation from a broad spectrum of interested people is essential. Open participation is grounded in democratic principles. Moreover, widespread participation results in greater understanding and acceptance of the process and the plan, which, in turn, increase the probability of successful implementation. Successful managers understand that the increased chance of success is reason enough to promote a process open to all who have a stake in the results, including neighborhood organizations, chambers of commerce, civic organizations, and unions.

The role of the local government manager in strategic planning is to act as organizer, coordinator, and facilitator of a process that will benefit the entire community. The local government manager most often provides the initial impetus for the strategic-planning effort and later continues to provide leadership and support. In return, the manager receives information that has a direct bearing on the future of the community—information that can be used to take advantage of strengths, correct weaknesses, maximize opportunities, and respond to threats as the community moves toward a less uncertain future. A special responsibility of the manager is to prevent the process—which can become bogged down in paper and swamped by detail—from overwhelming the intent of strategic planning.

Economic development

Local governments are extensively involved in economic development—in developing infrastructure, building cultural facilities, and fostering downtown renewal. Local governments compete to diversify their sources of revenue, increase employment opportunities for their citizens, develop a sustainable tax base, create a positive image for business growth, and attract new businesses. Gaining a competitive advantage is an art and a skill that local government managers need to sharpen.

Very few local jurisdictions can rely solely on the private sector to promote economic development. Businesses are participants in the process and can help develop innovative approaches to create and maintain jobs, but usually they do not develop the vision and plans necessary for long-term sustainability. Consequently, new public-private partnerships and formal collaborative efforts are on the rise, and the local government manager is in a unique position to assist the community in developing a plan for economic revitalization and viability.

Bryce Stuart, city manager of Winston-Salem, North Carolina, offers this description of his local government's cooperation with the private sector:

> With regard to economic development promotion in our community we have arrived at a division of labor that works well for us. The job of recruiting new business investors from outside the community through marketing is assigned to a not-for-profit corporation organized by the private sector. They provide the primary funding, and we contribute some public funds for their marketing budget. It's their job to take the prospective clients and seek to meet their various needs as best they can. We at the municipality are prepared to step up to the table with creative approaches to providing the customary infrastructure and services, and we also have loans and grants from public funds that we will consider applying if enough new tax base or new jobs are created.[18]

The new economic playing field

Local government managers must be careful not to limit their definition of economic development to attracting big-box stores, manufacturing plants, and large call-center operations. Managers must help the elected body understand that a major factor in economic development is helping local businesses grow. Existing businesses usually do not object to the local government bringing in new job opportunities or increasing the sales tax base as long as they have an opportunity to share in the growth and expansion incentives.

In addition to broadening the goals of economic development, the manager can lead the community to think beyond short-sighted solutions. Economic development activity frequently consists of offering financial incentives, such as tax abatements, to prospective new industries or to existing industries considering major expansion. It is difficult to measure the results of these incentives because many factors influence business location decisions. Sometimes, to the chagrin of the affected community, businesses enjoy incentives for a specific number of years and then leave town when the agreement ends. Also, local governments may be tempted to give away more in incentives than they receive in the form of new jobs and increased tax revenues.

Some communities are holding recipients of incentives accountable by, for example, tying payments, tax rebates, infrastructure improvements, and similar measures to specific milestones. Sometimes the industries are granted the incentives only after the project is complete and the goals established for the incentives have been met. To encourage new companies to hire residents, a local government can offer a specific dollar amount for every employee the company hires from the community. Some communities are retaining major industries already in residence by offering them incentives as well.

The manager's role in economic development

The local government manager, working with citizens and elected officials, develops the capital expenditure budget to help new businesses locate in the community and to help retain and expand existing enterprises. The manager must make sure the basic social and capital infrastructure are available to meet the needs of arriving businesses as well as the needs and desires of the businesses and residents already there.

Requirements may include improved streets, traffic-congestion relief, new parking places, upgraded recreational and cultural amenities, safe neighborhoods, streamlined administrative procedures for developers, land assembly for development, better public transportation, adequate water and sewer facilities, and improved data-transmission links. Carrollton, Texas, is one of many jurisdictions that have streamlined administrative processes to accommodate new building. Other communities have invested in fiber-optic networks, worked to reduce crime, or secured brownfields remediation grants to attract developers.

Creating the mechanisms that can address the many requirements of economic development in a coordinated and effective way is the manager's job. The manager must pull together the many interests involved in the community and help the elected body create a comprehensive and cohesive economic development strategy for the community.

The manager should also see to it that the community is kept informed of major economic development projects. Occasional press briefings that give the media the opportunity to ask detailed questions and other forms of open communication are especially important for large or controversial projects. The manager can also act as a facilitator for neighborhood groups and the developer when community issues have not been resolved. When necessary, the manager can act as a buffer for the elected body until all the issues are understood and tentative solutions have been reached.

The role of the manager in building the community is usually first approved by the elected body because the manager will be highly visible in this role. When the manager does not play a major role in economic development projects, the internal focus of the projects can become fuzzy and elected officials will not have a buffer to shield them if the project runs into trouble. Knowing whether to be in the background or in the forefront is part of having the political savvy necessary to manage the community.

I believe that part of the role of the manager is to be a realistic cheerleader, constantly pointing to the successes, but also working to manage the expectations of the public.

Cynthia Seelhammer

Most local government managers enjoy the economic development process. It is fun, exciting, challenging, and stimulating to compete in the new global economy, to make the community more livable, to provide the opportunity for more jobs, and to help create a broader, more resilient tax base. New businesses, especially those well known regionally and nationally, create a high level of excitement in the community—excitement that can be positive or negative depending on the history of the company and its potential new neighbors. On highly visible projects, local government managers must guide elected officials through the maze of existing and ad hoc neighborhood groups, special interest groups, and business and developer associations on their journey to the best policy choices.

This part of the job is called "issue anticipation," and it requires the manager to understand the desires of the elected body and of the community. It is the manager's job to be the risk taker who guides the elected body through the pros and cons of each economic development proposal, especially if the governing body does not want to be in the forefront of a controversial issue.

The local government manager should be the leader open to economic development opportunities, but, depending on the size of the community, managers should not necessarily get involved in the day-to-day activities of the project, particularly if a dedicated, professional economic development staff is available. Sometimes it is a distinct advantage for the manager to work behind the scenes and become the main negotiator only after ideas and concerns rise to the surface.

The notion of the city manager as a developer is based on my belief that the role is to help "develop" the hardscape and softscape of our communities, staff, and organization.

Raymond R. Patchett

Economic globalization

It is no longer viable to model the U.S. economy on factors that exist solely within geographic boundaries of the United States. Foreign trade, trade deficits, multinational corporations, and international finance all contribute not only to the national economy, but also to state and local economies. Economists, government officials, and business representatives no longer refer to a national economy; the global economy now affects everyone. For local government managers, this situation has two major consequences:

- Understanding the factors affecting state and local economic conditions has become more difficult. As the number and complexity of external forces that could affect their economies increase, state and local officials must include additional variables in their economic development programs—variables that may not be well or widely understood.

- Foreign competition is a growing concern. Competition can now come from Asian countries such as Japan, China, Taiwan, and India; from the growing number of European Union countries from Great Britain to Estonia; and from any number of developing countries. The immediate effects of global competition can be felt at the local level when a business closes or an attempt to attract a new technology-based business fails as a result of foreign competition, resulting in lost jobs and a reduced tax base. Communities with sizable numbers of manufacturers, particularly those depending on high technology, have become especially vulnerable to foreign relocations.

Increased global competition will require many local governments to adopt new economic development strategies designed to allow them to compete directly in the international arena. At an ICMA national conference, Darryl Griffin of Waitakere, New Zealand, described the Waitakere council's vision: "an eco-city that is sustainable, dynamic, and just. Waitakere wants to be known internationally as a sustainable city that celebrates and sustains its people, has a strong economic base, honors the environment, and builds on its culture and heritage.[19]

Global competition will continue to intensify. It will require local government managers to be more innovative and to work in a cooperative spirit with other governments in their region to provide the most favorable economic package they can to attract new business. Border cities are finding opportunities in their uniqueness. For example, the cities of El Paso, Texas; Las Cruces, New Mexico; and Ciudad Juaréz, Chihuahua, México, call themselves the "Border-Plex" and maintain interactive business relationships based on the Mexican maquiladora program, the North America Free Trade Agreement (NAFTA), shopping, and business services on the U.S. side of the border.

Technology and the information revolution

The United States has experienced a shift in employment patterns to information-based jobs as a result of international competition, rapid technological change, and an increased demand for knowledge and information. The U.S. Bureau of Labor Statistics reports that the number of information jobs in June of 2003 was 3.2 million, or about 2.9 percent of the total work force.[20]

Computer companies and companies that use computer-based technology need state-of-the-art telecom infrastructure if they are to locate in a community. Consequently, local governments have to offer highly skilled workforces able to meet the demands of computer-based and other high-tech jobs that are replacing the manufacturing jobs of the past. The labor pool and local job-training programs offered through the community college or the state economic development agency can act as major incentives for a company to locate in a new community.

Even with the shift to recruit high-tech industries, the local government manager must still be concerned about environmental issues, however. High-tech industries are sometimes very "dirty" because of the natural resources required to support the industry and the by-products of the manufacturing process.

Relocation competition

Some local governments look toward cooperation with nearby communities to achieve economic viability, but political realities sometimes get in the way if elected officials make pledges to invigorate older areas of the city, bring new job opportunities to the community, and increase the tax base. Until cooperation among jurisdictions and shared tax bases become the norm, competition will remain strong and sometimes create long-lasting tensions between the elected and administrative staffs of competing jurisdictions.

Convinced that attracting new business will create jobs and expand the economy, local officials continue to place business-relocation strategies at the heart of their economic development programs. Advertising campaigns in the best Madison Avenue style tout the community's virtues—a pleasant climate, a well-developed transportation system, cultural attractions, and proximity to entertainment opportunities such as sport teams. Government representatives attend trade shows and business conventions; some local governments even send trade missions to foreign countries.

As competition for relocating businesses intensifies, cities, towns, and counties develop and strengthen their incentive packages. Local governments use combinations of tax, financial, and special-service incentives to create business environments of lower costs and thus higher profits. Local governments often must include incentives in their economic development packages.

Economic incentive packages, especially tax reductions, rebates, and tax increment financing options, depend heavily on state regulations as well as local government assumption of risk.

> Economic development practices have evolved from a loose assortment of a limited number of inducements to the use of many diverse, yet highly focused incentives. They include but are not limited to land subsides, low interest financing, flexible zoning laws, infrastructure improvements, the use of land for private purposes, and the facilitated processing of building department bureaucracies.[21]

Another technique is the economic development district, often at the county level. Economic development strategies can be costly and risky, depending on the size of the project, the complexity of the issues to be worked out, and whether state or federal funding is used.

Debate continues over incentive packages that seek to attract or retain business. It is difficult to know for sure what part an incentive package plays in the decision-making process or how much is enough to attract the business. If both parties think they have gained from the transaction, it is probably the correct bundle of incentives.

When major national or regional businesses approach a jurisdiction for possible relocation assistance, it is a mistake not to hire the necessary experts, including lobbyists, public relations firms, financial experts, lawyers, and accountants. Those who propose the project as well as the other entities that may be competing for the development will seek their own advantages. The return on investment for professional services could far outweigh the up-front costs. Expert help will ensure the measure of trust and understanding that elected officials and the public will demand.

For most smaller economic development projects, however, the local government manager and the internal economic development team can provide the necessary information to assist elected officials with their decision about assistance and incentives. In smaller jurisdictions that do not have a development team, the manager can ask for assistance from a nearby university or college or the state's economic development agency.

Competition will continue to fuel the use of incentives. Few local governments are willing to risk eliminating incentives offered by competitors, but a local government that pursues a multifaceted strategy of business attraction, retention, and development increases its probability of success.

Local governments must also pay attention to variables such as the type of business, the location, the number and types of similar businesses in the community, jobs that will be available, and the image of the company. Not long ago, for example, large retail big-box stores were welcomed by many communities, which offered numerous incentives to attract them. Now citizens pack many council, town, and county chambers to oppose the big boxes. To avoid some of these problems, communities that wish to grow should develop economic plans and vision statements and review them every few years.

If a community does not achieve success when it pursues a specific company, it can take steps to improve its chances when another opportunity arises:

- Collect and review press clippings from the local newspaper and the newspaper of the jurisdiction in which the business located; study especially the chronology of events as they took place

- Ask the successful jurisdiction for a copy of the final agreement and the economic incentive package, which should be in the public record

- Call the president of the company with congratulations and request an interview to explore and compare community strengths and weaknesses as an assessment tool for the future

- Bring together community participants and professional advisers for a team review and to make suggestions for the next opportunity.

Regional approaches to economic development

There are wonderful success stories of regional cooperation and sharing when it comes to infrastructure projects such as wastewater and water facilities, landfills, street and bridge construction, and recreational and open-space amenities. Why are these efforts not duplicated when it comes to economic development activities? In some special projects, they are: "Proponents of regionalism have asserted that more optimal outcomes are achieved when local governments recognize their interdependencies and act in a coordinated way."[22] In some areas, counties have brokered business attraction successes that benefited a whole region.

In an ideal world, jurisdictions would offer fewer incentives and would share revenues to increase the tax bases of each participating jurisdiction. However, political boundaries and political processes still engender intense competition for large and highly visible projects such as car dealerships, hotels, malls, and sports facilities. The jurisdiction that lands the project is perceived as the only winner. Yet, there is another winner: the business or project developer that obtained the economic package that closed the deal.

Intergovernmental cooperation creates win-win development   For many years the town of Queen Creek, Arizona, and the town of Gilbert, Arizona, operated with an intergovernmental agreement (IGA) setting a mutual boundary in the unincorporated county land between them. Neither town could annex this land in the future. When a developer proposed a major residential development, golf course, and resort to be built on more than 1,000 acres of orange groves straddling the agreed boundary, the two towns had to reappraise the IGA. The developer wanted all the land annexed by Gilbert, the larger of the two towns, and did not want to deal with two different municipalities. A complication was that Queen Creek's general plan required low-density development and preservation of the orange groves, while Gilbert's plan allowed densities on its side of the property to be three times as high. The two communities amended the IGA to allow the entire development to annex into Gilbert. In return, the developer agreed to keep the lots on what would have been the Queen Creek side at a density of one home per acre, thus adhering to the spirit of the Queen Creek general plan. The developer adopted a citrus theme, ensuring that some of the ambiance of the orange groves would remain. The developer also agreed to pay Queen Creek $1,200 per house built on what would have been the Queen Creek side to make up for the loss to that town of development impact fees. And the two towns agreed to share all sales tax revenue from the golf course, resort, and ancillary uses for 10 years after construction.

Source: Cynthia Seelhammer, town manager, Queen Creek, Arizona, January 2003.

Memorandum of understanding for sharing retail sales revenues   In 1996, Tempe, Arizona, and Chandler, Arizona, found themselves in competition to build an outlet mall. One developer had optioned land in Tempe and another had optioned land in Chandler; both sites were along a major freeway, about seven miles apart. The developers understood that the economic viability of each project depended on being first and that only one outlet mall could be built. Both developers wanted economic incentives and a quick approval process.

At the encouragement of the developers and because both cities had a lot to lose in terms of revenues, prestige, and ancillary business developments near the proposed mall projects, the mayors of each city directed their city managers to develop a framework for a successful cooperative arrangement. Both city managers and their staffs were soon in the forefront of the negotiations between the two cities and the developers. The result was that the outlet mall was developed in Tempe, but a memorandum of understanding was signed to provide the city of Chandler some much-needed short-term revenue and some permanent revenue sharing between the cities in case the commercial development within either city turned out

to be unsuccessful. The agreement called for Chandler to receive an immediate reimbursement of its preliminary expenses and to begin receiving revenue from Tempe when the outlet mall was completed. In return Tempe was to receive revenue from Chandler when major retail developments were completed in that city. The developers benefited by joining forces to build one successful outlet mall and sharing in the economic benefits it produced.

At the beginning of 2003, the two cities discussed ending the perpetual revenue-sharing agreement because by that time both had successful commercial developments and they would be exchanging revenues of almost identical amounts but still generating significant accounting work and paperwork in the process. If one city's commercial development had been successful and the other's unsuccessful, the shared revenue would have been critical, but this was not the case.

Following on the precedent set by the two cities, Tempe and Chandler in 1998 signed another memorandum of understanding to share the revenue of a new car dealership, which located in Chandler near the border with Tempe.

Sources: Lloyd Harrell and Gary Brown, previous city managers of Chandler and Tempe, Arizona, conversations with author in February 2003.

What are the lessons learned from successful regional cooperation in economic development activities?

- Incentive costs that jurisdictions pay to attract or retain a business can be reduced
- Bidding wars become unnecessary
- Increased tax revenues that would have been completely diverted to another jurisdiction can increase the tax bases of all those in the region that participated
- The public sees government officials working together
- Elected officials receive credit for the cooperative arrangement
- Public-private partnerships can be effective
- Innovation and risk taking can bring great rewards
- Regional cooperation sets a precedent for future economic development projects.

Economic development decisions are based on relationships and not just on the money you're giving.

Lloyd Harrell

The return on investment

Before launching or continuing an economic development program, the local government manager must ask two key questions:

- Is economic development always in the long-term interest of the community?
- Is there always a community profit when the economic development ledger is balanced?

For many years the answer to both questions was a resounding "yes." The consensus was that an effective economic development program would produce a strong and expanded tax base.

After more than two decades of experience with economic development programs and a continued increase in the number of local governments actively involved in economic development, a growing number of managers are realizing that development has costs. In some cases those costs may outweigh the benefits.

Direct costs can be measured in terms of dollars and cents. Indirect costs are by-products of economic development and growth. Negative consequences can include increased demands for services, overburdened infrastructure, business closures as a result of increased competition from a large national company, and quality-of-life and environmental concerns. Indirect costs must be calculated in order to determine the net benefit from the new development along with the opportunity costs of the project.

Costs of employment   Economic development should create jobs, but not all new businesses bring new jobs for local workers. Many relocating businesses bring their top executive staff with them and offer their current employees the opportunity to move with the company, and their recruitment for new employee usually does not stop at the jurisdiction's boundary. Some local governments require companies to hire a specified number of employees who live in their jurisdiction in return for incentives. Some communities give specific cash amounts for hiring a certain number of local employees for a given period of time.

Increased demand for services   The capacities of municipal and county service delivery systems may have to be expanded to accommodate the increase in demand by the new businesses and the people they bring to the community. Other local government entities, such as school districts, may be especially affected by development. New growth should be able to pay for the increased services, but the ability of a city or county to respond to new service demands may be curtailed by tax abatements and other incentives that were a condition of the development agreement.

Overburdened infrastructure   Business development and population growth can place a significant burden on a jurisdiction's public buildings, parks and recreation facilities, water supply and sewage disposal systems, and the transportation system. Moreover, much of the infrastructure will need to be in place before the new business can begin operation. Expansion is particularly difficult in communities where the existing infrastructure must be improved simply to handle pre-growth demand. Unless a community is experiencing slow, gradual growth, it is far from certain that development will generate enough funds to finance infrastructure-related costs that result from development. The issues of infrastructure capacity and the financing of infrastructure improvement are important in any economic development plan. Many communities require infrastructure to be in place before development proceeds.

Impact on quality of life   Development proponents suggest that revenues generated by new economic growth can be used to improve the community's quality of life; they can fund low-income housing, recreational programs, and programs for the elderly, for example. Community officials may hope that new revenues can be used to strengthen and improve existing basic services such as solid-waste collection, street maintenance, and general customer service, but if revenue generation lags behind growth, existing resources must be stretched thin to accommodate demand. Even when growth generates enough new revenue to meet increased demand, it is unlikely that there will be excess revenue for previously existing problems.

Who pays the bill?   Residents of a community, not the developers, pay for most of the costs associated with growth. Established residents pay their portion through general and special taxes as well as user fees that defray the cost of maintaining and periodically upgrading the infrastructure they use. New residents, however, face a double whammy. They pay the same package of taxes and service fees that established residents pay, but they also pay an additional share of the costs of growth— either directly, through special assessments and impact fees, or indirectly, through the higher price they pay for property because of the passed-on costs of exactions and development fees.

Whether or not citizens or the media raise questions, local government managers must weigh the pros and cons of each incentive offer to make sure that it is fair. The challenge of economic development incentives is that outcomes can be both tangible and intangible. It is the intangible outcomes that are difficult to sell to the public.

The intersection of growth management, smart growth, and economic development

Growth management is a response to what are perceived as urban mistakes: urban sprawl, visual uniformity, traffic congestion, lack of open space, lack of public transportation, lack of diverse neighborhoods, and lack of sustainability. Growth management is often described by terms like smart growth, sustainable development, sustainable growth, and sustainable communities, which will be used interchangeably here. Growth management is a comprehensive term, but it is not always an appealing one; today's favored expression is smart growth.

Economic development and growth can have serious environmental consequences. For a growing number of state and local officials, businesspeople, neighborhood associations, and citizens, stopping growth is not the goal. Instead, forward-looking communities are developing smart growth alternatives. Smart growth is a new term, and it captures a new enthusiasm for good ideas that are not brand new. The objectives of smart growth do not differ greatly from the traditional objectives of land-use and density controls.

Objectives of smart growth

1. Mix land uses
2. Take advantage of compact building design
3. Create a range of housing opportunities and choices
4. Create walkable neighborhoods
5. Foster distinctive, attractive communities with a strong sense of place
6. Preserve open space, farmland, natural beauty, and critical environmental areas
7. Strengthen and direct development toward existing communities
8. Provide a variety of transportation choices
9. Make development decisions predicable, fair, and cost effective
10. Encourage community and stakeholder collaboration in development decisions.

Source: Smart Growth Network, *Getting to Smart Growth: 100 Policies for Implementation* (Washington, D.C.: ICMA, n.d.).

Smart growth objectives and techniques

ICMA's Smart Growth Network defines smart growth as "development that serves the economy, community, and the environment. It provides a framework for communities to make informed decisions about how and where to grow."[23] It aims to foster a positive business climate and reduce the negative consequences of development. In these and other ways it can actually enhance economic development.

A sustainable community can only be built in concert with those who inhabit it.
Richard Bowers

Smart growth requires planners to realize three main principles:

- First, a systematic approach to smart growth includes a comprehensive plan that sets forth a framework containing goals, objectives, and criteria for making decisions.

- Second, corporations and businesses seeking to relocate, firms reassessing their current location, and entrepreneurs considering new ventures are all interested in the business climate of potential sites for their operations. Business executives recognize that an area's business climate consists of far more than the local government's willingness to grant concessions and incentive packages in order to attract new business and expand existing operations. A free-for-all approach to growth in which anything goes and any business is considered fair game detracts from the local business climate in the minds of many private sector executives. An orderly plan and reasonable criteria for development that recognize the importance of quality of life for residents and corporate clients send a positive message to business executives. Certainly market access, labor costs, high-speed telecommunications, supplies, and transportation remain critical to private sector decision makers. However, various quality-of-life factors, ranging from education to recreation to diversity, are becoming increasingly important to businesses seeking to relocate, expand, or develop.

- Third, smart growth enhances economic development by reducing the negative effects that may result from business development and population growth. As businesses give increasing importance to quality-of-life factors, jurisdictions that offer smart growth will be more competitive than those that simply pursue development without concern for its potential impact.

Smart growth principles, the general plan, and design guidelines require constant attention and renewal. The manager should encourage the development of a community visioning process before the general plan and guidelines are developed. Everything follows from the visioning process. The local government manager must move the ownership of the community-building process into the community itself. "Admittedly, putting smart growth principles into action requires changes in the way communities function. It requires that local governments, lenders, community groups, zoning officials, developers, transit agencies, state governments, and others agree to a new way of doing business"[24] Only in this way can the community be sustained in the long run.

The objectives of growth management and smart growth are quite compatible with economic development if the overall goal is to combine development with the preservation or improvement of the community's quality of life. Most, if not all, of the objectives of smart growth would be welcome by businesspeople seeking to relocate, expand, or begin a business.

Political concerns

The roots of smart growth lie in the politics of environmentalism. Many early environmentalists wanted to stop growth. As concerns about growth became more widespread and began to appear on mainstream political agendas, the no-growth concept was modified to permit managed growth, which in turn evolved into smart growth principles.

The main obstacles that any smart growth plan is likely to encounter still come from the political arena. For example, some developers and homebuilder organizations lobby and pressure local elected officials not to add new requirements—often characterized as burdensome—to their projects that would increase costs to their buyers. Pragmatic and realistic managers and political leaders find that smart growth principles gain acceptance when they are combined with politically popular issues like economic development, quality of life, and sustainability.

Smart growth is a holistic approach to community building that involves improving the quality of life for those who want to make their city, town, or county a better place in which to live, work, and play. Because each community is different, there is no single formula for achieving smart growth. The community must rely on its own visioning process, including continuing, open, and meaningful dialogue with residents.

A comprehensive plan that includes smart growth, economic development, quality-of-life concerns, and sustainability has the potential for establishing a broad coalition that will champion smart growth policies. A smart growth process that is designed to promote planned, desirable development can provide a significant benefit for everyone. A community does not have to label its plan as a smart growth plan, but it needs to adopt the principles that best suit the needs of the community. Giving a name to a specific idea or principle is not the goal. Livability is.

Two examples of smart growth plans that have received wide support and are being implemented successfully are in Flower Mound, Texas, and Boulder, Colorado. The Flower Mound smart growth program is a comprehensive, community-based growth management strategy that adopted 29 criteria as a checklist to foster growth management. Boulder has been a leader in growth management and smart growth issues for more than four decades and, therefore, provides an effective case study for those searching for effective growth management ideas.

Community-building with citizens

Community building is the art, craft, and science of proactively involving the citizens in all phases of local government. It happens in both formal and informal settings, when citizens volunteer for boards, commissions, ad hoc committees, and community projects and services; attend citizen training programs; attend public civic and social events; communicate with their elected officials in an open, two-way process; and are generally happy that they live in the community.

Community building requires a spirit of inclusiveness. It is as simple and as complicated as allowing every resident to have a sense of belonging and a feeling of ownership in the governance process.

Why can some communities continually receive voter approval to pass bond issues? Pass a transit tax with no sunset provision? Attract and provide economic development incentives for large cultural and sports facilities? And re-elect the majority of the public officials that choose to run again? The answer in many cases is that most individual citizens identify with the community.

Indicators that the community feels connected include:

• A high degree of trust between the public officials and their citizens

• A high level of volunteerism among the citizens

- Neighborhood associations flourish and grow
- Annual citizen surveys show majority support for city projects and departments
- Ballot measures pass by large majority of the voters
- Consistently high voter turnout
- Residents attend and support community civic and social functions
- Civility the order of the day during public debates
- Community town hall meetings attract diverse residents
- Residents tell people outside the jurisdiction specifically where they live, as opposed to naming the county or general urban area
- More than two people show up at the final public meeting for adopting the budget.

The manager's role in community building

The secret to community building lies in the manager's sincere commitment and comfort with the processes of civic engagement, in other words, giving citizens and elected officials the opportunity to shape a vision that provides a sense of purpose and to recognize publicly those who participate in the process. It is important to have a vision that seeks to move from strictly business-driven principles to community-driven principles, provides a context for decision making, and is coupled with a strategy that can be shared by all. The role of the local government manager is to encourage and summarize but not control the final outcome.[25] Business as usual will not build a sense of community.

One key to community building is understanding what the community really cares about. The local government manager has to have a strong sense of social consciousness and be able to develop collaborative processes that include listening, encouraging, balancing ideas, and maintaining a sense of humility.

Local government managers must encourage critical thinking in the community. Eran Vigoda's definition of the nature of collaboration is a simple but direct statement of what collaboration means in today's political context:

> . . . [C]ollaboration which means negotiation, participation, cooperation, free and unlimited flow of information, innovation, agreements based on compromise and mutual understanding, and a more equitable distribution and redistribution of power and resources.[26]

Looking for new ways to engage citizens is especially critical in parts of cities and counties that are in decline—that have for a long time been bypassed by the marketplace and even by public investment. Even if neighbors are hostile toward the jurisdiction, the local government manager must respond with openness.

A major theme of this chapter is the importance of meaningful citizen involvement—from comprehensive planning, strategic planning, visioning, and smart growth to economic development and community-building activities. In summary, if the residents of your community were interviewed today, would they give your jurisdiction high or low marks for open communication and forming a collaborative relationship with them?

It is important for managers to understand that, even though the elected body employs the manager, local government managers work for the citizens of the community, and a legal and ethical bond requires that managers be inclusive in all they do. Communities provide abundant sources of ideas about the future and how to get there. It is up to the manager to tap into as many of these sources of advice as possible. Not only is this often an avenue for coming up with innovative ideas, it is also an excellent way of getting people committed to the planning process and to particular courses of action. After all, a plan created in a vacuum undoubtedly will remain a vacuum.

New communication techniques and innovative strategies

Successful community building or civic engagement—the terms are interchangeable—means finding new avenues for meaningful two-way communication. The continued rapid advancement in new communications technology will revolutionize this process in ways not envisioned today.

Electronic government (e-government) can have a tremendous, positive effect on how elected and appointed officials communicate with residents. It can be accomplished in real time, so that feedback on issues can be analyzed almost immediately. Results from an ICMA e-government survey indicate that 47.5 percent of cities and towns report that e-government has increased citizen contact with local government officials.[27] Bellevue, Washington, and Phoenix, Arizona, are two examples of cities that have positive, effective contact with their citizens and business communities via the Internet. Their e-government services are broad in scope, interactive, and are good examples of value-added services for those with Internet connections while the governments still maintain convenient access to existing services for those without.

Because large numbers of people do not own or know how to use computers, communities need multiple avenues to inform and communicate with residents: 24-hour hotlines for specific issues and complaints, around-the-clock local government cable programming, newsletters in several languages (depending on the makeup of the community), citizen academies or universities, public hearings in the neighborhoods, an ombudsman to help residents solve problems, neighborhood association training programs, and town halls. The list is long and growing.

Volunteerism is another important part of citizen involvement. There is no better way to learn about government than through volunteering for boards and commissions, mentoring programs, neighborhood cleanup projects, block watch committees, neighborhood associations, and government booster clubs or assisting part time in various departments of the jurisdiction. Current and future volunteers must be provided learning opportunities and adequate training. If the jurisdiction is large enough, it may be able to hire a full-time volunteer coordinator to develop and administer all volunteer programs. Citizens want to be involved in their community and will take the time to participate in issues and projects that they feel will make a difference in their lives. Opportunities are endless and limited only by our imaginations. Examples of jurisdictions that have well-developed and results-orientated volunteer programs that assist with city services and nonprofit organizations are Hillsborough County, Florida; Virginia Beach, Virginia; and Glendale, Arizona.

Relationships built on trust build better communities.
Steven S. Cleveland

Citizen training programs sponsored by the local government can also prepare citizens to take leadership positions within their communities and run for political office at the local and state levels. Training in citizen academies, city universities, and leadership programs can take place no matter how small the jurisdiction, with city staff, elected officials, and educators as presenters and trainers. Most city staff and others who donate their time to teach enjoy the opportunity to share information and ideas with citizens. The citizens, in turn, make a lot of new friends at city hall.

A number of innovative training programs take place at the local government level. Glendale, Arizona, has a formal training program for board members of private homeowner associations. In many communities, homeowner associations are proliferating and have governance activities of their own. When the developer turns over the homeowner association to the residents, it is probable that the new association board members have not had formal training in finances, hiring, contracting, utility obligations, dues structure calculations, complaint procedures, or dealing with problems that intersect with the local jurisdiction. Local governments form better partnerships with homeowner associations when they trust and know each other.

Public relations activities

Public relations activities in government are not intended to sell but to inform. Local government has an obligation to inform citizens of projects that will affect their lives before the project events take place. If an issue is to be decided by the public, even more information must be shared. The more controversial the project, the greater the amount of time that should be allocated for conversations with citizens. The manager must develop a working plan and decide how much effort to put into public relations for the issue at hand. This is where the manager's political savvy comes in.

Anticipating and framing issues are critical skills for the success of any project. Managers who wait too long will find that someone else has framed the issue first, making the process suspect and making it difficult to take the initiative. The objective of public relations is to give all stakeholders—even self-appointed ones—timely, accurate, and appropriate information about the issue as well as a voice in the process.[28]

A jurisdiction faces no bigger problem than losing credibility because it did not pay adequate attention to community involvement and the public relations process. Below is a checklist that many mangers might find appropriate.

Community involvement checklist

1. Determine if public involvement is needed or desired
2. Decide what level of involvement is appropriate
3. Develop an initial draft plan
4. Establish process objectives and boundaries
5. Establish authority and responsibility for the process
6. Establish discrete deliverables and expectations
7. Address internal resistance to involvement
8. Establish project reporting relationships
9. Develop timetables
10. Define the substantive issues
11. Create an initial project team.

Source: Lance Decker, *Over My Dead Body: Creating Community Harmony Out of Chaos: The Basic Training Guide for Managing Community Involvement* (Phoenix, Ariz.: LL Decker and Associates, 2001), 29.

Developing a positive legacy for the community

Two questions are fundamental:

- How can the local government manager effectively promote the future of the community?
- What roles should the manager play in light of the increasing complexity and uncertainty of the future?

The inability of traditional, comprehensive planning to deal with current issues has forced local managers to develop expertise in strategic planning, contingency planning, economic development, and smart growth concepts as they seek ways to guide their communities toward the future.

Managers must teach the importance of forming a vision of the community of tomorrow, the importance of initiating processes that promote that vision, and the importance of implementing plans and processes that link vision to action. These are logical and sequential activities from the perspectives of both planning and management. In organizations of the past, planners supplied the vision, managers initiated, and staff implemented. Today, however, local managers perform proactively in all three.

The activities discussed here require skills and attributes identified in ICMA's "Practices for Effective Local Government Management." Managers who master these skills will be able to promote the future of their communities.

Vision

The local government manager, whether in a large or small city or in a rural or urban county, works at the center of a complex set of public and private institutions that explicitly or implicitly, through action or inaction, make an impact on the community's future.

On the broadest scale, the manager's role involves facilitating—finding planning expertise and economic development expertise, creating a purposeful agenda for civic action, involving the local government and other public bodies in future-oriented processes, and supplying leadership. Developing a vision with community participation is important, but the manager must be flexible. When circumstances change, the vision changes as well as the strategy. Moreover, the professional local government manager is different from other chief executive officers in that the vision must be shared by elected officials.

Finding expertise   Despite their prominent role, managers cannot single-handedly plan the future of the community. Diligent care is required to develop a competent professional staff that can design plans and programs to achieve the desired future. Finding experienced, able individuals is by no means easy. Some governments may need the expertise of short-term consultants from the private sector as well as staff of local or regional universities or colleges to assist in planning and economic development. University public affairs departments, planning departments, and business departments often sponsor class projects that need fieldwork. They rarely charge a consulting fee and have minimal expenses.

Creating a purposeful agenda   Community agendas for action are known by many names—general plans, master plans, community development guides, goal documents, vision statements, and economic development strategies. Agendas are also designed for many purposes—to promote smart growth, to renew downtowns, to preserve a historical heritage, or to protect critical environmental areas. The process of creating public agendas and policies can be difficult at times because formulating and carrying out policy are woven into the political fabric of a community. (For more detailed discussions on creating public agendas and policy, see Chapters 2 and 6.)

Whatever it is called, the community agenda is fundamentally a document for purposeful action—a call for the community to do something. Helping to shape the community's agenda for action requires a manager to be a visionary who can act as catalyst and then let go. The manager's role is to:

- Open a community dialog about the future the community wants
- Provide the general direction and the enthusiasm for opening up avenues to creating and promoting the action plan and programs
- Ensure that the legal requirements—on the local, state, and federal levels—are met

- Be a teacher
- Be an enabler—encourage and summarize but not control the final process.
- Encourage a renewal of the vision process every five to ten years.

Providing leadership   Managers stand at the intersection of many contending interests that promote competing visions for the community. Moving the community forward and responding by creating consensus on critical issues demands that managers mediate the often conflicting views of various groups and interests.

Managerial leadership is a constant essential in the planning and promoting of the community's future. The local government manager is both a leader and a manager. Leadership is important in facilitating the creation of community goals and priorities, in ensuring council or commission involvement in directing staff analysis, and in relating promotion and planning to other activities of the jurisdiction. Also important is soliciting and responding to ideas—by observation and by structured and unstructured processes that involve the public, elected officials, community interests, staff, and department personnel.

The successful local government manager knows that promoting the future of the community involves a deep, personal understanding of the needs of human beings. The manager must be politically savvy and willing to assume the roles of broker, negotiator, and facilitator—and remain aware of competing and conflicting interests as well as opportunities to tap resources or foster coalitions and collaborators to promote overall community goals.

Initiation

Being a visionary is not enough. The manager must also be an initiator and an enabler who educates, oversees process, and implements. As an initiator, the manager gets involved in comprehensive planning, strategic planning, contingencies, economic development, and smart growth—all to achieve community goals and objectives.

Education   The manager as educator is an extension of the manager as leader. The manager must educate the general public, community leaders, neighborhood groups, staff, and elected officials about the importance of the community's future, a positive legacy, and the processes and techniques for success. Members of the public are more likely to support and participate if they understand the stakes and their role in promotion and planning.

Teaching can be subtle. Work sessions and retreats can explore and explain details of the community's future. The local government manager's annual or semiannual performance review is a good opportunity to clarify government visions and goals.

Organized meetings—less technical than those held with staff and council—of business leaders, civic groups, educational organizations, and neighborhood associations can inform the community about why visioning is critical, what goals the jurisdiction hopes to achieve, and how it plans to achieve them.

Extensive media campaigns—ads in local newspapers, e-mails to citizens, Web sites, cable television, inserts with utility bills, articles in the city and county newsletters, direct mail to residents, and town hall meetings—inform the community and encourage participation in visioning and planning.

Process oversight   Promoting the community's future brings together various departments and private as well as public citizens. But responsibility for oversight resides in the manager's office. Unlike comprehensive planning, with its defined and accepted series of steps, the methods of promoting a community's future vary among jurisdictions. A rural county may be able to use strategic planning alone to monitor critical issues and design action programs. A large city may combine strategic planning, contingency planning, development, and smart growth to promote the community's future.

Implementation A winning football coach cannot design an intricate game plan and then, on game day, discard the plan in favor of making-it-up-as-you-go. Some players may prefer the flexibility of making things up, and the team may still win the game, but uncertainty and disorganization increase the risk of losing.

The manager, too, must implement by linking planning and action. Action strategies cannot guarantee success, and new information or unanticipated events will likely cause course corrections. But success always requires implementation—whether through the budget process, other monitoring, public-private relationships, and plan review and revision.

Linking promotion, planning, and budgeting The typical 20- to 30-year time frame of comprehensive planning makes it difficult to relate the comprehensive plan to the yearly budget cycle. The much shorter time horizon of strategic planning and contingency planning make the link between planning and budgeting easier to attain. Managers can demonstrate to the elected body the need for funding improvements to the water supply and water reclamation system, for example, if the strategic plan identifies these public work projects as critical problems. Full support is even more likely if public works improvements can be tied to an economic development program to attract and retain business.

Capital improvements budgeting, which funds long-term, large-scale capital projects financed through public borrowing and amortized over a number of years, has been a major instrument of planning since the 1920s (see Chapter 5). Capital improvement programs (CIPs) allow for multiyear systematic scheduling of local physical improvements based on sound planning, public demand for the improvements, and the local government's ability to pay for the improvements. Effective CIP planning is essential if community infrastructure is to be maintained for use by residents and as part of the community's economic development efforts. Deterioration of infrastructure may deter new businesses from locating in a jurisdiction, discourage expansion of existing businesses, and contribute to businesses leaving for greener pastures.

The local government manager should require that the CIP be linked with the comprehensive and strategic plans and with economic development efforts. Forging this link is critical to effective implementation of short- and long-range plans and economic development objectives.

Linking the public and private sectors Economic development activities, because they offer excellent opportunities for ongoing relationships between the public and private sectors, often yield joint funding for programs that benefit both sectors. Economic development programs funded solely with public funds are not likely to receive approval of the elected body or the blessing of the public. A local government manager, in conjunction with elected officials, plays a key role in establishing and maintaining new public-private relationships. The city or the county must make sure that any one group cannot subjugate community goals, especially when the community has developed a smart growth plan as the guiding framework for economic development and quality of life.

Central to economic development is the truth that all dollars are interchangeable. This is the basis of negotiation between private interests and the local government. If a developer wants assistance from the local government and the local government wants to help, frequently the manager or the staff can identify cost savings or less costly interventions that will help the developer achieve a successful project. A parking variance, for example, to a developer might have the same financial impact as a cash grant.

For the entrepreneur, real estate development is an exercise in risk management—assessing potential risks, mitigating them where possible, and accepting them only when prudent—and interaction with local government is one of any developer's greatest risks. Uncertainties and delays associated with approvals and permits result in higher costs. A manager who can reduce that risk plays a very effective role in economic development. A developer prefers an honest analysis from government staff of the likelihood of getting approvals—even if the answer is negative—to going through a lengthy process with little chance of success.

Public-private partnerships have recently been described as an innovative approach to local economic development. The manager should recognize what the private development community has known for some time: local government is a partner in every development. Sometimes jurisdictions are even equity partners, but more often they are not. Nonetheless, jurisdictions ought to work with every developer as a potential partner and expect to be treated the same way.

Recap

- Promoting the community's future, creating a positive community legacy, and striving for economic viability and sustainability are important parts of the job of government manager.
- Rapid economic, social, demographic, and technological change make the future difficult to predict and plan.
- The local government manager plays a major role in shaping the vision of a community, from which all other planning phases flow.
- A local government's efforts to attract or retain business will depend on how well it competes in the global economy.
- Responsibility for promoting and planning the community's future must start with the local government manager.
- The local government manager is a major player in economic development, promotion, retention, and relocation efforts.
- Regional cooperation in economic development activities is becoming more important.
- To build a viable, sustainable community, a manager needs not only technical skills, but also political savvy.
- Public sector strategic and contingency planning begins with the recognition that a high level of participation is essential from a broad spectrum of community players.
- Many of the problems associated with development and growth can be alleviated through the wise application of smart growth principles.
- Local government managers are in the forefront of building the community and creating the mechanisms that allow these activities to take place in a coordinated and effective way.
- Community building is as simple and as complicated as allowing every resident to have a sense of belonging and a feeling of ownership in the governance process.
- Public relations activities should be designed not to sell but to inform.
- The local government manager is a leader, teacher, and facilitator in bringing together residents and businesses in an inclusive, participatory process as they develop and work toward the vision of the future community.

Exercise

The following is a practical exercise that will give the reader the opportunity to think through and apply the concepts in this chapter. After you complete your answers about how you would proceed, discuss your views with several colleagues. An exchange of views can point out differences and add meaning to the exercise.

Who? What? When? Where?

Assume you are a city manager in a suburban community of 75,000 residents, 10 miles away from a core city of 300,000 residents and adjacent to another city of 50,000 people. All three cities and the surrounding unincorporated areas are growing rapidly.

The cities have competed for economic development projects for the past eight years. After every announcement of a new economic development project, members of your city council believe there have been winners but they have been the losers. Council members in your city are now looking for a big win and indicate to you "it's our turn now."

Background

The first regional mall in your area was completed seven years ago in the large core city. It was a stand-alone project with no direct economic spillover for your city. The heated competition for the mall left lingering distrust among the jurisdictions.

You are currently involved in detailed negotiations with a developer to build the second regional mall, and your city is the favored location. There is tremendous, positive public anticipation about a forthcoming announcement. Your council has already discussed publicly the many benefits of the mall locating in your city—increased sales tax revenue, a new destination point for visitors, a stimulus for attracting other ancillary businesses, and boosting the image of the city.

Concerns

As the deal nears completion, you are approached by managers from the two neighboring cities who ask you to work together with them to develop a regional partnership in which new infrastructure costs could be shared, new regional bus routes could be developed, and a revenue-sharing formula would be developed for future joint large economic development projects in the future. The regional association of governments in your area is also asking your city to take the first step to bring the region together and set an example for the future.

Your elected officials see this project as more than fulfilling this year's economic goals; they see it as completing the community's vision of developing a vibrant, sustainable community.

Discussion

What is your recommendation to the city council and why?

Notes

1 N. Joseph Cayer and Lewis Weschler, *Public Administration: Social Change and Adoptive Management,* 2nd ed. (San Diego, Calif.: Birkdale, 2003), 88.

2 John and Carol Nalbandian, "Contemporary Challenges in Local Government," *Public Management* 84, no. 11 (December 2002): 6–11.

3 Jack W. Meek, Keith Schildt, and Matthew Witt, "Local Government Administration in a Metropolitan Context," in *The Future of Local Government Administration: The Hansell Symposium,* ed. H. George Frederickson and John Nalbandian (Washington, D.C.: ICMA, 2002), 145–153.

4 John Nalbandian, "The Manager as Political Leader: A Challenge to Professionalism?" *Public Management* 82, no. 3 (March 2000:): 7.

5 Jane Kazman, ed., *Working Together: A Guide for Elected and Appointed Officials* (Washington, D.C.: ICMA, 1999), 28.

6 Ibid.

7 "Practices for Effective Local Government Management," Washington, D.C.: ICMA, 2004. http://icma.org/main/bc.asp?from=search&hsid=1&bcid=120.

8 Jennifer Cheeseman Day, "Population Projections of the United States by Age, Sex, and Hispanic Origin, 1995–2050," publication no. P25-1130 (Washington, D.C.: U.S. Census Bureau, February 1996), 10.

9 Peter Calthorp and William Fulton, *The Regional City: Planning for the End of Sprawl* (Washington, D.C.: Island Press, 2001), 17–18.

10 Ron Starner, "Wired Cities," *Site Selection Magazine,* January 2001, 43–47.

11 See *Small Communities: Collected Best Practices* (Washington, D.C.: International City/County Management Association, 2002) for these and other examples of creative collaboration.

12 Steven G. Koven and Thomas S. Lyons, *Economic Development: Strategies for State and Local Practice* (Washington, D.C.: ICMA, 2003), 65–66.

13 Syracuse, N.Y., Web site, www.syracuse.ny.us/tnt.asp.

14 For additional information about comprehensive plans, see Charles J. Hoch, Linda C. Dalton, and Frank S. So, ed., *The Practice of Local Government Planning,* 3rd ed. (Washington, D.C.: ICMA, 2000) for a thorough discussion of comprehensive planning as well as other types of planning.

15 Cayer and Weschler, *Public Administration,* 141–142.

16 Jack Koteen, *Strategic Management in Public Organizations and Non-Profit Organizations,* 3rd ed. (Westport, Conn.: Praeger, 1997), 20.

17 Raymond R. Patchett, city manager, Carlsbad, Calif. provided the material in 2003.

18 Bryce Stuart, city manager of Winston-Salem, North Carolina, interview, March 2003.

19 Darryl C. Griffin (summary remarks presented at the ICMA annual conference, Philadelphia, Penn., 2003).

20 "NAICS 51: Information" (Washington, D.C.: U.S. Department of Labor, Bureau of Labor Statistics, 2004), www.bls.gov/iag/information.htm.

21 Roger I. Kemp, ed., *Economic Development in Local Government: A Handbook for Public Officials and Citizens* (Jefferson, N.C.: McFarland & Co., 1995), 1.

22 Julie Cencula Olberding, "Does Regionalism Beget Regionalism? The Relationship between Norms and Regional Partnerships for Economic Development," *Public Administration Review* 61, no. 4 (July/August 2002): 480–489.

23 *Getting to Smart Growth: 100 Policies for Implementation* (Washington, D.C.: ICMA, n.d.), i–ii.

24 Ibid.

25 Richard Bowers, former city manager, Scottsdale, Ariz., interview, March 2003.

26 Eran Vigoda, "From Responsiveness to Collaboration: Governance, Citizens, and the Next Generation of Public Administration," *Public Administration Review* 62, no. 5 (September/October 2002): 529.

27 Barbara H. Moore, ed., Academic Exchange (Washington, D.C.: ICMA, Fall 2002).

28 Lance Decker, *Over My Dead Body!: Creating Community Harmony Out of Chaos* (Phoenix, Ariz.: LL Decker & Associates, 2001), 28.

5 Essential management practices

Effective management involves selecting the right people for the right job; organizing them to expedite task accomplishment; identifying, budgeting, and spending funds consistent with the jurisdiction's capacities and priorities; and ensuring that the information infrastructure is adequate. This chapter addresses these separate but related aspects of management.

The chapter begins with a brief note on organization design and then looks at human resource (HR) management, financial management and budget development, and management of the information infrastructure.

Coordinating the work of departments, pursuing the priorities of governing bodies, recruiting and retaining skilled workers, managing fiscal resources, communicating with citizens, building partnerships with the business and nonprofit communities—local government managers do it all, over and over again. The work of the manager reaches deep into the hidden structure that keeps communities vibrant. Like a juggler with balls perpetually in the air, managers have three sets of resources for which they are continuously responsible: people, finances, and information. How they allocate each determines their capacity to accomplish goals, to be responsive to changing circumstances, and to ensure that each resource is mined to its fullest extent.

Organization design

The purpose of any organization, whether it is a public works department or an airport authority, is to bring people together so that they can accomplish a mission that cannot otherwise be attained. This requires organizing into work units so that efforts are coordinated and contribute to the success of the organization. Designing these parts so that they fit together offers the opportunity to think about what needs to be achieved and how that can best be accomplished. Managers have four sets of design elements at their disposal, and their configuration determines how well a department functions:

- **Human resources** The right people at the right place with the right skills, performance standards linked to rewards, authority commensurate with responsibility
- **Technology** The right equipment, efficient workflows, information technology that serves workers' needs
- **Organizational elements** Adequate resources; adaptable, flexible work units that correspond to jurisdiction goals
- **Interfacing elements** Public support, interorganizational networks, open communication channels.

When a new manager is hired, the temptation to reorganize surfaces. Sometimes reorganization is effective; sometimes it is not. But it is always disruptive, and it always carries a cost. In the short term, productivity plummets as employee energy turns to worries about how change will affect them. Relocating offices and modifying reporting channels changes the networks that employees have developed for getting their work done. Those who risk losing power, influence, or status will resist the change and endanger the likelihood that the reorganization will achieve its desired effect. Before undertaking a major reorganization, one must conduct a thorough analysis, seeking answers to the following questions:

- Why did the current design evolve?
- What problems will be resolved by a redesign?
- Who will gain?
- Who will lose?
- Will the redesign enhance service delivery?
- How long will it take to overcome the disruption caused by the change?

If answers to these questions lead to a decision that the benefits of redesign outweigh the costs, the local government manager can develop a consensus for change among those who will be affected by it and then proceed.

The human resource management function

First we turn to the hands and feet of government, the people who deliver services. If governance is anything at all, it is about people safeguarding and enabling the lives of others. This function involves service work, which means that public organizations operate less like well-oiled assembly lines and more like what they are—human beings in a group, with all the human foibles and frailties—who are doing the best they can to deliver services to citizens who understand their own needs far better than they understand the pushes and pulls that squeeze the jurisdiction's budget and capacity.

In a nutshell, the manager's challenge is to cause a group of strangers to join together to achieve goals that no one can achieve alone. The level of success affects the work climate, employee retention, communication patterns, morale, interdepartmental relations, and, ultimately, mission achievement. Those who lead, manage, and deliver public services are the human resources that make the jurisdiction work. As extensions of the manager, workers control the effectiveness of every decision made. A motivated, committed workforce achieves far beyond the sum of its parts. Conversely, a demoralized workforce unclear about goals will shut down the best-financed, most technologically advanced operation. Johanna Allyn, a manager for the Department of Social Services in Hanover County, Virginia, observed: "Everything we touch involves human beings. How you say what you say has never been more important."[1]

Nothing else matters if the right people are not in the right place at the right time to get the job done. It is people who breathe life into budget priorities, who maintain Web sites, put out fires, catch thieves, provide safety net social services, make traffic lights work, enforce zoning ordinances, fill potholes, collect taxes, and otherwise perform all those functions that communities demand. It is up to the manager to create a productive workplace that can deliver these services.[2]

The public workplace

Public administration is not business administration. Although the work of local government managers is to conduct the business of government, business and government differ significantly. One difference is in the nature of the workforce and notion of civil service. Because public work requires commitment to the public interest and to constitutional values, public workers are held to a higher standard than business employees, in both their personal conduct and the degree to which their job performance is open to public scrutiny. Moreover, public workers are expected to be representative of the citizens served, which means they should look like and be like the citizens of the community—an expectation that introduces an important variable during hiring and promotion: representativeness. The demographic characteristics of the jurisdiction's workforce should resemble the composition of the community. A city with a population that is 50 percent African American, for example, should have a city workforce throughout all ranks that is roughly 50 percent African American. A workforce that is 75 percent African American in the lower ranks but 75 percent white in the upper ranks fails to meet this standard.

I spent my first six years in Decatur as personnel director and feel very good about the diverse management team that we have been able to assemble. . . . And I don't mean diversity just in terms of race and gender. . . . He [the sanitation director] is an African American . . . who has a B.A. in mathematics and an M.A. in divinity. How many sanitation directors are ordained ministers?
Peggy Merriss

Why is representativeness necessary? Because employees bring to the workplace the perceptions and values of their associates. In a democracy that prides itself on equality, discussion and debate bring to light the varying perspectives of all groups of citizens. When all constituencies are represented in the workforce, the values of all citizens are present in decision making. Citizens' level of trust in government is higher, and, conversely, public officials' trust in citizens is higher as well. Representativeness in the workplace does not replace the need for town meetings and other open forums, however; instead it increases the likelihood that diverse views that emerge from meetings will be added to the decision calculus.

The term "strategic human resource management" refers to the new way of thinking about hiring, training, developing, and retaining valued employees. The HR function is no longer marginalized as a dotted-line staff function only peripherally related to strategic planning and performance; instead, a strategic approach realizes that HR is the lifeblood of the enterprise. Without the right people, even bountiful budgets miss their targets and sophisticated information technology goes to waste. With a strategic approach, the HR director works hand-in-glove with other directors to develop goals, strategies, workforce plans, and resource allocation. This approach expands the HR director's job and moves the focus beyond the traditional concerns of recruitment and retention, classification and compensation, performance appraisal, training and development, and labor relations to embrace capacity building, succession planning, and organization design.

Civil service principles   Civil service merit principles were established in 1883 when the Pendleton Act was passed by Congress to govern employment in the federal government. Over time, states and local governments also adopted these principles in an effort to separate public employment from patronage, prejudice, and favoritism. Although some confusion exists about the term "civil service" in local government because it often refers specifically to public safety personnel, the reference here is to the merit principles embodied in civil service. The manager must handle all matters of personnel on the basis of merit so that fairness and impartiality govern decisions of appointments, pay adjustments, promotions, and discipline. (See Appendix A, item 11.)

Merit principles

- Recruitment should draw from qualified individuals who represent all segments of the community; selection and advancement should be based on knowledge, skills, and ability and should take place in open competition in which every applicant has an equal opportunity to compete.

- Employees and applicants should be treated equitably, without regard to political affiliation, race, color, religion, national origin, sex, marital status, age, or physical handicap, and with proper regard for privacy and constitutional rights.

- Equal pay should be provided for work of equal value; appropriate incentives should be provided for excellence.

- Employees should maintain high standards of integrity, conduct, and commitment to the public interest.

- Employees should be retained on the basis of their performance; employees who cannot or will not improve their performance to meet standards should be separated from their jobs.

- Employees should be protected against arbitrary action, personal favoritism, or partisan coercion.

For all workers, it should be the employee's choice, not the employer's stereotypes, that determines the acceptance or rejection of employment and advancement opportunity. As enumerated in Title 5 of the U.S. Code at Section 2301, merit principles highlight the importance of representativeness, skills-based hiring, and fair treatment irrespective of gender, race, ethnicity, or any other type of "otherness."

Merit principles in civil service provide for equal opportunity in hiring and promotion, protection from capricious removal, and standardization of pay scales. They insulate workers from partisan political cycles by guaranteeing job security once a probationary period has passed; they categorize jobs so that equivalent levels of knowledge, skills, and abilities (KSAs) are compensated equally; they require job advertisements that give potential applicants an equal opportunity to apply; and they prescribe selection procedures that are based on an assessment of KSAs rather than on subjective criteria. The downside to this emphasis on fairness and equal opportunity is that it involves processes that require time—time to advertise, screen, rate, and select applicants.

Likewise, a manager has more control over employee output and loyalty if the jurisdiction uses at-will employment, which means that employees can be dismissed for any reason without notice or appeal rights. In most cities and counties, a set of job titles are reserved for just such a purpose. Personal staff assistants to elected officials are usually at-will positions to ensure loyalty to the person, not the post. Conversely, adherence to merit principles insulates workers from the necessity for personal loyalty and, instead, legitimates loyalty to the public good. Why is this necessary? Because elected officials come and go, but the day-to-day work of the jurisdiction must go on no matter who is in power.

The fact that election cycles recur on a regular basis differentiates public administration from business administration. Successful business enterprises almost never switch leadership every few years, especially to incoming executives who have little prior experience. Government has made cyclical turnover succeed by staffing itself with a cadre of workers who know the enterprise. Civil service protections represent a trade-off between fairness and speed. Although procedural delays frustrate both supervisors and workers, job protections have made government employment attractive for those who are motivated to serve the public yet desire insulation from the whipsaw of election returns. Jobs that would otherwise be held hostage to partisan or personal loyalty are relatively free from such coercion.

As with any business, no set of principles can replace effective supervision. In traditional civil service systems, employees are hired for a probationary period, during which the supervisor must orient, train, and appraise the worker's capacity to perform. Much of the criticism about civil service protection is wrongly placed on the system when, in fact, fault usually lies with the supervisor who fails to take responsibility for the unpleasant task of dismissing workers who do not or cannot perform. The probationary period provides freedom to dismiss the worker. Awarding permanent status to an incompetent worker is a supervision problem, not a civil service problem. Once employees achieve permanent status, they have property rights in the job, which means that any action to deprive them of this property invokes their right to due process. Grievance hearings consume time and energy, and unless the supervisor has a well-documented case, the employee is likely to prevail and be reinstated, embittered, and demoralized.

Another aspect of civil service's reliance on rules and fairness comes to the fore when a reduction-in-force is necessary. To give priority to those with more seniority and experience, the manager's discretion over positions to cut is limited to jobs, not people. The rules in jurisdictions give employees bumping rights. Permanent employees in jobs to be cut may bump a worker with less seniority in the same job category, or they may move down a rank and bump someone in a lower job class. The result is that a layoff initiated to cut personnel costs targets upper-level staff, but by the time bumping has cascaded through the unit, it may be the most junior assistant who loses the job. Such a system wreaks havoc among workers, each of whom is wary of being bumped by colleagues. The result is the expenditure of an inordinate amount of energy, a loss of productivity, and little financial gain.

Civil service reforms   All solutions produce their own problems; this is also the case with civil service reforms that, in the attempt to improve performance and efficiency, usually focus on:

- Increasing management discretion in regard to hiring, promoting, compensating, and disciplining
- Increasing flexibility and responsiveness in terms of filling vacancies and competing with the private sector for hard-to-fill jobs.

Reforms can take a number of shapes, including removal of job protection, bumping, or appeal rights; broadening job classifications; and revising the way that lists of eligible job candidates are developed. Changing one aspect inevitably affects others, however. Managers' goals of more discretion over selection, hiring, and dismissal differ from goals of staff for more flexible job requirements, flexible job classifications that permit staff to shift jobs, and higher pay limits. Although managers hear complaints from employees frustrated by civil service rules, often these same employees forcefully resist attempts to remove the protections such rules provide. Moreover, in jurisdictions that lack home rule, civil service reforms must be approved by state lawmakers, and the local manager may not think it worthwhile to expend political capital lobbying for reform that is controversial among staff.

A less confrontational tack is to make changes at the margins. Recent civil service reforms in local governments have included eliminating the rule of three—in traditional HR systems, only the names of the top three candidates from a list of eligible job applicants, as judged by numerical scores, are forwarded to the appointing authority for possible employment or promotion. Expanding the hiring choice to the top ten candidates or to all eligible candidates provides more managerial discretion. Another reform is broadening job classifications—called broadbanding—so that managers have broader discretion in job assignment and workers are less restricted in the precise definition of their job class. Another is to exempt from the system particular job classes, such as staff of elected officials. This establishes a small cadre of at-will employees while it maintains civil service protections for most jobs.

Some local governments remove specific classes of hard-to-recruit jobs from civil service and hire contract workers; or they partition a particular enterprise into a public authority to insulate it from election cycles while freeing it to develop its own HR system. These cannot be considered reforms of the system, however.

Lessons can be learned from the states of Georgia and Florida, each of which has modified its civil service systems in recent years and eliminated protections for some or all workers. Advocates argue that such reforms allow managers to bypass time-consuming regulations, fill vacant positions quickly, reward good performers with bonuses, and remove poor performers without entanglement in lengthy appeals. Opponents argue that such reforms politicize the workforce, cause excessive turnover after each election, destroy the psychological contract between worker and employer, and discourage the best and brightest from applying. Early evidence is that some of the best as well as some of the worst occur.

Of great interest to managers considering reforms should be whether the proposed reform will make it more difficult to hire and retain the best and brightest. Will occasional political seepage threaten the stability of the workforce and drive away workers whose partisan leanings differ from those in power? Are at-will workers less likely to speak truth to power and less likely to reveal performance problems? No consensus on these questions has yet been reached in the reform states, and similar issues will arise in reform cities and counties. Attempts to overcome the frustrations inherent in civil service will continue, and every solution will bring its own complications.

HR functions

Human resource management involves a number of functions, from recruiting, hiring, and retaining workers, to designing job classifications associated with equitable pay scales, to conducting performance appraisal and employee development. Much of the dynamism in the HR field is due to a confluence of factors that are changing the face of the workplace—the growing diversity of the population, that mothers with young children now remain in the workforce, and that workers with demonstrated family obligations are often protected by federal law. Managers must pay attention to the growing importance of case law as it defines and constrains what was once considered administrative prerogatives.

Recruitment and retention   Recruiting workers with the right skills and retaining trained workers are continuous challenges. The Internet is invaluable for recruiting outreach. Many jurisdictions now post job notices on their Web sites. Taking the job hunt to anyone with Internet access speeds the application process. For example, Englewood, Colorado, posts jobs on its Web site and applicants may complete and submit applications online (see www.ci.englewood.co.us). Many cities, although not equipped to manage online applications, post application forms in portable document format (PDF) on the Web so that applicants may print out the form, complete it, and fax or mail it. Some communities operate their own television stations and use them to broadcast job opportunities. For example, on WCOT, the television station operated by the city of Tallahassee, Florida, viewers see job vacancies posted several times each day along with a phone number to call and directions to the city's Web site where they can see additional information as well as download an application form.

More local governments are using contingent workers. One way to avoid the stalemate caused by a rigid classification and compensation system is to hire contract workers to perform functions that are project oriented, of short duration, or that require expensive-to-attain skills—such as health care—that do not transfer to other jobs. A local government can either establish a job classification for temporary or part-time workers that carries with it none of the benefits or protections of civil service or contract with a firm to provide temporary workers. The advantages are clear: flexibility and thrift. The disadvantage is that contract workers need not be committed to public service and to the citizens. With job security comes the psychological contract between employer and employee that builds commitment to the mission. Nevertheless, for short-term projects or to access skill sets that are difficult to recruit, contract workers are a popular alternative to full-time, permanent employees.

For tasks not needed year around, seasonal contingent workers are routinely employed: summer grounds crews, the snow removal corps, the seasonal pool staff, lifeguards at beaches, and summer playground leaders. Contract workers can also be used to staff projects that will be of short duration and to carry out technical work for which there is a short-term need. Hiring interns from local colleges and universities also fits into this category.

Once an employee is hired and trained, retention becomes the challenge. Few workers today expect to spend their careers with one employer. Labor costs rise each time an experienced worker walks out the door and a new person must be recruited, hired, and trained. Monitoring morale, keeping communication lines open, and providing opportunities for personal growth and career development help to reduce turnover. New organizational designs such as self-managed work teams (SMWTs, discussed later in this section), are tailored to accommodate the new demands of the changing workforce.

Succession planning   Preparing to fill vacancies in leadership positions is an area of human resource management where businesses do a better job than government. By identifying promising workers who have leadership potential and grooming them for promotion, a manager can minimize the lapse in performance that can occur when an experienced person leaves. Although strict job classification systems make it difficult to cycle those with management potential through a variety of jobs, the effort to add such an option is worth the time it takes. Without the staff in place to guide activities, financial and information resources go to waste.

The baby boomers who are dedicated to public service are quickly approaching retirement, and far fewer young people are following in their footsteps. This creates a large replacement gap in the public sector. This is particularly a problem in local government, which employs five out of every eight government employees.

Frank Benest

Management development programs become incubators for developing leaders at the same time that they provide personal and career growth for employees. Traineeships identify and groom talented people and prepare future leaders. Establishing a formal trainee program involves:

- Developing a method for identifying promising employees
- Collaborating with a nearby university's certified public manager program or master of public administration program to develop a curriculum
- Allowing time off to attend training
- Rotating trainees through offices for cross-functional training
- Providing leadership opportunities

Mentoring   A necessary component of retention and succession planning is to provide employees the opportunity to learn their way around the organization, acquire management skills, and develop leadership potential. Mentoring is a powerful tool for achieving this. Through a mentor, an employee learns existing rules and norms and acquires the savvy necessary for advancement. It also helps newcomers learn the ropes and integrate quickly into the unit. Although formal mentoring systems are used in some agencies, informal mentoring is often more successful. The most effective mentoring is done when experienced workers identify with junior workers, usually because they are reminded of themselves earlier in their careers. Senior staff take the newcomer under their wings, alert them to pitfalls, introduce them to influential people, and notify them of advancement opportunities.

Mentoring can play a large role in either retaining or repelling minority workers. Because mentors tend to help those who remind them of themselves, those of the local majority group tend to mentor those most like themselves and thus exclude members of the local minority group from the fast track. Diverse work teams that span departmental and hierarchical lines can lessen this problem. In addition, work teams can increase informal opportunities for networking among newcomers and old-timers, bringing majority and minority group members together and fostering mentoring relationships that, in the long run, work to the advantage of the entire organization.

Job shadowing—allowing an observer to accompany employees as they perform their duties—is another way to encourage mentoring. The observer learns about the tasks performed and the pressures and challenges of the job. By learning about the work first-hand, the observer has an opportunity to determine whether the job is a desirable career path. Job shadowing is effective at acquainting trainees and interns with work that is done. It also works well at the upper reaches of a jurisdiction, where it can acquaint leadership trainees with the mix of daily tasks that directors face.

Classification and compensation   One of the hallmarks of civil service is clear-cut job classification paired with equitable pay schedules. Job classifications ideally provide an objective rationale for compensation rates, create equity among employees, and guarantee that equal work is compensated equally. The downsides are that rigid classifications impede a manager's ability to take advantage of a worker's skills and strengths that fall outside the formal job description and prevent a worker's job enrichment. Correcting these problems requires time-consuming job reclassification. Collapsing groups of classifications into broad bands is one attractive solution.

Broadbanding   Broadbanding—grouping jobs together—has been implemented in jurisdictions such as Maricopa County, Arizona, and Charlotte, North Carolina. HR experts rely on O*NET (www.onetcenter.org), an online information source administered by the U.S. Department of Labor's Employment and Training Administration, to identify job families and place classes of jobs within relatively broad ranges rather than relegating jobs to narrow descriptions. Broadbanding gives managers the flexibility to promote and expand a worker's duties without having to reclassify the job. While this frees both workers and managers from rigid job classifications and permits more discretion in job assignments, the trade-off is that it requires more supervisory discretion and opens management to charges of favoritism from employees who believe they are not being treated fairly compared with others in their band.

To avoid the downside, training is essential. Those who make job assignment decisions must be aware of the latitude available to them and avoid unfairly privileging some workers over others. In other words, the drawbacks are precisely the reason that narrow job classifications were developed in the first place.

Skill-based pay   Skill-based pay is a new reward program that attempts congruency among an organization's values, goals, and culture. It is a fundamental departure from traditional pay systems that pay employees for the jobs they hold. In skill-based pay, employees are paid for skills they are capable of using and not for the jobs they are performing at a particular time. This system frees management from a rigid adherence to compensation systems that are pegged to narrow job classifications. In theory, skill-based pay encourages career development because an employee can see direct financial rewards for acquiring additional skills.

As with many innovations, skill-based pay works better in theory than in practice because subjective evaluations enter the compensation system, and, over time, an inequitable pay structure with corresponding claims of favoritism may evolve. Reginald Shareef describes a skill-based pay attempt in the state of Virginia's Department of Transportation and found that, unless there is a goodness-of-fit for all the systems that support skill-based pay, it fails.[3] In the case Shareef studied, alignment among recruitment, performance appraisal, and goals of the work teams was missing. By the time the program ended, it was considered a failure by both managers and employees. Although laudable, Virginia's experiment demonstrates the difficulty of reforming one aspect of the HR system without wholesale change elsewhere. On the other hand, some small jurisdictions such as Maryland Heights, Missouri, are experiencing some success with limited implementation of skill-based pay.

Performance appraisal   Performance appraisal is connected closely with worker retention, job classification, and compensation, but the perfect performance evaluation has yet to be developed. Evaluations should deliver feedback to employees, provide a starting point for supervisor-worker goal setting, establish a record of performance, and aid promotion and work assignment decisions.

Each new type of appraisal promises to overcome the frailties of its predecessor, yet it, too, fails to satisfy. Neither behaviorally anchored rating scales (BARS), nor critical incident reports, nor trait ratings, nor management-by-objectives rating scales changed employees' belief that they are rated subjectively rather than objectively; and supervisors believe that the evaluation formats prevent them from capturing realistically the performance of the worker. The more thorough the form, the more time it requires for completion. The more sophisticated the evaluation instrument, the more time-consuming supervisory training is required. And still the supervisor's attention is drawn away from the work of the unit in order to focus on the intricacies of the evaluation process. Experimentation with various formats continues regardless, always in an attempt to find an instrument that achieves its purpose.

One promising attempt to match the performance appraisal process to the work environment is 360-degree performance evaluation. This is a multisource assessment technique, and its strength is that it requires ratings by not only a worker's supervisor but also by peers and subordinates. It is especially useful for evaluating those who work in teams and who can succeed only if they work collaboratively, have good interpersonal skills, and are reliable teammates. Input from all their work colleagues presents a more comprehensive picture of performance than input from a supervisor only. The downside is that it is costly: such evaluations consume the time of multiple staff and create administrative burdens. Nevertheless, the concept moves the workplace a step closer toward integrating performance goals, workplace design, and individual performance, and it is more thorough than simpler instruments.

Focus on performance

A unit that is apathetic, unresponsive to change, and lacking in new ideas is unlikely to have any conflict, but it is also unlikely to have any energy. A unit that is disruptive, chaotic, and lacking in cooperation has too much conflict. Neither unit will be productive. The midpoint—where employees are self-critical, innovative, and eager to identify and solve problems—is the productive point. The term "organization development" captures the activities used to build capacity. As jurisdictions are challenged to maintain services while revenues shrink, capacity-building efforts focus on identifying and addressing human resource needs.

Public employees from solid-waste technicians to maintenance workers to firefighters to information technicians come to their jobs with skills ranging from manual-labor skills to highly sophisticated knowledge training. Encouraging high performance is not a one-size-fits-all matter. One of the most promising developments in recent years is the increasing diversity of the workforce. Another is the use of self-managed work teams. More traditional means of improving performance include training and reward programs.

Organizational development, known as OD, includes activities that facilitate planned, long-term changes in the attitudes and values of organizational members. In other words, its goal is to change organizational culture in order to improve performance. Training programs that emphasize interpersonal skills, collaboration, and socialization of new employees into the organizational culture help to integrate newcomers and minimize conflict. Organizational development encompasses those activities that prepare the organization for what is ahead; it trains employees about policies and procedures, plans organizational change, equips workers with new skills, and sensitizes them to changes.

Reframing management assumptions   Donna Douglas, director of social services, Hanover County, Virginia, commented: "I was managing successfully, but I was not addressing the future; I had to think differently about what I was doing." In the following year, she changed her management style from micromanagement to a team focus. She reframed her views on personnel to think of human resources as an asset, energized her workforce, and elicited a higher level of performance. "Anybody can do this and it will not cost one additional dollar to implement."

Source: Anya Sostek, "Managing Performance: People Power," *Governing* (January 2003): 54–55.

Although budgetary constraints and pay regulations make it difficult to award salary bonuses, managers have a number of ways to reward and recognize outstanding performers as examples for others to follow. Awards, for example, can include a designated parking spot, a plaque or photograph posted in a prominent place, a story in the office newsletter and on the Web site, or nicer office furnishings. Some jurisdictions hold an employee appreciation day or employee recognition breakfast to commemorate outstanding performance. Consistent, meaningful recognition builds a climate conducive to involvement, retention, and pride. Mollie Anderson, the Iowa personnel director, said, "We can't offer cars or country club memberships or large bonuses, but it is very honorable work and it is inspiring."[4]

Diversity   Diversity brings both challenges and strengths. Managers and employees from different generations and cultural backgrounds have different expectations about authority, rule making, and acceptable boundaries of behavior. Earlier generations, even including baby boomers, expected a tacit employer-employee contract that as long as they contributed to the organization, they would be promoted through the ranks and rewarded for their longevity. Full-time work was the norm. More recent entrants to the workforce bring different expectations.

Organizational justice   With the new generation of workers comes the concept of organizational justice—procedural fairness, the expectation that employer actions provide all workers with equal opportunity to compete and succeed, and that no category of worker bears a disparate burden. Systems that are perceived as fair by employees, even though they may be cumbersome, trump processes that produce an adverse impact on one category of workers. Sensitivity to this concept will help managers navigate around claims of discrimination and other avoidable problems.

Young entrants to the workforce expect higher levels of autonomy and discretion over their work than prior generations, an expectation that necessitates greater reliance on participative decision making and flattened hierarchies. Another difference is that women now remain in the workforce through their childbearing years; this increases the need for employers to provide alternative work arrangements such as flexible work hours, telecommuting, job sharing, cafeteria benefit plans, and convenient day care. Jurisdictions that employ large cohorts of baby boomers need to plan for succession, ensuring that trained workers are ready to step into posts about to be vacated through retirements.

Diversity creates more complexity and more ambiguity in processes, yet it also holds promise of greater productivity. To prevent miscommunication and conflict, managers benefit from a deeper understanding of cultures and workers' perceptions and expectations. In the short term, research shows that heterogeneous groups have more conflict and lower performance levels. Superficial diversity diminishes over time, however, as workers come to know one another as individuals rather than as members of a class. Demographically diverse work teams typically require a longer startup time than homogeneous groups; but once members of heterogeneous groups have worked together and develop a comfort level with one another, group output in terms of creative and sound decisions meets and then exceeds the output of homogeneous groups.[5]

Despite the slower startup time of diverse groups, heterogeneity positively affects team creativity and decision quality. Competing ideas and ideologies help to prevent groupthink. By injecting a degree of conflict and tension into team meetings, diverse membership contributes to airing alternatives and ideas that would otherwise be ignored or go unspoken. An additional bonus is that heterogeneous groups develop higher-quality ideas and solutions than homogeneous groups.

How things change!   Clara Gordon Rubin's career with the city of Seattle is an example of how much has changed. She went to work for the city as a typist in 1927. While working for the personnel department, she enrolled in night classes in public administration. In 1937 she was hired as a junior personnel examiner, the first woman to reach professional status with the city. In the late 1940s she received the highest score on the written test for chief examiner but was told the civil service commission would never hire a woman for that job. During the 1950s she played a key role in expanding job opportunities for African Americans and immigrants, and she was instrumental in making the city the first in the country to hire women as firefighters. She died in 2003 at the age of 94.

Source: *Observer-Reporter,* July 1, 2003, accessed online 7/1/2003, http://www.observer-reporter.com/278073010690090.bsp.

Demographic characteristics as well as differences in personal values and personalities have the potential to create fault lines—dividing lines that split a group into subgroups on the basis of one or more attributes. Fault lines deepen when personal characteristics combine with racial or gender differences. For example, if all women in a group are over 60 years old and all men are under 30, the gender and age fault lines align to form a chasm compared with a group comprising half women and half men, all of whom are of similar ages. The more distinct the fault line, the more divided the workplace becomes. Shallow diversity has more potential for productivity gains, but fault lines have more potential for performance losses.

Diversity brings additional perspectives and ideas and is a source of innovation and creativity, but fault lines exaggerate differences and introduce conflict. Diversity, by definition, includes multiple perspectives and experiences and correlates with task conflict, all the while it provides the potential for enhanced creativity. Severe conflict, however, can reduce satisfaction and stymie performance. If a work group is to take advantage of its diversity, it must learn to accept conflict over ideas while it disapproves of personal conflict. The negative effect of fault lines in a group diminishes as members accumulate common task experiences and mutual understandings. The most productive teams are usually those that have worked together longest.

Chapel Hill's participatory management   One of the characteristics of educated workers is that they expect to have a voice in decisions that affect their performance. Participatory management may have been one of several optional management styles in the past, but now it is the only acceptable style. Chapel Hill, North Carolina, for example, has a Human Relations–Management Relations Committee that meets on a monthly basis to receive information concerning personnel policies and to voice employees' concerns about personnel-related issues. The committee consists of a representative from each department and from all levels of the town's organizational structure. This committee plays a meaningful and substantive role in two-way communication between the town's administration and its employees.

Source: Stephen E. Condrey and Svitlana Slava, "Human Resource Management Best Practices: The Case of Chapel Hill, North Carolina (paper presented at conference on best practices in local government and development, Uzhhorod National University, Uzhhorod, Ukraine, August 17, 2001).

Self-managed work teams   Government workers equal or surpass private sector workers in education and intellectual skill because much public service work is knowledge work that requires workers to use their knowledge to do their jobs, in contrast with the private sector that uses labor to manufacture goods or perform tasks.[6] Knowledge workers perform their duties in the absence of close supervision, and they exercise discretion in their decisions. Zoning regulators, building inspectors, caseworkers, and law enforcement officers all exercise discretion every day.

Because government depends on knowledge work, no one can know all aspects of a job. Work teams are therefore increasingly popular. Team building brings people together to work interdependently toward the accomplishment of a goal. In its largest sense, the entire jurisdiction's workforce cooperates to achieve the overall goals. In a more functional sense, effective team building allows for cross-faulting strengths and weaknesses so that workers who are strong in one area but weak in another complement their colleagues with different strengths and weaknesses. Teams were once thought of as an OD intervention to help employees learn to work together more productively, but they are now used as relatively autonomous work groups called self-managed work teams (SMWTs).

Self-managed work teams, also known as self-directed teams, are relatively autonomous work groups in which the responsibilities and duties traditionally maintained by management have been transferred to the teams, thereby giving them full managerial control over their work. Because SMWTs replace reliance on top-down control with reliance on worker expertise and initiative, they move decision making to those who have first-hand experience with service delivery issues. The organization design morphs from a pyramid-shaped hierarchy to a flattened structure, and reliance on collaboration replaces reliance on individual performance.

These teams plan, organize, control, staff, and monitor themselves; they decide who works on what, where, and when; they control start-up and ending times, the pace of work, and goal setting; they are responsible for inventory, quality control, and work stoppage decisions; and they take action to remedy problems. Benefits of self-managed teams include less managerial overhead and more initiative, personal responsibility, creativity, problem solving, and self-reliance on the part of workers.

A 2002 study of U.S. cities with populations of 50,000 or more showed that 27.5 percent were using SMWTs (Table 5–1).[7] Of these, 80.4 percent reported adopting SMWTs to improve productivity. Other reasons for adopting SMWTs included:

- Improved morale
- Facilitated interdepartmental collaboration and decision making
- Enhanced employee initiative
- Helped workers perform their jobs better
- Flattened the organizational structure.

SMWTs are put together in a variety of ways. According to the study, some municipalities (counties were not studied) have adopted teams but have chosen not to allow full self-management. Others allow partial degrees of self-management, requiring management clearance before decisions are made that will have a budgetary impact. Still others allow some budgetary decision making but set a ceiling above which approval must be secured before moving forward. Each of these represents variations on the theme of SMWTs.

Of all cities that had adopted SMWTs, more than 85 percent were council-manager cities and over one-half had populations of 100,000 and above. Large cities possibly have more need for interdepartmental collaboration and flexible decision-making structures; they may also have enough latitude to experiment with teams. As shown in Table 5–2, managers report they and city employees rate SMWTs positively. They also believe that SMWTs reduce the cost of service delivery, increase

Table 5–1   Self-managed work teams in U.S. cities

Has your city adopted SMWTs?	
Yes	27.5%
No	72.5%
Why did your city adopt SMWTs?	
To improve productivity	80.4%
Productivity improvement and benchmarking	5.4%
Other reasons	14.3%

Source: Adapted from Mary E. Guy and Seung-Bum Yang, "Conditions for Effective Self-Managed Work Teams: Lessons from the U.S. Experience," in *Central-Local Relations and Local Government Reform in Korea,* ed. Byong-Joon Kim and Glen Hahn Cope (South Korea: Korea Association for Policy Studies, 2003).

Table 5–2   Satisfaction with self-managed work teams

	Mean	Standard deviation
City manager satisfaction	3.71	.82
Employee satisfaction	3.71	.84
Citizen satisfaction	2.94	.80
Cost reduction	3.20	.89
Quality improvement	3.40	.83

Source: Adapted from Mary E. Guy and Seung-Bum Yang, "Conditions for Effective Self-Managed Work Teams: Lessons from the U.S. Experience," in *Central-Local Relations and Local Government Reform in Korea,* ed. Byong-Joon Kim and Glen Hahn Cope (South Korea: Korea Association for Policy Studies, 2003).

the quality of services, motivate employees, and ease the work of the manager. Regarding citizen perception, one respondent stated: "Citizens don't care as long as they get city services and taxes are not increased." Another city manager wrote, "I don't think they [citizens] care. They only care about outcomes." Managers take note: when government works right, it is invisible. Only when services are not delivered in a timely fashion do citizens notice.

For performance innovations to work, there must be congruence among all facets of the HR system. If SMWTs are the goal, then pay increases must be attached to team rather than individual performance. Workers should be selected who thrive when working in close collaboration with others; performance appraisals should evaluate the performance of the team and the individual's contribution to it; and raises should be pegged to performance of the team, not to performance of the individual. In other words, subsystems should encourage and reinforce the behavior patterns that are sought.

Emotional intelligence   Emotional intelligence refers to a person's ability to perceive and express emotion and to regulate it in oneself and in others. It is linked to skill in managing one's own emotion as well as others', and it contributes to performance in all jobs where interpersonal relations are important. Many interpersonal skills required in public service jobs, including the ability to work with others, self-confidence, self-discipline, and personal initiative, rely more on emotional intelligence than on traditional intellectual skills. To some degree, the term emotional intelligence is a more specific name for what has been called "street smarts." Emotional intelligence influences team performance, and the shift in workplaces to SMWTs has increased the attention that emotional intelligence receives. The relationship between cognitive skill and individual performance is well known, yet only recently has the importance of affective skill been noticed.

Emotional labor   Related to the concept of emotional intelligence is emotional labor. Those who staff the counter at the information desk are expected to greet the 100th visitor of the day with the same sincerity and grace as they greeted the first. Those who staff the phone lines for city hall or the county courthouse are expected to be nicer than nice. Caseworkers must care about strangers; administrative assistants must perceive their directors' moods and respond accordingly. This work is relational in nature and is called emotional labor.

Emotional labor is applicable to both men's and women's work but it is the emotions, such as caring and nurturing, required for relational tasks that are most often invisible in job descriptions, performance evaluations, and salary calculations. However, these are the emotions that are a mainstay of interpersonal relations, that grease the wheels so that people cooperate, stay on task, and work well together.

Employees who exercise emotional labor are essential to work teams. Traditional job descriptions require only cognitive intelligence, and they disregard emotion work—making it invisible even though it is essential if customer satisfaction and citizen satisfaction are to be achieved.

Legal issues in the changing workplace

Managers are responsible not only for doing the right things but also for doing things right. Case law continues to evolve in the areas of employer liability for workplace violence, sexual harassment, safeguards for disabled workers and family and medical leave. It is most important to put in place sound, written policies; train all employees so they are knowledgeable about the policies; and follow the policies when incidents occur. The advice of a good city or county attorney is also integral. Jurisdictions lose in court when they fail to follow their own written employment policies.

Workplace violence   Local government workers fall prey to workplace violence more often than workers in other enterprises. Law enforcement officers, social service employees, teachers, housing inspectors, and public works employees are in high-risk jobs, as are health-care employees, especially nurses who work in public health-care facilities. The Occupational Safety and Health Act (OSHA) of 1971 dictates that employers are responsible for any condition that represents a hazard to the life, safety, or psychological well-being of employees in the workplace. States have adopted varying statutes or policies that apply OSHA principles to local government. Civil law holds an employer responsible for negligent hiring, retention, or supervision. Although the courts are reluctant to hold employers liable for all acts of violence against workers, there is consensus that an employer and/or a manager who is aware of a danger or a harm has a duty to protect an employee who, while acting within the scope of employment, comes into imminent danger of serious harm. For example, social workers in rural counties in North Carolina were fearful because they sometimes worked in isolated situations. Counties then issued them cell phones. This is a change that does not sound like much, but it was a morale boost as well as a safety precaution.[8]

There are four types of workplace violence: violence by people unconnected to the workplace (robberies), acts committed by people who are related in some way to an employee (domestic violence, stalking), violence between employees, and violence by clients. Although media stories highlight employee-on-employee violence, only a miniscule number of people are murdered by a disgruntled fellow employee. Most women killed at work are victims of domestic violence or stalkers. Most men who are killed are victims of armed robberies. Regardless of the cause, employers are responsible for providing a safe workplace and for planning for possible crises. Courts have thus far been reluctant to hold employers legally liable for harm to employees. This is an area where the law is evolving.

Employee-on-employee and client-on-employee violence emerges from a convergence of factors: an individual's propensity for violence; a situation that pushes that person beyond the capacity to cope constructively, such as job change or job loss, financial problems, personal hardship or family stress; and a setting in which it is possible to act. In all cases, the employer's vigilance and preventive measures are required by federal and civil law. Sound judgment, teamwork, reasoned decision making, collaborative information gathering, and compassion will often prevent workplace violence, but this assumes that everyone has learned how to identify potential trouble spots and how to act when they occur. An effective policy contains instruction about behavioral indicators of potential violence and actions to take. Some employers combine sexual harassment with general workplace conduct standards; see, for example, www.cityofseattle.net/personnel/rules/rule_1.htm for Seattle's workplace harassment policy.

A workplace violence policy should:

- Define workplace violence in precise, concrete language
- Provide examples of unacceptable behavior
- Express commitment to the prevention of workplace violence
- State precisely the consequences of making threats or committing violent acts
- Outline the process by which preventive measures will be developed
- Encourage reporting of all incidents of violence
- Outline the confidential process by which employees can report incidents, including the proper recipient of the information

- Assure that no reprisals will be made against those who report
- Outline procedures for investigating and resolving complaints
- Describe how information about potential risks of violence will be communicated to employees
- Commit to provide support services to victims of violence
- Offer an employee assistance program so employees with personal problems can seek help
- Commit to train all levels of personnel in the terms of the policy
- Commit to monitor and regularly review the policy.

Sexual harassment   Sexual harassment is a violation of the Civil Rights Act of 1964, which forbade discrimination on the basis of sex. For a number of years, few claims were filed and far fewer prevailed. This changed with the passage of the Civil Rights Act of 1991, which provided a framework more conducive to legal action. It set standards for employers when they attempt to justify discriminatory actions or policies based on business necessity; it shifted the burden of proof to the employer after the plaintiff has established a prima facie case; and it provides the right to a jury trial along with compensatory and punitive damages. Sexual harassment case law is evolving not in a straight line but as a progression of squiggles. Decisions differ on the basis of which court hears the case, the specifics of the complaint, and the arguments of the defense. There is consensus over the essential elements, however.

Sexual harassment is defined as unwelcome sexual advances, requests for sexual favors, and other verbal or physical conduct of a sexual nature when one of the following three conditions exists:

- Submission to such conduct is either explicitly or implicitly made a term or condition of an individual's employment
- Submission to or rejection of such conduct by an individual is used as the basis for employment decisions adversely affecting such an individual
- Such conduct has the purpose or effect of unreasonably interfering with an individual's work performance or creating an intimidating, hostile, or offensive work environment.

Case law has clarified two types of harassment on the job: quid pro quo and hostile environment. The former occurs when a direct demand is made for sexual favors in return for jobs, promotions, pay raises or the like; hostile environment harassment applies where no direct quid pro quo has been demanded but where conditions are permitted or encouraged by superiors that cause the employee to feel pressured into tolerating or participating in sexual behaviors.

Sexual harassment case law   The 1994 case of *Smith v. City of Mobile* (Civ. Action No. 94-0236-B-S [1994]) tested the sufficiency of Mobile, Alabama's sexual harassment policy and procedure in a hostile environment. Faced with serious charges of sexual misconduct by one of the city's supervisors, the city took immediate action by transferring the accuser to another department at her request so that the alleged harassment would cease immediately. A thorough investigation by an objective third party, although it did not bear out the charges of sexual harassment, included testimony from co-workers of both the alleged victim and the alleged harasser. Not finding sufficient cause to dismiss the alleged harasser, the city took the remedial action of reissuing its sexual harassment policy and ordered that it be posted conspicuously in every department. The court acknowledged the benefit of this action and found the city not at fault.

The Mobile case demonstrates how an employer can walk the fine line between a sexual harassment lawsuit from the victim and charges of wrongful discharge on the part of the accused. The court decreed that the city could be held liable only if it knew or should have known of harassment and failed to take action. Because the city investigated swiftly and acted to stop the harassment, the city avoided liability even though it did not discipline the harasser.

The 1995 case of *Fuller v. City of Oakland* (47 F.3d 1523 [9th Cir.]) presents a different outcome. The case tested the sufficiency of the employer's policies and procedures in an instance when the police department conducted an internal affairs investigation and offered the plaintiff a transfer. She refused the transfer, and the harassment later stopped voluntarily. The court found that the employer's actions were inconsistent with its stated policy of strong disapproval of sexual harassment; therefore the court judged that the city could not avoid liability.

The difference that gender makes becomes obvious in sexual harassment training sessions. Women perceive sexual innuendo and harassing behavior as more threatening than men do; this difference accounts for much of the confusion over acts that to women are harassing and to men are harmless. Training sessions that involve open communication about miscommunication are constructive venues for sensitizing employees to how the opposite sex perceives behavior. Combined with a policy and procedure statement with which all employees are familiar, training will help to prevent claims of harassment. An employer that has a sound policy and procedure in place, has trained its employees in the policy, and acts swiftly in accord with the policy when sexual harassment becomes known is likely to prevail if the claim progresses to legal action.[9]

Public work, private lives   Effective legislation reflects a nation's values and traditions. Two relatively recent laws, the Americans with Disabilities Act (ADA) and the Family and Medical Leave Act (FMLA), were written to ensure flexibility for employees who do not fit the mold of the perfect employee unfettered by family obligations, health problems, or physical limitations. The ADA was passed in 1990 to eliminate discrimination against individuals with physical or mental impairment that substantially limits one or more of the major life activities, individuals with a record of such an impairment, and individuals regarded as having such an impairment. The function of the law is to make employers disability blind as they make personnel decisions and disability conscious as they accommodate employee needs. Remedies for violations of the ADA are the same as for noncompliance with the Civil Rights Acts of 1964 and 1991. As the years pass, the law has been used to test not only an employer's reasonable accommodation to an employee's disability, but also to test an employer's liability in cases when an employee has an extended illness.

To establish a prima facie case of discrimination under the ADA, a plaintiff must show:

- He or she is disabled

- He or she is a qualified individual
- He or she was subjected to unlawful discrimination because of her disability.

The ADA of 1990, as amended by 42 USC §12101 et seq., prohibits covered employers from discriminating against an employee on the basis of known physical or mental impairments, provided that the employee is a qualified individual with a disability. A qualified individual with a disability must satisfy the requisite skill, experience, education, and other job-related requirements of the employment position and, with or without reasonable accommodation, the individual must be able to perform the essential functions of the position. Courts have chosen to interpret the law strictly—narrowly defining terms and usually deciding for the employer rather than for the plaintiff.

The Family and Medical Leave Act of 1993 (FMLA) covers all employers with 50 or more employees who are employed for at least 20 weeks during the year. Covered employees are entitled to 12 weeks of unpaid leave during any 12-month period for the recent birth or adoption of a child; to care for an ill child, spouse, or parent; or for the employee's own health condition that precludes working. Because FMLA was intentionally couched in somewhat vague terms, only partially clarified by the final regulations promulgated by the U.S. Department of Labor in 1995, employers must look to the courts for guidance in complying. The courts, in turn, look to legislative intent. The purposes of the act include:

- Balance demands of the workplace with the needs of families
- Promote stability and economic security in families
- Entitle employees to take a reasonable amount of leave for medical reasons; for the birth, adoption, or fostering of a child; or to care for a child, spouse, or dependent parent with a serious health condition
- Accommodate the legitimate interests of employers.

To state a claim under the FMLA, a plaintiff must prove three elements at trial:

- The employee availed himself or herself of a protected right under the FMLA
- The employee suffered an adverse employment decision
- There is a causal connection between the protected activity and the adverse employment decision.

The importance of policy and training   The rule of thumb for the manager in all these areas—workplace violence, sexual harassment, reasonable accommodation for disability, and family and medical leave—is that prevention is the best policy. Develop sound, written policies and procedures to govern workplace behavior. Communicate these policies to all employees in as many ways as possible, and make sure that written copies are accessible to everyone. Ensure that refresher training in these policies occurs on a regular basis. Most important, make sure everyone follows the policies.

A review of case law shows that complaints rarely have "clean margins." Instead, plaintiffs often claim simultaneous violations of ADA and of FMLA. Court testimony reveals managerial frustration with the employee's use of leave as well as employee perceptions that supervisors are spiteful. It is usually obvious that tensions mounted in the office before the event that resulted in the legal claim. Early action may nip problems in the bud.

Budgeting and managing financial resources

Failure to manage money wisely has shortened the careers of more than a few local government managers. Financial management comprises budget development and execution, debt management, revenue management, purchasing, short- and long-term cash and investment management, risk management, financial accounting and reporting, internal auditing, and management controls. All these elements should be integrated within one comprehensive financial management system. No one can be expert in all of these areas, but the successful manager has to know enough about each to build an effective financial management team.

All federal agencies, as well as some local governments such as Scottsdale, Arizona; Wayne County, Michigan; and Cook County, Illinois, have created the position of chief finance officer (CFO) to enable top financial managers to better contribute to the making of high-level strategic policy.

The ICMA Task Force on Continuing Education and Professional Development has identified competencies and skills in both budgeting and financial analysis.[10] Managers are expected to know about budgeting principles and practices, financial control systems, characteristics of revenue sources, ways to forecast revenues and expenditures, and to be skillful in communicating financial information. They must know how to assess the fiscal condition of their communities, be able to determine the cost-effectiveness of programs, and possess skills in the analytical techniques needed to compare alternative expenditure and financing strategies.[11]

I got into city management because of a desire to do public service. I started out in the numbers game and learning the money side of it. Most government is dictated by the budget.

Debra Brooks Feazelle

Monitoring financial health

A community should have a financial checkup from time to time. Just as physicians learn diagnostic frameworks to analyze the health of their patients, local managers need a diagnostic framework to discern the financial health of their governments and communities. Private companies that issue credit ratings for governments use their own proprietary diagnostic frameworks. For local managers, ICMA has developed an excellent diagnostic framework, the Financial Trend Monitoring System (FTMS).[12] It encompasses information about organizational factors, environmental factors, and financial factors.

Analyzing the organizational factors requires a top-level review of both legislative policies and management practices. A legislative commitment to "no new taxes" is an example of an organizational factor that can make it difficult to balance the budget when recession causes a drop in revenues. Environmental factors include national and regional economic conditions, unfunded state mandates, changes in citizens' attitudes toward taxes and services, and the potential effects of disasters and emergencies. Specific community needs and resources, tracked through community trends such as a growing or aging population, declining property values, or increased unemployment should be emphasized. Financial factors include revenues, expenditures, operating position, debt, unfunded liability, and capital plant. Annual reviews of these data and trends, perhaps at the outset of budget hearings or in conjunction with a review of comprehensive plans, can help elected officials think strategically about needs and priorities.

Budget development and execution

Budgeting is the set of activities that is necessary to develop, implement, and evaluate a plan for the provision of services and capital assets. The budget is that plan.

The budget is the most important plan of any government because through it, all other plans are accomplished. The Government Finance Officers Association (GFOA) gives Distinguished Budget Presentation Awards to local governments that demonstrate proficiency in four areas:

- As a policy document, a budget should provide a coherent description and rationale for major policies.

- As a financial plan, a budget should provide a consolidated picture of all operations: it should explain revenues, debt, expenditures, and projected year-end financial condition.

- As an operations guide, a budget should provide direction to operating managers and indicate the performance objectives and measures for which officials are to be held accountable.

- As a communication device, the budget must be useful to not only elected officials but also to citizens, the media, the business community, and other stakeholders as well.[13]

In the early 1930s, ICMA sought close linkages among planning, programming, and budgeting.[14] ICMA developed an executive management–oriented budget system that called for preparation of budgets and enactment of appropriations on a program basis and for the setting of goals and objectives. It emphasized the establishment of cost standards, performance measurements, and monthly reporting of accomplishments relative to costs. In that budgeting system, ICMA anticipated nearly every subsequent budget reform for the remainder of the twentieth century.

In the 1990s, ICMA participated with other national organizations in the establishment of the National Advisory Council on State and Local Budgeting (NACSLB). In 1998, the NACSLB released a set of recommended budget principles and 59 specific practices that closely mirror the budgeting system that ICMA had pioneered nearly seven decades earlier.[15] Now, for the first time, local governments have a comprehensive set of principles and practices around which they can organize their planning and budgeting activities. The recommended practices call for a goal-oriented approach to budgeting that encompasses planning, development, adoption, execution, and evaluation phases of the budget.

Framework for budgeting established by the NACSLB

- **Principle I**   Establish broad goals to guide government decision making
  Element 1. Assess community needs, priorities, challenges, and opportunities
  Element 2. Identify opportunities and challenges for government services, capital assets, and management
  Element 3. Develop and disseminate broad goals

- **Principle II**   Develop approaches to achieve goals
  Element 4. Adopt financial policies
  Element 5. Develop programmatic, operating, and capital policies and plans

  Element 6. Develop programs and services that are consistent with policies and plans
  Element 7. Develop management strategies

- **Principle III**   Develop a budget with approaches to achieve goals
  Element 8. Develop a process for preparing and adopting a budget
  Element 9. Develop and evaluate financial options
  Element 10. Make choices necessary to adopt a budget

- **Principle IV**   Evaluate performance and make adjustments
  Element 11. Monitor, measure, and evaluate performance
  Element 12. Make adjustments as needed

The NCSLB-recommended practices are not mandatory; they are recommended practices that can be used by governments to improve their own budget processes. Through the GFOA, local governments can now easily access Web-based examples of exemplary applications of each of the recommended budget practices that have been developed and applied in the field. For example, the use of citizen priority boards by the city of Dayton, Ohio, to obtain stakeholder input is cited as exemplary, as is Glendale, Arizona's long-range financial planning. It is likely that no local government could ever attain exemplary status in all areas of recommended budget practices, but these examples provide useful guidance.

Capital programming, project management, and debt management

Planning for the acquisition, maintenance, and replacement of capital facilities is usually reflected in a separate capital budget that complements the operating budget. Jurisdictions with a good capital programming and budgeting process keep abreast of the public infrastructure needs of the community—streets, sewers, schools, public buildings, computers, and communication networks, for example. Although the revenues and expenditures of an operating budget need to be balanced annually (borrowing beyond a budget year to finance current operations is a danger signal of fiscal crisis), it is prudent to incur long-term debt to finance some forms of infrastructure. A project that can generate its own revenues sufficient to offset many of its costs (such as a toll road, swimming pool, or performing arts center) is suitable as a capital project. Similarly, in rapid-growth communities, it is wise to borrow money to build larger projects (such as wider roads or bigger sewer lines) at the outset, rather than build too-small infrastructure that will have to undergo costly expansion later. With debt financing, future residents' taxes and user fees help pay for the facilities they will use.

Elected officials have a difficult job. They hear from neighborhoods that are angry about things like traffic problems, and they demand traffic lights and speed bumps. But the money is not always there to address the needs that citizens have.

Tom Mauk

When a jurisdiction decides to borrow money to finance capital projects, it needs to develop sound debt management policies. Debt must be managed wisely to obtain a good credit rating, and higher ratings save taxpayers money through lower interest rates. Government policies that identify criteria for incurring debt and that limit the debt that can be incurred are essential. When a government decides to market debt, it enters the arcane and highly sophisticated world of municipal finance,[16] a world inhabited by specialists—bond advisers, bond counsel, underwriters, mutual fund managers, and insurers. Specialized advice and counsel from experts who have solid track records are advised when entering this world.

Budgets, especially capital budgets, should be linked to a community's comprehensive plan and to its long-range functional area plans (e.g., transportation). Those plans, in turn, should be based on assessments of current and future community needs. Citizen participation and guidance are important in identifying those needs because failure to seek citizen participation increases the likelihood that voters will reject a capital project.

Once the needs for capital facilities are identified, they must be translated into specific projects for either the construction of new facilities or the maintenance of existing infrastructure.

Project management skills on the part of project managers are an essential component of good capital programming and budgeting. Project managers identify all activities that must be performed at each stage of a project, identify the resources needed to accomplish each step, assign responsibility for accomplishing them, and continuously monitor progress toward the project's completion. Fortunately, planners and budgeters can now use moderately priced project management software to plan, budget, and manage capital projects. Good project management seeks to avoid costly change orders to ongoing construction projects as well as the costly litigation that often accompanies major construction and technology projects.

Revenue management

Apart from an occasional sale of property and earnings from investments, jurisdictions have six ways to obtain revenues: taxing, charging user fees, levying fines, charging fees for permits, receiving federal or state intergovernmental transfers, and borrowing. Businesses and individuals can be taxed in three ways: when they obtain money (income taxes), when they spend money (sales taxes), and when they have some form of wealth (real or intangible property taxes). Most states sharply constrain the ability of local governments to tax sales and incomes, but in some states taxes that are not based on property have approached or passed property taxes in importance. Property taxes often lag behind the growth rates of local economies and are frequently insufficient to meet local needs. Consequently, managers are often instructed to search for new forms of revenues.

User charges are a popular alternate revenue source; they substitute for tax-based funding of some services. Solid-waste collection services were once commonly funded by property taxes, but user charges for those services are the norm in most local governments today. In locales with considerable amounts of new real estate development, where allowed by state law, local governments charge developers "impact fees" that are used to build infrastructure to support the new development. It is expected that developers, in turn, will pass the cost of fees on to buyers in the form of higher real estate prices. Utility franchise fees, paid by utility companies such as cable and telephone companies to do business within jurisdictional boundaries, are important revenue sources to many local governments.

Several criteria should be used to evaluate changes in revenue policies:

- *Adequacy*   Will the change yield the needed revenues? When taxes or other charges are levied on businesses, questions arise about whether the burden will be borne by business owners or be shifted to employees in the form of lower pay or to customers in the form of higher prices.

- *Overlapping burden*   How much do residents also pay to other governments? This is an issue that must be raised when a jurisdiction considers an increase in taxes—in sales taxes or property taxes, for example—that residents pay elsewhere.

- *Equity*   Is a revenue source fair? Local government managers must keep in mind that most jurisdictions have regressive revenue structures—they exact a larger portion of their incomes from the least affluent residents. If this is the fact and it is not disclosed, the least influential members of a community may be the most adversely affected without benefit of public awareness or debate. Some argue that managers are morally obligated to disclose the equity implications of revenue changes.

Forecasting future receipts is an often neglected aspect of revenue management. Good forecasting requires accurate records of past receipts and using them to build forecasts. Few local governments develop elaborate economic forecasting models that are commonly used at the state level. On the other hand, inexpensive software can be used by local governments to forecast revenues under varied sets of assumptions. Only those methods that staff can understand, and explain well, should be used. Also, managers should not hesitate to question and challenge the assumptions upon which revenue and expenditures forecasts are based. Experience has shown that good forecasters are those who are most likely to challenge their own assumptions.

Local leaders are often tempted to offer special deals—reductions in taxes or fees—to entice a company to locate nearby. When competition between governments leads to excessive giveaways, new development can lay an additional tax burden on taxpayers or cause underinvestment in education and infrastructure that are essential for building a high-wage economy. Effective managers ensure that their staffs carefully investigate the potential costs—not just the benefits—of offering financial deals to attract companies. (For more on economic development, see Chapter 4.)

Purchasing, privatization, and smart buying

Governments produce goods, such as roads, services, and recreation. Consequently, every government faces make-or-buy decisions. It must choose whether to produce things with its own employees or with outside contractors. Few would build a road with the jurisdiction's own workforce, but many use jurisdiction employees to maintain roads. Most hire their own police officers, but some contract with other governments to provide law enforcement. Purchasing (also known as procurement) is as old as local governments. The nature of purchasing is changing, however, due to electronic technology, especially the Internet and desktop computing, and the shift in popular attitudes in favor of privatization. Governments, therefore, are relying more heavily on purchasing to provide goods and services, and local governments must be smart buyers.

Government purchasing must be done scrupulously within a formal legal framework. Many governments once behaved like private businesses, which can buy from whomever they please, including close relatives; but the Progressive reform movement of a century ago produced a legal framework for purchasing that still prevails today. That framework requires governments to solicit bids in a competitive manner and award contracts on the basis of a formal analysis of objective factors such as costs, quality, and vendor reliability. When competition is limited, or one contractor is in a uniquely advantageous position to provide goods or services, purchasing regulations typically allow a government to negotiate a contract with that provider. Negotiated contracts are common for social services, where competitors are often few and government does not want to disrupt continuity of care. Unfortunately, it is common for disgruntled contractors or losing bidders to bring lawsuits against governments. Well-trained professional purchasing specialists can help to avert expensive legal proceedings.

Laws and regulations that govern procurement are often outmoded to the point that they inhibit some of the practices that produce the best value. For information technology, for example, the best way to get value for the taxpayer is to hire talented purchasing agents and create the conditions through which they can persistently press for value when they are buying electronically related technology and services.[17]

Government becomes a smart buyer when it creates a first-rate purchasing office imbued with a sense of value seeking. Such an office provides its buyers with the authority to work creatively with contractors to solve problems and to build performance incentives and measures into contracts. Smart buying, on the other hand, is far less likely to happen if bidders for contracts are allowed to use connections with elected officials to influence purchasing decisions. Purchasing laws should disqualify offending bidders.

Cash and investment management

Government managers have a stewardship obligation to assure taxpayers that their monies are handled carefully and invested wisely. Even small governments receive and disburse large amounts of money. Although the management of cash and investments is a specialized activity, it is still a management responsibility.

Well-managed governments will quickly consolidate cash receipts so that they can be invested rather than sit idle without earning interest. The flows of cash into and out of a government should be managed carefully to assure that

- The government is liquid (has cash on hand when it is needed)
- Investments are managed to produce reasonable yields
- The amount of risk associated with the government's investments is well understood and managed within carefully developed investment parameters.

If governments manage their own pension funds, the amounts invested can be large, and professional management of retirement funds is essential. Although locally managed retirement systems are common, many states enable local government employees to participate in a state-managed system. Various organizations, such as state associations for local governments, manage pension and related-benefits funds.

The governance structure should be capable of selecting sound investment managers, monitoring their progress, and deciding investment policy. Managers must guard against accruing large, unfunded pension liabilities, which come about by promising additional retirement benefits to employees such as police and fire fighters, but not allocating enough to make the needed investments in their pension funds. Monitoring unfunded pension liability is integral to the ICMA Financial Trend Monitoring System.

Risk management

Governments engage in activities that can cause substantial losses of money and even bodily harm. These activities should be managed in ways that reduce the likelihood of incurring such losses. The process of identifying risk and taking steps to avert losses is called risk management. Assessing the potential for losses associated with investments is integral to investment management. Other categories of loss that a community can face include property loss exposures, liability loss exposures, and exposures to employee injury. Risk management overlaps with disaster planning for the government's own continuity of operations.

Many actions of government employees can cause harm to citizens, and governments are often legally responsible for compensating citizens for that harm. Appropriate policies should be adopted to reduce the likelihood of causing harm. For example, to reduce the likelihood of harming innocent bystanders, police often adopt policies that authorize high-speed pursuit only to apprehend imminently dangerous violators such as armed robbers on a crime spree.

Risk managers should challenge any policies that sanction unnecessarily risky behavior. They should also ensure that all offices have well-crafted policies and procedures for dealing with workplace violence. Finally, risk management policies need to address questions of self-insuring, sharing risks with other governments in pooled arrangements, and purchasing catastrophic insurance coverage.

Financial accounting and reporting

Accountants are experts in capturing information about financial transactions, recording that information, analyzing it, and reporting it to stakeholders who need to know about a government's finances. It is their professional responsibility to work with management to design financial information systems that help managers monitor progress and make decisions. Nevertheless, friction sometimes occurs between managers and accounting professionals. To better manage this relationship, it is helpful if managers understand the role and responsibilities of accountants.

Good accountants pay close and careful attention to the details of what they do. The best accounting is that done according to a series of generally accepted accounting principles (GAAP) that describe specific procedures for accountants to follow and formats for the financial reports issued by a government. The recognized standards-setting authority for state and local governments in the United States is a nonprofit body known as the Governmental Accounting Standards Board (GASB). For accountants whose governments follow GAAP, a pronouncement by the GASB has the strength of a legal proclamation. Accountants in recent years have had to learn a new, more comprehensive, and more user-oriented format for reporting government finances. Failure to follow GAAP in all respects can lead to a qualified audit opinion—an accountant's worst nightmare—in which an outside auditor expresses reservations about the accuracy of financial reports and declines to give a clean opinion. If accountants feel that management wants to alter accounting procedures or make statements in a financial report that could jeopardize the prospects of getting a favorable audit, they feel professionally obligated to resist management.

Some individual accountants may simply resist changes that should in fact be made, perhaps because they are using outmoded accounting software that makes it difficult to serve the information needs of managers. Effective managers need to learn enough about accounting processes to recognize the difference between professionally responsible resistance and outright unwillingness to change.

Auditing and management controls

Effective managers learn not to fear auditors but, instead, to use audits strategically to improve the operations of a government. There are two categories of auditors: internal auditors who work for the jurisdiction's executive and external independent auditors. There are also two types of audits: financial audits that review a government's financial operations to assure that reports fairly present the status of its finances, and performance audits that focus on the processes, costs, outputs, and outcomes of programs. Each type of audit can also include a review of ongoing activities to assure that they are in compliance with legal requirements. Both financial and performance audits can provide valuable information to improve the operations of a government.

Newly appointed managers are sometimes wise to request that audits be done of the operations for which they are responsible. The information gained can be used to remedy problems before the manager has been on the job long enough to receive blame for them. Auditors are trained to look for weaknesses and shortcomings, but they can also be valuable for recognizing the strengths (called "noteworthy accomplishments" in the jargon of auditing) of an organization. Managers should encourage auditors to inform them of noteworthy accomplishments as well as shortcomings. Both types of information are essential for framing well-conceived strategies.

Auditors can be especially helpful to managers when they review a government's internal controls, which are also called management controls to underscore that managers are responsible for implementing them. Internal controls are the various rules and procedures, such as separating the receipt of cash from the disbursement of it, that are applied to prevent fraud, waste, and abuse of money and other resources. The best training programs on management controls emphasize that internal controls begin with an overall climate of ethics and stewardship that is encouraged by management. Without strong organizational commitments to ethical behavior and to the concept that all public servants owe their fellow taxpayers proper management of their money, the specific techniques that are collectively called internal controls could easily fail.

An effective financial management team

Managers are responsible for seeing that the components of a government's financial operation work together smoothly. One way of meshing these operations is to emphasize the development of an integrated financial management system, often referred to as an enterprise resource planning (ERP) system. The meetings and team building required to develop and implement such a system will often reveal junctures where problems exist and how differences in perspective can lead to struggles for authority. Local governments today are fortunate because good, commercial, off-the-shelf software exists around which a comprehensive system can be built. The manager needs to set the tone by regularly reminding all concerned that financial services should be customer oriented, in other words, all employees of the financial units of a government should be attuned to serving the needs of internal customers (the other units of a government) as well as external customers (the citizen-owners of a government). Effective management of financial resources requires effective management of both human resources and information resources. Developing an integrated financial management system makes that abundantly clear.

Managing information technology resources

Human resource management and financial management have long been essential components of local government administration; information technology (IT) is a newcomer. IT still suffers from the perception that it is for technically savvy managers, system analysts, programmers, and even webmasters to handle. The reality is that IT is integral to local government management at all levels. Arvada, Colorado, and Fairfax County, Virginia, are just two of many local governments that have adopted comprehensive IT plans, recognizing the strategic importance of IT to the mission of the organization.[18] Like Fairfax County, many medium to large local governments have added a chief information officer (CIO) to the management team.

IT performance criteria   *Governing* magazine's annual Government Performance Project evaluates city and county IT with these questions:

- Do IT systems provide information that adequately supports managers' needs and strategic goals?

- Do IT systems form a coherent architecture, and are strategies in place to support present and future coherence in architecture?

- Does the government conduct meaningful multiyear technology planning that includes an IT planning process that is sufficiently centralized, providing managers appropriate input into the planning process and creating government-wide and agency IT plans?

- Is IT training adequate for end users and technology specialists?

- Can the government evaluate and validate the extent to which IT benefits justify investment?

- Can the government procure needed IT systems in a timely manner with appropriate financial controls?

- Do IT systems support the government's ability to communicate with and provide services to its citizens?

Source: "How We Grade Them," *Governing* (February 2002): 37.

Now e-government (or e-gov), the common label for Web-based government applications, has brought IT to the forefront of every local government manager's agenda. Whether for promises of cost savings, better service, increased capacity, or a host of other benefits, e-gov efforts are trumpeted in every trade publication. Despite the good publicity, many of these efforts fail. A recent ICMA study finds that many of the expected benefits, such as cost savings and downsizing, have yet to be realized.[19] Government IT projects over the past three decades offer several lessons for managers:

- New technologies are not fundamentally different from those of the past. E-gov is a natural evolution of computing from 1970s mainframes, to 1980s PCs, to 1990s local area networks, to today's Web; and the same principles of management apply. Local governments still follow the same rules and procedures for budgeting, for example, but an automated budget process like the one used in Post Falls, Idaho, streamlines information gathering, saves paper, and makes it much easier for the city to share and explain budget information to citizens.

- Technology projects may fail because of poor technical understanding, inadequate financial resources, and poor project management, but they also falter because of poor attention to basic management issues like defining the client and training personnel.[20] If government staff do not learn to use a new imaging system, the local government's investment in hardware may be wasted.

- New technologies make it possible to deliver services in wholly new ways—sometimes called "business re-engineering." Simply topping an existing permit process with an online form, with no consideration for the efficiency of the process itself, fails to take advantage of IT benefits. "You need to spend time up front understanding and improving the process. The last thing you want to do is automate a bad process. You'll just get garbage at the speed of light."[21]

- Use of technology tends to follow an organization's way of doing things and support the existing political and policy structure.[22] New research on e-gov is already showing that organizations that are open and adaptable have greater success and are more likely to adopt e-gov approaches than less flexible organizations.[23, 24] Technology by itself will not usher major changes into government operations, and managers should be leery of anyone making such promises.

- It is a good idea to start small with IT innovations, especially e-government applications, in order to test the waters—to see whether the benefits justify the expense. For example, although the ultimate goal for a new Web service might be coordination across several agencies—fee payments online is one example—the manager should limit the initial application to a solution that minimizes the number of agencies involved. Once successful in a smaller area, the jurisdiction can expand the service.

Managers should be healthy skeptics, never forgetting the primary goals and values of public service. The job is to serve the public, not the technology. Managers do not need to understand technical details; they should focus instead on what technologies can do for the community. What are reasonable benefit expectations? What are the costs? Does the organization have the needed resources? Being IT savvy means understanding that technology involves not only technical issues but also managerial and policy issues.

What is e-government?   Most people immediately think of government Web sites when they think of e-government. E-government also applies to less-visible Web-based applications that improve internal local government processes like budgeting, asset management, traffic control, and procurement. According to an ICMA survey conducted in 2002, the majority of local governments with populations over 25,000 now use an intranet; almost two-thirds of those with populations over 10,000 use a geographic information system (GIS); and two out of five local governments now purchase equipment online.

According to the same 2002 survey, three out of four local governments maintain Web sites. The most common Web site applications, aside from sharing of general information, include online delivery of requested local government records, online service requests to the local government (for example, for pothole repair), and online communication with local government officials. Online payment of taxes, utility bills, and fees and online completion of permit and business license applications have been implemented by only a few local governments.

Sources: Evelina R. Moulder, "E-Government: Trends, Opportunities, and Challenges," in *The Municipal Year Book 2003* (Washington, D.C.: ICMA, 2003); Evelina Moulder, *E-Government: What Citizens Want; What Local Governments Provide*, Special Data Issue no. 5 (2002) (Washington, D.C.: ICMA, 2002); and Evelina Moulder, *Inside E-Government: Applications for Staff*, Special Data Issue, no. 6 (Washington, D.C.: ICMA, 2002).

Technical, managerial, and political concerns

The manager must consider technical, managerial, and political issues when managing IT resources. Stability of the technology is an example of an important technical issue: Is the technology being evaluated for purchase considered a proven technology? Avoid "bleeding edge" technology despite its tempting coolness factor. Will the technology integrate into existing hardware and software? Technical incompatibilities and complications can be costly to a jurisdiction that implements untried or very new technologies. Managerial issues concern personnel and training, deciding whether to outsource, developing an organizational structure for IT operations, and providing project planning and evaluation skills. Political and policy issues include citizen expectations, pressure from elected officials (who are being lobbied by vendors), and legal requirements for handling and providing information (which can sometimes conflict, as when citizen privacy collides with freedom of information).

Technical, managerial, and political issues are usually inseparable. For example, complex and overlapping questions arise when a jurisdiction ponders an online permitting application: Should it be built in-house or contracted out? If it is designed in-house, can it be maintained? If a vendor maintains it, how can accuracy, security, privacy, and information access be addressed? What exactly will the application do: provide electronic copies of applications for download or actually process them online? Should the application completely replace a paper process? Does that limit access to only citizens with Internet connections? Should the application be designed to handle multiple permitting processes across agencies, or just one? What if a council or commission member has a preferred vendor, or despises one, for reasons unrelated to the quality of their proposal? How will the application's operating costs be covered? Can cost savings be assumed? What about charging a user fee for the system? If so, how much should it be in comparison with any paper-based fees?

A geographic information system (GIS) is a good example of a technology that can bring privacy, efficiency, and effectiveness goals into conflict. GIS databases can expose AIDS patients and lead criminals to vulnerable children, but they can also help police pinpoint drug markets and chop shops. GIS greatly improves the manager's ability to communicate with staff, elected officials, and citizens; but managers must monitor carefully how it is implemented and always balance citizen privacy concerns. Managers will also face the issue of AVL, automatic vehicle location, which upsets both police officers and public works employees.

In sum, technologies should always be evaluated as applications that serve the public, directly or indirectly. The importance of remembering to address technical, managerial, and political concerns cannot be overstated. See page 142 for a description of Miami-Dade County touch-screen voting for a case in point.

Critical issues in IT management: What a manager should know

Lessons from the field provide insight into technical, managerial, and political concerns that are likely to be encountered in IT management. IT challenges arrive as project proposals for online permitting, webcasting of commission meetings, mobile meter reading, and automated budgeting. Proposals will come from all quarters—employees, vendors, elected officials, and citizens.

Complicating the landscape is the fact that what works for one jurisdiction may not work for another, if for no other reason than the level of resources and support varies from government to government. The Gartner Group, a respected government IT management consulting firm, notes that more than 60 percent of large IT projects fail.[25] Neglecting a basic evaluation of the potential application can be one cause of failure. Sophisticated evaluation techniques, many touted by vendors as proprietary methodologies, can be useful for very large applications; but for smaller projects, complicated methodologies can be overkill. The professional IT staff can produce a managerial summary instead. For the evaluation, a manager must keep in mind personnel capabilities and costs, possible benefits in terms of not only cost savings but also service improvement, the role of vendors, and the local government's relationship with vendors.

What personnel capabilities will be needed and what will be the cost? Estimating cost is tricky. Too often, hardware and software are assumed to be the only costs. Whether employees have the technical skill and time to build an application is usually considered in the evaluation, but the next question is often forgotten: Do employees have the time and expertise to maintain it? Hardware and software are not the major expenses of an application; training and maintenance are. Whether IT staff build the product or a vendor develops it, employees must like and understand it; otherwise the entire operation must be outsourced to reach its potential. Steven Reneker, CIO of Riverside County, California, says that 90 percent of the county's IT projects get resources only for hardware and software. Implementation, training, and maintenance costs have to be absorbed, which can result in reduced service levels.[26] Application support, training, and maintenance often take more than 50 percent of any budget, and such costs must be considered in any proposal.

What benefits can be expected? Traditionally, data processing and storage applications were evaluated by implementation timelines, potential political difficulties, and cost; and the lowest cost or best cost-savings was used. As newer IT applications promise measurable benefits, however, evaluation of potential and existing projects should be more sophisticated.

Experience demonstrates that promised savings tend to be exaggerated. For example, efficiency gains from an online system seldom reduce staffing costs. Pent-up service demands and the need to continue to offer services in the traditional way (to insure access to those with disabilities or without Web capabilities) often preclude staff reductions. The new application may also increase demand. And the new application must be supported.

Improved service delivery and better customer satisfaction are often cited as benefits of new technology, but in an era of tight budgets, local governments should do their best to demonstrate more tangible benefits with clear performance measures. These need not always be in monetary terms. For example, an online kennel for an animal shelter can be evaluated by tracking adoption rates. If the local government intends to reduce its printing costs by posting downloadable forms online, it must measure the demand for printed forms. Has it gone down? What about incorrectly completed forms? It may be that before the local government provided forms online, citizens completed the form onsite with staff assistance or review. If they download it, they likely completed it at home and then dropped it off, with a greater chance of error.

Benefits are sometimes intangible. For example, a GIS can improve decisions regarding land use, but it is difficult to quantify this benefit.

What will be the role of vendors? Government IT faces significant challenges in working with IT vendors. Many local governments do not require bids on professional services contracts—the category of much IT work—which increases the chances of pressures from elected officials and faulty vendor relations.

Miami-Dade voting machines   After the controversial 2000 presidential election, Miami-Dade County, Florida, purchased 7,200 touch-screen voting machines from Election Systems and Software (ES&S) for $24.5 million. The screens had never actually been used for a real election, and the contract terms included virtually no vendor on-site support. The 2002 primaries proved disastrous, with significant operational problems. The November general election went fairly smoothly, but only after the county mobilized massive numbers of workers at a cost of $5 million.

Despite the problems, Miami-Dade paid ES&S almost 90 percent of the contract amount after the primaries. County attorneys claim the company could have abandoned the jurisdiction before the November elections.

An ongoing investigation has prompted speculation that the inspector general's office may even recommend selling the voting machines back to ES&S or to another county.

Source: Karl Ross, "Payment for Vote Machines Disgusts Commissioner," *Miami Herald* (26 February 2003), 5B, www.herald.com.

Many jurisdictions also lack the technical expertise to adequately manage the procurement of technical systems. The manager is responsible for making sure that the government has good advice and a sound procurement process in place.

To avoid cost overruns, the local government needs to either avoid multiyear contracts for application development, especially contracts that extend beyond the political cycle, or retain the ability to back out if not satisfied with a vendor.

Finally, local government should look for vendors with government experience. E-gov success relies on a clear understanding of the uniqueness of government work; firms hoping to transplant a business application usually fail.

Critical issues in e-government management: What the manager needs to know

The public face of e-government, the local government Web site, is a visible communications tool that the manager will want to ensure is managed carefully. E-gov applications often are built on a *Field of Dreams* philosophy: "if we build it, they will come." Sometimes potential users do not rush to the product, and sometimes they overload the system. A series of management decisions will determine whether the outcome achieves a balance.

A local government need not develop its Web site from scratch. Many vendors offer full site development services. However, procurement of e-government applications poses special challenges. Local governments often have difficulties forming requests for services. Because e-gov is transforming the way government works, not just automating an online process, simply asking for bids to create a Web site is ambiguous and misses the point. Contracting for the work in stages is the best strategy. A local government manager can first bring in an outside firm to help re-engineer processes to be put online. Once an organization knows how it wants the process to work, the description should be outlined in a request for bids.

Many smaller governments get offers from vendors to host government Web sites for free or for dramatically reduced rates. These relationships can introduce problems. Citizens sometimes cannot discern whether such sites offer official government information or private marketing. Also, if a jurisdiction subsequently decides to create its own site, the vendor may balk at removing outdated information or relinquishing the Web address. If vendors host actual transactions for government, significant privacy and security concerns arise. Even a seemingly cost-free arrangement with an employee can cause problems if the employee leaves the government and takes away the necessary knowledge for maintaining the site.

Recognizing the needs of smaller local governments, many states offer assistance ranging from simple hosting to application development and support. Local governments should check with their state IT offices to learn whether such assistance is available. ICMA, in partnership with the Minnesota League of Cities, Qwest, and Microsoft, offers GovOffice, a Web site creation and content management system. (See www.govoffice.com.)

Managers need to ask a series of questions about any proposed Web applications:

Who are the customers and what are their expectations?   E-government applications can be government to government, government to business, or government to citizen. Of these, government-to-business applications (for example, licensing and building permits) are the most common. This framework clarifies the nature of the relationships and expectations, but it is simplistic: it ignores the reality that most applications should cut across these lines.

For example, consider a common government-to-business transaction: building permits. Builders can use the Web to file permit requests, check permit status, and schedule inspections. However, citizens can use permit data to check whether that lot clearing down the street has a permit or whether the contractor they are thinking of hiring to fix the roof is licensed. Other jurisdictions might reference the site to validate work histories and licenses cited in bid applications or license requests. This variety of potential customers was a key consideration for Santa Rosa County, Florida, when it developed its online building and contractor records system (see http://src.whinc.net/srpermits/index.html).

Application development should also consider customers' differing backgrounds and varying levels of computer expertise. For example, the Suwannee River Water Management District, in Florida, created three basic interfaces for its permit information: one for an average citizen, another for a commercial or industrial firm, and yet another for the agricultural and forestry community (see http://www.srwmd.state.fl.us/services/permitting/default1.htm). These divisions reflect different permits and different levels of understanding of the permit process. A citizen needs more help to understand which permits are needed for a boat dock or a water well, but a professional firm may just want to get to the form. The Suwannee Web page is not complicated, but it is unusual because it tailors a specific service to levels of customer sophistication.

The mix of customers and interests creates interesting although often treacherous political landscapes for local governments. Property tax records online cause realtors to howl that such access makes it easy to determine the last price paid for a house, but home buyers like it for the same reason. Some citizens consider online records an invasion of their privacy (although they know they are public data), and others happily use them to compare their assessed values with values of other property owners and perhaps complain of a high appraisal to the property appraiser's office. Likewise, building permits are not immune to political crosscurrents. Environmental groups may perceive, rightly or wrongly, that streamlining the permitting process for developers encourages development. Like so much of public policy, improved service delivery is not favored by everyone.

Privacy is a hot topic. Businesses want access to public records for marketing purposes, but citizens do not want personal information shared without their express consent. A number of legislative bills at the state level address the issue of corporate use of information and provision of government data to corporate interests. The concern is broader than e-government. Data matching and data mining allow far more personal details to be collected than ever before. Advocates of these techniques cite the benefits of better law enforcement and service provision, but the power of these techniques creates privacy risks.

The position of the business community is that a user must expressly deny—in other words, opt out of—the use of personal data for other purposes. Consumer groups argue that opting out is ineffective.[27] For government, an opt-in strategy is perhaps best: jurisdictions should have clearly stated privacy policies for their applications and charge one staff member with privacy policy management and enforcement. Such policies should coordinate with state laws, which tend to be stricter than federal requirements. Privacy concerns vary by application. For example, residents usually appreciate reminders to pay parking tickets, but e-mails about follow-up visits to a public health center can feel disturbingly invasive.

What are the lessons of all this customer diversity? Local government managers should determine the interest groups and customers that are affected by every IT application—their likely benefits, costs, and objections. Managers should not assume the person transacting the business is the only one reaping benefits or costs. The manager must ensure that a plan is developed that addresses negative concerns. How sensitive is the information and what are the privacy expectations of potential users? If a local government is new to e-government, it should first tackle problems with few conflicting interests and where customers can see a clear benefit and be supportive. It may be less cool to provide only downloadable forms—and not build a real-time permit application—but starting small conserves resources while it builds experience.

What do citizens need?   E-government applications should be built first around customer needs, not government agency needs: a simple idea, but its implementation is complicated because so many customer needs cut across agencies and governments. For example, a citizen who wants to report a pothole does not care whether the road in question is maintained by the town, the county, or the state; it is the ability to report the pothole at one central Web location that is important.

Residents rarely know which agency provides which services. For business permitting, interjurisdictional cooperation alleviates complexity of navigating through jurisdictional differences. Moreover, cooperation benefits local businesses and economic development efforts by minimizing the number of applications a business must make or at least providing one-stop shopping. Laura Larimer, CIO for the state of Indiana notes, "Citizens really shouldn't have to—and don't want to—understand the organizational structures of how government is delivering services. . . . We ought . . . to allow them to traverse those lines without having to understand our system."[28] However, coordination across organizational boundaries can be difficult, and lack of coordination can cause serious problems.

To design a successful online application, the local government must find out whether citizens really want to complete a task online, whether they have the access and the technical skills to use the proposed application, and how homogeneous they are in their expectations and needs. Many citizens do not have convenient access to the Web, they may have poor technical capabilities, or they may simply prefer personal interaction to computer interface. These challenges are usually greater among the elderly and the poor (the digital divide is discussed beginning on page 146).

Building permits: A tale of two counties   In the mid-1990s, a medium-size Florida county was one of the first to provide a sophisticated system for builders and contractors to file permits online. At a cost of almost $500,000, the application was a technical marvel for its time and generated lots of publicity at its launch. Yet, two years after its release, not a single permit had been processed through the system.

In 2000, another Florida county decided it wanted an online building permit application. Staff went to local industry association meetings and asked builders and contractors what they wanted. From those discussions, the country found the builders were far more interested in simply checking the status of filed permits than in completing them online. All parties agreed that such a limited application would be fast and cheap to build. This system has been a rousing success, and it has replaced an expensive phone-based system for checking permit status. The cost? Less than $10,000.

As of 2004, many areas provide successful online permitting systems, but timing and customer readiness are integral to success.

How user friendly will the application be? Residents will not use a new application if it is easier to do things the old way. This admonition is important to remember for complex tasks, even tasks that are complex simply because of long forms. Users do not like to complete more than one or two screens of information. Online forms that demand information that the citizen has to look up, such as a detailed job history, present a problem. Complicated or lengthy information entry must be carefully broken into manageable steps, allowing users to complete parts of the online forms at different times.

For example, when Santa Rosa County, Florida, decided to place a job application form on the Web, the county first investigated the nature of the existing application process. Applicants were usually current government employees, and employees commonly applied for several jobs over time. The county built a system that allows applicants to store their basic information across applications, which is a great help because more than 90 percent of an application is repeated in every submission. Applicants may change details, like home address, before new submissions. And applicants do not have to complete their forms in one online session, which is helpful when they have to find required information offline.

Jurisdictions with large non-English-speaking populations have to consider language. El Paso, Texas, for example, maintains a complete version of its Web site in Spanish.[29]

What about marketing? Sometimes low demand is just poor marketing; Citizens must know about a service. Complicated Web addresses are often to blame. Many local governments use Web addresses in the pattern of <www.ci.cityname. stateabbreviation.us> or <www.co.countyname.stateabbreviation.us>, but many use <.com> addresses instead. However, <.com> addresses make it difficult for citizens to tell an official government site from a commercial site. If a <.com> address is used for marketing, it should feed to an official site name that makes the legal authority clear to citizens. Fortunately, recent legal changes allow counties and cities to use <.gov>. The city of Boston used cityofboston.com for marketing but <www.ci.boston.ma.us> as well. Both addresses now take visitors to a <.gov>-style address recently made available to local governments: <www.cityofboston. gov>. For more popular services, separate Web addresses for each site are useful because they allow each to be marketed separately.

Local governments rarely have much marketing money, but budgets should not preclude cost-free marketing. Jurisdictions can plaster their Web addresses on letterhead, business cards, and utility payments and mention them on answering machines and phone support. Maybe the Web address cannot be placed on every license plate—the state of Pennsylvania does this—but publicity opportunities abound.

Human nature avoids change. Regardless of ease of use and absence of access fees, many still prefer to use walk-in services or call a live person for help. In Fairfax County, Virginia, CIO David Molchany laments that people still walk in to pay taxes instead of using the online system. Maintaining two approaches—the old-fashioned walk-in payment and the new online application—is expensive. Molchany, who hired a marketing director to promote the new, alternative kiosks and Web site, observed, "It's surprising that people still physically come to this building to pay taxes. We'd prefer they didn't do that. It takes a tremendous amount of resources."[30]

Hiring a marketing agent may seem extreme, but the idea has merit. Some level of marketing is essential to promote online access. Media coverage can promote the service and explain why—easier, more convenient, cheaper—it is to a user's direct benefit. Managers should be cautious about assuming the old, paper-based procedures will disappear overnight. Citizens without computer access need an alternative. This reality presents the next difficulty: customer accessibility.

Is there a digital divide in the community? Most Americans are online, but not all. For example, the city of Harrisburg, Pennsylvania, where about 32 percent of the residents are at or near the poverty line, waited until 2000 to launch its Web site. John Wright, a city council member, noted, "Cities spend a lot of money on Web sites, but a lot of urban people are never going to use them. There's a technology gap between the well-to-do and the non-well-to-do. It's a factor in determining how much of a Web presence you need."[31]

Citizen use of local government e-services   Percentage of users who say the Internet improves their interactions with local governments:

11%	A lot
19%	Some
18%	Only a little
48%	Not at all

Most popular activities performed at government Web sites are more informational than transactional:

77%	Get tourism and recreational information
70%	Research work for school
63%	Find out what services an agency provides

62%	Seek advice on a public policy or issue of interest
16%	File taxes
12%	Renew a driver's license or auto registration
7%	Renew a professional license
4%	Get a fishing, hunting, or other recreational license
2%	Pay a fine

How local government users rate the sites:

41%	Have visited the local government Web site; of those,
62%	Rate it excellent or good
38%	Rate it fair or poor.

Source: Pew Internet & American Life Project, cited in Ellen Perlman, "The People Connection," *Governing* (September 2002): 32–41.

The digital divide is not only an economic division, but is also racial, generational, and educational. For business, potential customers who do not have online access are simply an untapped market. For government, access becomes a serious issue of rights and equity. Nonusers correlate with specific demographic groups, and government cannot simply disregard groups of people. If the application taps basic needs and services, it is an even more significant issue.

Should the question of access be a reason not to launch an application? In most cases, no, not as long as traditional alternatives exist and careful attention is paid to improving access. For example, when Harrisburg moved onto the Web in 2000, officials used a federal educational grant to plan government-run cybercafes (although they did not serve food) to complement existing computer centers at libraries and schools.[32] Hardware and connections, however, are not enough. Access is not just about the equipment; it is also about technical knowledge. All too often, local governments launch public access computer banks and find them unused. Harrisburg, realizing this common mistake, included computer training in its cybercafes.

Training needs are partly application specific. For example, if the application targets professional activities and businesses, less training is required. If average citizens use the application (for activities such as paying a utility bill or a parking fine), the more the jurisdiction must plan for variations in background. Frequently, local governments find they must offer support, whether by phone, e-mail, or even online real-time chat, for many applications aimed at the general public.

Access issues also include the often confusing patchwork of policies and laws governing citizens with disabilities. Federal laws, such as the Americans with Disabilities Act and Section 508 of the Rehabilitation Act of 1998, are often cited as requiring IT development restrictions and accommodations. Despite these laws, government Web sites have, at best, a mixed compliance record. A 2002 Brown University study found only 27 percent of federal sites had some form of disability access, and state compliance ranged from Idaho at a poor 3 percent to Maine at 60 percent.[33] Why such low numbers? Reasons include legal confusion, development costs, political desirability for fancy sites that defy accessibility, and misunderstanding of proper development, especially among contracted vendors. The reality is that the applicability of much of the cited federal legislation to local governments is murky.[34] Even the often cited World Wide Web Consortium (W3C) guidelines and "Bobby-certified" rules (see http://bobby.watchfire.com/bobby/html/en/index.jsp) show clear conflicts with federal statutes. Amid confusion, concern over accessibility has launched a vast array of state policies and interpretations. The best strategy for managers is to consult with their state attorney general. Local governments should have clear, written policies driving application development.

Privacy primer: Some Web sites with advice

Electronic Privacy Information
   Center   www.epic.org

Privacy and American
   Business   www.panab.org

Privacy Leadership Initiative
   www.understandingprivacy.org

Privacy Rights Clearinghouse
   www.privacyrights.org

Online Privacy Alliance (a corporate representative)   www.privacyalliance.org

Source: Christopher Conte, "Getting to Know You," *Governing* (May 2002): 46–50.

Disability access should not be only about avoiding litigation. Governments have a moral obligation to assist as best they can. Many jurisdictions have learned that the best approach is to offer agencies carrots, not sticks. Rather than commanding compliance to a specific standard with correlating punishments, Illinois provides training on accessible Web design; Connecticut provides this training not only to government workers but also to consultants preparing applications for the state.[35] Such support alleviates two of the greatest compliance problems: development cost and understanding of proper design.

Can staff handle success?   Rather than too few users, the problem may be too many. Can staff handle an increase in service demands generated by the ease of Web access? Is there a citizen complaint form on the Web? Staff must be able to respond within a day. Overdemand leads to two problems: the shift from paper-based to online forms necessitates changes in work routines for those who receive the forms and process them; and online application processes increase the total volume of service requests. An overabundance of requests is a serious problem for governments where the supply of a service is strictly limited by budget constraints. Online park reservation applications can exacerbate workload problems in what is often an already over-taxed service unit. Online requests for utility hookups can also cause problems.

Demand can sometimes be controlled by levying a convenience fee, which is a charge for using the online application compared with a free paper-based process. The downside is that, although local governments are legally justified in charging user fees to pay for operating expenses or to regulate demand, such fees meet strong political resistance, especially where citizens and political officials believe the services should pay for themselves through increases in efficiency. Fees may be more acceptable when the primary users are businesses, the service itself is new, the service is perceived as a premium, and the fee is not an economic hardship.

Agencies may refuse to develop online applications unless they are allowed to recoup the costs. Sometimes the application fees are used to support the operation of an agency function, not just the cost of the application process. The worst public relations scenario is that a local government mandates use of the Web for a basic function (such as payment of property taxes) and then charges for this privilege.

The public library of Los Angeles County offers a for-pay research service online, handling requests such as criminal background checks and construction and marketing services. The application, "For Your Information," goes back to 1989. FYI's regular users include about 6,000 small businesses and 60 city governments.[36]

Recap

Human resources, when working together with financial resources and information resources, make it possible to pay competitive wages and maintain information services that meet the needs of the community. Managed well, these resources combine to achieve community goals, improve quality of life, and increase citizen satisfaction. These accomplishments are what good government is all about. For the manager, effectiveness means paying attention to detail while keeping the big picture in mind.

- A motivated, committed workforce will maximize financial and information resources.

- In strategic human resource management, the HR director works hand in glove with other department heads to develop goals, strategies, workforce plans, and resource allocation.

- Mentoring and succession planning are effective instruments in workforce development.

- Young entrants to the workforce expect higher levels of autonomy and discretion than prior generations of workers expected. This necessitates greater reliance on participative decision making and flattened hierarchies. Self-managed work teams are gaining broad acceptance because they capitalize on worker initiative, personal responsibility, creativity, problem solving, and self-reliance.

- Case law continues to develop regarding employer liability for workplace violence, sexual harassment, safeguards for disabled workers, and family and medical leave issues. It is important to have sound, written policies in place; ensure that all employees are trained and knowledgeable about the policies; and follow policies when incidents occur.

- The budget is the most important plan of any government because it is the plan through which all other plans are accomplished. A good capital programming and budgeting process keeps abreast of the public infrastructure needs of a community.

- Government managers have a stewardship obligation to taxpayers to assure that their monies are handled carefully and invested wisely. Internal controls begin with a strong organizational commitment to ethical behavior and to the concept that all public servants owe it to their fellow taxpayers to manage their money well.

- Financial trend monitoring enables leaders to keep abreast of important community trends such as declining property values or increased unemployment. Financial factors to watch out for include a deteriorating revenue structure, declining liquidity, growing debt, unfunded pension liabilities, and deterioration in the condition of the capital infrastructure.

- Forecasting future receipts is an often neglected aspect of revenue management. It requires keeping sound records of past receipts and using those to build forecasts.

- Governments engage in activities that can cause substantial losses of money and even bodily harm. These activities should be managed to reduce the likelihood of incurring such losses. The process of identifying risk and taking steps to avert losses is called risk management.

- Effective managers learn not to fear auditors but to use audits strategically to improve the operations of a government.

- Information technology touches all aspects of managerial operations, from tracking expenditures, to recording deeds, to providing direct citizen access to government.

- IT suffers from the perception that it is for technically savvy managers, system analysts, programmers, and webmasters. The reality is that IT is an integral part of local government management at all levels.

- Technology, by itself, will not usher in major changes in government operations. One of the great lessons of IT is that the real benefits come from redesigning how an organization does business. New technologies like e-government make it possible to deliver services in wholly new ways.

- An IT-savvy manager understands that technology involves not just technical issues, but also managerial and policy issues.

- Whether developed by internal IT staff or an external vendor, employees must like and understand new IT applications before they will use them.

- The digital divide exists. Many citizens still do not have convenient access to the Web, they may have poor technical capabilities, or they may simply prefer personal interaction to computer use.

- Techniques such as data matching and data mining allow far more personal details to be collected on individuals than ever before. These techniques are usually advocated in the name of law enforcement or better service provision, but the power of these techniques creates privacy risks.

- The history of government IT demonstrates that savings tend to be exaggerated. Managers should not assume that efficiency gains from an online system will reduce staffing costs.

Case in point

Mary Todd, a county commissioner for Taylor County, is encouraging the county to begin processing all permit processes online. She wants the county to begin by handling building and construction permits online, including filings to construct new homes and businesses as well as modifications to such properties. She has read a lot of news articles about how other jurisdictions are using the Web to save money and streamline operations. She wants the service to replace all paper-based permits in two years and is certain that this will bring cost savings—mostly via employment reductions—and reduced red tape.

Although the staff finds the idea appealing, they have many concerns. First, many employees in the building inspection and permit office fear that the service is designed to eliminate their jobs. Also, the director, John Littleton, fears his department will get swamped with calls from users not able to understand the system. Other department employees worry that many permits are complicated and require a lot of interaction with the permit filer to complete. Some permits also involve obtaining related permits from state agencies, for example, when water wells may be constructed for home sites where an environmental permit from the regional water management district must accompany the county filing.

Also, the two largest cities in the county have their own building permit office, and, for some permits, filers must submit requests to both the county and city. Currently, a streamlined paper process allows builders to file with either office for both city and county permits. However, if the county goes online, this ease of filing will no longer be possible unless there is collaboration with the respective cities and their staffs. Therefore, the process could actually become more complicated for builders in city jurisdictions.

Local builders have mixed opinions about Todd's idea. Large contractors tend to favor it, thinking the system will eliminate red tape. Small contractors think it will make it difficult to access file permits because they will have to learn the new system and then train employees to use it. They also like having county building department employees around to help them with technical details.

Budgeting is also an issue. The initial system is likely to cost at least $75,000 to construct, not counting the amount of staff time that will be required. The county already has pressing needs in what is proving to be a tight budget situation, and the budget has no slack. The $75,000 would have to come from an existing program. A couple of ideas have been proposed: one, unpopular with builders, is to pay for the conversion by increasing the current building permit fees until the new system is online; the other is to enter into an agreement with a vendor to construct it for free and give them the right to collect filing fees to recover their costs and make a reasonable return on their investment. The county's IT office does not favor the second idea because it places critical information, some of which has significant privacy and security issues, outside the county's direct control.

The county IT office is already understaffed and does not have the resources to build the new system. They would have to either hire new personnel or contract out the development. Once the application is developed, the building inspection employees will need significant training in its operation. They also suspect that the potential cost savings are exaggerated. Hence, they favor a test of some form and a thorough review of benefits and costs. Aware of the technology office's reluctance to move forward, Mary Todd has accused the IT office of stonewalling and views a pilot project as just a delaying tactic.

Questions:

1. What are the HR implications of this proposal?
2. What are the financial implications?
3. What are the information management implications?
4. What are the political implications?
5. As county manager, what actions should you take?

Notes

1 Anya Sostek, "Managing Performance: People Power," *Governing* (January 2003): 54.

2 For a comprehensive text, see Siegrun Fox Freyss, ed., *Human Resource Management in Local Government: An Essential Guide,* 2nd ed. (Washington, D.C.: ICMA, 2004).

3 Reginald A. Shareef, "The Sad Demise of Skill-Based Pay in the Virginia Department of Transportation," *Review of Public Personnel Administration* 22 (Summer 2002): 233–240.

4 Sostek, 54.

5 Faye Rice, "How to Make Diversity Pay," *Fortune* 130, no. 3 (1994): 78–83.

6 P. E. Crewson and J. F. Guyot, "Sartor Resartus: A Comparative Analysis of Public and Private Sector Entrant Quality Reanalyzed," *American Journal of Political Science* 41 (July 1997): 1057–1065.

7 Mary E. Guy and Seung-Bum Yang, "Conditions for Effective Self-Managed Work Teams: Lessons from the U.S. Experience," in *Central-Local Relations and Local Government Reform in Korea,* ed. Byong-Joon Kim and Glen Hahn Cope (South Korea: Korea Association for Policy Studies, 2003).

8 Katherine Barrett and Richard Greene, "The Prized Employee," *Governing* (May 2003): 78.

9 K. Smith, "Mobile Wins Sexual Harassment Lawsuit," *Alabama League of Municipalities* (March 1995): 16–19.

10 See Appendix B for ICMA Task Force on Continuing Education and Professional Development, "Practices for Effective Local Government Management"; for a comprehensive text on financial management, see Richard Aronson and Eli Schwartz, eds., *Management Policies in Local Government Finance,* 5th ed. (Washington, D.C.: ICMA, 2004).

11 For a comprehensive text on financial management, see Aronson and Schwartz, eds., *Management Policies in Local Government Finance,* 5th ed.

12 Karl Nollenberger, original text by Sanford M. Groves and Maureen Godsey Valente, *Evaluating Financial Condition: A Handbook for Local Government,* 4th ed. (Washington, D.C.: ICMA, 2003). An online supplement, *The IndiKit,* includes interactive spreadsheets that can be used to compile information annually and prepare worksheets and graphs that help to detect trends in financial health.

13 Government Finance Officers Association, "Distinguished Budget Presentation Award (Budget Awards Program)," www.gfoa.org/services/awards.html, accessed April 6, 2003.

14 Donald C. Stone, "Administrative Management: Reflections on Origins and Accomplishments," *Public Administration Review* 50 (January/February 1990): 4.

15 National Advisory Council on State and Local Budgeting (NACSLB), "Recommended Budget Practices: A Framework for Improved State and Local Government Budgeting" (Chicago, Ill.: GFOA, 1998), www.gfoa.org/services/nacslb/, accessed April 6, 2003.

16 The term municipal applies to debt issued by state and local governments generally, not solely to that issued by city governments.

17 Margaret Bowden and William Earle Klay, "Contracting for 21st Century Infrastructure," *Public Budgeting and Financial Management* 8 (Fall 1996): 384–405.

18 For two out of many examples of comprehensive IT strategic plans, see the Web sites of Arvada, Colorado, http://ci.arvada.co.us/forms/51321Information%20Technology%20Strategic%20Plan%20web.pdf; and Fairfax County, Virginia, www.fairfaxcounty.gov/gov/dit/itplan.htm.

19 M. Jae Moon, "The Evolution of E-Government among Municipalities: Rhetoric or Real," *Public Administration Review* 62 (July/August 2002): 424–444.

20 Ibid.

21 Paul Allsing, Maricopa County, Arizona, quoted in Diane Kittower, "Guide to Award-Winning Technology," *Governing* (October 1999): 46–52.

22 Kenneth Kraemer, *Managing Information Systems: Change and Control in Organizational Computing* (San Francisco: Jossey-Bass, 1989); J. Fountain, *Building the Virtual State: Information Technology and Institutional Change* (Washington, D.C.: Brookings Institution, 2001).

23 Eric Welch and David H. Coursey, "Factors in Perceived Web Success among Government Information Employees," working paper, 2003.

24 Moon, "Evolution of E-Government among Municipalities."

25 Blake Harris, "E-Government Failures Reflect Changing Workforce Needs," *Government Technology* (May 2002), www.govtech.net, accessed February 12, 2003.

26 Ellen Perlman, "The People Connection," *Governing* (September 2002): 32–41.

27 Christopher Conte, "Getting to Know You," *Governing* (May 2002): 46–50.

28 Ellen Perlman, "The People Connection."

29 See www.ci.el-paso.tx.us/esp_spanish.asp.

30 Ellen Perlman, "The IT Czar of Main Street," *Governing* (January 2001): 31–33.

31 Ellen Perlman, "Local Resistance," *Governing* (September 2000): 54–64.

32 Ibid.

33 Tod Newcombe, "Unequal Access," *Government Technology* (December 2002), www.govtech.net, accessed February 12, 2003.

34 Paul Bohman, "Section 508 Now in Effect." WebAim, www.webaim.org/news/show_item.php?nid=11, accessed March 2003; and Newcombe, "Unequal Access."

35 Shane Peterson, "An Inclusive Internet," *Government Technology* (December 2002), www.govtech.net, accessed online February 12, 2003.

36 Shane Harris, "E-commerce at the Library," *Governing* (April 2000): 56–58.

Policy implementation, productivity, and program evaluation

Local government managers strive to deliver programs efficiently and effectively. As the previous five chapters have explained, in order to do so, managers need to be leaders, models of ethical behavior, effective communicators, political savants, coalition builders, champions of community and economic development, strategic planners, and competent stewards of the community's resources. Managers need to play all of these roles in an ever-changing community environment. The contemporary condition of fiscal duress for local governments makes government roles particularly challenging.

Municipal and county governments remain the general-purpose public service delivery organizations of the U.S. political system. These governments have the highest levels of interaction with those governed, provide the daily essential services, and face high levels of citizen demand for accountability. Thus, local government agendas are extensive, diverse, and constantly changing. It is important to remember that, especially at the level of local governments, change is normal. Federal and state policies change, regional and local economies fluctuate, technology improves and brings new challenges, citizen needs and wants grow, and political and social values shift.

This chapter examines three aspects of the local government manager's responsibilities: policy implementation, productivity, and program evaluation. Each is essential for delivering efficient and effective services. First, however, is a discussion of agenda setting and policy formulation.

Agenda setting and policy formulation

Public policy is "whatever governments choose to do or not to do."[1] Normally, policy making is the responsibility of elected bodies—city councils, county boards, and the like. Local government managers also participate in policy making. The process of creating public policies is usually conceptualized as roughly sequential stages or activities. Thus, in professionally managed local governments, one sees the process (see Figure 6–1) as:

- *Agenda setting*   Process through which issues are brought to the attention of policy makers
- *Policy formulation*   Process of considering options for addressing the issue and adopting a specific course of action
- *Implementation*   Process through which adopted policies are put into action
- *Evaluation*   Assessment of whether or not policies perform as intended; also provides information on how to modify or improve policies.

These stages of the policy process are analytic constructions that are not always independent, distinct, and phased in the order presented here. Clearly evaluation can be used for formulation and after implementation. Similarly, it is difficult in practice to separate the process of agenda setting from formulation. Historically, the

Figure 6–1   Stages in
the policy process

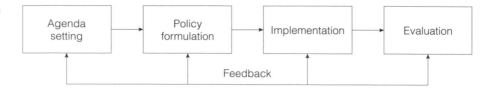

council-manager form of government attempted to separate the roles of the elected
body and the manager into, respectively, policy formulators and policy imple-
menters. In practice that distinction has proved to be neither realistic nor appropriate. Policy formulation and implementation overlap; each process informs and
affects the other. Instead, it is fruitful to look at the stages of the policy process as
structured opportunities to combine the professional expertise of civil servants with
citizen involvement, leadership with representative decision making, and experience-
based continuity with constructive and politically responsive change.

The remainder of this discussion will emphasize agenda setting and policy formulation; the other stages are addressed in subsequent sections. (Another perspective on these topics appears in Chapter 2.)

Setting the policy agenda

The policy agenda consists of those issues or problems that have come to the attention of the government as requiring scrutiny, deliberation, and some decision
regarding action (or possibly inaction). How issues reach the agenda can be a complex process, often involving a constellation of elected officials, interest groups,
individual citizens, lobbyists, professional associations, political parties, and others.[2]
Other levels of government can take actions that bring issues to local government
agendas. Mass media also have a role in bringing issues to the public agenda.
Although policy analysts disagree regarding the directness of media influence, it is
certainly true that selective attention to local issues by the mass media often alerts
citizens to new issues for government attention and encourages those who already
believe an issue should be addressed. Ultimately, however, elected officials and
interest groups usually exercise the greatest influence on the content of the jurisdictional policy agenda.

**I feel fortunate to be part of the growth of the community in a place where
people are getting things done. I'm [a cog in the wheel and] definitely not
the driver.**

Bruce Clymer

Policy professionals often distinguish between the systemic agenda and the
governmental (or institutional) agenda.[3] The systemic agenda is a discussion
agenda that includes general issues that receive public attention and discourse, but
it typically does not include proposals for specific action. For example, on the systemic agenda one might find discussion of the prevalence of street crime, a decline
in tourism, or violence in schools. In contrast, the government or institutional
agenda contains proposals for the adoption of particular solutions or goals by the
government. Local government managers are most concerned with the governmental policy agenda, which encompasses the issues on which the government
will take action.

In the setting of governmental policy agendas, the professional manager usually
assumes the role of an informed facilitator. The manager contributes knowledge of
the local political, social, and economic context; understanding of government pro-

cesses and procedures; memory of past and current policies; and interpersonal skills to the discussion. A public manager must be able to communicate articulately with all the actors involved and keep the discussion directed at the issues at hand.

It is a tenet of democracy that when elected officials and professional managers set the policy agenda, they attempt to maximize citizen participation. As informed facilitators, professional managers are expected to anticipate reactions from the community and accurately project levels of support for potential policies or future initiatives. If the manager knows the local political arena well; understands local economic and social forces; and is attuned to community leaders, activists, and media, the manager can exercise political leadership to pursue agendas and policies that might not be popular or salient to the public. Effective managers build networks of professional colleagues and rely on professional political and research sources to anticipate public reaction to ideas and policies and to identify important issues that might not otherwise reach the agenda.

Gatekeeping   The process of including or excluding items from the government agenda is called gatekeeping. Although it is sometimes exercised unscrupulously, ethical elected officials and managers practice gatekeeping for three legitimate purposes: to bring order to the local agenda, to group together issues that should be considered together, and to prevent the deliberative body from being overwhelmed by issues. Gatekeeping, therefore, requires expertise in strategic planning and management because of its short-range and long-range strategic management considerations. The manager must explore probable futures for the jurisdiction and alternatives for coping with them; this helps to reduce uncertainty as well as support the process of developing effective contingency plans for meeting identifiable social, economic, natural, and technological threats. Advanced contingency planning reduces the need for stressful and costly crisis management. (See Chapter 4 for more on planning.)

Managing agenda setting   The manager's role in agenda setting demands many skills and activities. Certain issues—employee benefits and compensation, internal budget allocations, and purchasing and contracting decisions—recur on virtually every local government policy agenda. In addition, new agenda items arise from new needs or from demands of citizens, politicians, interest groups, lobbyists, the media, or other participants in the agenda-setting process. New issues are generated by economic and social crises that produce calls to curtail services, initiate services (protection against terrorism), or maintain services in spite of budget shortfalls (education, child care, homeless services). In setting the government agenda, the manager must be able to communicate, set priorities, and identify alternatives.

Some agenda items are introduced with no mention of alternatives, and some are coupled with a single proposed solution or with several possible solutions. Agenda setting thus evolves into policy formulation as alternatives developed by a variety of sources—elected officials, citizens, public managers, lobbyists, interest groups, policy planning organizations, and the like—are brought forward for discussion.

Formulating policy

Regardless of when policy alternatives appear, the different levels of effort, cost, and complexity required for implementation of each alternative are usually examined. Thus, part of policy formulation requires consideration of avenues for implementation, and it is up to the professional manager to design implementation strategies for scrutiny or comparison at the formulation stage. Formulation then evolves into implementation because the strategies scrutinized when formulating a policy are likely to be the same strategies used when that policy is implemented.

Because the way a policy is formulated shapes the way it must be implemented, the more explicit and precise the formulation, the less distortion during implementation. Therefore, as part of policy formulation, the local government manager must perform two important functions.

First, the manager identifies prioritized goals and objectives for the policy or program in terms of available resources (or needed resources) and describes results to be created within a defined time frame. At this stage, goals represent the anticipated long-term results of the policy or program; outputs and outcomes are often described in intervals of five, ten, or twenty-five years of elapsed time. Objectives are more short term, usually specifying outputs and outcomes in a particular quarter or in a given year. This is the beginning of the process of marrying budget with policy.

Second, the manager develops plans for the accomplishment of the goals and objectives, specifying personnel, budget, location, equipment, facilities, and other operational features that will form the road map for implementation. The manager's ability to produce accurate and detailed plans insures that the costs of the policy or program are correctly established and that it addresses the problem intended.

The construction of action plans to chart the paths by which goals and objectives will be achieved falls to government managers. Often action plans represent the product of systems analyses and take the form of detailed flowcharts that associate time lines with particular tasks. Like the formulation of goals and objectives, action plan development is most successful when participation is broadest. Once action plan frameworks are created, it is necessary to associate administrative rules and procedures with the plan. In this way, formal authority and accountability are assigned, staffing is legitimized, and the stage is set for resources to flow at the policy implementation stage.

Implementation

Implementation—accomplishing objectives—is a central concern in policy formulation and a fundamental managerial responsibility. If the objectives set during policy formulation are to be accomplished, the policy-making process must include consideration of the problems and processes of implementation. Four managerial activities are basic to accomplishing objectives:

- Assigning responsibilities, delegating authority, and allocating resources
- Using functionally oriented management systems to coordinate organizational resources and performance
- Involving people in productive activity through shared performance targets and work processes and through training and the reinforcement of positive job-related behaviors
- Tracking progress toward results through intermediate productivity.

Communication is the essence of these four managerial functions. Taken together, they are designed to maintain an organization-wide exchange of information. Because many traditional government functions are no longer performed directly by government, and this trend is increasing, the discussion of implementation concludes with an examination of alternative delivery systems.

Responsibilities, authority, and resources

Assignment of responsibilities, delegation of authority, and allocation of resources are among the most important of the manager's activities. They also represent contradictions. Subordinate managers and nonsupervisory personnel need clear job assignments and the authority to carry them out, yet responsibilities often overlap, organizational boundaries blur, and authority is in constant flux. In this complex organizational environment, the manager attempts to create and maintain workable relationships. That effort requires an understanding of organizational structures and processes. It also requires active leadership to balance the twin requirements for stability and change.

Organizational structure   Organizations can be structured in many ways, but to keep the inevitable contradictions from resulting in chaos, managers need to draw on both hierarchical and open-systems organizational methods. To assign responsibilities, managers can use two concepts from the traditional hierarchical model as generally workable starting points:

* Specialization and organizational grouping by function (e.g., firefighting, law enforcement, planning) are the most commonly accepted bases for assignment of responsibilities; crime prevention is generally a matter for the police, and wastewater treatment is usually a function of the utility or sanitation department

* Authority needs to be specific to a function and commensurate with responsibilities.

These commonly accepted structural principles facilitate assignment of responsibility. Continuity and stability are usually maintained at the operations level because, in an existing organization, most responsibilities can be assigned on the basis of past practice and experience. The chief administrator does not need to make organizational changes when established routines work reasonably well and new functions readily fit existing patterns.

Often, however, new responsibilities do not fit current patterns. If prevention of crime related to drug use is a priority, for example, that function may need to be assigned to organizational units other than the police; it could be assigned to the health and recreation departments and the schools instead. Wastewater treatment may involve not only several departments of a local government but also relationships among several jurisdictions. Because of such complexities, matrix forms of project management sometimes work better than hierarchical structures. A project structure can be formed for such activities from various parts of the organization on the basis of the skills and expertise needed, regardless of the hierarchy.

There are practical limits on the complexity of matrix forms if the desired outputs and outcomes are to be achieved. Jeffery Pressman and Aaron Wildavsky, who studied policy implementation in Oakland, California, warned that designers of policy need to use the most direct means possible to accomplish their objectives. They noted that "since each required clearance point adds to the probability of stoppage or delay, the number of these points should be minimized wherever possible." Echoing Woodrow Wilson, they also concluded that policymakers should "pay as much attention to the creation of organizational machinery for executing a program as for launching one."[4] Two practical guides to assigning responsibility and delegating authority, therefore, are: (1) maximize functional expertise, and (2) minimize organizational and administrative complexity.

Allocation and utilization of resources   Once policy responsibility is assigned, the manager must see that the resources to perform the job are allocated and utilized. Generally, resource allocation relates to four basic administrative service areas: finances, personnel, plant and equipment, and information. One of the manager's hardest tasks is to maintain these service areas both as a service to line management and as a control system for general management. For example, in hiring personnel, management control may be enhanced by having a centralized system that standardizes most recruiting and hiring processes in a central personnel office. The line (department) manager, however, may find such a system inhibits the department's ability to hire good employees. If the system makes it difficult to employ the individuals most suited to doing the department's work, resources are not being allocated effectively, and service delivery and quality suffer.

Resource utilization—in this example, how personnel actually are used—rests in the hands of the department manager. Resource utilization is monitored in part by the local government manager's evaluation of service and program delivery, which will be discussed later in this chapter.

We now take a systematic approach to service delivery. . . . Service delivery is no longer based on who is complaining the most or the loudest. It depends on what is the best use of taxpayers' money.

Mark Ryckman

Resource utilization is successful if it accomplishes the desired results. Operational management, also known as results-oriented management, focuses on the outputs and outcomes of management activities. It requires specification, in operational terms, of the activities that fulfill government responsibilities. Thus, operations management might focus on the library's circulation of books, or responses to requests for information, or the public works department's maintenance of streets. In addition to the specification of outputs and outcomes, operations management includes planning the processes for achieving them. A flowchart or PERT (program evaluation and review technique) chart depicts the methods and resources used to provide the service. These charts help in making the most efficient use of resources by providing a view of how each step relates to another. They help to avoid overlapping and unneeded steps. Flowcharts also help to determine the time and resources needed to achieve the desired results. In addition, they facilitate identification of changes needed in an organization, procedures, or resources. Figure 6–2 shows a flowchart for processing a rezoning application.

For the local government manager, managing for results should be the overriding goal. To ensure that policies are implemented—and results attained—the manager must coordinate organizational resources and performance. This process is often referred to as functional management.

Functional management

Functional management (one of the components of ICMA's 18 best practices, see Appendix B) means that the manager must keep an eye on intraorganizational maintenance and development in order to coordinate activities among different units.

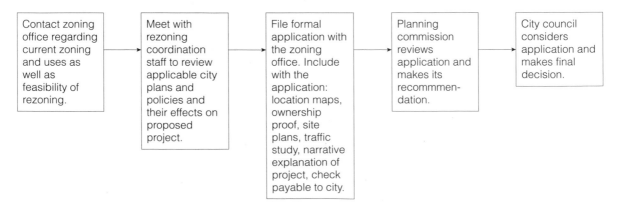

Figure 6–2   Flow chart for a rezoning application

Otherwise, competition for resources may become destructive to the organization. In short, attention must be focused on management processes, not simply on final results. In addition, while keeping the overall result in mind, the manager must also ensure that intermediate productivity controls are established for each department so that progress can be monitored and problems identified before they become crises.

Intermediate measures are particularly important in public service delivery. For example, police performance may be measured by the number of arrests made (output). Even though the number of arrests may be less important than reduced criminal activity or an increase in citizens' feelings of well-being, this intermediate measure provides time and cost comparisons required for important subfunctions and may reveal activities that should be changed or terminated before final results are in. Productivity and performance measurement are discussed in greater detail later in this chapter.

The functional management system allows organization-wide coordination and integration of activities. In turn, the manager can focus on key issues—cost-benefit trade-offs, contingency responses, and organizational procedures—and providing the resulting information available to others.

The police department, for example, may want to know the relative cost and effectiveness of foot patrols versus bicycle patrols. In addition, it needs to know how well each would respond to an emergency and what the procedures should be for deploying patrols to emergencies. The answers to all these questions are critical to effective coordination and integration of the department's efforts.

Coordination and integration depend on agreed work rules and performance targets. If they are not established through managerial leadership, they emerge through practice and become binding in fact. These rules must be related to function and kept up to date. They should be guides to behavior rather than limits on action, and they should be kept to the minimum necessary to achieve desired results. On occasion, explicit rules to establish limits on behavior may be required, often to meet legal or technical requirements.

Performance targets

Performance targets for work groups help supervisors improve service delivery (see the performance measures for Knightdale, North Carolina, on page 160). When individuals have performance targets, they may be useful indicators of the need for training, motivation, or discipline. Performance targets may also be used as a basis for reward, although this practice can result in counterproductive employee behavior, and it limits a manager's discretionary use of authority. Unions typically seek to control performance when quantified work standards are applied to individuals for compensation purposes; unionized workers may tend to work to the rules, becoming relatively rigid and inclined to contest management's decisions.[5]

Work process design Work processes in direct public service delivery are usually defined by those who perform the work. Internal processes may be designed more uniformly by management, which sees the needs of the whole organization. In either case, three factors must be considered in establishing work processes:

- Governmental functions
- Workers and their skills and needs
- People served or affected by the activity.

Managers generally should focus on work modules and work groups rather than on discrete units of work and individual workers. In short, as with performance targets, work processes need to be considered from the perspective of functional organizational management, not individual employee control.

Knightdale, North Carolina, finance department performance measures and workload indicator results

Measure/indicator	Target	FY 2000 actual	FY 1999 actual
Accounting			
Bank statement reconciled within 7 days of receipt	83%	83%	91%
Month closed out within 15 days of month end	83%	67%	75%
CAFR [comprehensive annual financial report] awards received since initial entry in 1991	N/A	9	8
Month-end financial reports complete within 20 days of month end	83%	67%	75%
Accuracy of bank deposits submitted to the bank	100%	99%	98%
Budget			
Annual operating budget submitted to GFOA by 3 months after budget is adopted	Yes	Yes	Yes
Number of budget amendments requiring council approval	N/A	28	16
Average accuracy rate in forecasting all major revenues	90%	99%	88%
Accuracy rate in forecasting ad valorem taxes	90%	96%	95%
Number of GFOA budget awards since first awarded in 1995	N/A	6	5
Investments: average rate of return on investments			
First Citizens	N/A	5.93%	4.27%
North Carolina Capital Management Trust-Cash Portfolio	N/A	6.37%	5.05%
Licensing			
Privilege licenses issued within 10 days of application, except during the billing month	90%	50%	95%

Source: Town of Knightdale, "Annual Budget; Fiscal year Ending June 30, 2001, at 88–90 (May 17, 2000)," in David N. Ammons, "Performance Measurement in North Carolina Cities and Towns," *Popular Government* 67, no. 1 (Fall 2001): 15.
Note to original table: Some data for the column, FY 2000 actual, did not meet target this year. The finance department installed new software for privilege licenses, all financial operations, and the utility billing process. Although the new software installation has been completed, the new system did cause some delays in our normal operations, and therefore staff did not meet all targets.

For results-oriented functional management to succeed, managers need to pay careful attention to how they organize for implementation of policies. Traditional theory assumes that the manager informs subordinates of what needs to be done and subordinates carry out the task because of the authority of the manager. Contemporary managers recognize that those who are responsible for achieving results should participate in deciding how to achieve them. Ultimately, the local government manager has the responsibility for results, but, in reality, local government employees share this responsibility.

Sharing authority with employees   Various forms of participative management attempt to engage members of the work organization in planning for attaining results.

Team management   In team management, parameters are established and a team representing all the units involved in the service or program are brought together to work on planning and organization. Typically, the team or task force has a specific objective in mind, and often a time line is established as well. The advantages of the team approach are that multiple perspectives are likely to emerge and the needs of various parts of the organization are considered in working toward objectives. Redundant efforts and counterproductive steps can be avoided. It is important that the expectations of the group be clearly defined; if they are not, the team may spend a lot of time in meetings that serve no useful purpose.

Project management   Project management is similar to the team approach, but it usually focuses on a specific problem or project. Again, it brings representatives from various parts of the organization together to work toward accomplishment of some task. Project management is particularly effective for programs involving several units of the organization.

Quality management   Another approach to involving people in planning for the achievement of results is quality management, or total quality management (TQM), a system adapted from the manufacturing sector for use in the public sector, with some good results. A major concern of quality management is the process for ensuring quality. Traditionally, evaluation techniques focus on the results or end service product. In the quality management approach, evaluation is continuous; this means that workers examine their activities to identify problems along the way instead of waiting until an activity is complete. Problems can be detected early and corrections made. This approach saves resources by reducing defects—the goal is zero defects—in products or services and by reducing time by lessening the need to go back and find out what went wrong.

An additional benefit of this approach is that the whole organization is brought into the process, and employees develop a stronger commitment to producing services of high quality. Productivity is likely to improve, and the people served are likely to perceive more interest in their concerns. Employees of the government are empowered if the manager is willing to give up some control and accept the full participation of subordinates in decision making and service delivery processes.

Empowerment also requires the manager to provide people the tools to work effectively. The most important of these tools are training and development. In addition, specific skills are often necessary for analyzing the work process and detecting errors or problems. In most quality management approaches, statistical process-control techniques—used to measure and correct variations in service level or quality—are very important. There also must be team training to focus on quality improvement from a group perspective.

There are many ways for management and labor to relate to one another. Some ways actually build a positive work environment that, in turn, contributes to the effective delivery of local government services. Others that are based upon distrust, enmity, and disagreement, however, injure the work environment and derail service delivery.

James Flynt

Learning organization model   The learning organization concept also has been used by local government managers as a way of adapting their organizations to the ever-changing environment. Learning organizations gain information from their environments and use the information to make internal changes, thus affecting the way the organization acts.[6] Local government managers have used this model to help adapt to citizen demands for better services without raising taxes. Learning organizations constantly reinvent themselves to better serve their citizens.

Balanced scorecard   The balanced scorecard management system builds on many other management approaches such as continuous improvement, employee empowerment, and measurement-based management and feedback.[7] The balanced scorecard provides continuous feedback about the internal organizational processes to

Checkpoints for avoiding the traps that can damage your TQM process

Trap 1: Short-term focus	Believe that TQM is a long-term journey, not a destination, and add a sense of urgency
Trap 2: The closed kimono	Don't place blame. Find fame when your employees bring quality problems out into the open
Trap 3: Quality improvement equals staff reduction	If quality improvement can result in a reduced staffing level, utilize attrition rather than termination
Trap 4: A green eyeshade only attitude	Believe that improved customer satisfaction will bring great benefits. Don't look only at the dollars and decimal points
Trap 5: Delegation	Total quality management leadership is too important to delegate
Trap 6: Ignoring the 85/15 concept	Believe that management must be involved in order to resolve 85 percent of your quality problems. Total quality management is not a "fix the worker" program
Trap 7: QI teams are the only way to achieve improvements	Use QI teams extensively, but supplement and complement them with other continuous improvement strategies. Minimal and selected use of quick-hit strategies is okay, but be careful
Trap 8: Training: Too little, too soon	Provide just-in-time training
Trap 9: Formal training only	Build a continuous learning environment
Trap 10: Solving world hunger	Break large issues down to those more solvable problems that can make the greatest difference
Trap 11: Lack of focus	Focus QI efforts on the key goals and CSFs of the company in order to advance more quickly toward your vision
Trap 12: A separate structure	Build a parallel quality organization, not a separate one
Trap 13: The quality department	Don't make the quality unit accountable for quality either implicitly or explicitly. Keep the unit small—an internal consulting staff group
Trap 14: Putting the test site on a pedestal	Showcase the test site carefully. Don't flaunt it or shove it down people's throats
Trap 15: Researching customers' satisfaction	Don't just check on how you are doing in the eyes of the customer. Check to see where you should be going in order to meet customers' needs
Trap 16: The split personality	Practice what you preach in order to shape the desired culture; what gets measured and rewarded gets done

Source: Thomas H. Berry, *Managing the Total Quality Transformation* (New York: McGraw-Hill, 1991), 209–210. This material is reproduced with the permission of The McGraw-Hill Companies.

allow continuous improvement in performance and outcomes. It focuses on four perspectives: learning and growth, business process, customer, and financial.

Tracking progress

Another important aspect of policy implementation, for the manager and for department heads, is tracking progress by means of intermediate productivity measures that indicate, for example, the level of recreational services in a given neighborhood. Automated information systems can help if they are oriented to the needs of central, departmental, and supervisory management. But relatively simple paper and oral reporting systems may serve just as well. For example, a calendar marked with target dates may serve adequately to track some timetables.

Tracking activities and results must be a sustained managerial activity—regular, but not merely routine. Periodic reports are a classic monitoring device. Some audits may need to be randomly scheduled and others selectively scheduled. An apparently spontaneous visit by the manager to an operating department can serve a constructive purpose, particularly when it is timed to highlight an important accomplishment, such as a significant increase in productivity.

Monitoring must be visible except in rare instances, such as investigations of theft, when security or privacy rights are involved. Whenever possible, the information gained from monitoring should be open to all concerned managers. Monitoring can serve as a positive organizational management mechanism rather than as a negative control if it is used to encourage employees by calling attention to their accomplishments and helping them identify areas for improvement.

Productivity   Productivity is defined in economics as the efficiency with which output is produced by the resources used, and it is usually measured as the ratio of outputs to inputs. To focus on effectiveness as well as efficiency, a broader definition is more commonly used in the public sector: the transformation of inputs into desired outcomes. Productivity improvement efforts in government, then, generally include actions to improve policies and services as well as operating efficiency.

A variety of productivity indicators exist: efficiency, effectiveness, responsiveness, quality, timeliness, and cost. Productivity indicators and the information they yield are useful only if they are employed to provide excellent public services, reduce costs, and make improvements when possible.

Productivity applied to investment of financial resources is a related concern. In the current economic environment, local government managers must give the returns on financial investment the same scrutiny as investments in service delivery and support services.

Three approaches to productivity improvement have been successful in the public and private sectors:

- Investment in capital resources and technology
- Strengthened management and work redesign
- Workforce improvement—working smarter and harder.

The second and third approaches relate primarily to improving internal management, which was discussed in the previous chapter. This chapter therefore discusses only investment in capital resources and technology; in addition it explores ways of overcoming obstacles to productivity improvement.

Use of technology in productivity improvement   The greatest increases in output generally have resulted from investments in capital resources (plant and equipment, for example) that make use of state-of-the-art technologies. In fact, in the discipline of economics, the prescription for improved productivity is greater technological efficiency in combining human, natural, and capital resources.

Five interrelated aspects of investment merit the attention of top managers:

The relation of investment to labor costs   Investment in scientific and technological advances and capital resources, along with readily available energy resources, has resulted in large increases in worker productivity. During the 40 years before the extended decline in improvement of productivity that began in the United States in 1968, output per worker increased an average of 3 percent per year, making possible large increases in worker compensation even in the fields outside those responsible for the increased output. Since 1968, the rate of productivity growth has fluctuated. In 1980, it reached its low point and then improved until 1986, when it began declining through 1988. In 1989–1990, the growth rate increased. From 1991 to 1999, the rate of productivity growth again declined. Since 2000, there has been an actual decrease in productivity. The decline in productivity growth, combined with higher labor costs, created incentives for further investment in labor-saving technology. Historically, local governments have been extremely labor intensive, with high workforce costs. The desire for a reduction in labor costs is a strong incentive for introducing technology. Effects on service quality and levels need to be carefully monitored.

Changes in services and public expectations resulting from technological advances   Investment typically results in new products and services as well as new technologies for more efficient production of existing products and services. In the private sector, new-product development is often preceded by market research to identify or change consumer demand. Traditionally, little comparable activity occurred in government. Local governments tended to focus only on production of existing services. Today's citizen surveys and other instruments help identify citizen demand and facilitate government's response. In addition, the greater involvement of citizens and groups in policy making helps educate them about the limits of government's ability to provide services. Thus, citizen demand changes as well.

Technological exchange and its impact on organizations   The usefulness of technology depends on organization size, structure, processes, and external connections. Some governments are too small to profit from some technologies. It makes no sense to acquire firefighting equipment for high-rise structures, for example, in a jurisdiction that has no buildings over three stories high. Experiences of other jurisdictions may or may not apply in a particular community; technological exchange must be evaluated case by case. Nevertheless, as a general rule, experience supports technological exchange and even the shared use of equipment to improve public service and reduce costs.[8]

Use of information technology in decision making   The technology involved in a geographic information system (GIS) is just one example of how modern integrated computer software and data warehousing facilitate management decision making and effective delivery of services.[9] A GIS (Figure 6–3) links many different types of data that pertain to a particular location or area. For example, when a building permit is requested, the GIS can bring up data about the entire infrastructure of the proposed area, types of buildings and businesses, crime rates, traffic patterns, and virtually anything else relevant to the decision. The public works department of Grand Rapids, Michigan, uses a system that permits the staff to map and log work on citizen requests and send an automatic response to the citizen when the work is done. The system combines GIS with mobile responders in the field. Systems like this save an immense amount of time and provide managers with a wealth of data to inform decision making.

Fairfax County, Virginia, developed a citizen relationship management (CRM) program that aggregates and disseminates information to all affected parties. By computerizing information on all county program activities, citizen complaints, and follow-up, the county can track its policies and their effects. Managers and decision makers have complete and accurate information on which to base their decisions and actions. Denise Souder, in *Public Management,* wrote, "A rising intolerance for system failure or for unreliable data is driving many local governments to change the way they do things."[10]

Automated budgeting systems provide similar advantages by linking information systems to allow sharing of data to improve decision making.[11] Automated budgeting enhances the processes of developing, preparing, analyzing, and evaluating budget requests. It also is used for developing budget recommendations and allocations and to control use of appropriated monies. Other automated financial

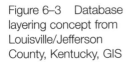
Figure 6–3 Database layering concept from Louisville/Jefferson County, Kentucky, GIS

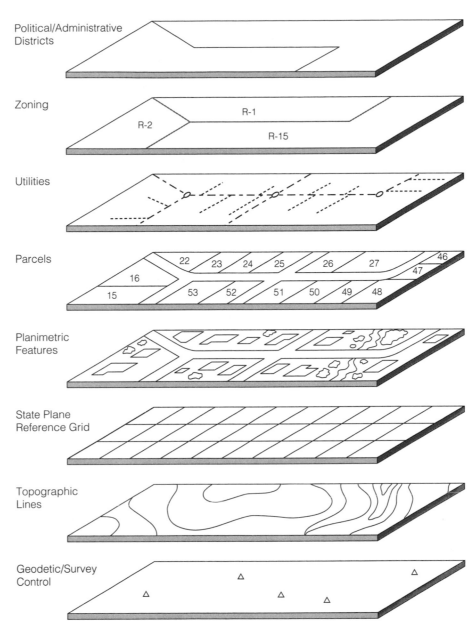

management systems are available to streamline payroll, preparation of financial statements, compliance with appropriations and policy, and maintenance of records (see also Chapter 5).

Cost savings and investment   Investments in equipment and technology are usually expected to yield cost savings. Savings resulting from investment in equipment should at least amortize outlays by the end of its useful life. If an investment is expected to improve productivity by reducing costs, then savings should yield a net return on the investment (including an amount equal to or exceeding the interest). However, improving services is also part of productivity improvement. Among internal service improvements are such things as raising the accuracy of revenue forecasts, reducing the average time to clear financial transfers, and reducing the cost to repair municipal vehicles. Citizens appreciate improvements in response times for addressing utility connections, increased cleanliness of streets and parks, speed in the repair of reported potholes, and reduced waiting time for purchasing permits. Improvements in these productivity measures mean increased citizen satisfaction with local government.

Overcoming obstacles to productivity improvement   With help from employees in identifying four common obstacles to improvement in local government, managers can take actions to overcome them:

Organizational constraints   Organizational constraints in government may derive from political and legal frameworks that cannot be easily changed. Often, however, the limiting factors are structural and procedural and, therefore, are amenable to change by management. A manager must strike a balance between the one extreme of centralization and uniform prescription of rules and procedures and the other extreme of dispersion of responsibility and differentiation of processes to suit every individual's wish. Current information technology makes it easier to exercise control without resorting to rigid and unchanging procedures. In addition, the manager can bring legal obstacles to the attention of elected officials for revision.

Resource limits   The manager must inform citizens and elected officials when resources limit policy, service, and productivity improvement. Cost-benefit assessment may show that reallocation of money, people, equipment, buildings, or other resources will improve productivity. When resource constraints are a major concern, local governments commonly tap into their reserves, increase fees for services, reduce staff, or reduce spending on infrastructure and maintenance.[12]

Information deficiencies   Information is one resource whose deficiencies are most subject to managerial correction. Three practical questions may help identify and eliminate barriers: Which data and analyses are needed? How is the information disseminated? How is it used? The department of planning in Lynnwood, Washington, has improved services for the public by integrating its geographic information and document imaging systems. The document imaging system allows the city to file information digitally instead of on paper. The electronic integration of information results in faster service for the citizen, with more complete information. Investment in information technology is currently of major importance in improving collection and dissemination of information (see Figure 6–4).

Disincentives   Although attention is often given to motivation and incentives, sometimes policy makers make productivity improvements in ways that alienate people; for example, they impose across-the-board budget cuts for both productive economizers and unproductive spendthrifts. Communication with employees is of utmost importance in identifying disincentives.

Government efficiency is another goal. There has been a clear transition from the traditional status quo to an openness to change amongst the city staff. It has been an interesting challenge, and I am heartened by the staff's responsiveness and willingness to make this transition. On my business cards are three words: "open," "agile," and "purposeful." To lead an organization of this size, I think it is essential that we are receptive to new ideas and not defensive.
Craig Malin

Alternative delivery systems

Although public services are typically delivered directly by local government, numerous alternative delivery systems have been used for years, ranging from food

Figure 6–4   Projected state and local information technology expenditures, in billions

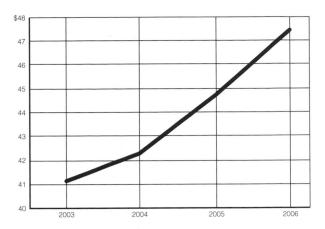

and recreation service franchises to virtually full-scale government by contract, as when urban counties provide almost all services to their small communities. During times of retrenchment, interest in alternative delivery systems increases as officials seek to reduce costs and offer different levels of service on the basis of citizens' willingness to pay.

When choosing alternative service delivery systems, local governments need to develop criteria for evaluating them. The criteria generally include

- Cost of service
- Financial costs to citizens
- Choices available to service users
- Quality and effectiveness of the service
- Distribution of services in the community
- Service continuity
- Feasibility and ease of implementation
- Citizen satisfaction
- Potential overall impact.

Alternative service delivery systems take many forms, described below and also in Chapter 7.

Privatization   Privatization of services, including contracting out and franchising, has become common in local government. Contracting out is the purchase of services from another government or private firm, for-profit or nonprofit. All or only a portion of a service may be involved. Small governments may obtain specialized services and gain advantages of scale by purchasing services. For similar reasons, a government may choose to sell services to neighboring governments. For example, urban county governments often sell computer, law enforcement, and fire services to local municipalities. Contracting out also allows the purchaser to take advantage of market competition to gain efficiency and cut costs.

Contracted services are usually those that are easily defined. Solid-waste collection and water services are easily defined, and both are often contracted privately. Day care, drug treatment, and transportation of disabled people are commonly provided by specialized contractors. Law enforcement, however, is more complex and rarely contracted out except to another general-purpose government.

Like special services contracts, franchises have been used for decades by local government. Franchises are typically awarded to exclusive or nonexclusive providers through competitive or negotiated bidding. Individual citizens usually pay directly for the service, such as for the food served at a sports arena owned by the local government or for an ambulance ride to a hospital. Governments generally charge a percentage of gross or net income as a franchise fee.

Joint ventures   Partnerships between local governments and the private sector have long been common, and they range from relatively modest programs to upgrade downtown storefronts to construction of large public facilities like airports and sports arenas. Usually the local government subsidizes the venture through tax incentives or the development of parking facilities or other public amenities. More recently, joint ventures to upgrade a community's telecommunications infrastructure are becoming common. For example, South Sioux City, Nebraska, partnered with the local cable company to build a fiber-optic network that provides high-speed Internet access to the city, to residents, and to businesses.

Local communities bank on being repaid through taxes on the earnings generated by increased employment and other multiplier effects of joint ventures. Sophisticated citizens, however, may question whether growth compensates for the changes in the environment and character of the community. The local government manager is challenged to accommodate conflicting perspectives on development; this challenge is discussed in Chapter 4.

Intergovernmental contracts and agreements   Local governments have a long tradition of engaging in intergovernmental agreements and contracts, although some states traditionally restrict them. In 1988, the city of Corvallis, Oregon, contracted with the county for repairs to its vehicle fleet, expecting to save as much as 20 percent on maintenance. Fire service is frequently provided under contract or by agreement by a large jurisdiction to smaller communities, and sometimes several units of government get together to provide service such as mass transportation when the need encompasses a large area and requires integration of service. Urban counties in California and Florida often provide municipal services to small communities via contracts or agreements.

Volunteer activity   Volunteer and self-help activity are important alternatives to direct public service delivery. For example, many sheriff's departments and fire departments depend heavily on volunteers. Josephine County, Oregon, uses volunteers for reception desks and filing in its library system and many of its county departments. Some cities, like Virginia Beach, Virginia, have developed robust volunteer programs that fill a wide variety of needs throughout the government and community.

Self-help includes neighborhood watch programs, neighborhood cleanup, and mutual assistance to mentally or physically disabled and elderly residents. Henrico County, Virginia, for example, organized a volunteer program in which seniors help one another, thereby reducing their dependence on the local government.

Volunteer and self-help programs reduce the demand for direct service by local governments, but they have other ramifications as well. For the local government manager, these efforts often bring new actors into the management and policy-making process. Neighborhood groups participate in the policy-making process, and local government managers need to be able to deal with them effectively, as discussed in Chapter 2. In addition, risk management issues may arise, and the manager should consider local government liability when deciding on the level of official responsibility to be assumed by volunteers.

The relationship between policy formulation and implementation

The policy implementation process is complex and involves the participation of many actors. The traditional assumption in public administration was that elected officials make policy and managers implement it, but that assumption no longer holds. If implementation is to be effective, it must be considered as part of the policy-making process. Plans for implementation and the policy's cost as well as benefits must be considered while policy is being made. Otherwise, the policy that is developed may not be realistic. Once developed, the policy depends on the involvement of the whole management team to be effective. Therefore, the effective local government manager must ensure that the management team assumes its responsibility for policy implementation. In addition, it is important to involve citizens and groups affected by the policy.

Evaluation

Evaluation is the collection and analysis of information regarding the efficiency, economy, and effectiveness of programs and organizations. The types of information collected, the types of analysis, and the uses of the knowledge produced vary, but the twin objectives of evaluation remain the same: assessing goal achievement and improving function. In a local government setting, the knowledge generated by evaluation may be used by managers and elected officials to accomplish at least four important tasks:

- Allocate scarce organizational resources
- Determine which goals are being met and which programs are performing as intended
- Identify specific reasons for successes and failures
- Adjust programs for additional improvement or terminate ineffective programs.

It is through these activities that managers monitor and innovate to insure that their program or department adapts to changes in internal and external environments and remains responsive to political forces and public needs.

Departmental vs. program evaluation

The evaluation of departments is generally considered separately from the assessment of programs. Departments are part of the organization of government itself and, consequently, are relatively permanent. They typically exist to execute service functions that remain relatively constant over time—for example, police departments, fire departments, water and wastewater, public works, and transportation. Programs, on the other hand, are subject to the ongoing public policy process and can change from year to year. Programs are often special or innovative means of accomplishing some particular goal or delivering a specific service. For example, many municipal fire departments run programs to deliver crisis counseling to victims of fires or medical emergencies.

Consequently, the options available to the decision maker as a result of an evaluation are different for departments and programs. For example, it is unlikely that an ineffective police department will be dissolved, but a counseling program that fails to deliver quality services might be discontinued. Another difference is that departmental evaluations tend to put more emphasis on changes in performance over time. The methodology and tools for conducting evaluation are largely the same for departments or programs.

Types of evaluation

Program evaluation is the systematic assessment of a program's or a department's goal achievement. Usually there is a longitudinal concern in the assessment, but a typical evaluation is conducted at one point in time to determine goal achievement

Data collection options for program evaluation

Technique	Data collection purpose	Evaluation purpose/phase	Flexibility	Intrusiveness for program evaluated
Sample survey	Study a few people to generalize statistically to larger group	Outcome: performance; Process: attributes, population exposed, effect identification	High: information obtained through questionnaire, telephone contact, personal interview	Low: no demands on staff, facilities
Experiment	Where evaluator can assign people to treatments, determines effect of program	Outcome: performance	Low: must meet standards for control groups, random assignment	High: potential to slow service delivery, must avoid treatment/service denial
Quasi experiment	Where evaluator cannot assign people to treatments, determines effect of program	Outcome: performance	Medium: must meet standards for control groups, no random assignment	Medium: potential to slow service/ treatment delivery
Archival data	Document inputs, outputs of any type	Outcome: effort, performance, adequacy, efficiency; Process: attributes, situational context, effect identification	High: if accurate records are available and machine readable	None: unobtrusive for staff, program participants
Intensive interviews	Study key actors to obtain in-depth information	Outcome: effort, performance, adequacy, efficiency; Process: attributes, effect identification, population exposed	High: time intensive, requires trained interviewers	Variable: to interview staff draws away from jobs; participant interviews unobtrusive for program
Observation	Document inputs, outputs, estimate outcomes	Outcome: effort, performance; Process: attributes, situational context, population exposed	High: time intensive, requires trained observers	Low: Operations observations must be conducted without treatment/ service interruption

over a defined prior period. Performance audits are a type of program evaluation, and sometimes it is implied that departments are subject to audits and programs are subject to evaluations. According to the U.S. General Accounting Office, a performance audit determines the economy, efficiency, and effectiveness of government entities, including their compliance with relevant laws and regulations.[13] Program evaluation, on the other hand, is the use of social science research methods to examine and document the effectiveness of social intervention programs.[14] The significant difference between the two types of evaluation seems to rest with professional disciplines of investigators (auditors tend to be accountants, evaluators tend to be social scientists), the scope of the research (audits tend to emphasize effectiveness, which is defined financially), and certifications available to investigators (auditors tend to be certified public accountants or certified internal auditors, but there is no certified program evaluator program).[15] Yet it is clear that both program evaluation and performance audits may address similar issues.

A third type of evaluation, policy evaluation or policy analysis, is the assessment of actual or probable impacts (outputs and outcomes) of a given policy.[16] Such analyses can be undertaken before implementation (dealing with probable products) or after (dealing with observed products); the analyses identify the likelihood of achieving intended effects, the production of unintended effects, costing features, and projected political and administrative impacts.

Clearly, the differences among performance audit, program evaluation, and policy analysis are a matter of focus and degree. Historically, performance audit is associated with financial and effectiveness assessments; policy analysis is usually narrowly focused on particular policies (though perhaps with multiple goals); and program evaluation is seen as a comprehensive assessment that may be directed by managers or elected officials. The similar thread is that all three are assessments (although foci and purpose may vary) that yield important managerial information. In the following discussion, the term "program evaluation" is used for all types of evaluation.

An evaluation agreement

The reasons for an evaluation—managerial good practice, jurisdictional tradition, or legislative or regulatory requirement (including sunset reviews)—may impact the scope, nature, and frequency of assessment. It is common practice to define an evaluation in a memorandum of understanding, in a statement of scope of work, or perhaps in legislation (for example, a sunset evaluation). This is to the benefit of the manager whose department or program is being evaluated and to the manager directing the evaluation. The formal written agreement should specify whether a department or a program is being scrutinized. A typical agreement addresses six issues: who will evaluate, the scope of evaluation, the type of access to people and records, the cost, the time frame, and important topics for the final report.

Performance measurement and management information systems

An important tool of evaluation, performance measurement is "the ongoing monitoring and reporting of accomplishments, particularly progress toward pre-established goals" that is the responsibility of government managers and department heads.[17] Program evaluation and performance audits document the process and outcomes of a particular program or department at a specific point in time. In contrast, performance measurement is an ongoing program that includes devising specific performance measures (or performance indicators) and continuously collecting information regarding these measures (see the chart on page 172 on fire service measures in Phoenix) that can be incorporated into managerial decisions regarding performance.[18] For example, a police department may collect information on the number of false-arrest lawsuits and their outcomes as one dimension for assessing the utility of existing written guidance on arrest procedures.

In the context just described, performance measurement is part of a management information system: the continual effort of managers to examine the efficiency, effectiveness, or economy of the services delivered by their program or department. Individual performance measures (e.g., number of uncontested arrests) can be used in a program evaluation, but performance measurement is a process separate from an evaluation.

A management information system may involve many different types of measures, some aimed at performance (outcomes and impacts), and others aimed at effort, process, efficiency, and similar dimensions. Montgomery County, Maryland, for example, uses a three-pronged approach of internal auditors, office of legislative oversight, and an inspector general to audit funds, performance, and fraud and waste, respectively. Although the concept of performance measurement is very popular among elected officials, program evaluators, and some managers,[19] its utility

Performance measures in fire services, Phoenix, Arizona, fire department

Function	Sample performance measures
Emergency medical services	Percentage cardiac responses less than 4 minutes Percentage paramedic recertification tests passed on first attempt Number of paramedic continuing education opportunities taught this quarter Number of equipment failures in the field this quarter
Emergency transportation services	Percentage of transportation fees collected Percentage of trauma transports reaching hospital in 5 minutes Average out-of-service time per ambulance per call by patient chief complaint Percentage of Code 3 trips that result in vehicular collision
Special operations: hazardous materials	Percentage of hazardous materials technician re-certification tests passed on first attempt Percentage of hazardous materials incident responses with responder lost-time injury Number of hazardous incident refresher classes taught this quarter Percentage of hazardous materials incident responses with agent identification in under 5 minutes
Fire suppression	Percentage fire incidents with initial response of first due crew in 4 minutes or less Percentage 3-1 fire incidents with command officer arrival 4 minutes or less Percentage fire incidents with damage confined to two rooms or less Percentage fire incidents with all-clear benchmark in 5 minutes or less
Fire prevention	Percentage of new construction plan reviews completed in 72 hours Number of new construction inspections completed per inspector by residential/commercial Percentage of schools in jurisdiction participating in urban fire safety instruction programs Number of public events staged/participated in for fire education this quarter

hinges upon the extent to which particular measures are actually used to accomplish managerial tasks and the degree to which it is integrated into a system that also accounts for aspects of program and department operation that are not related to performance.

The practice of performance measurement has its pitfalls.[20] Perrin has argued that well-chosen performance measures are useful for "monitoring performance, raising questions and identifying problems requiring management attention," but not for "assessing outcomes, determining future directions or for resource allocation." Perrin elaborates a variety of flaws in creating and using performance indicators, including serious issues like performance manipulation and goal displacement: "In Poland under communism, the performance of furniture factories was measured in tons of furniture shipped. As a result, Poland now has the heaviest furniture on the planet."[21] Perrin's complaint focuses not just on the way indicators are devised but also on the way they are used. Even proponents of performance measurement agree that, in the absence of a systematic framework for collating, evaluating, and examining performance indicators, the collection of data on the measures is not useful.[22]

Having good performance measures makes it easier to defend our resource allocations.

Don Gloo

In government, performance measurement is quickly becoming a fact of life. The provisions of the Government Performance and Results Act of 1993 require that federal agencies collect and report performance measures on programs. Thirty states have enacted legislation requiring that agencies engage in at least some level of performance measurement.[23] Cities and counties commonly practice performance measurement,[24] and as of early 2004, more than 100 local governments participate in ICMA's Center for Performance Measurement, a consortium formed to develop and benchmark performance measures for a wide variety of local government functions.

Performance indicators

Performance indicators themselves are multipurpose and can be used in the context of management information systems or program evaluation.[25] The creation of performance indicators—even with a management information system in place—requires careful attention. The guidelines below provide standard guidance for choosing and using performance indicators.

Guidelines for performance indicators

- Target what is meaningful within the context of the program or department. Involve managers, employees, and stakeholders (including citizens) in the process of identifying key indicators of performance and how they will be defined for the data collection process. The goal is to choose indicators that are less subject to misinterpretation or misuse, and more likely to reflect genuinely meaningful outcomes or impacts of the program or department.

- Identify and choose indicators over which the program or department staff exerts direct control. This goes far to ensure that changes in performance are reflected in changes in the level of the indicator. General indicators that are affected by the operation of many programs or people make it difficult to accurately attribute responsibility for changes in performance.

- Test selected indicators before the assessments. Use a trial implementation of information collection and then get feedback from those collecting data and those responsible for the operations that generate the data. Review the information, its interpretation, and the collection process for accuracy, effectiveness, and meaningfulness.

- Reexamine, revise, and update performance indicators regularly. As circumstances, missions, and organizational arrangements evolve, indicators must also evolve; otherwise information will be gathered that does not measure or reflect critical operations. The review process should be widely based, involving managers, employees, and stakeholders.

- Place outcome information in perspective. Finding that a performance indicator is low does not explain why or how performance may have changed. Further investigation of matters unconnected to performance—such as budget, process, personnel changes—is essential to diagnose organizational challenges and improve productivity.

Performance indicators tend to reflect output or outcomes. Measuring the quality of output and outcome may require, for example, going outside the organization or program to get citizens' subjective rating of the quality of services delivered by that department. It is difficult to capture process information with performance indicators, but the interpretation of outcomes and outputs may require process data. Awareness of the limitations of performance measurement is key; performance indicators cannot answer questions they were not designed to answer.

Performance measurement may lead to increased workforce productivity, but it is probably more important as an instrument for the examination and improvement of managerial decision making. By focusing on which tasks are to be performed or services are to be delivered, the manager can systematically identify appropriate strategies, tactics, and processes and allocate resources. The decision-making process is improved to the extent that attention is given to what is to be accomplished and how that accomplishment may be measured. Service is also improved. Citizens and clients benefit because they receive better service and are more able to hold government accountable.

Reasons for evaluation

Program evaluations may be undertaken for a variety of reasons and ordered by a variety of actors. Thus, an assessment may be required by legislation that establishes a program or a department or by administrative rules. In municipalities with internal audit departments, the manager's office may require that every department or some subset of a department's programs be evaluated regularly—perhaps every five years. Program or department directors may order an evaluation as a means of examining operations and improving productivity. Evaluations may be required as a condition of accepting state or federal funding. For example, when the U.S. Department of Housing and Urban Development provides municipalities with funds for safety and drug abuse programs in public housing projects, it requires that the programs be externally evaluated each year.

The auspices under which a program or department is evaluated usually affect the focus and possible outcomes of an evaluation. Sunset evaluations, for example, focus on determining the degree of goal achievement and may result in closure of the department or program if achievement is inadequate. On the other hand, evaluations commissioned by program managers balance emphasis between outcomes and process and typically aim at identifying tactics for improving program operation regardless of the level of goal achievement.

From a practical standpoint, it makes no sense to evaluate before some performance exists to be evaluated. It is important for managers who institute an evaluation of their own program or department to be certain that the conditions for an appropriate evaluation exist: that the program or department has operated long enough, with sufficient resources, to create a structure for achieving goals (or mission) and to generate meaningful outputs. In the technical literature, this is called an evaluability assessment.[26] Managers whose programs are evaluated at legislative or regulatory direction, or at the direction of their managers, should make sure that an assessment of evaluability is carried out. Also, any evaluability assessment by an evaluation team should be accompanied by the manager's own assessment. If the two assessments do not agree, or if the manager's assessment states that nothing yet exists to evaluate, then the evaluation team, the relevant manager, and those who directed the conduct of the evaluation need to communicate. When there appears to be an inadequate structure for goal accomplishment or inadequate output, the manager of the program or department usually documents the situation and provides an appropriate explanation. In such cases, the evaluation team may be asked to determine how the current state of affairs arose, not to conduct a more standard evaluation.

Emphases in evaluation

Program evaluations may emphasize either process, or outcome, or both.[27] Process evaluation, sometimes called formative evaluation, produces information about how or through what mechanisms and structure a program or department operates. Outcome or summative evaluation assesses whether goals have been achieved. Put another way, process evaluation shows how goals are accomplished while outcome evaluation reveals which goals are accomplished, and to what degree. Although outcome evaluation is generally considered critical, most evaluation professionals emphasize the need for balance with regard to process and outcome elements.[28] Conducting an outcome evaluation without including process elements can place an evaluator in the position of either knowing a program works and not being able to explain why, or knowing a program does not work but without a clue about how it might be repaired.

Sometimes legislatively required assessments focus on outcome evaluation to the exclusion of concern with process. Sometimes resources do not permit a multi-faceted evaluation design. Although such exigencies may require a narrower evaluation, managers of programs or departments that fail outcome evaluations should be aware that corrective action may require compilation of information regarding process.

Outcome or summative evaluation   The goal of outcome evaluation is to paint a complete picture of goal achievement in the program or department. A typical picture is composed of four assessments: effort evaluation, performance evaluation, adequacy, and efficiency evaluation. In the broadest sense, these four dimensions are performance standards against which programs or departments might be examined. Each standard is measured in terms of a variety of possible performance indicators.

Process evaluation   In large part, the purpose of process evaluation is to aid in the interpretation of results from other phases of a comprehensive evaluation. In particular, information about process offers a meaningful context for understanding performance evaluations. Process elements in an evaluation focus on understanding and documenting the structure, procedures, and mechanisms through which a program produces results. Process evaluations help pinpoint why successes and failures take place and, in so doing, contribute to the prevention of future failures. Furthermore, process evaluations identify and assess unintended impacts of program or department operation. Most process evaluations begin with the creation of a case or process flowchart. Such charts resemble decision trees or fault trees that specify all operations (decision and contact points) associated with the program or department of interest. An effective process evaluation looks at four dimensions of programs or departments: attributes, population served, situational context, and types of effects.

Equity

In evaluations of programs and policies, contemporary local government managers must always incorporate the criterion of equity in addition to the standard concerns of inputs, outputs, and processes. Equity is a challenging concept to apply at the policy level when different groups of citizens require different services to meet their needs. Managers should account in the evaluation process for such differences in needs and characteristics.

Costs and uses of evaluation

The process of evaluation—the use of management information systems, performance measurement, or program evaluation—is a critical source of information for the local government manager, but it can be costly and elaborate. Managers need to examine carefully the costs of evaluation (in dollars, time, and opportunities not pursued) to be sure that they are adequately balanced by the benefits of evaluation. Performance measurement as a day-to-day management approach regularly involves managers, whose time is valuable and limited; hence, the benefits of this approach should be weighed carefully against the cost in terms of time not available to other activities. The uses made of evaluation information largely determine the evaluation's benefits. Department-level managers may regularly use evaluation information. The manager's office and elected officials must also make constructive use of evaluation for it to fulfill its primary purposes of improving policies, services, and productivity.

Recap

- The chapter, setting the stage for a discussion of program management, describes various aspects of the manager's involvement in policy making: setting the agenda; gatekeeping; managing agenda setting; and designing plans for implementation that define goals, objectives, and priorities.

- Traditionally, local government managers have had to balance three major concerns in administering public policies: efficiency, effectiveness, and economy. Today, however, equity and ethics are receiving increased emphasis. This chapter examined three dimensions of local government program and service management—implementation, productivity, and program evaluation—to identify ways to address these concerns.

- Communication is essential to the success of managerial efforts to implement policy: through assigning responsibilities and allocating resources; using functional management to coordinate resources and performance throughout the organization; encouraging productivity through performance targets and reinforcement of positive job-related behavior; and tracking progress toward desired results. Quality management, employee empowerment, strategic planning, and productivity measures were examined.

- Alternative delivery systems, privatization, joint ventures, intergovernmental agreements, and volunteer activities are used regularly when local governments choose not to perform traditional government functions directly.

- Local governments have found success in improving productivity through investment in capital resources and state-of-the-art technologies. Rank-and-file workers and supervisors can often identify and eliminate many barriers to productivity, but cannot eliminate the systemic barriers of organizational constraints, resource limits, information deficiencies, and disincentives.

- Evaluation can improve a local government's decision-making processes, public policy, services, and productivity. The role of evaluation in program and service management, targets of and types of evaluation, costs and uses of evaluation, and several measures of organizational and program performance were presented.

Case study

Citywide customer service in Peoria

by Duane Otey

Citizens living in Peoria, Illinois, have long wanted and expected service equal to or exceeding the standards set by top-performing private organizations, so the concept of customer service is not new to the city. Peoria's managers and employees are encouraged to examine their respective customer service roles regularly and to renew their commitments to the citizens they serve. The city, which is dedicated to ongoing service delivery improvements, offers comprehensive customer service training and consultation assistance to all its employees.

Project objective   City administrators want to make further improvements in the way in which service is provided, to raise concern for special populations, and to increase efficiency by tapping into techniques of quality management, empowerment, teamwork, and benchmarking. To do these things, Peoria has partnered with citizens through community-based policing, open-space forums, neighborhood associations, citizens' training programs, and town-hall meetings. After considering their feedback, the city manager has called for a citywide emphasis on customer service. In response to this directive, we have interviewed staff and council to measure organizational needs and to help formulate the customer service program's structure. Although each individual had a different point of view, three common concerns emerged. Management should:

- Assess how city staff interacts with citizens.
- Enhance communication skills, as they are key to a successful customer service program.
- Ensure that employees are fully committed to the program.

Research   To benefit Peoria's program, the history of customer service in other local government organizations was researched. As we collected information, the elements of successful programs continued to surface. Although many local governments embrace components of customer service, here is a summary of

three communities that have put in place comprehensive programs.

Grand Rapids, Michigan

- Established a customer service focus in all areas of service.
- Established employee teams to offer input.
- Brought in representatives of private businesses to help train staff.
- Insisted that staff go the extra mile in serving others.
- Redesigned city hall to make it less of a rat maze and installed kiosks.
- Offered all employees name tags.
- Published a pocket-size, eight-page, waterproof city service directory for all employees.
- Believed, and believes, that if you give most staff the proper tools, they will do a good job.

Chesapeake, Virginia

- Began the "Year of the Citizen" program in 1991.
- Has established employee focus groups to answer questions like "What frustrates you?" and "How can we improve?"
- Trains new employees yearly.
- Has developed the *Customer Satisfaction Depends on Me* training handbook, course handouts, and a historic outline of the development of its customer service program.

Phoenix, Arizona

- Has appointed service-representative teams within each department to develop, administer, and evaluate customer service projects. The teams assess points of customer contact, service cycles, service blockages, and service delivery data and recommend improvements.
- Now, offers a one-day workshop entitled "Identifying Service Vision and Values" to department directors and top managers; a two-day "Systems and Structures Audit" workshop to service-representative team members; and a two-day "Building Customer Skills" workshop for all front-line workers.

Peoria's plan   Peoria's program was put in place last year to help employees focus their attention on delivering high-quality service and customer satisfaction, using a customer service model to raise the overall efficiency of the city at the systemic level. Because of the size of the organization and the complexity of its mission, full program implementation could take 12 to 18 months. It is the staff's intention, however, to maintain an emphasis on customer service indefinitely. Table 1 highlights the components of Peoria's program.

Classroom training is a critical component in conveying the customer service message. Peoria employees are required to attend a variation of the foundation course, "Providing Quality Customer Service," which covers the basic elements.

Department and division heads, supervisors, and key management personnel attend "Managing Customer Service Operations and Personnel."

Both courses help employees share a common vision of our service strategy. A series of elective courses also helps develop basic skill sets. Table 2 lists courses that will be featured under the customer service banner. And, to complement these activities, two new courses have debuted in 2000: "Executive School for Municipal Leaders" and the "Supervisor Development Series."

Duane Otey is citywide training coordinator, human resources department, Peoria, Illinois.

Table 1   Elements of Peoria's customer service program

Program component	Description
Classroom training	Two principal courses help employees understand basic customer service principles, while 14 elective courses develop the skill sets necessary to deliver good customer service.
Site visits and tours	Organizations within the community that have achieved exemplary customer service offer informational tours of their facilities, giving practical examples of how facility layout and appearance affect organizational efficiency and public perception.
Internal and external consultation services	A list of internal experts on various topics serves as the city's own speakers' bureau of internal consultants. These individuals help other divisions and departments with consultation and special training.
Training—library materials	The citywide training library has been stocked with new customer service materials, including videos, books, periodicals, cassettes, pamphlets, and brochures from localities throughout the country.
Public forums/ open-space events/ surveys	City departments sponsor citizen surveys and public hearings to gain insight into service delivery and aspects that need improvement. Employees are encouraged to attend the hearings for a greater awareness of citizen concerns and city issues.
Intra- and interdepartmental quality teams	Interdepartmental high-quality teams examine service delivery systems that require cooperation from two or more departments, and teams review internal systems. These teams are responsible for reviewing service objectives and taking steps toward process improvement.
Lecture series: help from the experts	Several one-hour presentations (a continuation of a breakfast series) feature customer service experts from local businesses, medical centers, and utility companies that have developed finely tuned delivery systems for customer services.
Performance measurement	Each department and division integrates measurable customer service objectives into its respective annual performance indicators (APIs). API statistics assist in measuring the progress of customer service activities.

Table 2   Customer service training courses and the times allotted to each

Course titles	Course times
Foundation courses	
Providing Quality Customer Service	3.5 hours
Managing Customer Service Operations and Personnel	7 hours
Elective courses	
Advanced Telephone Skills for Front-Line Operators	3.5 hours
Assisting Citizens with Obtaining City Services	1.5 hours
Basic Telephone Skills for Front-Line Operators	3.5 hours
Building Teams	7.5 hours
Conducting Focus Groups and Public Forums	7 hours
Developing Customer Service Questionnaires	6.5 hours
GO FISH!	3 hours
Increasing Communications	3.5 hours
Process Improvement	7 hours
Public Speaking	(2) 3.5-hour sessions
Serving Internal Customers	(2) 3.5-hour sessions
Serving All the Customers	2.5 hours
Understanding Personality Styles	3 hours
Verbal Judo	7.5 hours

Exercise

Assume you are the manager of a medium-sized municipality with a public transit department that operates its own buses and vans.

1. Specify the criteria you would use for measuring the performance of the department.
2. What processes would you use for actually conducting the assessment?

Now, assume you are the manager of a similar city that contracts for its public transit function.

1. What are the criteria you would use in evaluating bids to provide the service?
2. Are there differences between the criteria used in evaluating this service and those for the service in the city with its own transit department? If so, explain what they are and why different criteria would be applied.

Notes

1 Thomas R. Dye, *Understanding Public Policy,* 9th ed. (Upper Saddle River, N.J.: Prentice-Hall, 1998), 2.

2 John W. Kingdon, *Agendas, Alternatives and Public Policies,* 2nd ed. (New York: HarperCollins Publishers, 1995).

3 Charles F. Bonser, Eugene McGregor, and Clinton Oster, *American Public Policy Problems,* 2nd ed. (Upper Saddle River, N.J.: Prentice-Hall, 2000), 90.

4 Jeffrey L. Pressman and Aaron Wildavsky, *Implementation,* 2nd ed. (Berkeley: University of California Press, 1979), 143.

5 Chester A. Newland, "Labor Relations," in *Productivity Improvement Handbook for State and Local Government,* 2nd ed., ed. George J. Washnis, 503–529 (New York: John Wiley, 1980).

6 Peter M. Senge, *The Fifth Discipline: The Art and Practice of the Learning Organization* (New York: Currency/Doubleday, 1990).

7 Robert S. Kaplan and David P. Norton, *The Balanced Scorecard: Translating Strategy into Action* (Cambridge: Harvard Business School Press, 1996).

8 Public Technology, Inc., exists to assist local governments with technological exchange; see http://pti.nw.dc.us/.

9 Tony Leno, "Is GIS Good for Local Government?" *Public Management* (June 1989): 15–16.

10 Denise Souder, "CRM Improves Citizen Services In Fairfax County," *Public Management* 83 (May 2001): 14–16.

11 Jack Monahan, "Automated Budgeting Decision Support System," IQ Report, 34 (Washington, D.C.: ICMA, September 2002).

12 Michael A. Pagano and Christopher W. Hoene, "Cities Confront Tough Choices as Fiscal Conditions Decline—Economic Recovery Threatened," *Research Brief on America's Cities* (National League of Cities), no. 2003-2 (May 2003).

13 U.S. General Accounting Office, *Standards for Audit of Governmental Organizations, Programs, Activities and Functions,* 4th ed. (Washington, D.C.: Government Printing Office, 1988).

14 Peter Rossi, Howard Freeman, and Mark Lipsey, *Evaluation* (Newbury Park, Calif.: Sage, 1999), 4.

15 Dwight F. Davis, "Do You Want a Performance Audit or a Program Evaluation?" *Public Administration Review* 50 (January/February 1990): 35–41.

16 Evert Vedung, *Public Policy and Program Evaluation* (Piscataway, N.J.: Transaction Publishers, 1997).

17 Grover Starling, *Managing the Public Sector,* 6th ed. (New York: Harcourt Brace, 2002), 392.

18 Center for Accountability and Performance, *Performance Measurement: Concepts and Techniques* (Washington, D.C.: American Society for Public Administration, 1998).

19 R. L. Schlalock, *Outcome-Based Evaluation* (New York: Plenum, 1995).

20 Burt Perrin, "Effective Use and Misuse of Performance Measurement," *American Journal of Evaluation* 19, no. 3 (1998): 367.

21 Ibid., 368.

22 David J. Bernstein, "Comments on Perrin's Effective Use and Misuse of Performance Measurement," *American Journal of Evaluation* 20, no. 1 (1999): 85–93.

23 J. Melkers and K. Willoughby, "The State of the States," *Public Administration Review* 58 (January/February 1998): 66–73.

24 Evan Berman, Jonathan West, and Wang Xiaohu, "Using Performance Measurement in Human Resource Management," *Review of Public Personnel Administration* 19 (Spring 1999): 5–17; and Peter Kettner, Robert Moroney and Lawrence Martin, *Designing and Managing Programs,* 2nd ed. (Thousand Oaks, Calif.: Sage Publications, 1999).

25 Ronald Sylvia, Kathleen Sylvia, and Elizabeth Gunn, *Program Planning and Evaluation for the Public Manager* (Prospect Heights, Ill.: Waveland Press, 1997), 104.

26 Emil Posavac and Raymond Carey, *Program Evaluation: Methods and Case Studies* (Upper Saddle River, N.J.: Prentice-Hall, 1997).

27 Carol Weiss, *Evaluation* (Upper Saddle River, N.J.: Prentice-Hall, 1997).

28 Blaine Worthen, James Sanders, and Jody Fitzpatrick, *Program Evaluation* (New York: Longman, 1997).

7 Relating to other organizations

Jill, assistant to the city manager in charge of intergovernmental matters for a medium-sized suburb, spends nearly all day, every day, working with representatives of other governments and organizations. Her activities, mainly legislative matters, can be politically charged. Some weeks she focuses on telecommunications issues and interacts with a statewide coalition of city representatives and state legislators on relevant committees; she advocates not just for her city but for all cities in the region. She also periodically contacts administrators at the Federal Communications Commission for their interpretations of various regulations and possible advance notice of future agency policy. Other weeks find her addressing the problems of emissions and air quality. In addition to her frequent interaction with officials from the state department of environmental management and the U.S. Environmental Protection Agency, she develops regional air quality plans in consultation with scientists, local activists, and representatives from other cities, counties, and special districts. Critical metropolitan problems such as transportation and land use can also take up much of her time, resulting in much more extragovernmental activity. She describes her various activities as taking place "merely where my desk is located."

Jack is the director of the department of community development for a large central city. His duties require him to lead many development projects and programs that involve diverse populations. The primary responsibility of his office is to administer the various Department of Housing and Urban Development Community Planning and Development formula grant programs, including Community Development Block Grant (CDBG) funds and HOME Investment Partnerships. He works extensively with a nine-member citizens' advisory committee that prepares and reviews the city's consolidated plan, as well as with the local housing authority, builders, and groups who want to use the city's CDBG allocation. Jack also develops and maintains links with workforce development networks, regional university and research institutes, and organizations such the city's chamber of commerce that promote tourism. In addition, Jack's office also oversees funding relationships with human services agencies, including an adult day care, a children's advocacy center, and numerous charities providing emergency relief.

These examples show that governing is both a bureaucratic and a multiorganizational enterprise. It is bureaucratic in the sense that work takes place in single organizations that have defined hierarchies, clear divisions of labor, and a multitude of operating rules and procedures. It is also multiorganizational—and increasingly so. Cities, counties, special districts, and schools in metropolitan areas operate in a quasi-regional conglomeration, where problems that transcend the artificial geographical boundaries of each jurisdiction are addressed through coordination, collaboration, and exchange. Even a small, remote city or rural county spends a great deal of time working with state and federal governments, rural councils, and local organizations in order to increase development, regulatory compliance, and grants-in-aid. Local governments of all kinds and sizes develop strategies and produce goods and services through contractual agreements, partnerships, alliances, task forces, coalitions, networks, and good, old-fashioned intergovernmental activity.

Local governments relate not only to other local governments; they are also embedded in a much larger and more complex multigovernmental, multiorganizational environment. The ability of local governments to accomplish goals and solve problems is linked strongly, sometimes directly, to the capacities of other organizations. Citizens vote for persons to represent them within their city and county borders, and city and county governments hire personnel to work on behalf of the citizens, but more and more of today's governing involves extrajurisdictional relationships. That local government managers must operate across organizations as well as within hierarchies is now an accepted and expected part of public administration.

I try to spot a need and then create a mechanism to address that need.
Bryce A. Stuart

The number and variety of governments and nongovernmental organizations (NGOs) is so complex that a traditional administrative or legal focus on formal powers and constitutional structures offers an incomplete picture of the role and function of local governments. It is more appropriate today to examine the actual intergovernmental, interorganizational, and intersectoral relations that encompass all levels of government and the myriad public programs designed and administered by government agencies. Just as a local manager must be aware of the relationships prescribed by the U.S. and state constitutions, so too must the manager understand the number and variety of governmental units, the variety of public officials involved, the intensity of contacts among officials, and the importance of how relations vary across policy areas.

This chapter discusses the form and content of a local government's external relations. It first looks at changes in society that affect how local governments operate. Second, it examines the multitude of relationships with governmental organizations and NGOs, including the activities performed in both the vertical and horizontal environments. The chapter next examines how local officials manage their jurisdiction's external relations. It concludes with a list of suggestions for managing external relations.

The transformation of local government

Local governments have never operated in isolation. Much of the history of governing in the United States and in many other countries is rooted in citizens' strong preference for local rather than national solutions; and these solutions have traditionally involved charities, churches, and town associations as well as the legal and financial power and framework of the national and state governments.

The pace and quality of change in government in the twenty-first century is unprecedented, however. A radical transformation in how policy preferences are determined and program outputs are delivered has been occurring throughout the world. Although the bureaucratic organization seemed to be the ideal organizational structure during the industrial age, during the twentieth century, government increased in size and scope, and now an emerging form of organization is supplementing and in some cases supplanting the work of bureaucracies.[1] The new signature form—the collaborative network—is less rigid and more permeable than bureaucratic organizations. Local managers link across internal functions, jurisdictional and sectoral boundaries, and geographic boundaries. As the examples of Jill and Jack suggest, a local manager will often spend more time working externally than within the confines of the home organization.

Changes in society

External relations for local governments constitute a unique institutional form consisting of processes different from the spontaneous coordination of markets or the conscious management of hierarchy.[2] How can we account for such an organizational transformation? Futurists, business leaders, and contemporary organization theorists argue that the emergence of multiorganizational structures and processes is merely a reflection of a much more profound social change. In the world of the twenty-first century, power is more dispersed, work is increasingly despecialized, and preferences are diverse rather than integrated. A similar explanation asserts the importance of information and knowledge as a resource in organizational performance. The most valuable worker is one who possesses skills in problem solving and strategic brokering that may not always require reliance on hierarchical forms of organization.

Citizens' expectations of government reflect the society's increasing individuation and diversity. The problems and issues that society seeks to address collectively are often poorly defined, with unclear goals and, thus, imperfect solutions.[3] Bureaucratic agencies are best at fashioning technical and repetitious responses to emergent problems, but the "wicked" problems that are predominant in society do not lend themselves to such manipulation. Solutions to such problems typically lie outside of government, even as governments are held accountable for finding and implementing the solutions. Similarly, citizens often simultaneously—and somewhat paradoxically—demand more public action but less government.[4] Citizens expect government to fix problems but with limited resources, making the involvement of nongovernmental actors necessary for effective public action. Finally, increasing demands by citizens for solutions are accompanied by greater political demands for inclusion in the problem-solving process. The blunt act of voting is no longer sufficient for exerting a democratic influence on traditional policy makers. Policies are now often planned and formulated outside of legislatures in community groups, committees, and task forces. Many intergovernmental programs even mandate multiorganizational linkages as part of the implementation process.

New management perspectives

Public policy making is not a purely bureaucratic exercise. Public policy making in the twenty-first century is affected by new forms of collaboration, blurring of jurisdictional boundaries, extragovernmental alliances, and the interactions within a loose network of many organizations and institutions.

Collaboration "The process of facilitating and operating in multiorganizational arrangements for solving problems that cannot always be achieved, or achieved easily, by single organizations" is one definition of the collaborative model of management.[5] The term collaboration should not be confused with cooperation. Although both mean working jointly with others to some end, cooperation suggests that those working jointly seek to be helpful as opposed to hostile. A great deal of collaboration is cooperative, but collaborative relationships can also be tense, even combative. Some collaboration is voluntary, but other collaboration is mandated by the state and federal governments.

***Administrative conjunction*[6]** A de facto regionalism is emerging, not as a formal initiative embodied in a single government, but as a redefinition of the relationship between citizens and their government. The link between jurisdiction and public management is weakening. First, the borders of jurisdictions increasingly are porous.

The problems that citizens want addressed are seldom contained in a single municipality. Because people often work in one city, shop in another city, and vote in still another, they have few social, political, and financial commitments to the jurisdictions in which they live. Second, the largest cities, which are the central cities and inner-ring suburbs of metropolitan areas, have the greatest problems but the least capacity to solve them. Third, even as jurisdictional borders are becoming less relevant in defining problems, political leadership within jurisdictions is still more important than political leadership between the jurisdictions. Citizens vote for representatives whose success may, at least in part, be determined by the actions of elected officials in other communities. Finally, settlement patterns and voting behavior show that although people prefer fragmentation and they resist consolidation, they also want their metropolitan area to work and act like a single entity. These factors contribute to a set of external relations that can supersede the actions of a single government.

Regime theory   Regime theory of governing suggests that as complexity increases, nongovernmental actors become necessary components of a local delivery system. Multiple actors build long-lasting alliances to do what the government alone cannot do. Alliances or regimes do not prevent effective governing but instead provide necessary contributions to a city's capacity to govern. Governments must blend their capacities with those of various nongovernmental actors to be effective, and "government capacity is created and maintained by bringing together coalition partners with appropriate resources, non-governmental as well as governmental."[7] In essence, regimes increase the ability of local governments to design and implement public goods and services.

Social production   A community is a loosely coupled network of institutional arrangements and, as such, is characterized by a lack of coherence or control, and government no longer plays an exclusive role in coordinating and establishing control. Social production occurs in a complex, fragmented system of governments and NGOs when enough cooperation is developed to get things done.[8] Multiple institutions mean multiple, potentially conflicting preferences, but they also can lead to new possibilities and innovative solutions. The social production model reminds us that a synthesis of external resources, rather than a battle over compliance and discretion, is not only possible but also necessary for effective governing.

The external environment

Local government external relations are both vertical and horizontal. Vertically, local governments deal with regulations and seek access to available resources within the legal and administrative frameworks of the national and state governments. Vertical relations are pursued to achieve local goals with state and national resources, and vice versa. In many cases, local governments must find a balance between the national or statewide purposes embodied in an intergovernmental program and the needs of the local community.

Horizontal relations involve the array of public and private interests that often participate in the production of public services. The horizontal environment of a local government includes the policy-making resources held by NGOs, private agencies, and area local governments.

A local manager may be involved in managing across governmental boundaries (vertical relations) within the context of one program or project while simultaneously managing across organizational and sectoral boundaries (horizontal relations) within the context of another program or project. Operating simultaneously in each environment can also occur within the context of the same program or project.[9]

The extraordinary number and types of governmental organizations and NGOs in the United States are striking.[10] There are more than 87,000 units of government in the United States. In addition to the national government and the governments of the 50 states, there are 3,034 counties, 19,429 municipalities, 16,504 townships, 13,506 school districts, and 35,052 special districts. Approximately 21 million persons are employed directly by government in the United States, nearly 7 percent of the total workforce. State and local governments account for 18.3 million employees, 87 percent of the total. The number and proportion of state and local government personnel have been increasing since the middle of the twentieth century. In 1950, state and local government employees made up 54.4 percent of the public workforce; in 2002, that proportion was more than 87 percent. As if 87,000 governments are not complex enough, there were an estimated 1.2 million nonprofit organizations in the United States in 1998, with more than 7 percent of the workforce employed by these organizations. Millions more volunteer their time to nonprofit organizations such as charities and foundations. At least one-sixth of the population thus is involved in producing and delivering public goods and services to citizens.

Adding to the complexity of governing in the United States is the number of different functions performed by each type of local government. For example, counties are general-purpose governments that function on a level between the state and the municipality. One role counties play is to serve as an administrative arm of the state—managing such functions for the state as the state trial and appellate court system and the district attorney's office, assessing property taxes, recording deeds, and providing various health and welfare services such as child welfare and mental institutions. Municipalities are also general-purpose governments, but they vary tremendously in size and scope. As defined by the U.S. Census Bureau, a municipal government is a political subdivision within which a municipal corporation has been established to provide general local government for a specific population concentration in a defined area. Municipalities may limit or prohibit activity and property uses in order to protect the public health, safety, and general welfare.

School districts are single-purpose jurisdictions established to administer the public education of children. In most states, school systems are run by autonomous governments that have their own taxing, spending, and borrowing authority. Often their boundaries do not coincide with the boundaries of the community they serve, which adds to the fragmentation that is the hallmark of government in the United States.

Governments similar to school districts are special district governments. When citizens of a particular place desire to provide a single function or a limited set of functions, they can create a special government that suits their purposes and needs more effectively. Special districts are used most commonly for natural resource functions such as flood control, irrigation management, and wildlife and land conservation. Other uses include fire protection, housing, transportation administration, solid-waste administration, water, and sewage.

Vertical relations

Vertical relationships in the United States are defined in legal terms by the U.S. Constitution and the 50 state constitutions. The formal relationship between the national government and the state governments is federal, which means the exercise of power is divided between two levels of government. The U.S. Constitution grants some powers specifically to the national government (in Article I, Section 8, of the U.S. Constitution) and reserves others to the states (primarily in the Tenth Amendment). Some powers—including the power to elect representatives who make laws, raise revenue, and decide the purposes for which the revenue is raised—are held by both the national and state governments. First and foremost, federalism is a structural arrangement designed to accommodate simultaneously a strong, autonomous central (national) government and a system of strong, autonomous constituent (state) governments. The boundaries of the power distribution are essentially territorial, although the constituent territories reflect cultural diversity and thus varying packages of policy preferences. Federalism is viewed by some as a means to create and foster national unity while it preserves the respective integrities of its people.[11]

Federalism is also a process. In the United States, the division of power between the national and state governments is not static.[12] The structure provides the environment within which the power division can be debated, altered, and clarified through a continual process that involves the participation of both the national and the state levels of government.[13] As a result, the actual division of power has changed over time. During the nation's first several decades, there existed a so-called dual federalism within which each level of government claimed and maintained its own spheres of power and influence. Interaction between the levels was infrequent but competitive. Slowly since the middle of the nineteenth century and rapidly since the 1930s, a system of shared powers and a cooperative federalism has existed to varying degrees within different policy areas.

In our era of shared functions, both the national and state governments exercise significant decision-making power during the formulation of a given program, and officials from both levels of government exert significant influence over the administration and operation of that program.[14] Such sharing is seen by some people as the national government exerting undue influence in local affairs, resulting in a top-heavy, nation-centered relationship and reduced power in state and city governments.

One attempt at minimizing the regulatory reaches of the national government and restoring what some perceive as a balance to federalism in the United States and also in many other countries is devolution. Devolution is a term used to describe the shifting of policy responsibilities downward from the national government to states and local governments. The argument for devolution stems from a belief in local self-governance—that power, autonomy, and flexibility should reside as far down in the governmental system as is possible in practice. Through lobbying, repeated administrative requests, and often a lack of resources or unwillingness to spend money, some policy areas have been devolved from the national to the subnational governments. However, some critics of national-government policy making argue that devolution has heretofore been more philosophy than practice in the United States.[15]

State-local relations

The formal relationship between state governments and the local governments within each state is unitary. Unlike the power division of federalism, a local government possesses only those powers formally granted to it by the state. A state government creates a local government, specifically grants it autonomy in various administrative and policy areas, allows it to govern, and can legally abolish it. Local governments rarely can opt out of fulfilling state objectives. States shape the activities of local governments through the use of state mandates, and they may order local units to regulate private activities, provide services, refrain from using some types of taxes, limit tax rates, and use a particular personnel system.

Although national and state courts generally view local governments as legal creatures of their states, in practice, the amount of local government discretion varies by region, type of unit, and type of function performed. Generally, local units enjoy more discretion regarding their structure and organization than they do regarding the functions they perform or the ways they raise and spend revenues. Also, local governments are not powerless and can wield significant influence in state legislatures.

The states have substantial legal, financial, and administrative powers over local governments, but a host of factors often limits the willingness of state officials to use these powers. The tradition of local self-government is, for example, stronger in New England than in the South. Municipalities, on the whole, enjoy greater self-government than do counties and other units of local government. Fear of adverse reactions by the public and by local officials and concern that state action may produce negative results serve to restrain state intervention in many instances.

State and local agencies also cooperate administratively in many different policy areas, including economic development, human services, land use, transportation, natural resources, and the environment. States are dominant—no local manager would refute that—but the extent of dominance and the concomitant level of local discretion vary across policy areas.

For the first 140 years or so of governance under the U.S. Constitution, the state-local relationship was the paramount U.S. intergovernmental connection. Then, beginning in the 1930s, federal-state programs of the New Deal and the expanded intergovernmental partnership that resulted from the Great Society programs in the 1960s reduced slightly the significance of the state-local nexus, but recent trends have restored the subnational system. States provide nearly $300 billion in aid to local governments each year, and the amount increases, on average, much faster than the national inflation rate.[16] State aid accounts for more than 20 percent of all city revenues and approximately 40 percent of county revenues; and, in some states, state aid provides more revenue to school districts than the districts raise themselves through taxation and fees.[17] As a proportion of total state-local activity, state government own-source revenues, expenditures, and personnel increased substantially during the twentieth century, and since the 1970s in particular. Overall, the chief source of grant aid to local governments is state government.

Local managers understand that increasing aid means greater involvement and more strings attached by state government to local affairs. In many ways, state-local relations can be defined by the extent to which states make use of mandates to influence local government activity and achieve statewide policy objectives. Many local managers have little difficulty with the goals of many state mandates. In some cases, local managers who deal with unhappy community residents during the implementation of some unpopular programs actually welcome the political cover that mandates provide. But mandates that impose costs on the local government without providing accompanying funding or that do not reflect local preferences present the most serious obstacles for local governments. Compliance can be very expensive.

Other factors contribute to muddled state-local relations. The increase of federal-state programming and the concomitant de-emphasis of federal-local programs since the 1980s may have minimized the voice of local government. In addition, attempts to come to grips with the more intractable problems of modern life, greater pressure on states to deal with metropolitan problems, and the enhanced ability of states to raise greater amounts of tax money for revenue-sharing purposes have combined to put a strain on state-local partnerships.[18] Improving state-local relations has thus become a strategic goal of many states.

One national model for effective state-local relations is the Wisconsin governor's Commission on State-Local Partnerships for the Twenty-First Century (the Kettl Commission). The commission was charged with demonstrating the importance of state-local relations and devising proactive steps that can be taken to help configure a system from which each level can benefit.[19] Many other states have agencies and commissions that focus on state-local relations and seek to sort out state and local responsibilities.

Improving state-local relations in Wisconsin   In April 2000, the governor of Wisconsin, Tommy Thompson, launched the Commission on State-Local Partnerships for the Twenty-First Century (also known as the Kettl Commission). His charge to the commission was to think boldly and creatively, conduct nothing less than a mini–constitutional convention, and craft solutions that would launch Wisconsin's governments effectively into the twenty-first century. The commission was based on the idea that government leaders throughout the country recognize the central importance that state-local partnerships must play in providing an excellent quality of life for their citizens.

Although it was tempting to suggest that government boundaries needed to be redrawn or, perhaps, an entire level of government needed to be abolished, the commission concluded that those would be nineteenth-century answers to twenty-first-century problems. The problems of the information age do not call for new boundaries. Instead, they require innovative strategies to create seamless government for Wisconsin's citizens. After fifteen commission meetings, seven town meetings throughout the state, countless discussions with citizens and government officials, and electronic forums on the Internet over a period of nine months, the commission laid out its recommendations for how best to structure the twenty-first-century state-local partnership. The first three recommendations are:

- Wisconsin must immediately launch a major effort to rebuild its state-local partnership. The first steps in doing so require all members of this partnership, at both the state and local levels, to recognize the valuable role that all of the partners play and for all the players to work with their partners with an attitude of mutual respect.

- Wisconsin should launch a long-term, statewide effort to continue conversations among all members of the state-local partnership. There must be a constant, ongoing discussion of the system's basic problems and enduring values. The truly important effort must begin as the commission's work ends.

- The most important strategy for Wisconsin government in the twenty-first century is not redrawing the boundaries between governments but in strengthening the partnerships among them. Wisconsin's state and local governments need to focus much less on the boundaries of their programs and jurisdictions. They need to focus much more on how best to collaborate in solving their citizens' problems. Putting citizens at the center—with the reminder that the central purpose of Wisconsin's governments is to serve the state's citizens—is the basic compass that ought to guide the state-local partnership in the twenty-first century.

Source: *Wisconsin Blue-Ribbon Commission on State-Local Partnerships for the 21st Century* (January 2001), www.lafollette.wisc.edu/reform/report011001.pdf.

National-local relations

Although courts view local governments as legal creatures of their states, this legal condition has not prevented the establishment of direct ties between local governments and the national government. At various times in history, local governments have found the national government willing to help address problems facing local officials and willing to involve local officials in the shaping of national policies directed at these problems. The extensive contacts between the national government and local governments have grown up for a number of reasons:[20]

- Rapid urbanization and the growth of metropolitan areas resulted in local problems in cities that affect other cities. This so-called spillover effect is a primary justification for vertical government involvement in the subsidization and/or provision of public services.

- Up until the past few decades, states were unwilling or unable to respond to local demands, a situation that encouraged local officials to bypass the state and go directly to the national government with their concerns.

- National-local contacts have also been stimulated by the substantial influence wielded by officials from large cities. Organizations of local officials, such as the National League of Cities and the National Association of Counties, have been active advocates in Washington for their constituencies, which partly comprise large collections of urban voters.

- Perhaps the most important reason for the development of national-local relations has been need. The New Deal, born in the 1930s out of the devastation of the Great Depression, dramatically increased the scope of the national-local partnership. Local officials from all over the country, but especially from large cities, clamored for national assistance to meet the problems of unemployment, relief, housing, public works, and slum clearance. Following the depression years, direct national-city programs emerged in such areas as housing and urban development, which called for only minimal involvement of state governments. School districts, counties, and other units of local government also enjoyed relatively free access to national funds. The programs of the Great Society in the 1960s resulted in an expansive redefinition of intergovernmental relations to include an emphasis on local governments and nonprofit organizations as partners. National aid programs showed a pronounced shift in favor of urban and metropolitan areas: grant-in-aid outlays from the national government nearly doubled between 1964 and 1968, and the proportion of national aid channeled to local governments increased by more than 50 percent.

The shift in local governments' relationship with the national government has been well documented. While the demands of coercive regulations grew larger, the incentives for local involvement in achieving national goals were lessened. National aid to state and local governments peaked in 1978, declined in real dollars in 1982, and has since grown steadily but very slowly. Most important, in the early 1980s, nearly all significant national-local grants were eliminated except for entitlement programs such as CDBGs and some transportation funds. Direct aid to local governments went from nearly 30 percent of total aid in 1978 to less than 12 percent in the late 1990s. Similarly, during the 1960s, localities increasingly became the target of national regulations; this control did not abate during the 1980s, however, and it continues today even with more restricted funding.

One result of national cutbacks and the concomitant devolution revolution is embodied in the status of the funds given to states in the form of block grants, which are then allocated (passed through) to local governments. Counties are prime recipients of such funding, especially for social welfare, corrections, and environmental protection. The relationship between the original recipient, the state agency, and the secondary recipient, the associated county agency, thus becomes more important than the national-state linkage.

In spite of the shock to the intergovernmental system that began with decreases in federal funding in the late 1970s, the national-local relationship still is important and consequential. The Transportation Equity Act for the 21st century (TEA-21) emphasizes regional governance and metropolitan planning as it provides funds to state and metropolitan bodies. In fiscal year 2002, TEA-21 provided more than $31 billion for highway work and nearly $7 billion for mass transit, which is clearly a concern for a number of local governments. To address concerns about the regulatory might of the national government, Congress passed the Unfunded Mandates Reform Act in 1995, which ostensibly prohibits Congress from enacting any mandates above $50 million (adjusted yearly for inflation) unless funding is provided. Though the intent was laudable, local officials are quick to point out that federal preemption of regulatory authority has not diminished; in the area of telecommunications, for example, the Federal Communications Commission has diminished local control of public rights of way.

Homeland security is also an important and somewhat contentious issue for the national government and local governments. Local officials need funds to help cover the costs of new, unprecedented responsibilities in the nation's defense against terrorism, and they have turned to the national government for assistance to offset security costs incurred since September 11, 2001. Because of the planning requirements and staffing demands placed on local governments by national agencies such as the Department of Homeland Security and the Federal Bureau of Investigation, local governments are demanding technical as well as financial assistance.

Vertical activities

Local managers undertake several different types of activity in working with higher levels of government. Good intergovernmental management can promote local, regional, and national goals.

Seeking information   A primary vertical activity is contacting national and state governments for basic information. Information is an important policy-making resource when multiple participants hold other resources—finances, expertise, legal authority, and personnel. Information-seeking activities include obtaining and managing grants, but they also include transactions regarding the basic organization and operation of all intergovernmental programs. Some of this activity is conducted through official channels, but much is informal although just as significant.

Seeking funding   The core of intergovernmental activity is seeking available program and funding information. The frequency and intensity of such activity with the national government has diminished greatly since the late 1970s, and fewer cities receive grants from the national government than did in the 1960s and 1970s. However, state governments continue to be the primary donors to localities. In today's funding environment, many cities know all too well that participation in either the national- or state-level grant-in-aid system has become extremely difficult. Searching the *Catalog of Federal Domestic Assistance* is a regular activity for local managers who are adept at seeking information by increasing their contacts, improving their knowledge of the targeting of funds, garnering greater support from external groups, and paying more attention to program detail and quality.

Administering programs   Local government managers also contact national and state officials to seek program guidance, clarify administrative matters, and reach mutual understandings. Local governments and higher-level donors may share the same general goals but differ over the details of local implementation. Effective managers are able to develop agreement on the nature of problems, search for and forge joint solutions, and implement decisions through joint action.[21] Much of the information transacted in the vertical realm concerns basic program accommodations, adjustments, and other routine matters on specific problems that rarely cause conflict once local managers and the other government's representatives discuss them.

Seeking technical assistance   Because program operations can place demands on a jurisdiction that it might not be able to meet with its existing capabilities, local managers ask for technical assistance that enhances their ability to implement a given program. Often the activity is informal, such as when a state official explains a new geographic information system (GIS) program to a local administrator. States also provide formal technical assistance programs to communities. The Iowa Community Betterment Program, for example, provides technical assistance to community groups and local volunteers in cities to help them organize, plan, and implement a community improvement or service project. The Southwest Washington

Vertical relations in a small town

Ithaca, Michigan, manages its regulatory framework when it can. The city regularly negotiates with federal and state officials. Although concerned and often frustrated by unfunded mandates, it takes a proactive stance on most of these issues.

For example, when officials from the public works department became concerned about health and safety regulations, the city asked the Michigan Occupational Safety and Health Administration to carry out an inspection audit, which was discussed, negotiated, and then followed.

When the Michigan Department of Natural Resources informed the city that several city streets would have to be closed, blocking industrial and retail access, while the state repaired streets, Ithaca called in the department supervisor for a meeting. Ithaca was able to negotiate a solution: no more than two of the

proposed streets would be closed at one time.

City officials also proposed to the department of natural resources an alternative storage pond for the water reservoir so the city could expand its industrial park without having to build a water tower. This action ultimately required a U.S. Environmental Protection Agency waiver of rule, which was obtained.

Another example of adjustment-seeking activity occurred in the early 1990s when EPA Superfund project officials arrived in town to test for lead on city property. The initial cost to the city would have been $2 million for mitigation, but the city negotiated with the state attorney general and department of natural resources to reduce the city's liability to in-kind costs only.

Source: Robert Agranoff and Michael McGuire, *Collaborative Public Management: New Strategies for Local Governments* (Washington, D.C.: Georgetown University Press, 2003), 76–77.

Health District provides the physical locations of existing public water supply wells in critical aquifer areas to assist cities in locating all such wells. The EPA offers a program—the agency calls it a Swiss army knife for environmental planning—that is a one-stop introduction to a wide range of environmental issues and decisions that affect small to medium-sized communities.

Seeking regulatory relief Restrictions placed on local government activity and conditions attached to intergovernmental aid programs by the national and state governments are often unwieldy for cities. Such regulations and conditions may cause local agencies to calculate the project's political and economic costs and benefits. When the calculation results in an apparent loss to the local government, managers can take steps to get relief and move a program forward. Managers may conclude that it is worthwhile to seek relief from standards that adversely affect local interests and thus request some form of asymmetrical treatment or program adjustment that is not technically within standards, rules, or guidelines but nonetheless advances the goals of both the higher governmental level and local manager. This involves the common practice of a government seeking to change the application of a regulation or standard to a particular situation if it impedes a specific project or effort.[22]

When rules and other mandates are impediments to achieving the aims of a program, neither the local government nor the higher-level government will benefit. Certainly conflict occurs, but a workable solution will be found not through turf battles or stalemates but through collaborative relations. In this regard, working with, rather than deferring to or acceding to, national or state officials can result in a successful adjustment for both parties. In many cases the regulating government or donor government may deny the request for an adjustment, but it is always worth the request. A mutually beneficial solution will rarely result from coercion.

Managers can seek relief from regulations or statutes through lobbying and developing regional interlocal coalitions. The Texas Coalition of Cities for Utility Issues (TCCFUI) is an example of such a coalition. In the field of telecommunications policy, its board monitors legislative activity at the state government level and rule promulgation at the Federal Communications Commission and informs its members—approximately 110 cities—of the effects of these intergovernmental actions. Where possible, TCCFUI also lobbies relevant state legislative sub-committees with jurisdiction over telecommunications issues.[23]

In an era when performance measurement has become a valued managerial principle, recipient governments often are forced to balance an audit mentality (the donor government tries to ensure legal and procedural compliance) and an evaluation approach (the donor government focuses on performance and effectiveness). Local managers sometimes seek to trade off strict compliance in exchange for greater discretion, which allows them to achieve program goals by focusing on outcomes instead of process. For example, many national and state economic development programs award localities in terms of numbers of jobs or new investment and are flexible in the enforcement of reporting and compliance. Cities, counties, and public-private development corporations regularly seek changes in business development programs in order to attract specific types of companies.

Horizontal relations

The complexity of governance in the twenty-first century is most evident at the local level. In 2003, there were 362 metropolitan statistical areas and 560 micropolitan statistical areas in the United States.[24] Approximately 83 percent of the U.S. population lived in metropolitan statistical areas in 2003, compared with less than 63 percent in 1960; and another 10 percent lived in micropolitan areas. Metropolitan areas are not only growing in number and in population, but the large metro areas are growing larger. Nearly two-thirds of the metropolitan population lives in areas that have a population of at least 1 million.

Growth in metropolitan areas has meant accelerated fragmentation of local governments. More than 40 percent of the nation's local governments are now located in metropolitan statistical areas, a proportion that has doubled since 1972. The average metro area encompasses more than 100 local government units. For example, the Dallas-Fort Worth Consolidated Metropolitan Statistical Area contains 461 local governments, including 199 cities, 134 special districts, and 116 school districts—more than one government unit for every 1,000 citizens. The Cincinnati metropolitan area is even more fragmented, with 242 cities and townships, 125 special districts, and 84 school districts stretched across 15 counties in parts of three states—one local government unit exists for every 450 citizens. The Chicago metropolitan area has more than 1,200 local governments.

In highly urbanized regions, it is virtually impossible to deal with major transportation and environmental issues on a jurisdiction-by-jurisdiction basis. Rather, a coordinated and cooperative approach is required for comprehensive, effective and efficient results. Similarly, local governments are discovering that they can better utilize limited resources, in many cases, when they participate in jointly sponsored projects and programs to serve their citizens' common needs.
Mike Eastland

The consequence is that the natural boundaries for needed services are not the same as arbitrary jurisdictional boundaries, especially in metropolitan areas. Managers have to come up with economically efficient, administratively effective, and equitable ways and means of handling the problems, programs, and processes that spill over municipal and county boundaries. Local managers have found that most of these issues can be addressed only through horizontal, multiorganizational activity.

The effect of metropolitan fragmentation is a much debated issue. Some argue that the existence of a large number of separate governments creates problems such as duplication of services, taxing and service inequities, ruinous competition resulting in giveaways to large businesses, public confusion over which government is responsible for what, and an inability to focus effectively on areawide problems. This "reform view" of metropolitan fragmentation also points to the lack of coordination among local governments. Others argue that a having a large number of local governments is desirable because it allows citizens to choose the lifestyle and level of services they want, and it keeps government more accessible and accountable to the people. Competition among local units keeps taxes low and encourages efficiency. From this perspective, the local political system is like a marketplace, where citizens can shop around for the combination of services they want.[25]

Horizontal relations are not just a metropolitan phenomenon. Rural communities face challenges related to structural changes in economic and social life: low skill and resource densities, lack of specialized expertise and information, isolation and limited access to urban amenities, and an overspecialization of local economies.[26] These internal forces have contributed to dwindling populations, relatively low wages, above-average incidences of poverty, and a declining institutional infrastructure in cities located outside metropolitan areas. Counteracting or adapting to trends within this rapidly changing environment requires new governing relationships. For example, in the early 1990s, a series of horizontal, rural-based networks emerged in Nebraska to pull together diverse rural interests while focusing on specific projects. Networks that were formed included eight regional groups of rural service providers, a development academy that conducts educational and training programs, a computerized interactive information and communications vehicle among rural communities and service providers, and a number of working groups to explore new programs and development tools.[27]

The question, in administrative terms, is "how do we devise a system of local governments large enough to handle area-wide problems and small enough to remain responsive to the needs and desires of neighborhoods and other small areas?"[28]

Horizontal activities

Managing horizontally means working the highly interdependent local policy process, pooling resources, building bases of support, and determining feasible courses of action.[29] Cities and counties operate horizontally because their capacity to make decisions is highly dependent on other organizations' resources to achieve their goals. With the days of federal government abundance long past, key policy-making resources are increasingly held by many players, most of which are located horizontally within or apart from the city. Even within the context of a vertical program such as a grant, local government managers need to work with other local interests in developing policy strategies. Cities also engage in leveraging as they blend private nonprofit and for-profit resources with public resources.

Like vertical intergovernmental relations, horizontal activity can be formal, such as an agreement between two cities to share in the delivery of a service, or it can be more informal, such as a plan among several NGOs for a course of action and a role in decision making. Some arrangements may enable routine coordination, others provide a means of solving specific problems.

Interjurisdictional agreements   Formal horizontal collaboration includes: (1) interlocal service contracts between two or more units of government in which one pays the other for the delivery of the service to the residents of the jurisdiction of the paying government, and (2) joint service agreements between two or more governments for the joint planning, financing, and delivery of a service to

Cost savings through interlocal agreements in Utah

- Cities that are members of an equipment pool in Utah can rent equipment (and the personnel if needed) from other cities. Under an interlocal agreement, each participating city lists its equipment and an hourly cost (the cost is listed with an operator and without an operator).

- The cities of Provo, Spanish Fork, Salem, Nephi, and Levan—all members of the Utah Municipal Power Agency—buy power as a group for a better price than they could each get separately.

- Working through an interlocal agreement, Springville, Spanish Fork, Payson, Salem, and Santaquin have been sharing GPS and GIS technology and services since 1997. In 2001, their cost was only $36 per hour compared with the $120 per hour it would cost for an independent consultant.

- Springville, Mapleton, Spanish Fork, Salem, Elk Ridge, Payson, Santaquin, Genola, and Goshen work through an interlocal agreement to save money in chip seal operations. The cost to bid chip spreading before the agreement was $1.05 per square yard. Since the agreement, the cost is 64¢ per square yard.

Source: Utah Technology Transfer Center, "Interlocal Agreements Save Money," *On The Move* (quarterly newsletter) 15 (Summer 2002).

the residents of all participating jurisdictions. Many variations of interlocal agreements (ILAs) are used to overcome the problems of fragmentation, especially duplication of service and lack of resources. Interlocal agreements are used extensively in metropolitan and rural areas to provide police and fire protection, detention facilities, libraries, solid-waste disposal, criminal laboratory services, and joint use of facilities.

Localities commonly transfer service responsibilities from one local government to another—the direction is typically from cities to counties—as allowed by state law. To avoid overlap and fragmentation, counties in various parts of the country have assumed responsibility from cities for services such as jails, libraries, street repairs, and animal control. Los Angeles County promotes its services to cities on a contract basis; the most popular service is the county's extensive crime lab.

A sample of interlocal agreements in San Antonio, Texas

- **Animal control services**   The city's metropolitan health department provides animal control services to residents in unincorporated Bexar County. These services include dispatching for stray and/or unwanted dogs and cats, catching and kenneling all dogs and cats brought to the animal control facility, investigating animal-bite complaints, providing 10-day rabies observations of animals that have bitten a person, and providing humane and appropriate disposal of unclaimed dogs and cats. Services are based on a fee for service (including disposal, euthanasia, adoption, and dispatching) and reimbursement of expenses for staff and related materials.

- **EMS services (suburban cities)**   The San Antonio fire department provides, by contract, EMS services to residents in various suburban cities including Balcones Heights, Castle Hills, Helotes, and Windcrest. The fee is based on a pro rata share of the operating budget and incorporated cities' electrical connections.

- **Tax collection consolidation**   In 1998, the city of San Antonio and Bexar County consolidated property tax collections. The Bexar County tax assessor-collector is now responsible for computing and publishing the effective tax rate, establishing the tax roll, preparing and mailing all tax statements, and receiving payment of taxes for the city of San Antonio.

Source: San Antonio Office of External Relations.

Contracts and partnerships Local governments and NGOs engage in formal partnerships and contracts. In public-private partnerships, each sector shares in planning, funding, and delivering public services. There is burgeoning interest in public-private partnerships in economic and community development projects. Other creative public-private partnerships are formed in such areas as public works and utilities, infrastructure development, environmental management, park maintenance, and libraries.

In many states, local economic development corporations combine the funding and legal authority of government with the innovation, expertise, and contacts of the private sector. Since 1987, the city of Denton, Texas, has maintained a formal partnership with the city's chamber of commerce. The economic development staff at the chamber lead the marketing efforts, while the city department of economic development manages business retention and provides technical and advisory support. The partnership is funded partly through an annual pledge from the Public Utility Board, and the balance is raised through additional investments made by conscientious citizens, interested businesspeople, and other stakeholders. The state of Texas allows such partnerships and encourages cities to create separate organizations to plan and manage various development projects.

Throughout the latter half of the 1990s, Beloit, Wisconsin, worked in a partnership with a nonprofit redevelopment association to transform an area of blight on the Rock River, which runs through the heart of town, into a combination civic center–industry site and a moderate- to low-income housing area. The association, known as Beloit 2000, mobilized neighborhood groups, the business community, local elected officials, and the city administration for its goals. The county government contributed tax funds. Both the city and county governments used their state-authorized powers to establish tax-increment finance districts, grant tax abatements, and reduce or eliminate regulations that had thwarted development.[30]

Some so-called partnerships are actually contracting arrangements in which the government pays NGOs to provide a good or a service; the government then does not share the responsibilities of service provision. The primary reason for entering into contracts with NGOs is cost savings through lower labor costs and/or management innovation.[31] In June 1997, Riverside County, California, entered into an agreement with a private company for the day-to-day management of its 25-branch library system. Just one year after the partnership was formed, library hours were expanded by 34 percent, staff were added, salaries were maintained, the materials budget increased by 33 percent, and circulation increased by about 10 percent—all at the same level of funding. Some cities, like Hinesville, Georgia, contract with private firms to manage nearly all local government public works and provide waste and wastewater services, garbage collection, street sweeping, and fleet vehicle maintenance.

Other horizontal mechanisms Interlocal agreements, partnerships, and contracting are the most common horizontal activities, but jurisdictions use a variety of others as well. To assure citizens of access to a service or a good that the local government decides not to pay for, a government can award a private firm a franchise to perform a certain service or provide a good. The firm then charges citizens—customers—directly for the service or good. In return for exclusive access to customers, the franchisee will often pay a fee to the government. The price charged to the customer is typically negotiated and regulated by the local government. Examples of franchises include common utilities (electricity, natural gas, water, and sewage), mass transit, telephone service, and cable television.

In coproduction, local governments work with citizens to provide goods and services. Coproduction occurs in volunteer fire departments, primary and secondary education programs, and adopt-a-park projects sponsored by local parks and recreation departments. A growing number of community groups and neighborhood associations not only assist local government in providing traditional services, but also offer services not provided well, or at all, by government. Neighborhood crime watches are an example of such voluntary service.

About partnerships   In an environment of change, partnerships are prized because they extend an organization's capacity to marshal diverse skills and other resources to address problems that do not ordinarily fall within the organization's scope of services. Partnerships can provide added capacity at little cost and permit an organization to add value to existing structures and people.

The challenges of partnerships are great, however:

• Who defines the problem the partnership is supposed to address?

• How are partnerships convened?

• How is accountability established?

• How do the different cultures of the organizational partners help or hinder achievement of a common goal—especially when the partners come from different sectors?

• Can the partnerships be sustained without being ultimately incorporated into a new or existing organization?

Source: John Nalbandian and Carol Nalbandian, "Contemporary Challenges in Local Government," *Public Management* 84 (December 2002): 6–11.

Regionalism

As metropolitan areas grow larger, as the number of special districts increases, and as "wicked" cross-boundary problems become more prevalent, regional activity has in many cases superseded jurisdiction-based activity. Observers of intergovernmental cooperation conclude that relationships among local units of government can be improved by regional initiatives and by solutions that are formalized and institutionalized in a particular structural arrangement or agreement. Examples of regional activities include county-based solutions, councils of governments, government mergers, and tax-sharing agreements.

County solutions   One commonly prescribed reform is reducing the number of special districts and authorities in favor of multipurpose and politically accountable units of government. Special districts and authorities play positive roles in providing needed environmental, transportation, housing, and other services. They make it possible for government to target costs to specific groups of people and thus avoid general increases in property taxes. At the same time, however, they add to the fragmentation of government and to problems of political accountability. Moreover, functions provided by special districts or authorities may be equally well provided by multipurpose, regional governments such as counties.

County governments provide a viable entity when the goal is a shifting of responsibilities to multipurpose, politically accountable entities with broad metropolitan or regional jurisdiction. An improved role for the county is particularly feasible in single-county metropolitan areas. The larger jurisdiction of counties, compared with municipal governments, makes them potentially better able to deal effectively with problems such as environmental protection and transportation. Compared with special authorities, counties offer well-established general-purpose governments directly accountable to the voters. Shifting responsibilities to the county may also provide economies of scale and a broader and more stable tax base.

Councils of governments   In sprawling areas extending into two or more counties, councils of governments (COGs), of which counties are a part, could be more suitable than counties as units of multipurpose regional government. COGs are voluntary or state-mandated associations of governments. A majority of the regional councils in the United States serve governments in specific metropolitan areas or groups of metropolitan areas. Membership varies greatly. The Metropolitan Washington Council of Governments serves ten cities in seven counties and the District of Columbia. The Ohio, Kentucky, Indiana Regional Council of Governments has 198 community and 8 county members located in three different states. The Council of Fresno County Governments is composed of only the city governments located in Fresno County, California.

The role played by COGs in intergovernmental planning and the coordination of nationally aided projects varies from state to state. Most councils act as clearinghouses and are catalysts for regional problem solving. In many cases, they are the only organization that generates plans for metropolitan areas. In addition to their roles in long-range intergovernmental planning, COGs provide various types of technical assistance under contract to member governments.

Although COGs historically have been the principal instruments for addressing regional problems, most COGs play only an advisory role in regional policy making, and their decisions have little binding authority over member units. At the same time, COGs show considerable potential for comprehensive horizontal problem solving. At times, finding a solution has meant involvement of not only local government but also other actors and institutions in the community critical to the resolution of conflict. For example, in addition to serving county and city governments, the Southeast Michigan Council of Governments also has eight educational members, including two community colleges.

Local government mergers   One rare but available response to local fragmentation is a city-county merger. Only four such consolidations occurred during the 1990s. The most recent consolidations were the Kansas City, Kansas–Wyandotte County merger in 1998 and the Louisville–Jefferson County merger in 2003. The latter joins Lexington–Fayette County in Kentucky, the only state to have its two largest local governments exist as city-county mergers. For the most part, mergers of this type consolidate all political and administrative functions into one governing body, thereby eliminating service duplication, equalizing service provision, and providing clear accountability. Such drastic attempts at restructuring are typically opposed by communities that perceive consolidation as a loss of political power and by incumbent local officials who stand to lose their jobs. In spite of the difficulties of securing local support, city-county mergers are often proposed when a metropolitan area experiences fiscal stress.

Tax sharing   Tax-sharing agreements also address regional issues. In a typical setup, two or more jurisdictions share an earmarked percentage of revenue, usually from property taxes or sales taxes. Some participants share funds from new developments, which reduces competition over economic development projects. As the administrator of tax collection and disbursement, a county government or other regional entity often takes part in tax sharing agreements.

Metropolitan districts   Some regional bodies are configured as metropolitan special districts that perform diverse functions although many are established to address specific, related functions such as land use, area planning, and development. The best known district of this sort is the Metropolitan Service District in Portland, Oregon, which is a multipurpose government operated by directly elected officials. The Twin Cities Metropolitan Council in the Minneapolis–St. Paul region of Minnesota works with all area municipalities and townships. Compared with the Portland district, the Twin Cities Metropolitan Council has relatively limited administrative impact.

Tax sharing among district communities in the Meadowlands   In zoning on a regional basis, the possibility of financial inequities arises. For example, if a large section of Community A is zoned for a park and a large section of Community B is zoned for a major office, residential, or warehouse project, then Community B should share some of the benefits derived from development.

A tax-sharing plan for the Meadowlands region in New Jersey was designed in 1972 to balance these inequities so that the region could be developed as a unit with town-to-town equality. Each community receives a proportionate share of the property taxes from post-1970 development, regardless of where it occurs. Essentially, communities share the benefits of development rather than have winners and losers in the competition for economic development. The commission receives no money from the fund; it serves merely as the routing agent.

Source: New Jersey Meadowlands Commission, "Tax Sharing in the Meadowlands District," www.meadowlands.state.nj.us/tax.html.

Managing external relations

External relations do not emerge spontaneously as self-sufficient, automated linkages. Multiorganizational activity is both operational and strategic and depends, in large part, on the actions of a local manager. Multiorganizational relationships depend on various leaders at various times performing various roles, all of which may be necessary for effective governing. In each local jurisdiction, the local manager ultimately is held accountable for the satisfactory delivery of public goods and services.

Characteristics of external relations

External relations for local managers involve interdependence, a variety of actors, a dedicated purpose, and the presence of multidimensional management.

Interdependence   In multiorganizational settings, each actor is dependent on at least one other actor for key resources. When these dependent relationships multiply and are reciprocal, a shared interest in a policy solution develops. The greater the interdependence among actors, the greater the need for coordination and collaboration.[32] Interdependence implies that all actors have mutual needs and each has something to gain through involvement with the others.

Variety of actors   Local government managers must work productively with a variety of actors who have their own goals and strategies but who must adapt their preferences to achieve the network goal. No one actor has enough power to determine the strategic actions of the other actors (although the government manager is more equal than the others). Linkages can be created with representatives from government, nonprofit, and for-profit organizations; with administrators or other staff; with elected officials and board members; and with members of the community and interested individuals from other jurisdictions. Any organization that can help solve a pressing problem should be included. Cost savings that partnerships with private agencies can bring are widely acknowledged, and NGOs have been an integral component of service provision since President Lyndon B. Johnson expanded federal partnership during the creative federalism period of the 1960s. The George W. Bush administration has also asserted its desire to involve faith-based organizations in governing.

Dedicated purpose   External networks emerge for a specific purpose. Some relationships—such as subcontracting or borrowing arrangements—are "obligational," and some interlocal contracts and privatization efforts exist for this limited, but still multiorganizational, type of exchange. Relationships that are forged for implementing grant programs or complying with vertical mandates can also be classified as obligational.

Other external relations are "promotional"; interests can be pursued through political alliances like the Texas Coalition of Cities for Utility Issues or through marketing alliances and research consortia like the city of Denton–Denton chamber of commerce partnership (described earlier in this chapter).

The most complex types of external relationships are systemic production networks, "clusters of organizations that make decisions jointly and integrate their efforts to produce a product or service."[33] A systemic production network must develop strategy, mechanisms for operation and implementation, and some means for determining whether expected results are being accomplished.[34] A great deal of local management occurs in such networks for programs in areas such as community and economic development, social services, land use, transportation, and emergency management. Examples of systemic production networks are collaborative efforts like the State Rural Development Councils[35] that are organized around federal, state, and local governments, tribal councils, and NGOs, and the more complex implementation structures such as those in the mental health field.

Multidimensional management   Although some perceive multiorganizational networks as being so decentralized that management happens by accident rather than by intent, the truth is quite the opposite. Because of the number of actors dedicated to a defined purpose, networks can be considered "leaderful."[36] Multiorganizational relations typically exhibit multiple power centers with reciprocal relationships, many suppliers of resources, diffused responsibility for actions, massive information exchanges among actors, and the need for information input from all actors.[37] Coordinating these persons and activities requires management of legal, political, technical, and financial issues.[38]

A local government operates within a legal framework, and laws—for example, contracts or interlocal agreements—govern the formal structure of multiorganizational activity. Federal and state regulations, the formal distribution of funds across actors, or national grant program mandates may control multiorganizational activity.

In many contexts, external management involves the political skills of conflict resolution, diplomacy, negotiation, and consensus building. Local managers must strike political bargains with network members, some of whom may have only limited support from their citizens. For example, a proposal for a child care center created by a partnership of three local nonprofit agencies in North Texas met with opposition from a neighborhood association. If the city council had allowed the center to be built and had granted all the necessary permits, city administrators would have needed to build bridges between the partnership and the neighborhood. Local managers may also have to expend political capital on maintaining support for a network operation within the home organization.

Managing external relations often has a technical dimension, and it is necessary to continually update information and collect data on key developments in relevant subjects. Negotiating interlocal agreements for fire protection, for example, requires knowledge of firefighting capacity, equipment needs, response time, and many other factors. Establishing provider networks for health services requires knowledge of medical needs and the administrative capacity of potential providers. In addition to such specialized knowledge, managers working in multiorganizational settings must know how to conduct needs assessments, develop strategic plans, write budgets, and evaluate outcomes, and they must possess strong programming and implementation skills.

Managing external relations also has a cost dimension. Operating in multiorganizational settings takes considerable time and effort, and good managers will reduce the costs of collaboration as much as possible. The lower the predicted costs for a potential actor, the greater the probability of cooperation. Any manager who has participated in multiorganizational arrangements understands that collaborative decisions are usually the most effective, making the effort worth the cost.

Community collaboration in rural France   A human services volunteer group active in six rural communities in central France operates a mobile day care center featuring a *ludothèque,* a lending library for games. A van loaded with games, driven alternately by two nursery school teachers, stops for at least one afternoon a week in each of the six participating communities. The modest budget of the mobile game room is funded by member families as well as a prorated subsidy from the welfare fund of the six participating communities. Each of the six communities in the Ille-et-Vilaine district makes available a school or community center facility where the van pulls up to accommodate the local children. A total of some 200 children now participate. The *ludothèque* has become a convivial weekly meeting place for both mothers and their children.

Source: "Child-Friendly Communities: The Mobile Game Room of Mordelles," *Public Innovation Abroad,* January 1998.

The key for the local government manager is to understand how and why each organization contributes to the network effort. The key questions are managerial and strategic in nature: How does a local official make sure the right people are involved? How is it possible for a network to work jointly to fashion the best solution?

Strategic approaches to external relations

Managing across governments and organizations involves operating in a complex system of rules, regulations, and standards—and taking advantage of opportunities. The local manager must mobilize forces within and outside of the community, acquire the resources needed to carry out a program or project, access information about external opportunities and constraints, and work with persons over whom they have no formal authority. To achieve success, a manager can choose among three primary management approaches: compliance, bargaining and negotiation, and networking.

Compliance   As the previous analysis of national-local and state-local relations suggests, a considerable amount of managerial time is spent meeting program intent and expectations. A primary aspect of multiorganizational governing is local compliance. Clearly, local governments have a large incentive to comply when implementation of vertical programs is based largely on reporting, review, and audit. Many local governments seek financial resources to subsidize or create new programs. Given the limits on the availability of resources, need and fierce competition can result in a grab-the-money mentality, and maximum local discretion is not a priority.

Administrative rule making and regulatory programs are similarly designed with the expectation of full compliance. Often the benefits of compliance, measured in terms of political capital or simply time, far outweigh the costs of negotiation and bargaining. Sometimes local governments do not have the organizational capacity for negotiation and bargaining. Furthermore, many national programs are forged in the midst of conflicting goals and unclear intent, resulting in initial administrative confusion and overlapping program authority. Top-down management through centralized decision making and mandated local actions sometimes is the most efficient way of dealing with such problems.

Top-down compliance approaches rarely involve horizontal relations unless national or state programs mandate such relations. Empirical research has shown that when local governments pursue grants from higher levels of government, they interact far less with other jurisdictions and community organizations. However, many state requirements force local governments into interlocal agreements.

In many programs, any action beyond total compliance is unacceptable. National policies exist to achieve national goals, just as state policies exist to achieve regional goals. The more than 75 conditions attached to all national aid are nonnegotiable, as are direct orders or mandates by the national government that are designed to protect the rights of citizens. Hundreds of state mandates require administrative compliance, leaving local governments with little more than the political arena in which to seek local discretion. Although debates rage about whether federalism should include top-down mandates, in practice the local manager is wise in some instances to simply follow orders. Compliance is a legitimate multiorganizational management approach.

Bargaining and negotiation Compliance management is the appropriate local government approach when the national or state government possesses the information, expertise, finances, and capacity to control policy output. In many program areas, however, governments depend on each other for effective governance instead of on remote control from the top of the system. State governments often depend on the actions of the local government to achieve state objectives. A local government needs financial or other resources and may look to the state for assistance, but the state cannot always hold that need over the head of the locality and demand conformity. The granting state agency needs solid applications that reflect good planning and demonstrate administrative capacity. Similarly, local governments may have leverage over state actions in some areas because the latter simply may not have the time, the inclination, or the legal authority to intervene in local operations.

Locally initiated, jurisdiction-based management sets the scene for bargaining, negotiation, and mutually beneficial solutions. Grant programs may come with conditions, but the local manager may also view programs as opportunities to bargain with the donors.[39] If a local government desires some type of relief from a higher government's conditions or rules, it can take one of two actions: either ignore the standards and defy the granting government, thus risking penalties; or constructively engage the grantor to make special accommodations. Because both local and higher-level program managers understand that action ultimately must conform to the goals of the higher-level program at the same time that higher-level managers depend on local managers to achieve conformity, a negotiated approach to management is the most effective.

If a local government desires some type of relief from a higher government's conditions or rules, it can take one of two actions: either ignore the standards and defy the granting government, thus risking penalties; or constructively engage the grantor to make special accommodations. Because both local and higher-level program managers understand that action ultimately must conform to the goals of the higher-level program at the same time that higher-level managers depend on local managers to achieve conformity, a negotiated approach to management is the most effective.

Bargaining and negotiation lead to a solution that is multilateral, not command and control. Thus, although the critical measure of policy success in compliance management is the extent to which managers carry out the demands of the granting government, a negotiated-management approach is judged successful when local managers are provided with sufficient policy discretion, resources, and autonomy to concurrently meet these demands and fulfill local needs. When a local manager calculates the planned benefits and potential costs of each available program and resource, the manager can negotiate and bargain rather than accommodate and acclimate.

Managers who adopt the bargaining mentality not only for grants and regulations but also for other vertical and horizontal relationships must pursue the needs of their jurisdiction first. External demands by outside vertical agencies can be only a secondary concern for them. For such jurisdiction-based management, the achievement of a local goal and the completion of a particular task are paramount.[40] Instead of attempting to go it alone in the face of potentially debilitating mandates, the local manager will strategically involve other jurisdictions and other key actors as a means of achieving the goals of each.

Networking Many external linkages among local governments take place in network-like arrangements of various players, within which no player possesses the power to determine the strategies of the other actors but where the local manager is held accountable for the network solutions that emerge. Although each actor comes to the network with different types and levels of technology and resources and with individual operational goals and policy strategies, all focus on mutual strategic goals.

Networks enable joint decisions and collective actions to some degree.[41] The solutions that result from network management benefit not only the local government but other parties as well.

Joint decision making is not particularly efficient, but a network of participants may produce better decisions because of the larger supply of information and a new commitment and interaction as they are stimulated by alternatives they would not have considered otherwise. If the basic challenge of making policy and strategy in the twenty-first century is to deliver policy outputs that are consistent with all societal interests, then a policy decision that emerges from a network process may provide the best possible route to success.

Management tasks

Involving the right people, framing the rules of engagement for the relationship, mobilizing the support of participants, and facilitating an effective process for productive relations are four primary tasks of managing a local government's relationships with other governments and organizations.

Creating multiorganizational relationships The most important management task in external relations is getting the right collection of persons and resources to achieve the goal.[42] Including the correct number of persons as well as all relevant interests is integral in determining the effectiveness of external relations. The manager must identify participants for the network and include key stakeholders in the process. Effective managers know the important contacts, the linkages that make them important, and the dimensions of various arrangements within which governing can occur. The skills, knowledge, and resources of potential participants must be assessed and engaged. Removing persons who are not performing as desired also appears to be an important component of management; introducing new actors in order to shift the operating dynamic of the multiorganizational arrangement is a common prescription.

The numbers and types of multiorganizational relationships depend on the purpose of the policy. The manager must constantly bear in mind the lineup of potential collaborators, even when the number actually engaged is small. The manager who sits on community boards, volunteers, inventories local government resources, and attends and holds workshops and informational meetings on relevant issues will automatically know who has which resources. Simply put, the manager must know something about the work of different professions and occupations and be ready to use this knowledge.

When appropriate, local managers can invite national and state officials to meetings, provide them with updates on progress, and report successes. Also when appropriate, local managers can include representatives of professional and technical associations or solicit technical assistance and advice from specialists.

Establishing rules of engagement Managing external relations also requires establishing the structure of the network, the formal roles of the participants, and the ground rules for participation.[43] Local managers arrange, stabilize, nurture, and integrate the multiorganizational structure to aid in the formation of linkages and in the management of the network when effectiveness diminishes or is suboptimal. Establishing the rules of engagement involves facilitating the internal structure and position of the participants, influencing the prevailing norms of the network, and altering the perceptions of the network participants.

The manager might suggest viewing a problem differently or recommend an alternative decision-making mechanism. A manager cannot draw up an organizational chart for a network, but a manager can help establish the roles of each participant at any given time. Clarifying various actors' roles, responsibilities, and boundaries is not the same as asking "Who's in charge?" A useful approach is to identify which actors have primary responsibility for the tasks required for a joint solution to a problem.

A manager can introduce new ideas to the network and thereby create (or celebrate) a shared purpose or vision.[44] A manager can also frame and champion an explicit shared purpose or program rationale that provides the motivational glue that secures the network and helps people who would otherwise not work together find mutual understanding. Similarly, developing explicit criteria the network can use to evaluate its work facilitates mutual understanding of operating and performance guidelines. Participants should draft plans within the multiorganizational arrangement, not beforehand; plans should not be predetermined instructions for activity.

Mobilizing support In addition to selecting the right persons and establishing the rules of engagement, managing external relations often requires inducing individuals to commit to the joint undertaking—and to keep that commitment.[45] A manager must be able and ready to sell an idea, project, or a set of ideas or projects to representatives of other organizations. Collaboration does not come automatically, and the more the potential collaborators perceive demands on agency autonomy, power, and resources, the more resistant they may be. The decision in favor of a joint effort requires persuasion that participation or partnering will be of mutual benefit.

Motivated people are the key to organizational success. The ability of organizational actors to operate together within a single network depends less on a shared belief system, an ideology, or a common world view than it does on a shared motivation embodied in the project or program itself. Reminding network members and external stakeholders of the purpose of the activity and broadcasting network success are common and sometimes ongoing tasks for achieving motivation and thus building support for the activity. Inducing a sense of urgency is another way to develop support. Public opinion and organized-group pressure can help demonstrate the urgency of a problem and thereby enhance the possibility of concerted action toward a solution. In addition, the ability to manage networks is related to the internal support and cooperation of the manager's primary organization. A manager in city government, for example, should have the cooperation of the city council and the government's chief executive.

Facilitating interaction Managing external relations also requires creating the environment and enhancing the conditions for favorable, productive, and purposeful interaction among all actors in the partnership.[46] It is important to help the various participants—who can have conflicting goals and different perceptions or dissimilar values—to fulfill the strategic purpose of the relationship. The strategies of each participant and the outcomes of those strategies are influenced by the patterns of interactions that have been developed. Establishing relationships that result in achieving the network's purpose is the aim of the manager. Effective behaviors to accomplish this include facilitating and furthering interaction among participants, reducing complexity and uncertainty by promoting information exchange, providing incentives for cooperation, developing helpful rules and procedures of interaction, helping the network to be self-organizing, and engendering effective communication among participants. The effective manager seeks to lower the cost of interaction, which can be substantial in network settings.

The manager should communicate freely and openly with all actors. All information should be read, digested, circulated, and explained to all actors. Exchanges of information and expressions of interest are prerequisites for establishing trust and respect, which are the lifeblood of effective multiorganizational settings. In many local governments, top administrators and elected officials have to make considerable efforts to gain the trust of officials from other jurisdictions who possess needed resources. Trust may not necessarily require a harmony of beliefs, but it does depend on mutual obligation and expectation.[47] Synthesizing the relationship to achieve a collective goal depends on it.

Guidelines for managing external relations   Know who the important contacts are and the linkages that make them important. The list can and will change as the scope of the relationships changes.

When applicable, involve officials from other governments. At the very least, invite these officials to attend meetings and provide updates on progress.

When applicable, involve participants from professional and/or technical associations.

Seek expertise from external sources as much as possible.

Expand external relations to foster innovation and gain more information.

Reduce the costs of collaboration. The lower the costs affecting the collaborative players, the greater the probability of cooperation.

Demonstrate the urgency of solving the problem.

Clarify roles and responsibilities for all linkages among the players. Identify which participants have primary responsibility for which part of the tasks required to solve a particular problem.

Build an effective administrative structure into every collaborative arrangement.

Develop operating standards, guidelines, and plans within the collaborative structure, not before it is convened.

Create a unified program rationale to act as the motivational glue for the participants.

Establish a strong linkage between what the network intends to do and what actually occurs.

Clearly link program objectives to strategies and action steps.

Develop short- and intermediate-term systems for monitoring and evaluation.

Promote long-term solutions.

Communicate openly and frequently. Exchanges of information and expressions of interest across governmental and organizational boundaries are prerequisites for establishing trust and respect.

Read, explain, and circulate information to all network members.

Ensure that all correspondence is well written. Write in clear concise sentences and make all correspondence appealing.

Continually update information on key developments and changes in your program area. Share data, studies, and articles related to changes in the program area and the possible resources available to the network.

Allow the network to serve as a resource center and information resource on program information.

Recap

- The external environment of local governments is multiorganizational, multi-faceted, and complex. Local governments do not just relate to other organizations; they depend on external organizations and are a part of a larger, less geographically bounded governing process than in the past.

- The emergence of complex external relations locally can be attributed to larger, society-wide forces based in instant information exchange and an increasing reliance on networks of all kinds—both economical and technological. Critical resources include not just finances but also information, expertise, and other forms of human knowledge. Citizens also demand that governments solve nettlesome problems with limited resources.

- The capacities required to operate successfully in multiorganizational settings are different from the capacities needed to succeed at managing a single organization. Theories that inform local government management can no longer focus simply on hierarchical processes in single organizations. Local managers operate extensively in multiorganizational settings and require new perspectives on effectiveness.

- A local government's external relations exist in a vertical context, with emphasis on levels of government, and in a horizontal context, where the players are local and represent multiple interests within the community. In practice, a manager rarely differentiates between these two relationships except to determine which entities possess needed policy-making resources.

- Local governments pursue a number of activities with vertical governments, including seeking program information and pursuing adjustments to cumbersome regulations. The local manager is not always successful at making these adjustments, but, more often than not, solutions are worked out that benefit both the local government and the higher-level government.

- Local government officials must confront problems that spill over into neighboring jurisdictions at the same time they are faced with governmental fragmentation that makes it difficult to design effective solutions. Many horizontal mechanisms can overcome the problems of fragmentation; these include interlocal agreements, partnerships, and councils of governments.

- Local managers know that complying with the regulations of external governments is often the only course of action. Opportunities usually exist, however, for bargaining and negotiating with donors and regulating governments. Networks offer a structure in which participants can fashion joint, mutually beneficial solutions.

- External relations are managed and will be successful if there is a broad base of involvement, the participants demonstrate a commitment to the process, roles and responsibilities of network participants are established, and the manager is able to facilitate a free flow of information and ideas.

- Overall, managers must recognize the advantages of operating externally and learn how to capitalize on the many different resources available from external sources.

Exercise

Emergency management in the suburbs

The city of Outer Ring is seeking to turn crisis into opportunity. Recent terrorist attacks and threats, a tornado that destroyed two neighborhoods in a nearby town, and the recent retirement of the veteran fire chief has forced Outer Ring to address a great concern of its citizens: disaster and emergency management. This city of 45,000, located at the periphery of a rapidly expanding metropolitan area of 1.6 million people, has always been satisfied with its police and fire operations. Response times for 911 calls are outstanding, and citizens view the very capable staff of firefighters and police officers as highly valued members of city government. The city's admiration is demonstrated each year when the city celebrates the anniversary of the heroism displayed during the Great Package Warehouse fire of 1983.

But the world is not the same in the twenty-first century. City council members have recently pressured the city manager and the manager's emergency staff to assume a greater role is planning for emergencies. They ask: Would Outer Ring be prepared to deal with a tornado or other natural disaster? A terrorist attack? Would city staff be in a position to assist other communities? Does the community have the capacity to make sure that a troubled teen cannot inflict violence in a public school? As city staff honestly and soberly answered "no" to each of these questions, the city manager knew what needed to be done. It wasn't clear how to accomplish the task, however, and the manager turns to you to help make it happen.

A new position of emergency management coordinator is created, and you are hired for the job. Similar positions are being created in the small and large cities that border yours, each of which is facing the same need for planning and management of disasters and other emergencies. You are armed with a strong mandate from the city manager and the explicit support of the city council, but you are faced with the pressure that such support can impose. You have been promised adequate staff to implement your plans, but you also understand that a focus purely on internal management concerns may be insufficient for the task at hand. Your actions during the first 30 days will be critical to your success.

Questions

1. How important are external relations for the city's emergency preparedness?
2. Who (which organizations) should be contacted? What roles will each play?
3. What is your role in managing external relations? What actions should you take? Which of the guidelines for managing external relations (on page 204) will be the most important for your success?

Notes

1 Jessica Lipnack and Jeffrey Stamps, *The Age of the Network* (New York: Wiley, 1994).

2 Walter W. Powell, "Neither Market nor Hierarchy: Network Forms of Organization," in *Research in Organizational Behavior,* ed. Barry Staw and Larry L. Cummings (Greenwich, Conn.: JAI Press, 1990), 295–336.

3 Laurence J. O'Toole, "Treating Networks Seriously: Practical and Research-Based Agendas in Public Administration," *Public Administration Review* 57 (January–February 1997): 45–52.

4 Joseph W. Whorton and John A. Worthley, "A Perspective on the Challenge of Public Management: Environmental Paradox and Organizational Culture," *Academy of Management Review* 6 (1981) 357–361; Charles T. Goodsell, *The Case for Bureaucracy: A Public Administration Polemic,* 3rd ed. (Chatham, N.J.: Chatham House, 1994).

5 Robert Agranoff and Michael McGuire, *Collaborative Public Management: New Strategies for Local Governments* (Washington, D.C.: Georgetown University Press, 2003).

6 H. George Frederickson, "The Repositioning of American Public Administration," *PS: Political Science and Politics* 32 (1999): 701–711.

7 Clarence Stone, "Urban Regimes and the Capacity to Govern: A Political Economy Approach," *Journal of Urban Affairs* 15 (1993): 1–28.

8 Clarence Stone, Kathryn Doherty, Cheryl Jones, and Timothy Ross, "Schools and Disadvantaged Neighborhoods: The Community Development Challenge," in *Urban Problems and Community Development,* ed. Ronald F. Ferguson and William T. Dickens, 339–380 (Washington, D.C.: Brookings Institution, 1999).

9 Agranoff and McGuire, *Collaborative Public Management.*

10 All government data are from the U.S. Census Bureau, *2002 Census of Governments* 1, no. 1, "Government Organization," GC02(1)-1, (Washington, D.C.: GPO, 2002). All nonprofit sector data are from *The New Nonprofit Almanac in Brief* (Washington, D.C.: Independent Sector, 2001).

11 Daniel J. Elazar, *American Federalism: A View from the States,* 3rd ed. (New York: Harper and Row, 1984).

12 Russell L. Hanson, *Governing Partners: State-Local Relations in the United States* (Boulder, Colo.: Westview Press, 1998).

13 Deil S. Wright, *Understanding Intergovernmental Relations,* 3rd ed. (Belmont, Calif.: Wadsworth, 1988).

14 Morton Grodzins, *The American System: A New View of Government in the United States,* ed. Daniel J. Elazar (Chicago: Rand McNally, 1966).

15 Alan Ehrenhalt, "Devolution's Double Standard," *Governing* 16 (April 2003): 6.

16 Virginia Gray and Peter Eisinger, *American States and Cities* (New York: Longman, 1997).

17 David B. Walker, *Rebirth of Federalism: Slouching toward Washington,* 2nd ed. (New York: Seven Bridges Press, 2000).

18 Joseph F. Zimmerman, *State-Local Relations: A Partnership Approach* (New York: Praeger, 1983).

19 See *Wisconsin Blue-Ribbon Commission on State-Local Partnerships for the 21st Century* (January 2001), www.lafollette.wisc.edu/reform/report011001.pdf.

20 David C. Nice and Patricia Fredericksen, *The Politics of Intergovernmental Relations,* 2nd ed. (Chicago: Nelson-Hall, 1995).

21 Robert Agranoff, *Intergovernmental Management: Human Services Problem Solving in Six Metropolitan Areas* (Albany, N.Y.: State University of New York Press, 1986).

22 Agranoff and McGuire, *Collaborative Public Management.*

23 See Texas Coalition of Cities for Utility Issues, www.tccfui.org/.

24 The Office of Management and Budget (part of the Executive Office of the President) defines an official metropolitan statistical area in terms of population size and commuting patterns, with such an area having "at least one urbanized area of 50,000 or more population, plus adjacent territory that has a high degree of economic and social integration with that core as measured by communities ties." A micropolitan statistical area is based in the same principle of population and integration, but it is centered on an urban cluster of at least 10,000 but less than 50,000 population. All figures for metropolitan and micropolitan areas are from "Revised Definitions of Metropolitan Statistical Areas, New Definitions of Micropolitan Statistical Areas and Combined Statistical Areas, and Guidance on Uses of the Statistical Definitions of These Areas," OMB Bulletin no. 03-04 (Washington, D.C.: Office of Management and Budget, June 6, 2003), www.whitehouse.gov/omb/bulletins/b03-04.html.

25 Charles M. Tiebout, "A Pure Theory of Local Expenditures," *Journal of Political Economy* 64 (October 1956): 416–424.

26 Robert Agranoff and Michael McGuire, "The Administration of State Government Rural Development Policy," in *Handbook of State Government Administration,* ed. John J. Gargan, 385–420 (New York: Marcel Dekker, 2000).

27 Corporation for Enterprise Development, *Rethinking Rural Development* (Washington, D.C.: Corporation for Enterprise Development, 1993).

28 Nice and Fredericksen, *The Politics of Intergovernmental Relations.*

29 Agranoff and McGuire, *Collaborative Public Management.*

30 Ibid.

31 Donald Kettl, *Sharing Power: Public Governance and Private Markets* (Washington, D.C.: Brookings Institution, 1993).

32 Donald Chisholm, *Coordination without Hierarchy: Informal Structures in Multiorganizational Systems* (Berkeley: University of California Press, 1989).

33 Catherine Alter and Jerald Hage, *Organizations Working Together* (Newbury Park, Calif.: Sage, 1993).

34 Robert Agranoff, "Human Services Integration: Past and Present Challenges in Public Administration," *Public Administration Review* 51 (1991): 533–542.

35 Beryl A. Radin, Robert Agranoff, Ann O'M. Bowman, Gregory C. Buntz, Steven J. Ott, Barbara S. Romzek, and Robert H. Wilson, *New Governance for Rural America: Creating Intergovernmental Partnerships* (Lawrence: University Press of Kansas, 1996).

36 Lipnack and Stamps, *The Age of the Network.*

37 Kenneth Hanf, Benny Hjern, and David O. Porter, "Local Networks of Manpower Training in the Federal Republic of Germany and Sweden," in *Interorganizational Policy*

Making: Limits to Coordination and Central Control, ed. Kenneth Hanf and Fritz W. Scharpf, 303–341 (London: Sage Publications, 1978).

38 Robert Agranoff and Michael McGuire, "Managing in Network Settings," *Policy Studies Review* 16 (1999): 18–41.

39 Helen Ingram, "Policy Implementation through Bargaining: The Case of Federal Grants-in-Aid," *Public Policy* 25 (1977): 499–526.

40 Agranoff and McGuire, *Collaborative Public Management.*

41 Catherine Alter and Jerald Hage, *Organizations Working Together* (Newbury Park, Calif.: Sage, 1993).

42 Michael McGuire, "Propositions about What Networks Do and Why They Do It," *Public Administration Review* 62 (September–October 2002): 599–609; Barbara Gray, *Collaborating: Finding Common Ground for Multiparty Problems* (San Francisco: Jossey-Bass, 1989); Erik-Hans Klijn, "Analyzing and Managing Policy Processes in Complex Networks," *Administration and Society* 28 (1996): 90–119.

43 Walter J. M. Kickert, Erik-Hans Klijn, and Joop F. M. Koppenjan, "Introduction: A Management Perspective on Policy Networks," in *Managing Complex Networks,* ed. Walter J. M. Kickert, Erik-Hans Klijn, and Joop F. M. Koppenjan (London: Sage Publications, 1997), 1–13; Myrna P. Mandell, "Network Management: Strategic Behavior in the Public Sector," in *Strategies for Managing Intergovernmental Policies and Networks,* ed. Robert W. Gage and Myrna P. Mandell, 29–54 (New York: Praeger, 1990); O'Toole, "Treating Networks Seriously."

44 Myrna P. Mandell, "Intergovernmental Management in Interorganizational Networks: A Revised Perspective," *International Journal of Public Administration* 11 (1988): 393–416; David O. Porter, "Accounting for Discretion in Social Experimentation and Program Administration," in *Do Housing Allowances Work?,* ed. Katherine L. Bradbury and Anthony Downs, 110–137 (Washington, D.C.: Brookings Institution, 1981).

45 Judith E. Innes and David E. Booher, "Consensus Building and Complex Adaptive Systems: A Framework for Evaluating Collaborative Planning," *Journal of the American Planning Association* 65 (Autumn 1999): 412–423.

46 Robert Agranoff and Michael McGuire, "After the Network is Formed," in *Getting Results through Collaboration: Network and Network Structures for Public Policy and Management,* ed. Myrna P. Mandell, 129–153 (Westport, Conn.: Quorum Books, 2001); Karen Mossberger and Kathleen Hale, "Information Diffusion in an Intergovernmental Network: The Implementation of School-to-Work Programs" (paper delivered at the annual meeting of the American Political Science Association, Atlanta, Georgia, September 2–5, 1999); Laurence J. O'Toole, "Strategies for Intergovernmental Management: Implementing Programs in Intergovernmental Management," *International Journal of Public Administration* 11 (1988): 181–210.

47 Charles F. Sabel, "Studied Trust: Building New Forms of Cooperation in a Volatile Economy," in *Industrial Districts and Local Economic Regeneration,* ed. Werner Sengenberger and Frank Pyke, 228–262 (Geneva: International Institute for Labor Studies, 1992).

8 Leading a manager's life

In the first seven chapters you have seen the nature of the work of a local government manager. Still interested? The previous chapters have described the work done by a local government manager—engineering local democracy to make it work for all citizens, building community, facilitating governance, and managing local government resources to achieve excellence in public facilities and services. The chapters described who the work is done for (citizens and elected officials) and who it is done with (other public service professionals). It is also important to understand the values and beliefs of local government managers as reflected in the ICMA Code of Ethics (Appendix A) and the behavior of managers as they do their work.

James Svara has described five characteristics of that behavior:

- Basing decisions on need rather than demand
- Serving the long-term interests of the community
- Promoting equity and fairness
- Recognizing the interconnection among policies
- Achieving broad and inclusive citizen participation.[1]

Two more characteristics of managers' work behavior are scrupulous political neutrality and seeking continuous improvement in all aspects of the work. If you feel you would enjoy doing this work with these values and beliefs and these characteristics, you should still be interested.

The life of a local government manager is exciting, demanding, and stressful. This chapter examines the demographics of the profession, identifying the practitioners in the early years of the twenty-first century and the opportunities for new entrants. It explores the appeal of the career, and it reviews some of the sources of satisfaction reported by managers themselves. The chapter describes preparatory educational programs and advises how to get started and chart a career path. It explains the typical stages of a career and typical dilemmas and decisions: mobility, competing for positions, employment agreements, pressure for resignation or being fired, choices among the variety of managerial positions available, and midcareer transitions to outside positions. The personal and family life of a typical manager is important, and the ability of managers to cope with stressful situations affects not only their effectiveness but also the level of enjoyment and satisfaction they are likely to derive from a career in local government management. Every manager must periodically assess personal competencies, desires, values, personality, and preferred management style.

A manager's motivation

The local government management profession continues to be dominated by white males who are well educated and in their advanced middle years. Despite more than 30 years of affirmative efforts to diversify the profession, approximately 95 percent of the practitioners are white. Females made up 1.0 percent, 5.0 percent, and 12.0 percent in 1974, 1989, and 2000, respectively, while minorities accounted for 1.0 percent in 1989 and 5.0 percent in 2000. "Given the increasing diversity of American cities one may conclude that the profession will be faced with the need to diversify its ranks in order to provide leadership to city councils that will become increasingly diverse."[2]

I thought I wanted to be a lawyer until I went to work for the city of Abilene and was influenced by a dynamic mayor and city manager. I decided I had the skills and was tough enough to live in the glass house of city management, and could be a multi-tasker and handle the stress of the job."
                                                                    Rickey Childers

---

The aging of the profession exacerbates normal job turnover. Between 2000 and 2002 the percentage of managers over the age of 50 increased from 42 percent to 51 percent, and many managers transition to positions outside of the profession as they reach their 50s, at midcareer. Each year, on average, a total of about 300 chief executive officer (CEO), chief administrative officer (CAO), and chief operating officer (COO) positions open, in addition to positions at the department director and assistant levels.[3]

The profession of city/county manager will be one of increasing opportunity in the next decade. Minorities entering the profession will continue to receive support for their career development through the National Forum for Black Public Administrators (NFBPA) (officially supported by ICMA since 1985) and the Hispanic Network (established as a formal affiliate of ICMA in 1991).

Practicing managers offer many reasons for their attraction to local government and their decision to remain in service:

- The opportunity to perform work that is important
- The opportunity, even at a young age, to influence crucial community decisions
- The opportunity to engage in work that is varied and has a visible product
- The high-profile nature of local government issues and activities
- The challenge to succeed where success is never guaranteed, and in an environment requiring a high tolerance for ambiguity
- The opportunity to take charge of a complex operation
- The opportunity to have a positive impact on a community and on individual citizens.

Almost two out of three managers responding to the 2002 ICMA survey, "State of the Profession," stated they were satisfied or highly satisfied with their jobs, and 92 percent (up from 89 percent in 1991) reported they were at least "moderately satisfied." Only 1.1 percent reported dissatisfaction (a decrease from 2.2 percent in 1991). Fewer than 9 percent reported a voluntary job change in 2002, and fewer than 0.5 percent were fired; fewer than 2 percent were forced to resign, and approximately 2.5 percent were under pressure to resign. For the past decade, more than 75 percent of managers reported that their councils were supportive or highly supportive of their performance in the manager's position, while fewer than 1 percent of the councils were "not supportive." These findings are affirmed by a recent survey to which over 90 percent of responding managers reported receiving performance evaluations that were "greater than satisfactory."[4]

I've always wanted to make a difference in the world. I started out as a candy striper at age 13. I didn't realize until I went to work for the city of Plano that I could truly impact people's lives on a daily basis by working in local government. Once I came to that realization I knew that my true calling was city management. Being a city manager allows me to make a difference in the world around me.

Julie Johnston

In 2002, the average salary for city managers was $89,001. It was $69,404 for city administrators, $99,243 for county managers, and $85,848 for county administrators. These figures compare with the average annual compensation of $65,624 for executive, administrative, and managerial positions in private industry in the United States,[5] although that average is not for chief executives alone. Doing work that can make a difference in people's lives, for bosses who appreciate it, in a relatively stable environment, for greater than average compensation—good reasons to still be interested in the profession of local government manager as a career.[6]

A manager's career

Careers in local government management are shaped in a variety of ways. Individuals from dissimilar backgrounds with assorted occupational experiences and varying levels of formal education in many disciplines can all become managers. Some successful managerial careers have been built on unusual foundations. The 2002 survey, "State of the Profession," reported that although 51.7 percent of managers came from positions in local government (including 16.6 percent who had the term "assistant" in their former title), 34.1 percent came from positions in business or from other backgrounds. The value that drives this diversity of backgrounds is a commitment to representative democracy bolstered by a belief that local elected officials should be able to select any qualified individual to manage the business of the local government.

The profession in recent years has been busy refining the term "qualified."[7] In the early years of council-manager government in the United States, most local government managers were trained as engineers. The country was busy building its physical infrastructure, and the job of these new managers was still largely undefined. As the expectations for the manager were clarified, the profession came to define itself by the legal definition of the position held by an individual manager, administrator, coordinator, or assistant and by the commitment of each manager to the accepted values of the profession as expressed in the ICMA Code of Ethics. With time, patterns of preparation and entry into the profession changed, leading to the observation in 1982 that "the ideal training for a city manager today seems to consist of an undergraduate degree in the liberal arts, graduate work in public administration, and on-the-job training as interns or assistants in city management."[8]

From 1991 through 1993, ICMA engaged its members in a comprehensive "Dialogue on the Profession," which portended a significant shift in the definition of the profession. In addition to the position and the values held by the individual, professionalism would increasingly be defined by the individual's competence in the knowledge, skills, and abilities considered necessary for the local government manager that were identified through the comprehensive dialogue and originally called simply "practices." At the time, 27 practices were identified, and by 2002 they had evolved into the "competencies and skills" listed in Appendix B, now grouped into 18 management practices. As a result of the dialogue, two guidelines were added to ICMA's Code of Ethics; the guidelines encourage members to periodically self-assess their competencies and commit at least 40 hours per year to professional development activities based on the required competencies. The ICMA University was established to offer professional development opportunities to the members.

Between 1994 and 2002, ICMA developed the first assessment instruments designed by local government managers to evaluate their competencies. The Applied Knowledge Assessment explores the level of knowledge an individual possesses, and the Management Practices Assessment uses a 360-degree review process to help a manager personally examine the everyday application of that individual knowledge. In 2000, ICMA initiated a voluntary credentialing program enabling individuals to gain a recognition as a "credentialed manager" through approval by a peer-review board of members and the ICMA Executive Board. Approval is based on a combination of education, experience, periodic assessment, and a measured commitment to ongoing professional development. The rites of passage into and through the local government management profession have been changed by improved definitions of "qualified." Still, the final decision on entry into the professions remains with local elected officials.[9]

Career paths

A traditional career path takes a prospective local government manager from an entry-level position as an intern or administrative assistant, through the ranks to the position of department director or assistant manager, and then to appointment as a local government manager. This tradition has changed dramatically over the past three decades, however. Far more career choices are available today, and management professionals can select the level of overall responsibility they wish to accept in an organization and the specific nature of the work they wish to do. In addition, as the work of local government has broadened to include the entire scope of governance, management professionals have increasingly moved in and out of the profession throughout their careers.

The nature of the work of a department director or an assistant differs dramatically from that of the professional who holds the top job with the title of manager, administrator, coordinator, deputy mayor, or other appointed executive title for the overall local government. Those who serve in these positions as chief executive, administrative officer, or operating officer for the entity focus on the external responsibilities of management.[10] Department directors and assistants focus on the internal responsibilities, emphasizing a specialized field such as public works, public safety, financial management, or planning and development. Those who focus on these specialized areas tend to settle in jurisdictions with larger populations and feel less need to relocate to move up in their profession. The CEO, CAO, and COO focus on external relationships with citizens, elected officials, and business and other special interest groups; and they are more visible and more vulnerable to being forced to move on and move out of the community than are those who operate as department directors and assistants.

A decision to concentrate on a specialty or remain at a certain management level is far from unusual. For example, Dan Johnson, who served as manager of Carrollton, Texas, became assistant city manager in Richardson, Texas, and enjoyed the lower profile. Mike Lecher moved from city manager of Winooski, Vermont, to city manager of Sedona, Arizona, then to the position of deputy city manager of Tucson. Paul Wenbert returned to Mesa, Arizona, as deputy city manager eleven years after beginning there as an intern; along the way, he served as the manager in Newton, Iowa, and Villa Park, Illinois. All are local government managers regardless of the level or specialty each has chosen.

Opportunities outside the traditional positions are increasingly available. Several examples might make the point. Curtis Branscome, former president of ICMA and manager of Decatur, Georgia, left the traditional career path to become executive director of Stone Mountain Memorial Association, a self-supporting state authority that is responsible for Georgia's Stone Mountain Park; Bob Herchert, former manager of Fort Worth, Texas, and a vice president of ICMA, moved into senior management positions in banking and health care enterprises before becoming president and CEO of a major engineering firm; Angela Griffin began her career in the United Kingdom and became the chief executive of Redditch, England, before moving to New Zealand to serve as manager of the capital city of Wellington. She now serves as an adviser to local governments in developing and democratizing nations. The author of this chapter has his own version of career diversity, having been not only a city manager and the executive director of ICMA but also a dinner theater producer and entrepreneur. All of this movement within the profession, among various levels of responsibility and various degrees of specialization, and in and out of the profession has enriched the professional lives of those who choose this career.

Career planning

Career development is an important matter; each step deserves the same care and consideration a manager devotes to major projects on the job. Steady progression to increasingly responsible positions within an organization or from one organization to another rarely just happens. Normally, a candidate must take steps to become qualified for a desired position, develop contacts, develop and nurture a career-support network, prepare for the specific position sought, and approach each opportunity knowledgeably and with confidence. Preparing carefully and presenting oneself effectively will not guarantee appointment to a desired position, but failure to do so makes the likelihood of appointment extremely remote.

Education

Preparation for a successful career in local government management typically includes advanced education. In 1971, seven of every ten local government managers possessed at least a bachelor's degree. Fewer than two decades later, the number was up to nine of every ten;[11] and, even more striking, the percentage with graduate degrees had more than doubled—from 27 percent to 64 percent. The 2000 "State of the Profession" survey reported that these percentages were holding constant.[12] Although the undergraduate degrees possessed by local government managers show study in a variety of fields, today the preference is for a master's degree in public administration (MPA) or a closely related field (for example, government administration, city management, city planning, urban affairs). Almost two-thirds of those with graduate degrees report concentration in one of these specialties.

The trend toward graduate degrees will probably continue because it reflects a real increase in competence. A study now several years old showed that 97 percent of local government managers with reputations for productivity or innovation had graduate degrees compared with 64 percent of all local government managers; and 61 percent of the productive, innovative managers possessed an MPA or a closely related degree.[13]

Advice to job candidates   Prepare to compete in the future for desired jobs:

- Build skills, experience, and accomplishments
- Avoid excessive job-hopping, especially later in career

Develop contacts:

- Job references
- Influential individuals within the profession
- Search firms.

Consider carefully your choice of references.

Be discreet; but when it is time to move, let the right people know.

Be selective about considering a new position—but only as selective as your circumstances will allow.

Be candid about your strengths, weaknesses, accomplishments, and failures. Make it clear that you have learned from your experiences—good and bad.

Avoid excessive credit taking and blame laying.

Be prepared for a comprehensive interviewing process; be prepared to substantiate accomplishments and skills.

Do not be surprised to encounter an industrial psychologist, simulation exercises, or videotaping during the screening process.

Do not assume that you have to convince a search firm that you are the number one candidate; there will probably be no ranking among the finalists prior to consideration by the hiring body.

Being named as a finalist is a compliment, but do not let up; you must work at establishing a favorable relationship with the hiring body.

Avoid the pitfalls that prevent some candidates from ever making the finalist list:

- Applications for positions you are not qualified to hold; do not allow delusions of grandeur to interrupt a steady progression through the next logical job
- Scattershot applications
- Poorly prepared resumes and letters

Do not be reluctant to apply for a job that interests you even if you do not match the specified qualifications exactly, especially if the qualifications are unusual and you think you are particularly strong in at least one of the specified areas.

If an executive search firm is involved, use it as a source of information about the position, the community, the organization, and the desires of the hiring body.

A candidate's presence, image, appearance, demeanor, courtesy, and impressions conveyed are all subjective—and also very important.

Do your homework on the jurisdiction.

Approach each stage of the selection process seriously; do not wait until the final stage to begin considering factors that should have been contemplated much earlier and might result in withdrawal from candidacy.

Source: David N. Ammons and James J. Glass, updated by David N. Ammons, *Recruiting Local Government Executives: Practical Insights for Hiring Authorities and Candidates* (San Francisco: Jossey-Bass, 1989), 189.

The accrediting association for public affairs programs is the National Association of Schools of Public Affairs and Administration (NASPAA). NASPAA standards call for flexibility in the design of master's programs to meet constituent needs and stipulate that the primary objective of the graduate program must be "professional education preparing persons for leadership and management roles in public affairs, policy, administration."[14] In addition, an internship is integral to the degree programs of NASPAA member universities. NASPAA also stresses community involvement and has a long history of working jointly with ICMA on appropriate professional education. Thus, the trends in local government management credentials and the programs offered by universities offering public affairs programs are complementary.

Early opportunities

Even with limited experience, many prospective local government managers are eager—and sometimes overeager—to find a prestigious job with an impressive title and extensive responsibilities. Nevertheless, less glamorous choices may better serve their long-term career interests. Often more important than title and starting salary for the enhancement of one's competitiveness for the next career step are the nature of the job, the opportunity to test and develop skills, the possibilities for advancement, the opportunity to learn from a respected mentor, and the reputation of the employing government.

The aspiring manager will be competing for future positions with very talented colleagues and, in some cases, friends who will be just as eager to have the position. Early in a career, the prospective manager should take care to do the following three things.

Build a record of accomplishment   Position title, number of employees supervised, and size of budget managed—these are not the measures that will help one compete for a position with greater responsibility and greater compensation. Instead, it is critical to assume responsibility for a specific issue, problem, capital project, or service area, especially during the first few jobs. If the responsibility is not assigned, the early-career manager should seek out an assignment that will lead to measurable results; that is what builds a professional reputation for accomplishment. As one competes for higher positions, a record of early results is fundamental. In almost all cases, a record of tangible, measurable accomplishments is more valuable to a prospective employer than a background of general experience.

Build relevant experience   Advancing in the local government management profession involves building on previous experience. Some early-career experiences seem to steer young staff toward finance, human resources, or planning and economic development. A combination of experiences in one of these fields frequently fascinates a young professional and is the motivator to build a career of increasing responsibility in a specialized field, which often culminates in a department director's position. Others try out positions that support elected officials in their policy making or constituent representation responsibilities, and they develop a keen interest in support or generalist administration roles. These individuals are frequently interested in assistant positions that come with increasing responsibilities. A smaller number remain focused on the top appointed administrative posts in local government. They deliberately try to vary their early assignments so as to gain a broad exposure to all the concerns facing a local government. All of these options are legitimate, and all result in positions as a professional local government manager.

In addition to the degree of specialization and the level of management responsibility desired, there are several other variables to consider when deciding which early experiences to build upon. The first of these is size. ICMA recognizes communities that have established positions of overall general management responsibility through the council-manager form or some other scheme of organization. In 2003 there were 3,387 communities recognized, and 45 percent had populations of 10,000 or less. In smaller communities, the top manager may be the only manager; a decision to focus experience and career on small communities means much greater exposure to the daily details of a government's operations. Larger communities involve more staff and specialist management positions with more internal upward mobility and greater responsibilities for coordination.[15]

Another variable affecting careers is community type. Rural, independent, and suburban communities are all recognized by ICMA, along with a large number of central cities in which special challenges and opportunities arise from broad demographic and economic diversity. Managing in a central city/urban center involves skills that are different from those required in suburban communities, and those skills need to be built and sharpened through early experiences.

Finally there is the question of where a professional manager wishes to live. Mobility is a factor in the profession, but most managers limit their movement to communities within the same state in order to build on experience with state laws, customs, and traditions. Some managers do make interstate moves, but they are a distinct and declining minority. At the other end of the spectrum is the handful of managers who spend their entire careers in one jurisdiction.

Learn to compete   Managers interested in moving up in their local government or moving out to manage another local government discover quickly that competition for the most desirable positions is fierce. The strongest contenders establish the foundation for their candidacy early by securing an advanced education, gaining the appropriate experience, and building the record of accomplishments noted above. In the future, becoming and remaining an ICMA credentialed manager will also be an advantage. This foundation, coupled with a reasonably keen knowledge of the recruitment process and an ability to present oneself effectively, enhances the odds of a competitive standing in the job market.

Candidates for local government managerial positions must know the steps in the standard recruitment process conducted by governing bodies for the top job and by the chief appointed official and personnel departments for other professional management jobs. Frequently they must also know the practices of executive search firms. Most small local governments continue to solicit applications for the position of top appointed administrator by advertising in the region, statewide, and nationally (the latter through the biweekly *ICMA Newsletter*), screen résumés of candidates; conduct reference and background checks; and interview finalists. Most jurisdictions with medium and large populations use search firms to enrich the candidate pool and strengthen the screening process. Top managers and personnel departments also use these firms for assistant and department director positions.

Executive search firms dramatically change the nature of the recruitment and selection process. They become another party in the process, and those ready for a new assignment would be well advised to identify the major firms and let them know of their interest and availability. In addition to improving the candidate development and screening process, the firms have played a significant role in negotiating employment agreements for successful candidates. This has undoubtedly been a factor in the increasing number of such agreements and the increased stability in the profession.

Mobility

The local government profession has always required its practitioners to move from one community to another as they seek increasing responsibility, improved compensation, and new experiences—and as they are no longer welcome in their current position and community. Recent evidence indicates that these perceptions of necessary mobility may be exaggerated at the beginning of the twenty-first century. The average tenure of managers in a council-manager city has been lengthening over the decades. In the 1960s the average tenure was 3.5 years; in the 1970s, 4.4 years; in the 1980s, 5.4 years; and in 2000, 6.9 years.[16] One recent survey of managers reported: "The mean for the number of cities a city manager has served is

2.15 with a median of 2 and a mode of 1. Consequently, the conclusion drawn from these data is that even though there is the perception that city managers go from city to city, and other national statistics show that the city management profession is a transient one, the descriptive statistics of this study do not support the prevailing perception."[17]

Stability in the profession may be increasing for a number of reasons. The increasing use of employment agreements with severance provisions for termination without cause may be encouraging greater patience by councils. The prevalence of two-career couples could be hindering voluntary movement because the spouses of managers cannot pick up and move on as they used to. The growing number of professional positions and department director positions in mid-size and large communities may encourage practitioners to seek broader responsibilities within the existing local government in order to avoid the costs of relocation.

In addition, as the average age of managers has increased, managers have become sufficiently vested in their local or state pension programs to create a strong incentive to stay put to maximize pension benefits rather than start over in a new plan. Thus, any move is likely to be within the same state. Older managers also mean older children will be reluctant to relocate. The combination of pension, children in high school, and two-career families can be a tremendous deterrent to voluntary mobility, and strong severance provisions are a limit to involuntary mobility.

The ICMA Code of Ethics has always discouraged a great deal of mobility and job hopping. A guideline for Tenet 4 (Appendix A) requires managers to commit at least two years to any position they have accepted, and a pattern of short-term assignments can result in censure for violation of the Code of Ethics. Two situations that may increase the perceived mobility of the profession are the large number of very small communities served by a manager and the tendency of managers who have been fired to take positions in communities that have a history of high turnover. In the first case, many small communities lack the resources to retain a talented manager even though many would like to do so; the manager must, in fact, move out to move up. This is an unfortunate consequence of the fragmented nature of local government in the United States, but many of these communities have been excellent starting places for career managers, and the communities have been well served by the changes brought by new managers.

Those managers who move too quickly to reenter the profession after being fired or forced to resign place themselves in jeopardy of being fired again if they choose a community where the political culture is not ready for professional management. Managers who have been terminated or forced to resign—especially if this job roiling happens more than once—should step back for a careful personal and professional assessment of their strengths and weaknesses as a local government management professional. Patience and careful research are needed to try to assure a better match between the individual's skills and a community's needs. Such a careful, reflective, analytical approach to finding the next job is easier if the individual has accumulated reasonable savings to cover living expenses during this difficult transition period. It used to be said in the profession that it would take at least one month to find a new position for every $10,000 in salary sought. That is probably a bit optimistic today; therefore, careful, conservative personal financial management geared to creating and maintaining the requisite nest egg is essential.

Employment agreements

Because city and county managers serve at the pleasure of elected officials, they are vulnerable to removal from office with little or no notice. As a result, many have requested and received employment agreements—in the form of a contract, a letter of agreement, or an ordinance or resolution—that clarify and formalize terms of employment. Among the typical items addressed in an employment agreement are duties of the manager, termination procedures, severance pay, periodic performance evaluation, salary, and fringe benefits.

ICMA has been promoting employment agreements for managers for several decades, and the number of such agreements has increased dramatically. Between 1992 and 2002 the percentage of managers responding to ICMA surveys who indicated they had an employment agreement of some kind increased from 40 percent to 69.5 percent.[18]

Severance pay and performance evaluation are crucial in these agreements. ICMA has advocated severance provisions that provide at least six months' salary following termination without cause, and this amount has been provided in most agreements. A task force finishing its work in 2003 reported that increasingly the time period is a full twelve months, and some jurisdictions are providing even more generous severance pay provisions. ICMA's Model Employment Agreement suggests that the employing body or individual commit to at least an annual review of the performance of the professional manager and that the employing agency commit to support continuing professional development activities such as memberships, conferences, workshops and seminars, and publications to improve the skills of the practitioner. Thus, the model agreement not only encourages more employment security for the individual manager, it also promotes better management by requiring annual performance reviews and promoting continuous improvement through professional development. Employment agreements are far less common for assistants and department directors because they are employees of the top manager and the general employment rules for the local government apply to them. Their positions are also less subject to the volatility of politics.[19]

The new job

Steps taken early in a new manager's tenure, even before the official starting date, can be important to long-term success. Before reporting for duty, a manager needs to learn the specific issues and expectations for the new position. If it is in a community new to the manager, the professional manager must get to know that community and its government by reviewing the local charter and organization chart; reading the local government coverage in the local newspaper; and examining budgets, financial statements, and major reports before arriving on the job. ICMA's *First Time Administrators Handbook* provides sound advice helpful to all who are entering a new job:

- Gain the trust of council and community
- Get to know colleagues in the management of the government
- Meet with all department directors as soon as possible
- Be yourself
- Get to know other local government managers in the area
- Be ethical, visible, and fair
- Establish good relations with the media.[20]

Managers moving from one community to another are also well served by avoiding the syndrome of "We did it this way in _____." Building on prior experience is essential as a career develops, but implying that your former government did things better is an invitation to poor relations and poor support from your new colleagues.

Build on prior experience and introduce new approaches, but keep the sources to yourself.

Another negative might be described as too much use of "I" and too much reliance on a command-and-control style early in a new position. Seeking opinions and advice from new colleagues who have been in the government and involving and including them in decision making will build the teamwork and support essential for success in local government. Most managers have long rejected a command-and-control style, but the unfamiliar circumstances and the desire to make a quick impression and to demonstrate ability to use the authority implied in any management position sometimes drive managers to an unfamiliar style that, in fact, slows their assimilation into a new setting.

When to move on

The excitement that a new manager feels when hired, the energy generated by new challenges, and the honeymoon with a supportive governing body may begin to fade after the first year or two on the job. Saying no to enough special interests may gradually gain the new manager a group of detractors. Eventually, new governing body members are elected, perhaps after campaigning on the need for change, and some of them may express privately—or perhaps even publicly—a desire for their own manager. Sometimes community satisfaction and the confidence of the governing body remain firmly intact, but the manager's enthusiasm wanes after several years; the manager may begin to feel that the major challenges associated with the job have been met. In either case, it may be time for the manager to look for new challenges and new opportunities.

In the absence of pressure from the governing body or other, sometimes subtle, signs of growing displeasure, deciding whether to remain with a particular local government can be difficult. Nevertheless, the decision to remain or leave an organization is made over and over by countless people in various occupations, not just local government managers. Career consultants Barry and Linda Gale report that "above-average" persons typically decide to change jobs approximately eight times during their careers.[21] They suggest careful consideration of important aspects of one's current job as well as personal attributes (see their list of personal values on page 220). Their advice, adapted to apply to local government managers, suggests consideration of the following factors:

- Interpersonal relationships with the governing body, the chief elected official, department heads, and other influential individuals
- Office politics
- Personal values and skills, and the degree to which they are compatible with one's current job
- The direction in which the local government is headed and the likelihood that one's contributions will be rewarded in a fashion that is meaningful
- The stress of one's current situation
- One's willingness to take risks or try something new, perhaps an entrepreneurial endeavor
- One's willingness to undergo the inconvenience and disruption—both personal and professional—of making a move.

Sometimes the manager decides to stay. A manager who is well suited to and challenged by the current position and appreciated by the local government employer need not feel pressured by some rule of thumb that says local government managers should change jobs every six or seven years.[22]

Personal values relevant to career choice   From the following list of job-related values, select the six that hold the most attraction for you:

Above-average income

Adventure

Appreciating beauty

Artistic impression

Change

Community involvement

Competition

Contact with people

Creativity

Excitement

Expanding knowledge

Fast pace

Feelings of belonging

Flexibility of schedule

Helping others

Helping society

Independence from supervision

Influencing people

Location

Making decisions

Mental challenge

Moral fulfillment

Physical challenge

Power

Precision

Recognition

Security

Stability

Supervisory responsibility

Working alone

Working under pressure

Working with others

How many of the values you selected does your present job satisfy?

Source: Adapted from Barry and Linda Gale, *Stay or Leave* (New York: Harper and Row, 1989), 39–41. Copyright 1989 by Barry and Linda Gale. Reprinted with permission of HarperCollins.

IT

The least enjoyable time in a professional local government manager's career is the time of being "IT"—in trouble or in transition. Every aspect of these times is before the public, and the manager's family must also suffer the indignity of performance criticism and, unfortunately, personal attack. It would be nice if people could disagree without being disagreeable, but the media glare and the open nature of local government focus attention on any negative. This is the most unpleasant part of the manager's job.

The program helps preserve and share some of the wisdom and lessons gained over the careers of senior members of the profession. It is an important, on-the-ground source of support for communities considering the council-manager form of government.

Mark Achen

To cope with these challenges, it is most important to recognize the signs that usually signify a time of trouble. A number of very senior managers have reported that they never saw the problems developing before they were summarily dismissed from the job. Spotting the signs early might help to avoid that final action, or at least it will help to initiate preparation for moving on in a career. Bill Mathis, an industrial psychologist, suggests seven symptoms of a manager in trouble:

- Unwillingness to fire or move a department director or key employee
- Change in personal effectiveness

- Unwillingness to read or adapt to the political environment
- Becoming a target for what's wrong with the community
- Distancing—detachment from problems and people
- Power conflict between the professional manager and the elected officials
- History of environmental dishonesty—not playing by the public rules.[23]

When a manager reads one or more of these signs, it is time to reread the previous section.

"In transition" is the euphemism ICMA uses to describe a manager who has been fired. When another professional person loses a job, often only the family knows; but when a local government manager is fired, everyone knows. Recovering from the perceived humiliation of that action—no matter how unjustified—is extremely difficult. A manager who has been fired must go through a mourning period similar to the loss of a loved one. Denial, anger, sadness, and finally acceptance are all phases through which the manager must pass, and denying or fighting any phase delays the entire process. Some fired managers feel it is their obligation to "save the community from this outrage and protect the citizens who are supporting me." Almost every fired manager receives support from friends, neighbors, and those who feel the firing was unjust. It is rarely enough to cause the council or any other employer to change the decision, and fighting delays getting through the adjustment period.

They ought to call Range Riders the Rough Riders—because you usually need them most when the going gets rough.

Bob Jasper

Personal and professional support for a manager in these difficult situations is available from ICMA. A manager sensing trouble or already fired should contact ICMA, which can generate a strong support network and provide literature tailored for local government managers.[24] In 22 states ICMA sponsors 77 Range Riders—retired managers with significant experience who have volunteered to serve as counselors for active managers who want their advice. After a manager has used these support services to navigate the adjustment period, the number-one priority is often finding the next job. Every manager who is IT needs to think through whether moving back into local government service is the right thing to do after such a shock—for both the manager and the manager's family. Most managers do return to public service. They are committed to their career choice and are not discouraged by a bad experience.

Although being IT is a part of the local government management profession, it is important to remember that in any one year less than 4 percent of management professionals find themselves in these situations. A majority of managers complete successful careers without ever being IT.

The work and life of a manager

The workweek of a typical local government manager is meaningful, frenetic, challenging, demanding, and stressful. The demands are in some ways similar to executive work in any field of endeavor, with complications added by the public nature of the work as well as the role ambiguity, role conflict, and role overload that characterize the work.

Role ambiguity

The manager is expected to be an expert administrator who carries out the policy directives of the governing body—even when those directives are imprecise or contradictory, even when resources are insufficient, and even when sufficient authority to perform the task has not been granted. The manager is expected to render sound policy advice; yet many managers believe it wise to refrain from public acknowledgement of a substantial role in the policy process. In some cases, local government managers are denied the authority to appoint and remove department heads and may even possess few realistic options for preventing subordinates from going over their heads to the governing body; nevertheless, managers are expected to maintain control over the entire administrative operation.

Role conflict

Under conditions of ambiguity, role conflict may be extensive. Council members have expectations regarding the manager's role that may differ from those of the manager, professional colleagues, subordinates, and citizens, or that may deviate from professional norms or even charter prescriptions. For example, the assumption that the manager has full authority over operating departments occasionally collides with council expectations that the manager will assume a more subservient or "responsive" role on sensitive matters, deferring to the council in such cases. Failed attempts by city managers to remove police chiefs—their nominal subordinates in most council-manager governments—are legendary. Such occurrences dramatize the commonplace disparity between the role formally assigned to the post of manager (in this case, management of all municipal operations, including the authority to appoint or remove the chief of police) and the role that the city council may expect the manager to play.

Role overload

Role overload is apparent in the hectic pace and long workweek typical of the local government manager's job. (Surveys have found the typical workweek to average 53–57 hours.[25]) Like chief executives in other fields, local government managers rush from task to task throughout the day: a breakfast meeting with community leaders, a staff meeting back at the office, a half hour to dictate responses to letters or answer a few phone calls, a quick visit with a department head to discuss the concerns of a commissioner, lunch at a civic club, an afternoon that proceeds at much the same pace, an evening meeting, and a briefcase full of memos and reports to read at home. Such schedules create a pressure-packed formula for overload; yet considerable evidence suggests that people attracted to the job of chief executive may actually thrive on the frantic pace—right up to the point of burnout.

My daily prayer while serving as a local government chief executive was "God grant me courageous councilors and staff who are not afraid of making mistakes."

A. Jeffrey Greenwell

In his seminal study of executive roles and work activities, Henry Mintzberg concluded that executives not only tolerate a work situation characterized by fragmented tasks, brevity in nearly everything they do, and almost constant interruptions, but actually prefer that mode of operation for at least four reasons. First, they fear any other pattern would deny them the constantly updated information vital to their effectiveness. Second, they become accustomed to great variety in their work and grow to enjoy it. Third, most of their activities are related to problems or opportunities they consider important; accordingly, they are reluctant to abandon personal involvement in any of them. And, fourth, they recognize that some duties can be performed only by the chief executive and cannot be delegated.[26]

Personal life

Three aspects of a local government manager's work exacerbate the usual pressures felt by any executive: a pervasive lack of privacy, a lack of job security, and the consequent almost constant threat of forced mobility. As the operations of local government have become increasingly transparent and media coverage of local officials has become intense, managers cannot expect to shelter any aspect of their personal lives from public scrutiny. Salaries and benefits are set through public action by the council. Because the manager is a public figure, the manager's personal life may be a subject for media coverage. Criticism of performance is offered in public, causing the family to share in any resulting frustration. Life in a fishbowl can become tiresome.

The lack of job security has been a natural result of the formulation of the council-manager plan: while the council-manager form gives significant authority to an appointed official (the manager), it also makes certain that that manager has no guaranteed term or tenure and can be removed by the employing body at any time for any reason. Absence of job security, coupled with the reality that elected officials submit to the judgment of the voters every two to four years and the current manager's advocates can lose, lead the professional manager to recognize that a move may be required at any time. Although this forced mobility may be somewhat overstated today, it is still a prerequisite that an aspiring manager accept the possibility of relocation.

Most managers truly enjoy their jobs and balance the challenging work with a variety of hobbies and activities. Doug Harman, former manager of Alexandria, Virginia, and Fort Worth, Texas, is an avid collector of toy soldiers and a historian of the wars and battles they represent; he is also an amateur cartoonist. Chip Morrison, former manager of Auburn, Maine, enjoyed dropping his normal public persona by acting in community theater presentations. Debra Brooks Feazelle of Port Lavaca, Texas, runs in Susan G. Komen Races for the Cure, with a goal of completing all of them in the country. ICMA life member John Goss is true to his California base when he plays jazz saxophone; and Steve Bonczek of Beaumont, Texas, is a model railroader. Programs of state associations of managers show that golf is almost a religion for managers who enjoy the outdoors; the concentration required helps them forget the job while they compete with friends. Tennis is another sport for managers who enjoy competition. It is no surprise that many managers serve as volunteers in the arts, sporting activities, health care, affordable housing, and other quality-of-life initiatives.

Family life

Being part of the family of a local government manager requires special sensitivity and a willingness to support the public service career of the manager as well as the ethical constraints that accompany it. Spouses may find their career and job choices limited by potential conflicts of interest. Jobs that may be perceived as possibly conflicting with the requirements of the local government manager position include: newspaper reporter, real estate developer, and even jobs in the fields of the arts or health care if the employer is funded by the city government. Active participation in politics by a spouse can also cause problems that strain a marriage; in fact, many spouses were attracted to their manager partner because of a shared interest in public affairs. For couples who are both committed to a profession, career conflicts can be even more complicated, and the growing prevalence of dual-career couples may be one of the factors reducing voluntary job change in the profession.

City managers must be able to patiently and expertly respond to all criticism involving city activities, suffer the consequences of city decisions or indecisions not necessarily under their control, work extraordinarily long hours, and subject their families to some of the same pressures.
David R. Mora

Managers' children are not exempt from special pressures and must learn at an early age that their manager-parent has an important job in the community. Performance at school may subject a child to "You should have known [done] better, you're the city manager's child." This can burden a child, and the situation requires special support from both parents. Other children may hear their parents criticize the city government and/or the manager and take it out on the manager's child by teasing and ridiculing; this again calls for special parental support. Both children and spouses carry an added burden as they are expected to be ready at any time for contact with elected officials, media personnel, or the general public. In many ways they are volunteer citizen service representatives because the home telephone can ring at any time for the city manager. Children must develop patience, courtesy, and often a good sense of humor.

The potential for forced relocation is a special challenge that calls for good, open communication on the subject as soon as children are old enough to understand. Intermittently uprooting a family, combined with the realization that the impetus for the move may come suddenly, can cause stress in a family, especially when the children are teenagers and family members have become attached to the community.

The unmarried manager

Unmarried managers, while they have many of the same concerns as married managers, often find demands to be even greater and more complex. If a single manager is divorced, family relationships can be a source of pressure; if the manager lives in the same community as his or her children and ex-spouse, the pressure may be intensified. Life in the goldfish bowl can be particularly difficult for unmarried managers in small communities; their social lives are so public that they seek social relationships in other communities to avoid gossipy hometowners. For single managers, life can be especially lonely. These managers may need to make a special effort to develop a support network of colleagues and friends (perhaps from other communities) with whom they can discuss both job-related and personal issues.

Work and life balance

The overwhelming majority of local government managers and their families enjoy rich, well balanced, rewarding lives. They cope with the special challenges of the profession as they recognize they are close to the heart of their community and the work of the manager is improving the residents' quality of life. The number of second- and third-generation managers is growing; children of local government managers are energized by their parents' public service commitment. The profession is demanding and stressful, and occasionally this stress can overwhelm a manager or a family member. Recognizing the symptoms of burnout (see page 225) is as important as building and maintaining personal and professional support networks.

Symptoms of burnout

Physical symptoms

Fatigue, physical depletion, exhaustion

Sleep difficulties (e.g., insomnia, night-mares)

Back pain

Gastrointestinal problems (e.g., stomach-aches, appetite loss, bowel difficulties)

Headaches

Colds and flu

Behavioral symptoms

Job turnover

Poor job performance (e.g., neglectful, mistake-prone, often requiring supervisory discipline)

Absenteeism/tardiness

Overeating or oversmoking

Extended work breaks

Workplace theft

Prone to workplace injury

Use of alcohol or drugs (e.g., tranquilizers)

Attitudinal symptoms

Cynicism

Callousness

Pessimism

Defensiveness

Intolerance of clients

Lack of confidence regarding personal effectiveness or accomplishments

Lack of commitment to profession

Desire to escape from people or avoid going to work

Reduced expectations

Negative attitudes toward self or life in general

Reduced satisfaction with role and daily activities (personal and professional)

Low job satisfaction

Emotional symptoms

Depression

Guilt

Anxiety

Nervousness

Emotional depletion

Anger

Irritability

Tearfulness

Hopelessness

Loneliness

Interpersonal symptoms

Work interferes with family life

Defensive escape or avoidance of clients (e.g., refusal to answer phone, hanging up on callers)

Verbal attacks or even physical violence toward others

Increased tendency to complain of work problems to family and co-workers ("staff gripes")

Fewer friends

Preference for solitary activities

Lower level of marital satisfaction

Lower quality of personal relations with friends and family

Tendency to display negative emotions and withdraw from spouse or family

More likely to disagree with spouse about children's discipline

Spouse more likely to feel depressed and shut out

Tendency to feel less involved in family matters, more distant from children, and misunderstood by spouse about pres-sures of job

Note: The relationship of burnout to general physical health and job satisfaction has been explored extensively. All other symp-toms listed, though supported by initial research, should be regarded as probable symptoms.

Source: Adapted from Sophia Kahill, "Symptoms of Professional Burnout: A Review of the Empirical Evidence," *Canadian Psychology* 29 (July 1988): 184–197. Copyright 1988 Canadian Psychological Association. Reprinted with permission.

Support networks

Support networks made up of family, friends, and professional associates can rein-force other stress-management strategies. Close confidants who can help a manager assess a stressful situation and design a control strategy to deal with the source, who can provide honest and trusted advice to a manager tempted by escape strategies, and who can encourage and perhaps participate with the manager in an exercise or health maintenance program can be of major benefit.

Few people other than local government managers themselves fully grasp the problems and pressures in their environment. Their job is the only one of its kind in their jurisdiction; no one else shares precisely the same perspective. Nevertheless, a support network can be formed of persons who understand at least part of the pressures and who have the manager's interest at heart. The crucial element of a support network is someone—often a spouse—who offers unconditional support, a sympathetic ear, and, ideally, an unshakable emotional foundation.

Trusted department heads or other work associates—especially those whose mutual interests and personalities bind them to the manger in a friendship extending beyond their occupational ties—may form part of the support network. They, more than most others, understand the problems and pressures of their shared work environment. Colleagues who hold similar positions in other communities may be another important element of the network. They can offer camaraderie at professional association events and expert advice on difficult or sensitive issues. Whether they offer serious advice or simply swap war stories, professional colleagues can help a manager view matters philosophically and keep events in perspective. Finally, personal friends who have no occupational ties can offer diversion, relief from daily pressures, and an outsider's view of troublesome matters, even if their grasp of the manager's professional world is limited. Personal friends who share a common spiritual faith may be especially comforting, particularly during trying times when managers face unfair public criticism, emotional upheaval of a family crisis, or a sudden job loss.

The support of colleagues provided through a variety of networks has helped me throughout my career, providing both professional and personal counsel. Serving as state association president in Pennsylvania and as a member of the ICMA board has expanded my horizons and shown me that there is never a reason to be lonely at the top.

Tom Fountaine

ICMA has helped develop and maintain a series of professional support networks available to local government managers. There are 48 state associations of managers and 11 associations that are especially supportive of assistants. The state, and even substate, management associations encourage assistants to get together professionally. Professional associations also provide support for women—who are currently still in the minority among managers—in the local government management profession. The National Association of County Administrators (NACA) is open to professional managers who work in county governments, and the National Association of Regional Councils welcomes directors of regional councils. Those who practice local government management as department directors will find a plethora of professional associations in the fields of, for example, finance, personnel, and public works. The National Forum for Black Public Administrators and the Hispanic Network have already been mentioned. Finally, a great many local and regional groups provide a venue for managers to work together on common interests and support each other personally as well as professionally. Local government professionals have a tendency to bond; they recognize that, although the profession can be a lonely one, no manager need be alone.

Career suitability

A person must consider four personal questions when evaluating a career or job choice:

- First, what is the real nature of the work—not the title or the popular perception of the job, but what really happens on the job? The first seven chapters describe the nature of the work, and in this chapter we explore the behavior characteristics displayed by those who do the job (Appendix B) and the values they hold (Appendix A). The work requires visioning and communicating (the two basic skills of leadership);[27] interpersonal and group interaction; and continuous problem solving. The work finds no easy answers and requires a high tolerance for ambiguity.

- Second, who is served? Would you enjoy working for those people? Citizens and elected officials are in charge of the work of a local government. They must be served and served well. Elected officials must submit themselves to the judgment of the voters every two to four years, and those voters frequently choose change. This fact requires a manager to submit almost every aspect of life to public scrutiny and limits the right of privacy for the individual and family. Because change at the top is always a possibility, limited job security and the potential for forced mobility to another community must also be accepted. Respect for representative democracy and the elected officials who participate is essential, and this requires a scrupulous political neutrality that can be frustrating; a local government manager is in the middle of the political action yet must remain neutral in the contests. Finally, the public nature of the job requires adherence to the highest personal ethical standards as well as the professional obligations set by the Code of Ethics of the profession (Appendix A). Managers have been censured by ICMA and removed from office by their jurisdictions for personal behavior that would be acceptable for those who live a more private life.

- Third, who is the work done with? A manager works with and often leads committed public service professionals and dedicated public servants who offer a broad variety of services to the public. This environment requires a genuine respect for the work of government—for those who serve and those who are served. A skeptic about the value of government may suffer in this field of endeavor. Do you really believe that government is a force for good?

- Finally, how well is the work compensated? Although the average salary of a local government manager is well above the average for a worker in the United States who has some managerial or administrative responsibility, it is well below the average for private sector managers and professionals who do similar work. This fact requires a manager to plan personal finances carefully and, with the acceptance and support of the family, be willing to accept a comfortable but far-from-affluent or -opulent life style.

A good match?

A recent study of managers' style preferences, with the Myers-Briggs Type Indicator, found that three style preference out of a total of sixteen constituted 49 percent of all managers' preferences. The ISTJ (introverted, sensing, thinking, judging) style was indicated by 23 percent of managers who responded to the survey. Persons who prefer this style have been described as practical, logical, thoughtful, matter-of-fact individuals who are traditionalists and stabilizers. They have also been described as "doing what should be done." A smaller number, 14 percent of managers, indicated a preference for the ENTJ (extroverted, intuitive, thinking, judging) style. They have been described as "life's natural leaders." And 13 percent indicated a preference for the ESTJ (extroverted, sensing, thinking, judging) style—"life's administrators."[28] These three types—who might otherwise be seen as moralists, leaders, or administrators—probably comprise the major types found in the local government management profession. They meet the combination of dedication to continuous improvement, independence, and commitment described as "the reformer" on page 228. However, these three types together describe only half of all local government managers. The profession has room for a variety of work styles—the key is to know what yours is.

I have gone through personal and professional challenges during my career—from the loss of my first wife to cancer to moving to serve different towns in Maine—but this profession has given me both the support I have needed and the opportunity to improve the quality of life for neighbors in towns I have loved.
                                                                                      Don Gerrish

---

The reformer   A reformer is one who sets forth cheerfully toward sure defeat.

It is his peculiar function to embrace the hopeless cause when it can win no other friends and when its obvious futility repels that thick-necked practical, timorous type of citizen to whom the outward appearance of success is so dear.

His persistence against stone walls invites derision by those who have never been touched by his religion and do not know what fun it is.

He never seems victorious for if he were visibly winning he would forthwith ceased to be dubbed "reformer."

Yet, in time, the Reformer's little movement becomes respectable and this little minority proves that it can grow, and presently the Statesman joins it and takes all the credit, cheerfully handed to him by the Reformer as a bribe for his support.

And then comes the Politician, rushing grandly to the succor of the victor.

And all the crowd.

The original Reformer is lost in the shuffle then, but he doesn't care—

For as the great bandwagon which he started goes thundering past with trumpets, the crowd in the intoxication of triumph leans over the side to jeer at him—a forlorn and lonely crank, mustering a pitiful little odd lot of followers along the roadside and setting them marching while over their heads he lifts the curious banner of his next crusade.

Richard S. Childs, executive director, National Civic League, 1927.

Know thyself

Local government management is a profession that requires continuous self-evaluation and enrichment of personal competencies. ICMA suggests that all members "periodically assess their competencies" and has worked with managers to develop two instruments—the Applied Knowledge Assessment and the Management Practices Assessment—to assess knowledge about the skills required for success and the practical application of that knowledge.

Aspiring managers should take the Applied Knowledge Assessment at least once early in a career and periodically thereafter every decade or so. Results from the first 1,700 assessments indicate that the greatest strengths of managers are in media relations, functional and operational expertise and planning, and technological literacy. On the other hand, many managers' knowledge of quality assurance, citizen service, financial analysis, democratic advocacy, and citizen participation could be improved. Those preparing to enter the profession should develop competence in the substantive areas deemed most important by elected officials. Careful review of current literature and job advertisements can give a clear indication of elected officials' priorities. Those considering entry should take the Applied Knowledge Assessment early so as to target their personal professional development.

It is too early to report any results from the Management Practices Assessment, but some managers, with reported success, are beginning to use this 360-degree instrument in their annual performance evaluations. Annual assessment by the council or employing official is a vital tool for a manager who wants to continuously update personal knowledge of performance. It is surprising—yet not surprising—how many managers and councils resist the annual evaluation. The evaluation must be conducted in public in many states, or the results must at least be reported to the public, which can engender criticism by the public and open the door for community controversy. Many individual members of councils have never participated in a performance evaluation, and conducting one as a group almost seems unnatural, or very difficult at best. In addition to using ICMA's Management Practices Assessment as a tool to make the job a bit easier for the council and to introduce the traits and competencies that the profession deems appropriate for evaluation, some managers have encouraged their councils to use the services of a professional facilitator to help make the assessment a bit smoother for both parties. Whether one uses the instrument, a facilitator, or both, the annual evaluation is critical for the relationship and for the individual manager's self-knowledge.

A local government manager leads a challenging and fascinating life . . . doing varied and interesting work that improves the quality of life for all residents in the community. Working for elected officials and with dedicated public servants has been a truly rewarding career. I would do it again in a heartbeat.
Bruce Romer

A fourth assessment tool beyond the Applied Knowledge Assessment, the Management Practices Assessment, and the annual performance evaluation is the Myers-Briggs Type Indicator, which attempts to identify "the 16 personality types that determine how we live, love, and work." Many managers have used the assessment to help identify their own strengths and weaknesses, and some have asked their families, management teams, and councils to take the assessment with them to improve team understanding.

Recap

- Local government management is a career that offers immense opportunities for meaningful public service. It continues to draw capable men and women who are attracted by the chance to use their skills for community good and by the opportunity to see the tangible products of their work.

- The education required as preparation for the profession consistently involves a quality undergraduate experience in the liberal arts or in a business program followed by study for an MPA. Career paths in the profession have come to vary greatly depending on the degree of specialization desired (department directors are usually specialists) and the extent of overall management responsibility sought (those who prefer the job of assistant manager choose a lesser degree of responsibility than does the CEO, CAO, or COO). Each of the paths chosen is legitimate, and practitioners of local government management are all professionals regardless of title, specialization, or organizational level.

- Competition for jobs in the profession is intense, and an ambitious practitioner must build a record of measurable accomplishment, understand the recruitment and selection process in the profession, and be prepared to move up or out while it is still the choice of the individual.

- Life as a local government manager is exciting, varied, and fast paced, and it requires constant attention to balancing personal, family, professional, and job demands while living life in the public spotlight. These pressures can occasionally result in burnout. Managers must pay attention to the signs of burnout and the mechanisms for handling stress.

- An examination of individual attributes and personality traits often reveals those who may be more or less suited for dealing with the difficulties inherent in local government management. Such an examination also provides evidence of the prevalence of various personalities within the field. Despite some common problems and some common characteristics, differences do exist in the needs and expectations of local governments. A manager who is suitable for one locality may be less suitable for another. It is the individual who must decide whether the pressures are tolerable—or even stimulating—and whether the many sources of satisfaction in local government management provide sufficient reward.

Leadership self-assessment

Take a minute to look at yourself as a leader. Do you have the qualities to make a valuable leader to your group? Answer the questions associated with leadership attributes, skills and knowledge and put yourself to the test. After you have looked at yourself as a leader, answer the questions at the end.

Attributes . . .

- Do I view problems as opportunities?
- Am I a priority setter?
- Am I customer focused?
- Am I courageous?
- Am I a critical and creative thinker?
- What is my tolerance for ambiguity?
- Do I have a positive attitude toward change?
- Am I committed to innovations that are best for children?

Skills . . .

- Do I debate, clarify, and enunciate my values and beliefs?
- Can I fuel, inspire, and guard the shared vision?
- Can I communicate the strategic plan at all levels?
- Do I recognize the problems inherent to the planning process?
- Do I ask the big-picture questions and "what if"?
- Can I support the staff through the change process?
- Do I encourage dreaming and thinking the unthinkable?
- Can I align the budget, planning, policies, and programs with the city's goals and vision?
- Do I engage in goal setting?
- Can I develop and implement action plans?
- Do I practice and plan conscious abandonment?
- Do I transfer the strategic planning process to planning?

Knowledge . . .

- Do I know council roles and responsibilities in planning and implementing plans?
- Do I know the strategic planning process, short- and long-term planning tools?
- Do I know the council and city vision, beliefs, and mission?
- Do I know the relationship of the budget to city planning?
- Do I know local, state, and national factors that affect local government?
- Do I know the best practices and research on improving service delivery?
- Do I know the process of change and paradigm shifts?
- Do I know the strategies to involve and communicate with the community?

What trait were you proud to say describes you? • Was there any trait you would not consider desirable? • What trait are you trying to make more descriptive of you?

Source: Used with permission from "Leadershp Self-Assessment" in the *Education Leadership Toolkit,* an online publication at http://www.nsba.org/sbot/toolkit/LeadSA.html. Copyright 1997, National School Boards Association. All rights reserved.

Notes

1 James Svara, quoted in Bill Hansell, "Professional Management: A Significant Contribution of the Council-Manager Form of Government," *Public Management* (May 2002): 24.

2 George L. Hanbury II, "The Function of Leadership Styles and Personality Types among City Managers" (Ph.D. diss., Florida Atlantic University [UMI/ProQuest Digital Dissertations, AAT no. 9998892], May 2001), 163.

3 State of the Profession Survey Results, 2000 and 2002, reported in *ICMA Newsletter,* various issues.

4 State of the Profession Survey Results, 1992–2002, reported in *ICMA Newsletter,* various issues.

5 *Compensation 2002: An Annual Report on Local Government Executive Salaries and Fringe Benefits* (Washington, D.C.: ICMA, 2002); and U.S. Department of Labor, Bureau of Labor Statistics, "Occupational Wages in the United States as of July 2002" (Washington, D.C.: Bureau of Labor Statistics, June 2003).

6 Hanbury, "The Function of Leadership Styles."

7 State of the Profession Survey Results, 2002, reported in *ICMA Newsletter,* various issues.

8 Richard J. Stillman II, "Local Public Management in Transition: A Report on the Current State of the Profession," *The Municipal Year Book 1982* (Washington, D.C.: ICMA, 1982), 163.

9 ICMA Report of the Task Force on Continuing Education and Professional Development (Washington, D.C.: ICMA, 1994).

10 Henry Mintzberg, *The Nature of Managerial Work* (Englewood Cliffs, N.J.: Prentice-Hall, 1980).

11 Tari Renner, "Appointed Local Government Managers: Stability and Change," *The Municipal Year Book 1990* (Washington, D.C.: ICMA: 1990), 41–52.

12 State of the Profession Survey Results, 2002.

13 David N. Ammons, "Reputational Leaders in Local Government Productivity and Innovation," *Public Productivity and Management Review* 15 (Fall 1991): 19–43.

14 "Standards for Professional Masters Degree Programs in Public Affairs, Policy, and Administration" (Washington, D.C.: National Association of Schools of Public Affairs and Administration [NASPAA], 2003), Standard 1.3, http://www.naspaa.org/accreditation/seeking/pdf/OFFICIAL_DOCUMENTS_2003_standards_only.pdf.

15 "Inside the Year Book," *The Municipal Year Book 2002,* xii.

16 Douglas J. Watson and Wendy Lassett, "Long Serving City Managers: Why Do They Stay?" *Public Administration Review* 63 (January–February 2003): 71–78.

17 Hanbury, "The Function of Leadership Styles," 164.

18 State of the Profession Survey Results, 2002.

19 In addition to the ICMA model agreement, see also Ron Holifield, *The Public Executive's Complete Guide to Employment Agreements* (Tampa, Fla.: Innovation Groups; and Washington, D.C.: ICMA, 1996).

20 *First Time Administrators Handbook* (Washington, D.C.: ICMA, September 2000).

21 Barry and Linda Gale, *Stay or Leave* (New York: Harper and Row, 1989).

22 Arlene Loble, "Becoming a Risk Taker—and Then a City Manager," *Public Management* (March 1988): 19.

23 Bill Mathis, "Seven Signs of a Manager in Trouble" (Washington, D.C.: ICMA, December 1990).

24 See Betsy Sherman, "ICMA Support to Members in Transition," *Public Management* (1992), accessed online at http://www.icma.org/main/ld.asp?from=search&ldid=14491&hsid=1; Michael Roberto, "10 Points of Change during Transition; or, Can Someone Throw Me a Rope in This Quicksand?" *Public Management* (June 2001), 15; http://www.icma.org/upload/library/IQ/500599.htm; and Jerry W. Johnson and Nolan Brohaugh, "The Emotional Aspects of Job Loss," *Public Management* (January 1992): 6; http://www.icma.org/main/ld.asp?from=search&ldid=14488&hsid=1.

25 Respondents to a 1985 survey reported average workweeks of 56.6 hours for city managers and 52.7 hours for assistant managers; see David N. Ammons and Charldean Newell, *City Executives: Leadership Roles, Work Characteristics, and Time Management* (Albany: State University of New York Press, 1989). Local government managers reported an average workweek of 63 hours in 1980; see Stillman, "Local Public Management in Transition."

26 Henry Mintzberg, *The Nature of Managerial Work.*

27 Warren Bennis and Burt Nanus, *Leaders: The Strategies for Taking Charge* (New York: Harper & Row, 1985).

28 Hanbury, "The Function of Leadership Styles," 121; Sandra Kriebs Harsh, *MBTI Team Building Program* (Palo Alto, Calif.: Consulting Psychologists Press, 1992); and Otto Kroeger and Janet M. Thuesen, *Type Talk* (New York: Dell Publishing, 1988).

APPENDIX A
ICMA code of ethics
with guidelines

The ICMA Code of Ethics was adopted by the ICMA membership in 1924, and most recently amended by the membership in May 1998. The Guidelines for the Code were adopted by the ICMA Executive Board in 1972, and most recently revised in September 2002.

The mission of ICMA is to create excellence in local governance by developing and fostering professional local government management worldwide. To further this mission, certain principles, as enforced by the Rules of Procedure, shall govern the conduct of every member of ICMA, who shall:

1. Be dedicated to the concepts of effective and democratic local government by responsible elected officials and believe that professional general management is essential to the achievement of this objective.

2. Affirm the dignity and worth of the services rendered by government and maintain a constructive, creative, and practical attitude toward local government affairs and a deep sense of social responsibility as a trusted public servant.

   Guideline
   Advice to officials of other local governments   When members advise and respond to inquiries from elected or appointed officials of other local governments, they should inform the administrators of those communities.

3. Be dedicated to the highest ideals of honor and integrity in all public and personal relationships in order that the member may merit the respect and confidence of the elected officials, of other officials and employees, and of the public.

   Guidelines
   Public confidence   Members should conduct themselves so as to maintain public confidence in their profession, their local government, and in their performance of the public trust.

   Impression of influence   Members should conduct their official and personal affairs in such a manner as to give the clear impression that they cannot be improperly influenced in the performance of their official duties.

   Appointment commitment   Members who accept an appointment to a position should not fail to report for that position. This does not preclude the possibility of a member considering several offers or seeking several positions at the same time, but once a bona fide offer of a position has been accepted, that commitment should be honored. Oral acceptance of an employment offer is considered binding unless the employer makes fundamental changes in terms of employment.

   Credentials   An application for employment or for ICMA's Voluntary Credentialing Program should be complete and accurate as to all pertinent details of education, experience, and personal history. Members should recognize that both omissions and inaccuracies must be avoided.

   Professional respect   Members seeking a management position should show professional respect for persons formerly holding the position or for others who might be applying for the same position. Professional respect does not preclude honest differences of opinion; it does preclude attacking a person's motives or integrity in order to be appointed to a position.

   Reporting Ethics Violations   When becoming aware of a possible violation of the ICMA Code of Ethics, members are encouraged to report the matter to ICMA. In reporting the matter, members may choose to go on record as the complainant or report the matter on a confidential basis.

   Confidentiality   Members should not discuss or divulge information with anyone about pending or completed ethics cases, except as specifically authorized by the Rules of Procedure for Enforcement of the Code of Ethics.

Seeking employment   Members should not seek employment for a position having an incumbent administrator who has not resigned or been officially informed that his or her services are to be terminated.

4. Recognize that the chief function of local government at all times is to serve the best interests of all of the people.

Guideline

Length of service   A minimum of two years generally is considered necessary in order to render a professional service to the local government. A short tenure should be the exception rather than a recurring experience. However, under special circumstances, it may be in the best interests of the local government and the member to separate in a shorter time. Examples of such circumstances would include refusal of the appointing authority to honor commitments concerning conditions of employment, a vote of no confidence in the member, or severe personal problems. It is the responsibility of an applicant for a position to ascertain conditions of employment. Inadequately determining terms of employment prior to arrival does not justify premature termination.

5. Submit policy proposals to elected officials; provide them with facts and advice on matters of policy as a basis for making decisions and setting community goals; and uphold and implement local government policies adopted by elected officials.

Guideline

Conflicting roles   Members who serve multiple roles—working as both city attorney and city manager for the same community, for example—should avoid participating in matters that create the appearance of a conflict of interest. They should disclose the potential conflict to the governing body so that other opinions may be solicited.

6. Recognize that elected representatives of the people are entitled to the credit for the establishment of local government policies; responsibility for policy execution rests with the members.

7. Refrain from all political activities which undermine public confidence in professional administrators. Refrain from participation in the election of the members of the employing legislative body.

Guidelines

Elections of the governing body   Members should maintain a reputation for serving equally and impartially all members of the governing body of the local government they serve, regardless of party. To this end, they should not engage in active participation in the election campaign on behalf of or in opposition to candidates for the governing body.

Elections of elected executives   Members should not engage in the election campaign of any candidate for mayor or elected county executive.

Running for office   Members shall not run for elected office or become involved in political activities related to running for elected office. They shall not seek political endorsements, financial contributions or engage in other campaign activities.

Elections   Members share with their fellow citizens the right and responsibility to vote and to voice their opinion on public issues. However, in order not to impair their effectiveness on behalf of the local governments they serve, they shall not participate in political activities to support the candidacy of individuals running for any city, county, special district, school, state or federal offices. Specifically, they shall not endorse candidates, make financial contributions, sign or circulate petitions, or participate in fund-raising activities for individuals seeking or holding elected office.

Elections in the council-manager plan   Members may assist in preparing and presenting materials that explain the council-manager form of government to the public prior to an election on the use of the plan. If assistance is required by another community, members may respond. All activities regarding ballot issues should be conducted within local regulations and in a professional manner.

Presentation of issues   Members may assist the governing body in presenting issues involved in referenda such as bond issues, annexations, and similar matters.

8. Make it a duty continually to improve the member's professional ability and to develop the competence of associates in the use of management techniques.

Guidelines

Self-assessment   Each member should assess his or her professional skills and abilities on a periodic basis.

Professional development Each member should commit at least 40 hours per year to professional development activities that are based on the practices identified by the members of ICMA.

9. Keep the community informed on local government affairs; encourage communication between the citizens and all local government officers; emphasize friendly and courteous service to the public; and seek to improve the quality and image of public service.

10. Resist any encroachment on professional responsibilities, believing the member should be free to carry out official policies without interference, and handle each problem without discrimination on the basis of principle and justice.

Guideline

Information sharing The member should openly share information with the governing body while diligently carrying out the member's responsibilities as set forth in the charter or enabling legislation.

11. Handle all matters of personnel on the basis of merit so that fairness and impartiality govern a member's decisions, pertaining to appointments, pay adjustments, promotions, and discipline.

Guideline

Equal opportunity All decisions pertaining to appointments, pay adjustments, promotions, and discipline should prohibit discrimination because of race, color, religion, sex, national origin, sexual orientation, political affiliation, disability, age, or marital status. It should be the members' personal and professional responsibility to actively recruit and hire a diverse staff throughout their organizations.

12. Seek no favor; believe that personal aggrandizement or profit secured by confidential information or by misuse of public time is dishonest.

Guidelines

Gifts Members should not directly or indirectly solicit any gift or accept or receive any gift—whether it be money, services, loan, travel, entertainment, hospitality, promise, or any other form—under the following circumstances: (1) it could be reasonably inferred or expected that the gift was intended to influence them in the performance of their official duties; or (2) the gift was intended to serve as a reward for any official action on their part.

It is important that the prohibition of unsolicited gifts be limited to circumstances related to improper influence. In de minimus situations, such as meal checks, some modest maximum dollar value should be determined by the member as a guideline. The guideline is not intended to isolate members from normal social practices where gifts among friends, associates, and relatives are appropriate for certain occasions.

Investments in conflict with official duties Member should not invest or hold any investment, directly or indirectly, in any financial business, commercial, or other private transaction that creates a conflict with their official duties.

In the case of real estate, the potential use of confidential information and knowledge to further a member's personal interest requires special consideration. This guideline recognizes that members' official actions and decisions can be influenced if there is a conflict with personal investments. Purchases and sales which might be interpreted as speculation for quick profit ought to be avoided (see the guideline on "Confidential information").

Because personal investments may prejudice or may appear to influence official actions and decisions, members may, in concert with their governing body, provide for disclosure of such investments prior to accepting their position as local government administrator or prior to any official action by the governing body that may affect such investments.

Personal relationships Member should disclose any personal relationship to the governing body in any instance where there could be the appearance of a conflict of interest. For example, if the manager's spouse works for a developer doing business with the local government, that fact should be disclosed.

Confidential information Members should not disclose to others, or use to further their personal interest, confidential information acquired by them in the course of their official duties.

Private employment Members should not engage in, solicit, negotiate for, or promise to accept private employment, nor should they render services for private interests or conduct a private business when such employment, service, or business creates a conflict with or impairs the proper discharge of their official duties.

Teaching, lecturing, writing, or consulting are typical activities that may not involve conflict of interest, or impair the proper discharge of their official duties. Prior notification of the appointing authority is appropriate in all cases of outside employment.

Representation   Members should not represent any outside interest before any agency, whether public or private, except with the authorization of or at the direction of the appointing authority they serve.

Endorsements   Members should not endorse commercial products or services by agreeing to use their photograph, endorsement, or quotation in paid or other commercial advertisements, whether or not for compensation. Members may, however, agree to endorse the following, provided they do not receive any compensation: (1) books or other publications; (2) professional development or educational services provided by nonprofit membership organizations or recognized educational institutions; (3) products and/or services in which the local government has a direct economic interest.

Members' observations, opinions, and analyses of commercial products used or tested by their local governments are appropriate and useful to the profession when included as part of professional articles and reports.

APPENDIX B
Practices for effective local government management

In 1991 the ICMA Executive Board convened the Task Force on Continuing Education and Professional Development to identify the competencies and skills required of an effective local government manager. During a process facilitated by the task force, ICMA members agreed that the following Practices are essential to effective local government management. For convenience, the Practices were originally organized into eight groupings. With the development of the Management Practices Assessment, it became clear that for professional development purposes the practices more clearly fall into 18 "core content areas," as shown below. These are the same Practices that members developed and approved. They are simply organized differently.

1. **Staff effectiveness**   Promoting the development and performance of staff and employees throughout the organization (requires knowledge of interpersonal relations; skill in motivation techniques; ability to identify others' strengths and weaknesses). Practices that contribute to this core content area are:
   - **Coaching/mentoring**   Providing direction, support, and feedback to enable others to meet their full potential (requires knowledge of feedback techniques; ability to assess performance and identify others' developmental needs)
   - **Team leadership**   Facilitating teamwork (requires knowledge of team relations; ability to direct and coordinate group efforts; skill in leadership techniques)
   - **Empowerment**   Creating a work environment that encourages responsibility and decision making at all organizational levels (requires skill in sharing authority and removing barriers to creativity)
   - **Delegating**   Assigning responsibility to others (requires skill in defining expectations, providing direction and support, and evaluating results)

2. **Policy facilitation**   Helping elected officials and other community actors identify, work toward, and achieve common goals and objectives (requires knowledge of group dynamics and political behavior; skill in communication, facilitation, and consensus-building techniques; ability to engage others in identifying issues and outcomes). Practices that contribute to this core content area are:
   - **Facilitative leadership**   Building cooperation and consensus among and within diverse groups, helping them identify common goals and act effectively to achieve them; recognizing interdependent relationships and multiple causes of community issues and anticipating the consequences of policy decisions (requires knowledge of community actors and their interrelationships)
   - **Facilitating council effectiveness**   Helping elected officials develop a policy agenda that can be implemented effectively and that serves the best interests of the community (requires knowledge of role/authority relationships between elected and appointed officials; skill in responsibly following the lead of others when appropriate; ability to communicate sound information and recommendations)
   - **Mediation/negotiation**   Acting as a neutral party in the resolution of policy disputes (requires knowledge of mediation/negotiation principles; skill in mediation/negotiation techniques)

3. **Functional and operational expertise and planning (a component of service delivery management)**   Practices that contribute to this core content area are:
   - **Functional/operational expertise**   Understanding the basic principles of service delivery in functional areas—e.g., public safety, community and economic development, human and social services, administrative services, public works (requires knowledge of service areas and delivery options)
   - **Operational planning**   Anticipating future needs, organizing work operations, and establishing timetables for work units or projects (requires knowledge of technological advances and changing standards; skill in identifying and understanding trends; skill in predicting the impact of service delivery decisions)

4. **Citizen service (a component of service delivery management)**   Determining citizen needs and providing responsive, equitable services to the community (requires skill in assessing community needs and allocating resources; knowledge of information gathering techniques)

5. **Quality assurance (a component of service delivery management)**   Maintaining a consistently high level of quality in staff work, operational procedures, and service delivery (requires knowledge of organizational processes; ability to facilitate organizational improvements; ability to set performance/productivity standards and objectives and measure results)

6. **Initiative, risk taking, vision, creativity, and innovation (a component of strategic leadership)**   Setting an example that urges the organization and the community toward experimentation, change, creative problem solving, and prompt action (requires knowledge of personal leadership style; skill in visioning, shifting perspectives, and identifying options; ability to create an environment that encourages initiative and innovation). Practices that contribute to this core content area are:
   - **Initiative and risk taking**   Demonstrating a personal orientation toward action and accepting responsibility for the results; resisting the status quo and removing stumbling blocks that delay progress toward goals and objectives
   - **Vision**   Conceptualizing an ideal future state and communicating it to the organization and the community
   - **Creativity and innovation**   Developing new ideas or practices; applying existing ideas and practices to new situations

7. **Technological literacy (a component of strategic leadership)**   Demonstrating an understanding of information technology and ensuring that it is incorporated appropriately in plans to improve service delivery, information sharing, organizational communication, and citizen access (requires knowledge of technological options and their application)

8. **Democratic advocacy and citizen participation**   Demonstrating a commitment to democratic principles by respecting elected officials, community interest groups, and the decision making process; educating citizens about local government; and acquiring knowledge of the social, economic, and political history of the community (requires knowledge of democratic principles, political processes, and local government law; skill in group dynamics, communication, and facilitation; ability to appreciate and work with diverse individuals and groups and to follow the community's lead in the democratic process). Practices that contribute to this core content area are:
   - **Democratic advocacy**   Fostering the values and integrity of representative government and local democracy through action and example; ensuring the effective participation of local government in the intergovernmental system (requires knowledge and skill in intergovernmental relations)
   - **Citizen participation**   Recognizing the right of citizens to influence local decisions and promoting active citizen involvement in local governance

9. **Diversity**   Understanding and valuing the differences among individuals and fostering these values throughout the organization and the community

10. **Budgeting**   Preparing and administering the budget (requires knowledge of budgeting principles and practices, revenue sources, projection techniques, and financial control systems; skill in communicating financial information)

11. **Financial analysis**   Interpreting financial information to assess the short-term and long-term fiscal condition of the community, determine the cost-effectiveness of programs, and compare alternative strategies (requires knowledge of analytical techniques and skill in applying them)

12. **Human resources management**   Ensuring that the policies and procedures for employee hiring, promotion, performance appraisal, and discipline are equitable, legal, and current; ensuring that human resources are adequate to accomplish programmatic objectives (requires knowledge of personnel practices and employee relations law; ability to project workforce needs)

13. **Strategic planning**   Positioning the organization and the community for events and circumstances that are anticipated in the future (requires knowledge of long-range and strategic planning techniques; skill in identifying trends that will affect the community; ability to analyze and facilitate policy choices that will benefit the community in the long run)

14. **Advocacy and interpersonal communication**   Facilitating the flow of ideas, information, and understanding between and among individuals; advocating effectively in the community interest (requires knowledge of interpersonal and group communication principles; skill in listening, speaking, and writing; ability to persuade without diminishing the views of others). Practices that contribute to this core content area are:
   - **Advocacy**   Communicating personal support for policies, programs, or ideals that serve the best interests of the community

- **Interpersonal communication**   Exchanging verbal and nonverbal messages with others in a way that demonstrates respect for the individual and furthers organizational and community objectives (requires ability to receive verbal and nonverbal cues; skill in selecting the most effective communication method for each interchange)

15. **Presentation skills**   Conveying ideas or information effectively to others (requires knowledge of presentation techniques and options; ability to match presentation to audience)

16. **Media relations**   Communicating information to the media in a way that increases public understanding of local government issues and activities and builds a positive relationship with the press (requires knowledge of media operations and objectives)

17. **Integrity**   Demonstrating fairness, honesty, and ethical and legal awareness in personal and professional relationships and activities (requires knowledge of business and personal ethics; ability to understand issues of ethics and integrity in specific situations). Practices that contribute to this core content area are:
    - **Personal integrity**   Demonstrating accountability for personal actions; conducting personal relationships and activities fairly and honestly
    - **Professional integrity**   Conducting professional relationships and activities fairly, honestly, legally, and in conformance with the ICMA Code of Ethics (requires knowledge of administrative ethics and specifically the ICMA Code of Ethics)
    - **Organizational integrity**   Fostering ethical behavior throughout the organization through personal example, management practices, and training (requires knowledge of administrative ethics; ability to instill accountability into operations; and ability to communicate ethical standards and guidelines to others)

18. **Personal development**   Demonstrating a commitment to a balanced life through ongoing self-renewal and development in order to increase personal capacity (includes maintaining personal health, living by core values; continuous learning and improvement; and creating interdependent relationships and respect for differences).

APPENDIX C
Declaration of ideals

The International City/County Management Association (ICMA) was founded with a commitment to the preservation of the values and integrity of representative local government and local democracy and a dedication to the promotion of efficient and effective management of public services. To fulfill the spirit of this commitment, ICMA works to maintain and enhance public trust and confidence in local government, to achieve equity and social justice, to affirm human dignity, and to improve the quality of life for the individual and the community. Members of ICMA dedicate themselves to the faithful stewardship of the public trust and embrace the following ideals of management excellence, seeking to:

1. Provide an environment that ensures the continued existence and effectiveness of representative local government and promotes the understanding that democracy confers privileges and responsibilities on each citizen.

2. Recognize the right of citizens to influence decisions that affect their well-being; advocate a forum for meaningful citizen participation and expression of the political process; and facilitate the clarification of community values and goals.

3. Respect the special character and individuality of each community while recognizing the interdependence of communities and promoting coordination and cooperation.

4. Seek balance in the policy formation process through the integration of the social, cultural, and physical characteristics of the community.

5. Promote a balance between the needs to use and to preserve human, economic, and natural resources.

6. Advocate equitable regulation and service delivery, recognizing that needs and expectations for public services may vary throughout the community.

7. Develop a responsive, dynamic local government organization that continuously assesses its purpose and seeks the most effective techniques and technologies for serving the community.

8. Affirm the intrinsic value of public service and create an environment that inspires excellence in management and fosters the professional and personal development of all employees.

9. Seek a balanced life through ongoing professional, intellectual, and emotional growth.

10. Demonstrate commitment to professional ethics and ideals and support colleagues in the maintenance of these standards.

11. Take actions to create diverse opportunities in housing, employment, and cultural activity in every community for all people.

Annotated bibliography

1 The profession of local government manager: evolution and leadership styles

Behn, Robert D. *Leadership Counts.* Cambridge: Harvard University Press, 1991. Looks at the skills and behaviors required to be a successful public sector executive.

————. *Rethinking Democratic Accountability.* Washington D.C.: Brookings Institution, 2001. Proposes new models and perspectives for defining accountability and performance. Borrows from theories of program evaluation and performance appraisal; develops the notion of 360-degree accountability.

Bok, Sissela. *Lying: Moral Choice in Public and Private Life.* New York: Vintage Books, 1999. Expands the author's 1978 analysis of the importance of truth telling in society and in public policy. The book is a careful analysis of the distinction between "lies" and "untruth" and the danger of not appreciating the limited circumstances under which even an untruth is permitted.

Burns, James McGregor. *Leadership.* New York: Harper & Row, 1978. Reconceptualizes the notion of leadership by introducing the idea of "transformational" leadership, which embodies the effort to change organizations by redirecting and refocusing the organizational mission and culture.

Caddy, Joanne. *Citizens as Partners: Information, Consultation and Public Participation in Policy-Making.* Paris: OECD, 2001. A handbook on how to establish and affirm citizen participation and information sharing; accessible how-to guide for use by public officials.

Carnevale, David G. *Organizational Development in the Public Sector.* Boulder, Colo.: Westview Press, 2003. Examines the humanistic and conceptual foundations of organization development in order to explore why organization development is so often advocated but so rarely implemented.

————. *Trustworthy Government.* San Francisco: Jossey-Bass, 1995. Explores the role of trust in the exercise of leadership and in developing successful and effective organizations; draws from insights gained through experience in the public sector and in labor relations.

Cooper, Terry L. *An Ethic of Citizenship for Public Administration.* Englewood Cliffs, N.J.: Prentice-Hall, 1991. A thought-provoking analysis of democratic values and how those values can serve as the basis for new approaches to citizen service.

Cox, Raymond W., III. "Creating a Decision Architecture." *Global Virtue Ethics Review* 2, no. 1 (Summer 2000). Develops a framework for incorporating democratic and community values into public sector decisions to facilitate and confine the exercise of discretionary judgment.

French Peter A. *Ethics in Government.* Englewood Cliffs, N.J.: Prentice-Hall, 1983. Careful analysis of public sector ethics; explores the problem of decision making and the role of ethics in decisions. Examines ethics from the perspective of the chief executive, career employee, and legislator.

Gilman, Stuart. "Public Sector Ethics and Government Reinvention: Realigning Systems to Meet Organizational Change." *Public Integrity* 1, no. 2 (Spring 1999). Addresses the ethical and moral concerns of public officials, whether elected or appointed. Explores the ethical implications and problems of the reinvention movement and new public management movement.

Kiel, Douglas. *Managing Chaos in Government.* San Francisco: Jossey-Bass, 1994. Uses the perspectives of chaos theory to develop an innovative approach to managing in complex organizations.

Nalbandian, John. *Professionalism in Local Government: Transformation in the Roles, Responsibilities, and Values of City Managers.* San Francisco: Jossey-Bass, 1991. Transformations in the roles of managers owing to political developments and the simultaneous demands for professionalism and political acumen; roles, responsibilities, and values as the base for managerial professionalism.

National Civic League. *Model City Charter,* 8th ed. Denver: National Civic League, 2003. The latest revision of the city charter model first published in 1915. Acknowledges renewed interest in the mayor's office while continuing a preference for council-manager government; emphasizes the professionalism of local government managers.

Paul, Amy Cohen. *Future Challenges, Future Opportunities: The Final Report of the ICMA Future Visions Consortium.* Washington, D.C.: ICMA, 1991. Areas of change, implications, and strategies for coping; future managerial skills needed; and advice on structuring a community visioning process. See also *Managing for Tomorrow: Global Change and Local Futures.* Washington, D.C.: ICMA, 1990. A look at trends in futures studies, with the message that anticipation of future events makes for a smoother administration in the present.

Rohr, John A. *Public Service: Ethics and Constitutional Practice.* Lawrence: University of Kansas Press, 1998. Traces the evolution and development of this well-known ethics scholar's views on public sector ethics by representing previously published works into a coherent and rich analysis of contemporary ethics.

Selznick, Philip. *Leadership in Administration.* Berkeley: University of California Press, 1957. Classic analysis of the role of organizational mission, "organizational" character, and leadership in creating effective organizations.

Stillman, Richard J., II. *The Rise of the City Manager: A Public Professional in Local Government.* Albuquerque: University of New Mexico Press, 1974. A classic history of council-manager government, including discussion of the special problems of urban administrators in highly diverse environments.

Svara, James H. *Facilitative Leadership in Local Government.* San Francisco: Jossey-Bass, 1994. Provides a conceptual framework for understanding manager-council and manager-mayor relations by examining the actual experiences of city managers.

Wildavsky, Aaron. *Speaking Truth to Power.* New Brunswick, N.J.: Transaction Books, 2002. Author expands his 1987 study of policy analysis and explores the role and responsibility of the policy analyst in relation to political leadership and political decision making; equal applicability of the lessons across a range of public sector positions.

2   Achieving effective community leadership

Browning, Rufus P., Dale Rogers Marshall, and David H. Tabb, eds. *Racial Politics in American Cities.* New York: Longman, 1990. Examines the participation of African-Americans and Hispanics in 11 cities: Atlanta, Birmingham, Boston, Chicago, Denver, Los Angeles, Miami, New Orleans, New York, Philadelphia, and San Antonio.

Eggers, William D., and John O'Leary. *Revolution at the Roots: Making Our Government Smaller, Better, and Closer to Home.* New York: Free Press, 1995. An extensive argument for the value of smaller governments and privatization. Review of efforts to introduce competition into local government management in large mayor-council cities (with little attention to the accomplishments of council-manager cities).

Ehrenhalt, Alan. *The United States of Ambition.* New York: Times Books, 1992. An examination of the "new breed" of elected official in local and state government; argues that elected officials are increasingly activist, professional politicians for whom reelection rather than governing is the primary goal.

Florida, Richard. *The Rise of the Creative Class: and How It's Transforming Work, Leisure, Community and Everyday Life.* New York: Basic Books, 2002. Examination of how the "creative class" is contributing to the development of the economic and social revitalization of cities; provides evidence of the importance of fostering diversity in order to attract and retain creative-class workers.

Katz, Bruce, and Robert E. Lang. *Redefining Urban and Suburban America: Evidence from Census 2000.* Washington: Brookings Institution Press, 2003. Examination of changes during the 1990s: whether central cities are making a comeback, growth patterns in suburbs, and changes in the comparison between cities and suburbs.

Kettl, Donald F. *The Transformation of Governance: Public Administration for Twenty-First Century America.* Baltimore: Johns Hopkins University Press, 2002. Elaboration of how globalization, devolution, and decentralization are changing the governmental process in the United States.

Mouritzen, Poul Erik, and James H. Svara. *Leadership at the Apex: Politicians and Administrators in Western Local Governments.* Pittsburgh: University of Pittsburgh Press, 2002. A major comparative study of city managers and their equivalents in 12 countries in Western Europe, Australia, and the United States. Contributions to policy and community leadership and the relative influence of officials in budgeting and economic development are compared.

Nalbandian, John, and Carol Nalbandian. "Contemporary Challenges in Local

Government." *Public Management* 84 (December 2002): 6–11; and "Meeting Today's Challenges: Competencies for the Contemporary Local Government Professional." *Public Management* 84 (May 2003): 11–15. Examinations of the major issues facing city and county managers and the competencies needed to address them.

Newell, Charldean, and David N. Ammons. "Role Emphasis of City Managers and Other Municipal Executives." *Public Administration Review* 47 (May/June 1987): 246–252. Study of the factors that contribute to the success of city managers in large cities; compares conditions in the 1960s and 1980s.

Pavlichev, Alexei, and G. David Garson. *Digital Government: Principles and Best Practices.* Hershey, Pa.: Idea Group Publishing, 2004. Examination of the theory of e-government, and a review of how digital government practices are being incorporated into government.

Pelissero, John P., ed. *Cities, Politics, and Policy: A Comparative Analysis.* Washington, D.C.: CQ Press, 2003. Textbook on urban government and politics comprising essays by leading scholars on a range of topics including citizen participation and community power.

Putnam, Robert. *Bowling Alone: The Collapse and Revival of American Community.* New York: Simon & Schuster, 2000. An influential study of how community patterns are changing in the United States, and the importance of "social capital."

Schwarz, Roger. *The Skilled Facilitator: A Comprehensive Resource for Consultants, Facilitators, Managers, Trainers, and Coaches,* 2nd ed. San Francisco: Jossey-Bass, 2002. A thorough examination of the theory of facilitative leadership and how it can be used in a governmental organization in a consultative role as well as in a managerial role.

Svara, James H. *Official Leadership in the City.* New York: Oxford, 1990. A comparison of the roles of mayors, council members, and administrators in mayor-council and council-manager cities; includes an examination of the nature of community leadership provided by each type of official.

———. "The Shifting Boundary between Elected Officials and City Managers in Large Council-Manager Cities." *Public Administration Review* 59 (January/February 1999): 44–53. An update of earlier work on the relative contributions of council members and city managers to urban governance; shows the increasing role of city managers in shaping the city's agenda.

———. *Two Decades of Continuity and Change in America's City Councils.* Washington, D.C.:

National League of Cities, 2003. Analysis of responses from national surveys of city council members in 1979, 1989, and 2001; provides information about those whom council members represent, the performance of councils in addressing community needs, and a comparison of the mayor and city manager as executives.

———. "U.S. City Managers and Administrators in a Global Perspective." Chap. A4 in *The Municipal Year Book 1999.* Washington, D.C.: ICMA, 1999. Results of the 1997 survey of city managers and city administrators in the United States; shows how U.S. managers are distinctive and similar to managers in 13 other countries.

Thomas, J. Clayton. *Between Citizen and City.* Lawrence: University of Kansas Press, 1986. A study of the incorporation of neighborhood organizations and the citizen participation initiatives of city government in Cincinnati, Ohio.

3 Enhancing the governing body's effectiveness

Carlson, Margaret S., and Anne S. Davidson. "After the Election: How Do Governing Boards Become Effective Work Groups?" *State and Local Government Review* 31 (Fall 1999): 190–201. Discusses the challenges that governing bodies face in developing an effective working relationship among members; offers an intervention that promotes a better understanding of roles and expectations for various officials.

Crosby, Barbara C. "Leading in a Shared-Power World." In *Handbook of Public Administration,* edited by James L. Perry, 613–631. San Francisco: Jossey-Bass, 1996. Offers nine key leadership tasks in a leadership framework appropriate for finding solutions in a world in which no "single person, group, or organization has the power to resolve any major public problem."

DeSantis, Victor S., and Tari Renner. "City Government Structures: An Attempt at Clarification." In *The Future of Local Government Administration: The Hansell Symposium,* edited by H. George Frederickson and John Nalbandian, 71–83. Washington, D.C.: ICMA, 2002. Offers new typology of local government form, consisting of seven variations based on 1996 survey data; response by City Manager Peggy Merriss.

Feiock, Richard, and Christopher Stream. "Local Government Structure, Council Change, and City Manager Turnover." In *The Future of Local Government Administration: The Hansell Symposium,* edited by H. George Frederickson and John Nalbandian, 118–129. Washington,

D.C.: ICMA, 2002. Reviews explanations of managerial turnover and explains how turnover on the governing body affects managerial tenure; response by City Manager Matthew J. Kridler.

Fisher, Roger, and William Ury. *Getting to Yes: Negotiating Agreement without Giving In.* New York: Penguin Books, 1991. Offers the principled method of negotiation as an alternative to traditional positional forms of negotiation; is especially useful as a way of resolving conflict among governing body members.

Frederickson, H. George, Gary A. Johnson, and Curtis Wood. "Type III Cities." In *The Future of Local Government Administration: The Hansell Symposium,* edited by H. George Frederickson and John Nalbandian, 85–99. Washington, D.C.: ICMA, 2002. Uses survey data to identify a form of government called the "adapted city" that mixes features of the council-manager and mayor-council forms; response by City Manager Eric Anderson.

Green, Richard, Larry Keller, and Gary Wamsley. "Reconstituting a Profession for American Public Administration." *Public Administration Review* 53 (November/December 1993): 516–524. Features a classical definition of professionalism and argues in favor of founding public administration upon notions of governance and the role professionals play as institutional leaders.

Ihrke, Douglas M. "City Council Relations and Perceptions of Representational and Service Delivery Effectiveness." In *The Future of Local Government Administration: The Hansell Symposium,* edited by H. George Frederickson and John Nalbandian, 3–19. Washington, D.C.: ICMA, 2002. Analyzes survey data from city council members in New York and Wisconsin to determine how demographic characteristics, government structure, and representational behavior affect perceptions of representational and service delivery effectiveness; response by City Manager Del D. Borgsdorf.

MacManus, Susan A. "The Resurgent City Council." In *American State and Local Government: Directions for the 21st Century,* edited by Ronald E. Weber and Paul Brace, 166–193. New York: Chatham House Publishers, 1999. Summarizes developments affecting city councils in the 1990s and reviews important research on local governing bodies.

MacManus, Susan A., and Charles S. Bullock III. "The Form, Structure, and Composition of America's Municipalities in the New Millennium." In *The Municipal Year Book 2003,* 3–18. Washington, D.C.: ICMA, 2003. Reviews and interprets data from ICMA's Form of Government Survey, with a focus on mayors and governing bodies.

Mouritzen, Poul Erik, and James H. Svara. *Leadership at the Apex: Politicians and Administrators in Western Local Governments.* Pittsburgh: University of Pittsburgh Press, 2002. Reports how appointed local government chief executives working in 14 countries understand the nature of their work and view the performance of elected officials, and how these views are related to institutions and political culture.

Nalbandian, John. "Facilitating Community, Enabling Democracy: New Roles for Local Government Managers." *Public Administration Review* 59 (May/June 1999): 187–197. Explores how the profession evolved in the 1990s and suggests that facilitative leadership and community building are the "anchors" for contemporary professionalism.

Svara, James H. "City Council Roles, Performance, and the Form of Government." In *The Future of Local Government Administration: The Hansell Symposium,* edited by H. George Frederickson and John Nalbandian, 215–229. Washington, D.C.: ICMA, 2002. Discusses results of survey research on how city council members perform their jobs and the effect that the form of government has on their behavior; response by City Manager Julia D. Novak.

———. "The Roles of the City Council and Implications for the Structure of City Government." *National Civic Review* 90 (Spring 2002): 5–23. Presents five models of governing body performance: board of trustees, board of directors, board of delegates, board of governors, and board of activists; and the advantages and disadvantages of each model.

Thomas, John Clayton. *Public Participation in Public Decisions: New Skills and Strategies for Public Managers.* San Francisco: Jossey-Bass, 1995. Develops a model of how to involve the public effectively and reviews useful approaches and practices.

Wheeland, Craig M. "Council Evaluation of the City Manager's Performance: An Inventory of Methods." Chap. A1 in *The Municipal Year Book 2002.* Washington, D.C.: ICMA, 2002. Reviews the results of a 2000 survey of city managers in the United States that reports on the methods that the managers' governing bodies use to evaluate the managers' performance; assesses the effectiveness of the various methods.

———. "Mayoral Leadership in the Context of Variations in City Structure." In *The Future of Local Government Administration: The Hansell Symposium,* edited by H. George Frederickson and John Nalbandian, 59–67. Washington, D.C.: ICMA, 2002. Features a typology of mayoral leadership styles that is based on data from the 40 largest cities in the United States; response by City Manager David Mora.

Zaner, William, ed. *Elected Officials Handbooks.* Washington, D.C.: ICMA, 1994. The five books feature advice on setting goals for action, building a policy-making team, setting policies for service delivery, setting policies for internal management, and pursuing personal effectiveness.

4 Promoting the community's future

Cayer, N. Joseph, and Lewis Weschler. *Public Administration: Social Change and Adaptive Management,* 2nd ed. San Diego: Birkdale Publishers, 2003. Analyzes the difficult and changing environment in which today's public administrators must operate; also provides a well-balanced overview of the field of public administration.

Childs, Richard S. *The First 50 Years of the Council-Manager Plan of Municipal Government.* New York: National Municipal League, 1965. A classic from the "father of the council-manager plan." Lays out the foundation of the plan and the role relationships as perceived by the originator of the plan.

Decker, Lance. *Over My Dead Body! Creating Community Harmony Out of Chaos: The Basic Training Guide for Managing Community Involvement.* Phoenix: LL Decker and Associates, 2001. A comprehensive and systematic approach to developing community "buy in" and a basic training guide for managing community involvement from the very beginning of the process; provides a checklist of items to consider at each phase of the community involvement process.

Frederickson, George H., and John Nalbandian. *The Future of Local Government Administration: The Hansell Symposium.* Washington D.C.: ICMA, 2002. A compendium of issues; each issue is first discussed by an academician and then receives a response from a city manager. Discusses and defines competencies required for effective local government management. Captures the probing questions that need to be discussed as the council-manager form of government continues to evolve. A must read.

Johnson, Spencer. *Who Moved My Cheese? An Amazing Way to Deal with Change in Your Work and in Your Life.* New York: Putnam, 1998. Notes that all organizations are going through change; lays out principles of change in a delightful and meaningful way. Simple, succinct, and straightforward; opens up the imagination to how different attitudes and personalities affect change. Applies to the organization as well as to one's personal life.

Kazman, Jane G., ed. *Working Together: A Guide for Elected and Appointed Officials.* Washington, D.C.: ICMA and National League of Cities, 1999. A workbook to assist in collaboration between elected and appointed officials to maintain and build their communities. Detailed, practical information for understanding role relationships between elected officials and staff. The workbook contains a number of excellent self-assessment questionnaires and numerous activities to assess role relationships with elected officials.

Koteen, Jack. *Strategic Management in Public and Nonprofit Organizations: Managing Public Concerns in an Era of Limits,* 2nd ed. Westport, Conn.: Praeger, 1997. A full understanding of strategic planning, the strategic agenda, and the role of the chief executive as master of change. Gives both theoretical and practical advice.

Koven, Steven G., and Thomas S. Lyons. *Economic Development: Strategies for State and Local Practice.* Washington D.C.: ICMA, 2003. A comprehensive and informative guide to understanding the role of managers in developing economic development strategies. A primer on attracting and sustaining viable economic development projects.

Moore, Mark H. *Creating Public Value: Strategic Management in Government.* Cambridge: Harvard University press, 1995. Good use of case studies; thoughtful discussions of creating public value and understanding political management and the accompanying challenges. Insight into the roles of public managers.

Nalbandian, John. *Professionalism in Local Government: Transformations in the Roles, Responsibilities, and Values of City Managers.* San Francisco: Jossey-Bass, 1991. Discussion of how the roles and responsibilities of city managers have changed, especially the new and expanded roles of the city manager in the political process. Also describes the coalition building that managers need to undertake to be effective.

Nalbandian, John and Carol. "Contemporary Challenges in Local Government." *Public Management* 84, no. 11 (December 2002): 6–11. Looks at emerging trends that will shape the future for local government professionals; discussion of challenges in modernizing the organization to build community.

Vigoda, Eran. "From Responsiveness to Collaboration: Governance, Citizens, and the Next Generation of Public Administration." *Public Administration Review* 52 (September/October 2002): 527–540. Comprehensive review of the ideas and theories of collaboration and what it means to involve community stakeholders.

Wheatley, Margaret J. *Leadership and the New Science: Learning Organizations from an*

Orderly Universe. San Francisco: Berrett Koehler, 1992. A proactive and stimulating discussion of leadership and management as seen through the eyes of science. Challenges assumptions about organizations and how they evolve and grow. Thought-provoking book that discusses management "outside the box."

Whyte, David. *The Hearts Aroused: Poetry and the Presentation of the Soul in Corporate America.* New York: Currency Doubleday, 1994. A new way to look at and understand how organizations affect people's lives. Poems and histories that relate to the organizations of today; results are "mind opening and challenging." A very different view of the individual in an organization; has everything to do with promoting the community's future.

---

5   Essential management practices

Andersen, David F., and Sharon S. Dawes. *Government Information Management: A Primer and Casebook.* Englewood Cliffs, N.J.: Prentice-Hall, 1991. Although dated, a fine collection of management and policy cases that includes structuring government IT operations, personnel practices, data archiving, security, and privacy.

Aronson, J. Richard, and Eli Schwartz, eds. *Management Policies in Local Government Finance.* Washington, D.C.: ICMA, 2004. ICMA "Green Book" covering a broad range of issues and practices in local government financial management.

Bland, Robert L., and Irene S. Rubin. *Budgeting: A Guide for Local Governments.* Washington, D.C.: ICMA, 1997. A practical guide written for managers and budget staff; includes specifics about many aspects of preparing and presenting budgets; actual exemplary practices featured.

Braverman, Mark. *Preventing Workplace Violence: A Guide for Employers and Practitioners.* Thousand Oaks, Calif.: Sage, 1999. Explains actions an employer can take to identify the likelihood of workplace violence; includes a sample policy and procedure.

Cherniss, Cary, and Daniel Goleman. *The Emotionally Intelligent Workplace.* San Francisco, Calif.: Jossey-Bass, 2001. Provides a solid foundation for understanding what emotional intelligence is and why it is a valuable skill in the workplace.

Folger, Robert, and Russell Cropanzano. *Organizational Justice and Human Resource Management.* Thousand Oaks, Calif.: Sage, 1998. Outlines the various perspectives on organizational justice, defines what it is, and

explains the human resource implications and ramifications.

Fountain, Jane E. *Building the Virtual State: Information Technology and Institutional Change.* Washington, D.C.: Brookings Institution Press, 2001. Excellent examination of government organizational and institutional interactions and change in the use of new information technology.

Garson, David, ed. *Handbook of Public Information Systems.* New York: Marcel Dekker, 1999. Broad essay collection on the uses of and issues in information technology in government; includes policy, strategic planning, application case studies (local, state, and federal) related to particular technologies, including GIS. A new edition is expected in 2004.

Gauthier, Stephen J. *Evaluating Internal Controls: A Local Government Manager's Guide.* Chicago: Government Finance Officers Association, 1996. A guide directed at the concept that managers are responsible for seeing that internal controls—the policies and procedures that are needed to prevent resource waste, abuse, and fraud—are put into place.

Government Finance Officers Association. Elected Official's Guide Series. Chicago, Ill.: GFOA. A plain-language series of booklets for elected officials on topics such as auditing, issuing debt, investments, retirement plans, buying financial system software, the GASB 34 model for financial reporting, internal controls, multiyear budgeting, negotiating and costing labor contracts, purchasing, revenue forecasting, and risk management.

Gutman, Arthur. *EEO Law and Personnel Practices,* 2nd ed. Thousand Oaks, Calif.: Sage, 2000. Valuable resource that alerts employers to the law and employer liability when HR practices fail to comply.

Kamarck, Elaine C., and Joseph S. Nye Jr., eds. *Governance.com: Democracy in the Information Age.* Washington, D.C.: Brookings Institution Press, 2001. Widely cited collection of essays on the role of e-gov in democratic governance.

O'Looney, John. *Wiring Governments: Challenges and Possibilities for Public Managers.* Westport, Conn.: Quorum Books, 2002. Strategic orientation to the e-gov challenges for public managers; in a prescriptive style, discusses fitting technology to the needs and current practices of an organization.

Petersen, John E., and Dennis R. Strachota, eds. *Local Government Finance: Concepts and Practices.* Chicago, Ill.: GFOA, 1991. A GFOA equivalent and companion to ICMA's "Green Book"; a bit dated but still a principal reference on a wide range of financial management topics.

Reese, Laura A., and Karen E. Lindenberg. *Implementing Sexual Harassment Policy: Challenges for the Public Sector Workplace.* Thousand Oaks, Calif.: Sage, 1999. Explains what sexual harassment is, how it affects performance, and what employers need to do to fulfill legal obligations.

6 Policy implementation, productivity, and program evaluation

Ammons, David. *Municipal Benchmarks: Assessing Local Performance and Establishing Community Standards,* 2nd ed. Thousand Oaks, Calif.: Sage, 2001. Provides practical suggestions for examining municipal services and performance; identifies standards for most municipal functions.

Barrett, Katherine, and Richard Greene. *Powering Up: How Public Managers Can Take Control of Information Technology.* Washington, DC: CQ Press, 2001. Real-world examples of effective information technology; gives managers specific direction in effective use of information technology.

Chelimsky, Eleanor, and William Shadish. *Evaluation for the 21st Century: A Handbook.* Thousand Oaks, Calif.: Sage, 1997. Wide-ranging compendium of persistent issues facing evaluators, special attention given to likely changes in future. Primarily for professional evaluators, but some applied chapters as well.

Cochran, Clarke E., T. R. Carr, Lawrence C. Mayer, and N. Joseph Cayer. *American Public Policy: An Introduction,* 7th ed. Belmont, Calif.: Thomson/Wadsworth, 2003. A basic text on public policy making, implementation, and evaluation, with an introductory chapter on policy analysis. Substantive chapters apply analytical framework.

Cooper, Phillip J. *Governing by Contract: Challenges and Opportunities for Public Managers.* Washington, D.C.: CQ Press, 2003. Focuses on how managers can best develop, manage, and monitor contracts with a particular emphasis on the intergovernmental system.

Kaplan, Robert S., and David P. Norton. *The Balanced Scorecard: Translating Strategy into Action.* Cambridge: Harvard Business School Press, 1996. Step-by-step explanation by the concept's developers of how to build and use the balanced scorecard.

Lavery, Kevin. *Smart Contracting for Local Government Services: Processes and Experiences.* Westport, Conn.: Greenwood

Group, Inc., 1999. Examines the practical aspects of contracting for local public services; identifies successful and unsuccessful experiences.

Leeuw, Frans, Ray Rist, and Richard Sonnichsen. *Can Governments Learn? Comparative Perspectives on Evaluation and Organizational Learning.* Piscataway, N.J.: Transaction Publishers, 1999. Excellent integration of evaluation issues with the problem of managing a government organization; one of few books that shows means of linking evaluation with organizational development.

Levin, Henry, and Patrick McEwen. *Cost-Effectiveness Analysis: Methods and Applications.* Newbury Park, Calif.: Sage, 2000. Easy-to-understand and -use approach to cost analyses; some theory, but largely practice oriented. The perfect reference book on analyzing program costs.

Madison, Anna-Marie. *Minority Issues in Program Evaluation.* San Francisco: Jossey-Bass, 1992. An older book but the only book in print that deals with minority issues as they impact evaluators. Examines the range of practical evaluation concerns when minority employees and citizens are affected by evaluations.

Moynihan, Daniel Patrick. *Miles to Go: A Personal History of Social Policy.* Cambridge: Harvard University Press, 1996. Definitive insider view of the conduct and particularly the utilization of evaluation results. Focuses on federal programs and examines the factors that promote and impede evaluation-driven governmental decision making.

Newcomer, Kathryn E., ed. *New Directions for Evaluation, Using Performance Measurement to Improve Public and Nonprofit Programs.* San Francisco: Jossey-Bass, 1997. One of few books to integrate concepts of performance measures into evaluation processes and problems. Discusses construction and interpretation of measures and shows how measures can be fitted into an ongoing jurisdictional evaluation plan.

O'Looney, John A. *Outsourcing State and Local Government Services: Decision-Making Strategies and Management Methods.* Westport, Conn.: Quorum Books, 1998. Guidance for state and local managers with specific, practical steps to use in outsourcing services.

Posavac, Emil, and Raymond G. Carey. *Program Evaluation: Methods and Case Studies,* 5th ed. Upper Saddle River, N.J.: Prentice Hall, 1997. Effective at elaborating each phase of evaluations and explaining precisely what must be done to accomplish important milestones. Includes well-chosen case studies to illustrate measurement techniques; nonexperimental, quasi-experimental, and true experimental designs; and qualitative evaluation.

Rossi, Peter, Howard Freeman, and Mark Lipsey. *Evaluation.* Newbury Park, Calif.: Sage, 1999. Classic encyclopedia of evaluation philosophy and technique. Covers every aspect of evaluation design and utilization in intricate detail.

Rusaw, A. Carol. *Leading Public Organizations: An Integrative Approach.* Orlando, Fla.: Harcourt, 2001. Reviews leadership theories and concepts with an explicit focus on the public sector. Includes interactive exercises.

Sylvia, Ronald, Ken Meier, and Elizabeth Gunn. *Program Planning and Evaluation for the Public Manager.* Prospect Heights, Ill.: Waveland Press, 2002. Addresses the use of evaluation results by managers in organizations. Focuses principally on formative evaluation, but summative practices and issues are covered also. Excellent integration of strategic planning and systems approaches with evaluation and management.

Weiss, Carol H. *Evaluation,* 2nd ed. Upper Saddle River, N.J.: Prentice Hall, 1998. A revision of the classic 1972 edition. Addresses both theoretical and practical aspects of program evaluation. Discussions of measurement and experimental design are balanced by reviews of evaluation planning and report construction. Effective discussion of ethics in evaluation and a review of the utility and use of evaluation results.

Yukl, Gary. *Leadership in Organizations,* 5th ed. Upper Saddle River, N.J.: Prentice Hall, 2002. Examines theories and research on leadership and suggests ways for improving leadership skills.

7   Relating to other organizations

Agranoff, Robert, and Michael McGuire. *Collaborative Public Management: New Strategies for Local Governments.* Washington, D.C.: Georgetown University Press, 2003. Provides an in-depth look at how city officials from 237 cities within five states work with other governments and organizations to develop their cities' economies and what makes these collaborations work. Explores the complex nature of collaboration across jurisdictions, governments, and sectors.

Bardach, Eugene. *Getting Agencies to Work Together.* Washington, D.C.: Brookings Institution Press, 1998. Exposes the difficulties of getting government agencies to work together, demonstrates how linkages can be made, and offers ideas for managers interested in developing interagency collaborative networks.

Campbell, Andrew, and Michael Goold. *The Collaborative Enterprise: Why Links across the Corporation Often Fail and How to Make Them Work.* Reading, Mass.: Perseus Books, 1999. Written by business strategy experts and focuses on establishing and seizing synergies across departments, business units, and companies.

Chrislip, David D., and Carl E. Larson. *Collaborative Leadership.* San Francisco: Jossey-Bass, 1994. From empirical research that demonstrates how to create, initiate, and sustain a constructive, collaborative process.

Conlan, Timothy J. *From New Federalism to Devolution: Twenty-five Years of Intergovernmental Reform.* Washington, D.C.: Brookings Institution Press, 1998. Update of author's classic text that provides an in-depth analysis of three major presidential and congressional reforms intended to remake American intergovernmental relations.

Drucker, Peter. *Management Challenges for the 21st Century.* New York: Harper Collins, 1999. A look at major trends facing managers; discussion of knowledge workers and the inherent interdependence that characterizes the landscape of managing in the twenty-first century.

Fountain, Jane E. *Building the Virtual State: Information Technology and Institutional Change.* Washington, D.C.: Brookings Institution Press, 2001. Popular volume that documents how the introduction of one collaborative policy instrument—coordination through information technology—can be constrained by the form of institutions attempting the coordination.

Gray, Barbara. *Collaborating: Finding Common Ground for Multiparty Problems.* San Francisco: Jossey-Bass, 1989. An early look at solving multiparty disputes with collaborative mechanisms.

Independent Sector. www.independentsector.org/ (primary Web site for information on nonprofit and volunteer sectors).

Institute for Public Private Partnerships, Inc. www.ip3.org/ (Web site of a consulting firm specializing in bringing together the public and private sectors for economic development).

International City/County Management Association (ICMA). www.icma.org/main/topic.asp?tpid=29&stid=73&hsid=1 (links to ICMA reports and articles on regionalism).

Kickert, Walter J. M., Erik-Hans Klijn; and Joop F. M. Koppenjan, eds. *Managing Complex*

Networks. London: Sage, 1997. Theoretical treatise on the monumental shift from hierarchical management to managing policy networks.

Peters, Tom. *Liberation Management*. New York: Knopf, 1992. Magnum opus that documents dozens and dozens of new collaborative structures in business.

Radin, Beryl A., Robert Agranoff, Ann O'M. Bowman, Gregory C. Buntz, Steven J. Ott, Barbara S. Romzek, and Robert H. Wilson. *New Governance for Rural America: Creating Intergovernmental Partnerships*. Lawrence: University Press of Kansas, 1996. Case studies and analyses of a new-governance model that emphasizes decreased federal control in favor of intergovernmental collaboration and increased involvement of state, local, and private agencies.

United Nations Development Program. www.undp.org/ppp/ (site with links to the use of public-private partnerships in international programs sponsored by the UNDP).

United States Advisory Commission on Intergovernmental Relations. www.library.unt.edu/gpo/acir/acir.html (electronic archive of all publications from the commission).

Wondolleck, Julia M., and Steven L. Yaffee. *Making Collaboration Work: Lessons from Innovation in Natural Resource Management*. Washington, D.C.: Island Press, 2000. Based on extensive research in the field of natural resources; offers a set of lessons on the role of collaboration in natural resource management, explains why collaboration is an essential component of resource management, and explains how to make it work.

8   Leading a manager's life

Ammons, David N., and James H. Glass. *Recruiting Local Government Executives: Practical Insights for Hiring Authorities and Candidates*. San Francisco: Jossey-Bass, 1989. Primary focus on how to recruit the top-level manager and how top manager candidates can prepare; elements of what makes an effective local manager; some attention to roles of managers.

Ammons, David N., and Charldean Newell. *City Executives: Leadership Roles, Work Characteristics, and Time Management*. Albany: State University of New York Press, 1989. In-depth analysis of the roles local government managers play; based on a survey of chief executives and principal assistants in U.S. cities. Context in which managers work; exploration of their roles in local government.

Benest, Frank, ed. *Preparing the Next Generation: A Guide for Current and Future Local Government Managers*. Washington, D.C.: ICMA, 2003. Prepared by and for practitioners. Helps current and would-be managers understand the call of public service, the basics of getting a job, and strategies for professional development. Includes case studies.

Bennis, Warren, and Burt Nanus. *Leaders: The Strategies for Taking Charge*. New York: Harper and Row, 1985. Straightforward look at the components of effective leadership based on interviews with corporate executives. Emphasizes results orientation, vision, and credibility.

Gale, Barry and Linda. *Stay or Leave*. New York: Harper & Row, 1989. Includes a series of tests for a self-assessment of the advisability of remaining in or departing from one's current job.

Hanbury, George, II. "The Function of Leadership Styles and Personality Types among City Managers: An Analysis of 'Fit' and Tenure." Ph.D. diss., Florida Atlantic University, May 2001. Available through UMI/ProQuest Dissertation Services, UMI/ProQuest number AAT 9998892. Important academic study that addresses the manager as person, the manager's behavior, tenure, and success.

Holifield, Ron. *The Public Executive's Complete Guide to Employment Agreements*. Tampa, Fla.: Innovation Groups and ICMA, 1996. Includes both a book and a diskette with sample wording for employment agreements; discusses merits of such agreements, getting concurrence from the governing body, and negotiations.

International City/County Management Association. *Internship Toolkit*. Washington, D.C.: ICMA, 2002. www.jobs.icma.org/documents/internip_toolkit.pdf (discusses internships that are appropriate in a local government and offers guidelines and examples of how to create an internship program).

Klarreich, Samuel H. *Work Without Stress: A Practical Guide to Emotional and Physical Well-Being on the Job*. New York: Brunner/Mazel, 1990. Highly readable book on coping with stress, written largely from a psychological perspective; emphasizes overcoming stress derived from irrational thinking by developing an ability to "counter-think."

Kroeger, Otto; Janet M. Thuesen, and Hile Rutledge. *Type Talk: How 16 Personality Types Determine Your Success on the Job*. New York: Dell Publishing, 2002. One in a series of related books that focus on self-typing coupled with prescriptions for behavior. Emphasizes understanding the workplace and thriving in it.

Leiter, Michael P., and Christina Maslach. *Preventing Burnout and Building Engagement: A Complete Program for Organizational Renewal.* San Francisco: Jossey-Bass, 2000. One of a series of books, pamphlets, and workbooks by these experts in burnout. Guides management team members through a checkup to spot warning signs in the organization.

Levinson, Daniel J. "A Conception of Adult Development." *American Psychologist* 41 (January 1986): 3–13. Summarizes the formulations of the author, a noted expert in the field, regarding life course, life cycle, and the adult development of the life structure in early and middle adulthood.

Matteson, Michael T., and John M. Ivancevich. *Managing Job Stress and Health: The Intelligent Person's Guide.* New York: Free Press, 1982. A detailed yet practical book on stress, primary sources of stress, prescriptions for dealing with stress, and the development of personal action plans for maintaining physical and mental health.

Mills, James Willard. *Coping with Stress: A Guide to Living.* New York: Wiley, 1982. A series of simple suggestions and exercises for managing life's stresses.

Mintzberg, Henry. The Nature of Managerial Work. New York: Harper & Row, 1973. Classic study of managerial roles based on observation: five case studies used to define what managers actually do.

Nalbandian, John. "Educating the City Manager of the Future." In *The Future of Local Government Administration: The Hansell Symposium,* edited by H. George Frederickson and John Nalbandian, 249–260. Washington, D.C.: ICMA, 2002. One of many excellent papers presented by a prestigious group of scholar-authors and responding local government managers in honor of the retiring director of ICMA. Focuses on the interface between practice and academe and what the public affairs programs must provide in the future.

About the authors

N. Joseph Cayer is a professor of public affairs at Arizona State University. He has published books and articles on various aspects of public administration, with an emphasis on public personnel and human resource management. He taught previously at the University of Maine and has served as director of the Center for Public Service at Texas Tech University and director of the School of Public Affairs at Arizona State University. He received his Ph.D. in political science from the University of Massachusetts and a master of public administration degree and a bachelor's degree from the University of Colorado.

Raymond W. Cox III is chair of the Department of Public Administration and Urban Studies at the University of Akron. He is the author of approximately 30 academic and professional publications, including two books. His recent work has focused on issues of management theory and discretion in decision making and has included publications addressing personnel systems and police ethics. He is a "pracademic" with more than 16 years of government service, including four as chief of staff to the lieutenant governor of New Mexico and five at the National Science Foundation, complementing 14 years as a faculty member. He received his Ph.D. in public administration and policy from the Virginia Polytechnic Institute and State University.

David Coursey is an associate professor in the Askew School of Public Administration and Policy at Florida State University, where he directs the graduate information technology concentration. His publications in such journals as *Journal of Public Administration Research and Theory* and *Public Administration Review* are numerous, and he has managed the development of approximately 75 government Web site applications for a broad array of local and state governments. He is also a regular speaker for *Government Technology* magazine at its annual conferences. He received his doctorate in 1991 from the Maxwell School at Syracuse University and his master of public administration degree in 1987 from the University of Alabama at Birmingham.

Mary E. Guy holds the Jerry Collins Eminent Scholar Chair in the Askew School of Public Administration and Policy at Florida State University. She is past president of the American Society for Public Administration, a fellow of the National Academy of Public Administration, and editor in chief of the journal, *Review of Public Personnel Administration.* She has written numerous books and articles on subjects pertaining to the management of public agencies, especially in regard to productivity and human resource issues.

William H. (Bill) Hansell is a native Pennsylvanian who graduated from the University of Pennsylvania in Philadelphia with a bachelor's degree in economics and a master's degree in government administration from the Fels Institute at the Wharton School. He served in local government management in four Pennsylvania communities, including eight years as administrator of the city of Allentown. He then spent 21 years as an association executive, two with the Pennsylvania League of Cities and nineteen as ICMA's fifth executive director. He is a fellow of the National Academy of Public Administration and a trustee of the Financial Accounting Foundation.

William Earle Klay is a professor in the Askew School of Public Administration and Policy at Florida State University. His research often looks at the future of society in order to identify the problems that will challenge and shape government. A certified government financial manager, he has recently sought ways to link performance reporting and financial reporting. His several years of practitioner experience include service as a U.S. Army officer, a financial systems specialist, a policy analyst, and a senior planner. His Ph.D. is from the University of Georgia.

Michael McGuire is an associate professor and director of the master of public administration program in the Department of Public Administration at the University of North Texas. He is the coauthor of *Collaborative Public Management: New Strategies for Local Governments;* and he has published numerous articles on collaborative policy making and managing in intergovernmental and interorganizational network settings, the composition and performance of economic development strategies, and capacity building in rural communities. He holds a bachelor's degree in political science from the University of California at Irvine and a Ph.D. in public policy from Indiana University.

Charldean Newell is Regents Professor Emerita of Public Administration, University of North Texas. An honorary member of ICMA, she served on the ICMA University Board of Regents and the Credentialing Advisory Board. She is also an honorary member of the Texas Municipal Clerks Association. She chaired the public utilities commission, civil service commission, and a major charter revision commission for her community. A member of the National Academy of Public Administration, she received the Staats Career Public Service Award from the National Association of Schools of Public Affairs and Administration. Coauthor of four books, she has also authored numerous articles and reports.

Ronald W. Perry is professor of public affairs at Arizona State University. He completed his Ph.D. in sociology at the University of Washington, spent a decade at the Battelle Memorial Institute (Seattle), and has taught at Arizona State University for the past 20 years. His research and teaching interests focus on evaluation research, emergency management, personnel, and human resources. He has published 16 books and more than 100 referred articles on various topics in emergency management, human resources, and public management.

James H. Svara is head of the Department of Political Science and Public Administration at North Carolina State University. He has been a professor in the department since 1989 and previously taught at University of North Carolina–Greensboro. In his research and

teaching, he specializes in local government politics and management and has a special interest in the roles and relationships of elected and administrative officials. He is a fellow of the National Academy of Public Administration and an honorary member of ICMA.

Martin Vanacour served the cities of Phoenix, Arizona, and Glendale, Arizona, for 37 years and recently retired after 17 years as city manager of Glendale. He is chief executive officer of Dynamic Relations, a management consulting company, and an adjunct professor at Arizona State University. He is a nationally known speaker and facilitator specializing in council-manager relations. He has received numerous awards for his contributions to the city management profession. Vanacour received his bachelor's degree from the State University of New York at Buffalo, a master of public administration degree from New York University, and a Ph.D. from Arizona State University.

Craig M. Wheeland is an associate professor of political science at Villanova University, where he is chair of the Department of Political Science and directs Villanova's master of public administration program. His research interests include leadership by elected officials and professional administrators in city and suburban governments, collaborative problem-solving approaches, and municipal government institutions. His publications have appeared in *Public Administration Review, Administration & Society, American Review of Public Administration, Public Productivity & Management Review, State and Local Government Review, Public Integrity,* and *The Municipal Year Book,* among others. He received a master of public administration degree from the University of South Carolina and a Ph.D. from the Pennsylvania State University.

Sources of quotations

The following list gives the sources of the boldface quotations that appear throughout the book and the affiliation—or past affiliation—of the person quoted, at the time of the quote. If the quotation was taken from a publication, a short reference to the publication is also provided.

Mark Achen   Colorado Range Rider and interim city manager, Centennial, Colorado.

Gordon Anderson   Assistant city manager, Santa Monica California.

Michael Ball   Chief executive and town clerk, Worthing, West Sussex, England. Quote on p. 26/"Positive Public Relations: A Very British Approach," *Public Management* (May 1991): 14.

Frank Benest   City manager, Palo Alto, California. Quote on p. 119/*Preparing the Next Generation: A Guide for Current and Future Local Government Managers,* by Frank Benest (ICMA, 2003), 34.

Wally Bobkiewicz   City manager, Santa Paula, California.

Del Borgsdorf   City manager, San José, California.

Richard Bowers   Former city manager, Scottsdale, Arizona.

Charley Bowman   Former city manager, Xenia, Ohio.

Alex Briseño   Former city manager, San Antonio, Texas. Quote on p. 48/"Briseño's Work Respected Even by Critics," *San Antonio Express-News,* 9 July 2000.

Rickey Childers   City manager, Longview, Texas.

Jan Christofferson   Executive officer, Placer County, California. Quote on p. 11/*Public Management* (July 2003): 27.

Steven S. Cleveland   City manager, Goodyear, Arizona.

Bruce Clymer   City administrator, Gothenburg, Nebraska. Quote on p. 154/*Public Management* (August 2003): 26–27.

Larry Comunale   Township manager, Lower Gwynedd, Pennsylvania.

Anton "Tony" Dahlerbruch   Deputy city manager, Beverly Hills, California.

Jan Dolan   City manager, Scottsdale, Arizona.

Kevin Duggan   City manager, Mountain View, California. Quote on p. 12/"When a Council-member Crosses the Line," *Public Management* (November 2002): 8.

Mike Eastland   Executive director, North Central Texas Council of Governments, and former city manager, Carrollton, Texas.

Terry Ellis   City manager, Peoria, Arizona.

Debra Brooks Feazelle   City manager, La Porte, Texas.

James Flynt   City manager, Alameda, California. Quote on p. 161/"Mending Labor-Management Relationships," *Public Management* (August 2003): 18.

Tom Fountaine   Manager, State College Borough, Pennsylvania; ICMA vice president.

Toby Futrell   City manager, Austin, Texas.

Don Gerrish   Town manager, Brunswick, Maine; ICMA past vice president and president.

Don Gloo   Assistant city manager, Urbandale, Iowa.

A. Jeffrey Greenwell   Chief executive, retired, Northamptonshire, England; former president of SOLACE, and vice president of ICMA.

C. A. Harrell   Former city manager, Norfolk, Virginia; past president of ICMA. Quote on p. 23/1948 presidential address to ICMA; quote on p. 59/"City Manager as Community Leader," *Public Management* (October 1948): 291.

Lloyd Harrell   Former city manager, Chandler, Arizona.

Bob Jasper   Administrator, Mesa County, Colorado.

Julie Johnston   City manager, Oak Point, Texas.

Mark M. Levin   City administrator, Maryland Heights, Missouri.

Jim Ley   County administrator, Sarasota, Florida. Quote on p. 59/"OPX . . . The Beginning," *Public Management* (December 2002): 14.

Craig Malin   City administrator, Davenport, Iowa. Quote on p. 166/*Public Management* (May 2003): 21.

John L. Maltbie   County manager, San Mateo, California.

Leonard Martin   City manager, Carrollton, Texas.

Tom Mauk   Former city manager, La Habra, California.

Peggy Merriss   City manager, Decatur, Georgia.

David R. Mora   City manager, Salinas, California.

Julia D. Novak   Vice president, Organization Management Partners, Inc., Cincinnati, Ohio, and former city manager, Rye, New York. Quote on p. 76/*The Future of Local Government Administration,* edited by H. George Frederickson and John Nalbandian (ICMA, 2002), 229.

Dave Osberg   City administrator, Hastings, Minnesota. Quote on p. 5/*Public Management* (January/February 2003): 28.

Raymond R. Patchett   City manager, Carlsbad, California.

Bill Pupo   Former city manager, Surprise, Arizona.

Bruce Romer   Chief administrative officer, Montgomery County, Maryland; and past president of ICMA.

Mark Ryckman   City manager, Corning, New York. Quote on p. 158/*Public Management* (March 2003): 20.

Gary Sears   City manager, Englewood, Colorado.

Cynthia Seelhammer   Town manager, Queen Creek, Arizona.

Bryce A. Stuart   City manager, Winston-Salem, North Carolina.

James Thurmond   City manager, Missouri City, Texas. Quote on p. 67/"The Council-Manager Relationship," *Public Management* (September 2002): 24.

Les White   Former city manager, San José, California. Quote on p. 58/"Remember Your Mentors," *Public Management* (June 2003): 10.

O. Wendell White   Former city manager, Charlotte, North Carolina. Quote on p. 75/ "Identity and Excellence: Role Models for City Managers," by Craig Wheeland, *Administration and Society* (November 1994): 295.

Roland Windham   County administrator, Charleston County, South Carolina. Quote on p. 68/"Identity and Excellence: Role Models for City Managers," by Craig Wheeland, *Administration and Society* (November 1994): 295.

Illustration credits

Chapter 2

Table 2–1: Adapted from James H. Svara, "U.S. City Managers and Administrators in a Global Perspective," *The Municipal Year Book 1999* (Washington, D.C.: ICMA, 1999), Table 3/6.

Table 2–2: Computed from survey conducted in 2001 by James H. Svara for the National League of Cities.

Table 2–3: Prepared from data in James H. Svara, "Mayors in the Unity of Powers Context," In *The Future of Local Government Administration: The Hansell Symposium,* ed. H. George Frederickson and John Nalbandian, eds. (Washington, D.C.: ICMA, 2002).

Table 2–4: James H. Svara, *Two Decades of Continuity and Change in American City Councils* (Washington, D.C.: National League of Cities, 2003), 18, Table III.4.

Table 2–5: Calculated from Census 2000 Summary File 1 (SF1).

Chapter 4

Table 4–1: Charldean Newell, ed., *The Effective Local Government Manager,* 2nd ed. (Washington, D.C.: ICMA, 1993), 139.

Figure 4–1: Raymond Pachett, city manager, Carlsbad, California, February 2003.

Chapter 5

Tables 5–1 and 5–2: Adapted from Mary E. Guy and Seung-Bum Yang, "Conditions for Effective Self-Managed Work Teams: Lessons from the U.S. Experience," in *Central-Local Relations and Local Government Reform in Korea,* ed. Byong-Joon Kim and Glen Hahn Cope (South Korea: Korea Association for Policy Studies, 2003).

Chapter 6

Figure 6–4: "Information Technology Trends," provided by Gartner Dataquest, *2003 State and Local Sourcebook* (Washington, D.C.: *Governing,* 2003), 104.

Chapter 8

Leadership self-assessment: Adapted from self-assessment by the National School Boards Association, Alexandria, Virginia; www.nsba.org/site/index.asp.

Index